Conflict and Compromise in Multilingual Societies

Volume 2, **BELGIUM**

Kenneth D. McRae

The author of an authoritative work on this topic in Swiss society now draws a comprehensive picture of Belgium's linguistic demarcations. Firmly rooting the discussion in an historical background, the author discusses group images and attitudes and the constitutional and institutional framework for multilingualism that exists in Belgium. Yet, as the title of the series would suggest, conflicts do lead to compromises, and the study concludes with a penetrating look at contemporary problems in Belgium—problems stemming from the very richness of multilingual culture. This analysis of Belgium is concerned not only with conflict between language groups as such, but with evolving relationships between language diversity and economic development, language diversity and distributional fairness, language cleavage and other societal cleavages, and the implications of language diversity for democratic politics.

The book is the second volume in a projected multi-volume work examining four multilingual Western democracies. After the studies of Switzerland and Belgium, the volumes to come will focus on Finland and Canada.

Kenneth D. McRae, Professor of Political Science, Carleton University, Ottawa, is a Past President of the Canadian Political Science Association and a Fellow of the Royal Society of Canada; he served as a research supervisor for the Canadian Royal Commission on Bilingualism and Biculturalism. His publications include Switzerland: Example of Cultural Coexistence; The Federal Capital: Governmental Institutions; Consociational Democracy; *an edition of Jean Bodin's* The Six Bookes of a Commonweale; *and* Conflict and Compromise in Multilingual Societies, Vol. 1, *Switzerland (WLU Press, 1983).*

CONFLICT and COMPROMISE in Multilingual Societies

Belgium

Kenneth D. McRae

Wilfrid Laurier University Press

Canadian Cataloguing in Publication Data

McRae, Kenneth D. (Kenneth Douglas), 1925-
    Conflict and compromise in multilingual societies

(The Politics of cultural diversity ; 1-2)
Bibliography: p.
Includes index.
Partial contents: v. 1. Switzerland — v. 2. Belgium.
ISBN 0-88920-133-1 (v. 1, bound). — ISBN 0-88920-173-0
(v. 1, pbk.). — ISBN 0-88920-163-3 (v. 2, bound). —
ISBN 0-88920-195-1 (v. 2, pbk.).

1. Multilingualism — Case studies.   2. Socio-
linguistics — Case studies.   3. Languages —
Political aspects — Case studies.   4. Language
policy — Case studies.   I. Title.   II. Series.

P115.M37 1984   305.7   C84-098201-1

Cover design: Polygon Design Limited

WILFRID LAURIER UNIVERSITY PRESS
Waterloo, Ontario, Canada   N2L 3C5

86 87 88 89 4 3 2 1

Printed and bound in Canada by John Deyell Company

Contents

BELGIUM

List of Tables

List of Maps and Figure

Maps

Figure

Preface

This volume constitutes the second of four case studies investigating in some depth the circumstances that have given rise to political tensions between language communities in four multilingual Western democracies. The first volume examined the case of Switzerland; the third and fourth will deal with Finland and Canada, respectively. While the primary emphasis of the inquiry as a whole is on factors that have generated or intensified conflict and on those that have moderated or regulated it, the full scope of the inquiry goes beyond an elemental concern with domestic peace and stability to look at other objectives of these four societies and how far these objectives have been realized by their component language groups. Thus each of the studies attempts to deal not only with conflict between language groups as such but also with evolving relationships between language diversity and economic development, language diversity and distributional fairness, language cleavage and other societal cleavages, and the implications of language diversity for democratic politics.

A secondary aim of the inquiry is to provide a foundation for assessing more carefully some of the hypotheses about linguistic diversity and about plural societies in general that abound in the current literature of the social sciences, often with insufficient evidence or explanation. Examples of these hypotheses include the view that linguistic diversity is a barrier to economic development; that multilingual or multicultural societies are more prone to conflict or even doomed to subcultural violence; that linguistic conflicts once begun are inherently more "intractable," and less amenable to compromise solutions, than other conflicts. There may or may not be sound foundations for such views, but the point is that there is a scarcity of serious case studies of multilingual societies—particularly among the advanced Western democracies—against which to test them. The aim of this study of Belgium and of its three companion volumes is to provide better empirical foundations for evaluating these generalizations in specific settings. A shorter study, tentatively planned as a brief concluding volume, will examine some of the general implications of these four case studies for social science theory and for public policy.

The rationale for the selection of these four countries and for the organization followed in the case studies is developed at some length in the General Introduction to the inquiry as a whole (Volume 1, 1-33). For a full discussion the reader is referred to this introduction, but its essential features are summarized in this volume's brief Introductory Note, which explains the analytical framework common to all four studies. The four cases chosen for study are not representative for all multilingual societies but represent a distinct subgroup. All four are characterized by (1) high levels of economic development, (2) Western-style political democracy, (3) moderate linguistic pluralism (with formal legal equality for two or more languages), and (4) relatively low levels of overt violence between language groups as measured by comparative indicators. The all-important question to be examined is how they have managed to combine these characteristics in a way that has so far eluded many other plural societies. A secondary question is why they have differed among themselves or even from one time period to another in their respective levels of intergroup hostility, conflict, and violence.

The most obvious feature of this second volume is that it is longer than the first, a characteristic that can be linked to its portrayal of major social and linguistic change. Whereas the case of Switzerland highlights political stability and conflict management, that of Belgium exemplifies a major social upheaval and a realignment of major linguistic communities extending over more than a century. The dynamics of this change call for close attention, and one prominent feature of the Belgian scene has been successive waves of highly detailed language legislation to give effect to an evolving linguistic relationship between Francophones and Flemings. The primary focus of this attention must be on the two turbulent decades of linguistic and constitutional reform from 1961 to 1980, but the earlier phases of the language conflict are also important as aids to understanding present difficulties.

Nomenclature is a sensitive question in Switzerland, but much more so in Belgium. For Belgian place-names, I have generally tried to follow the official language of the region, even when that seems a little strange in English. Thus the text prefers Brugge over Bruges and Leuven over Louvain because it seems to me that to perpetuate English forms based on the French versions of these names is to deny something for which the Flemish Movement has fought for more than a century. For officially bilingual Bruxelles/Brussel, one can fortunately take refuge in the neutral English form of Brussels, and a few other English forms (e.g., Antwerp for Antwerpen) are well established and unlikely to give offence. For regions or provinces, the term Flanders is so well established by long historical usage that Vlaanderen might appear pedantic, but Wallonia is still an awkward neologism that is perhaps better left as Wallonie. For names of organizations and their acronyms, I have usually preferred the French form, if a choice was necessary, on the purely pragmatic ground that it would be more recognizable to an English-speaking reader. With this one exception, I have tried hard to maintain balance and neutrality in nomenclature, though perhaps without total success. A list of acronyms used in this volume and the corresponding titles will be found in Appendix A.

Another minor problem is the spelling and alphabetization of surnames beginning with De/de and Van/van. Dutch and Belgian practices appear to diverge on this point, and a rapid check of other published volumes revealed no fewer than seven distinct conventions governing capitalization and indexing. In the midst of such diversity, I have tried to follow as far as possible the forms used by the authors themselves. In any case, an author with a Scottish surname has little right to complain about variations of this kind.

Like its predecessor, this volume has left me deeply indebted to a lengthy list of individuals and institutions. Though the printed sources for the study of Belgian language questions are far more ample than the works listed in the bibliography can begin to convey, I have also been given much valuable information and insight in interviews and discussions with public servants, ministerial staffs, military officers, politicians, academics, researchers, and ordinary citizens. Since all these interviews were conducted with the understanding that there would be no attribution of sources, I would like to thank these informants collectively and anonymously, but nevertheless with deep appreciation, for the vast amount of time and trouble that they have taken to educate me about their country.

Certain individuals deserve special acknowledgement. Among the foremost is the late Val Lorwin, whose infectious enthusiasm for the smaller European democracies and for Belgium in particular has left a whole generation of scholars in his debt. I must also mention several friends and patient mentors in Belgium, most notably Maurice-Pierre Herremans, Senator Lode Claes, Albert Verdoodt, Jozef Nuttin, Xavier Mabille, Fernand Keuleneer, Jean Beaufays, and Baudewijn Meeus. The first three read the entire manuscript and offered many valuable suggestions for its improvement. I also thank several colleagues in North America for sharing with me their interest and expertise in Belgian studies, including Jacques Brazeau, Sam Clark, Maureen Covell, David Rayside, Elizabeth Swing, and Aristide Zolberg. While all of them have helped make this work a better one, they cannot be held responsible for any defects that remain.

I am further indebted to some dozen libraries and archives for access to source materials. Foremost is the Bibliothèque Royale Albert I in Brussels, an admirable national library and a hospitable workplace during several research visits. I would also mention the libraries of the universities of Leuven and of Brussels (ULB), of the Institut national de statistique, of Statistics Canada, of the newspaper *Le Soir* in Brussels, and the National Library in Ottawa. I thank Jean-Claude Deheneffe for data from the Belgian Archives for the Social Sciences (BASS), and the Centre d'étude belge des supports de publicité for permission to use data from the 1969 media survey.

Closer to home, my thanks and appreciation go to Annie Knox, who typed virtually the entire manuscript; to Ruth Kelvey, who has typed the final stages of this volume as well as the beginning of Volume 3; and to Christine Earl, who prepared the maps. I have been assisted by Joseph Rizzotto in the calculation of some of the tables and by Alex Ing in computer runs on the data sets. I am also grateful to Sandra Woolfrey, Director of Wilfrid Laurier University Press, for continuing support for a project of long duration, and to her staff at the Press.

The early stages of research on this volume and its predecessor were made possible by a Canada Council Leave Fellowship and by further Canada Council grants for research and travel assistance. The bulk of the manuscript was written during tenure of a Killam Research Fellowship. This book has been published with the help of a grant from the Social Science Federation of Canada using funds provided by the Social Sciences and Humanities Research Council of Canada. A further grant from the Faculty of Graduate Studies and Research of Carleton University helped to meet the costs of typesetting the numerous complex tables in this volume. It is a pleasure for me to acknowledge these sources of research support and aid to publication.

One of the minor but interesting sidelights of any research project is how the researchers themselves fare in their field work. When Shepard Clough investigated the history of the Flemish Movement in the 1920s, his research in Belgium led to a press campaign against him, two police investigations, and a "short prison detention" (Clough, 1930, vi). Val Lorwin's work during the 1960s was untroubled by the police, as far as I am aware, but he too was criticized in the press for interference in Belgian politics. Reactions to my own research in the later 1970s ranged from strong encouragement to passive indifference at worst, and the only press mention that I know of was benign. This could be construed as lack of zeal on my part, or it might be taken as a portent that the struggle between the Belgian language communities is at last inching towards settlement.

Whatever its current direction, the *question communautaire* has remained in full evolution even while this volume has been in the press. The year 1985—an election year in Belgium—has brought both new tensions and new accommodations, and the more important of these have been noted below, some in the text or as footnotes, others in a brief postscript (see Appendix B, 340-41). I am indebted to the Canadian Embassy in Brussels and to the Belgian Embassy in Ottawa for assistance at many points of the inquiry, but especially for documentation on these recent developments.

Ottawa, Canada   K. D. M.
November 1985

Introductory Note: Towards a Common Framework of Analysis

As indicated in the Preface, the four case studies of this inquiry are organized around a common outline of questions to be investigated. The outline and the rationale for these questions are developed at some length in the General Introduction in the first volume, along with a more general analysis of the incidence of multilingual and multicultural states in the world as a whole (see Volume 1, 1-33). While limitations of space preclude repetition of that chapter here, it may nevertheless be useful to begin this second volume with a brief sketch of the plan of organization that is common to each of the four case studies. One can also suggest how each of the categories of analysis will yield data or findings that can then be related to some of the more common theoretical propositions in the literature of the social sciences.

The central objective of the inquiry is to identify and analyze the factors that generate or increase linguistic tensions and those that help to overcome or reduce those tensions. The common framework for each case study groups together these factors under four broad headings: (1) historical traditions and developmental patterns, with special reference to the evolution of linguistic diversity; (2) the social structure of the language communities, and relationships between linguistic cleavage and other societal cleavages; (3) the perceptions and attitudes of the language communities, and how these attitudes have been mobilized in the political system; and (4) constitutional and institutional arrangements for languages and language groups in the public and private sectors. Each of these four categories becomes the basis for a separate chapter in each volume, but the internal organization of these chapters necessarily varies slightly from one volume to another because of different experiences of multilingualism. To permit greater flexibility and to present these differences more fully, each volume also contains a fifth chapter on the most salient contemporary issues, problems, or conflicts involving the language communities, with no special effort at comparability between countries.

In tracing *historical traditions*, we are interested in the extent of shared historical experience among the language communities; in the continuities

1

and ruptures in those traditions; in the formative elements that have shaped the political cultures. One should note the emergence of linguistic awareness and the processes by which this happened. One should trace the impact on the language communities of such "modernizing" processes as industrialization, urbanization, and political integration. As well, one should be sensitive to the international context and how it influenced the language communities.

These historical patterns can then be reviewed in the light of various hypotheses about linguistic conflict. For example, one can observe whether language tensions in Belgium have been associated with modernization (or with too rapid or asymmetrical modernization); with industrialization and the rise of an industrial working class; with foreign invasion, or changes in the international environment; or with other long-term developmental factors. Unlike the Swiss example, the Belgian case saw the emergence in the nineteenth century of significant subcultural nationalism in the form of the Flemish Movement, which in turn generated organized Walloon reactions. Further, since Belgium has been for centuries a cockpit of European warfare and diplomacy, one may reasonably look for connections between the rise of the Flemish Movement and the emergence of modern Germany as a great power. On the side of conflict management, one may examine how far modern linguistic pluralism in Belgium rests on an earlier pluralism of social orders and mercantile cities that was common to the northern and southern Netherlands.

Of the factors included under *social structure*, the most prominent are the relative size, stability, and spatial distribution of the language communities, as well as patterns of language contact and individual bilingualism. The languages are also important in themselves, especially the relationship between dialect forms and standard language, the social status of the languages both domestically and internationally, and their availability for highly specialized areas of communication. The relationship between language divisions and other significant societal cleavages, most obviously those based on religion or social class, should also be noted. Finally, because economic inequality has been viewed as a potent source of social conflict since the time of Aristotle, we must study closely the occupational patterns and the general economic situation of the respective language groups.

The possible theoretical implications of these structural factors are immediately obvious. One may examine whether linguistic tensions have been diminished by cross-cutting cleavages of religion or class or other social characteristics, and whether they have been accentuated by disparities of income or wealth. Has differential social mobility been a factor in conflict? Can linguistic tensions be traced to changes in the relative socioeconomic status of language groups, or to changes in their level of social or political mobilization? The Belgian case offers extensive materials for testing such hypotheses, but it is also complex enough that the facts must be established with some care.

For the study of *perceptions and attitudes*, a logical starting point is to examine how the groups view themselves and each other, and whether these images are congruent with one another. The degree of consensus or dissensus on basic values, on political issues, and on the procedural rules of the political system can also be charted. One area of special concern is attitudes towards cultural diversity itself. This section of the inquiry also includes in each case some attention to the pattern of mobilization and expression of these attitudinal differences through political parties and interest groups. To include such questions in the same chapter may seem somewhat arbitrary, but there are practical organizational reasons for doing so.

Findings from this part of the inquiry may be related to a variety of assumptions and hypotheses in sociology and social psychology: for example, that conflict arises from basic attitudes of superiority and inferiority; from perceptions of disadvantage in relation to some particular reference group; or from a perceived incongruity between one's status as a member of a particular language group and other statuses. Of interest also is the question of multiple loyalties, and how far loyalties to a language group may be felt to be either compatible or incompatible with loyalties to the polity as a whole or to other groups. Another approach suggested by recent literature on political integration debates the question of how far consensus on values is a prerequisite for a stable polity.

In the Belgian case the attitudinal dimensions are rich in potential sources of conflict. Feelings of superiority and inferiority are not difficult to find, and when Belgium is compared with Switzerland its cross-group stereotypes and sympathy ratings are more negative. Intergroup differences on political issues have been frequent and strong. Unlike the Swiss case, where language affiliation has had a minimal impact on politics, the Belgian party system since the 1960s has been increasingly mobilized around and defined by the language division.

The accommodation of language diversity through *constitutional and institutional arrangements* involves examination of a wide range of public bodies and private organizations. Formal constitutional and legal recognition of languages and of language communities has both symbolic and practical consequences. Institutional recognition may cover the full range of public institutions—that is, the legislature, the executive, the public service and public corporations, the judiciary, the armed forces, and also subordinate levels of government. Some areas, such as education, culture, or the mass media, are particularly sensitive for multilingual societies. While most language regulation concerns the public sector, linguistic intervention in the private sector is often more controversial and deserves special attention.

The theoretical relevance of these institutional arrangements most often lies in the degree of political participation and/or autonomy that they grant to members of the various language groups. These members may be recognized only as individuals, or in some collective sense as a group. They may be incorporated into the polity either as a minority with limited rights or privileges, or as full and equal partners. In any given public body they may be recognized through a formula for power-sharing, or through some degree of group autonomy, or their position may be left to chance. One widespread device for group autonomy is federalism or administrative decentralization. Where territorial divisions are not appropriate for this purpose, some countries have experimented with nonterritorial federalism or with informal segmentation at the level of parties and interest groups. A full listing of possible institutional options of this kind will not be attempted here. While institutional arrangements can seldom be identified as primary causes of linguistic conflict, they can serve to moderate or regulate it, or to exacerbate it if they function badly.

The current institutional situation of Belgium is more than usually complex, in that recent constitutional reforms offer a dual perspective of an older highly centralized political system and an emerging less centralized one. In the early 1980s the latter is far from being fully implemented and is therefore difficult to evaluate. Another prominent feature is highly detailed language legislation in several sectors, which makes any significant description of Belgian institutional arrangements considerably longer than for most other countries. Finally, Belgium has made serious efforts to regulate certain aspects of language usage in the private sector.

It must be emphasized once again that this common framework of analysis is intentionally loose and open-ended. It is intended to serve as an organizational pattern, but not as a barrier or limitation to the inquiry. As noted in Volume 1, the problem is to combine sufficient theoretical rigor for comparative purposes with freedom to pursue new insights as each case study unfolds. It seems important that the common framework should not close off or distort the discussion of what is unique or different in each country. For this reason the first four chapters in each volume are structured loosely enough to accommodate differences both in data and in emphasis, and the fifth chapter is even more oriented towards problems specific to the country in question. Thus while Switzerland has strains and tensions that illustrate the working of decentralized federalism (Volume 1, 185-227), the problem areas in Belgium reflect attempts to impose a uniform, symmetrical, central language policy on the country as a whole (below, 275-321).

Although the framework divides the factors to be studied into four broad categories for purposes of presentation and analysis, it should be noted that important relationships may exist *across* these categories. For example, perceptions of economic disparities at the attitudinal level may be at variance with present structural realities because they may be based upon memories of past economic relationships or even on outright misperceptions. The aim of this volume, as of the other three case studies, is to integrate all these factors and their subtle interrelationships into a comprehensive portrait of a single country. This phase of the inquiry is much less concerned with cross-country comparisons. While this volume makes a number of comparisons with the Swiss experience described in Volume 1, most comparisons with the two following cases of Finland and Canada, together with more systematic comparative analysis of all four cases, are postponed for the later stages of the inquiry.

Belgium

Jack wold be a gentilman if he coude speke frensske.
> English medieval proverb, cited in F. Louckx, *Wetenschappelijk onderzoek van de taaltoestanden in de Brusselse agglomeratie* (Brussels, 1975), Preface.

On traitera et proposera toutes affaires concernant le pays de Flandre dans la langue dudit pays.
> Article 18 of the Charter of Flanders, February 11, 1477, cited in J. Des Cressonnières, *Essai sur la question des langues dans l'histoire de Belgique* (Brussels, 1919), 178.

L'Union fait la Force/Eendracht maakt Macht.
> Belgian national motto, 1831 (Constitution, Article 125).

Les premiers principes d'une bonne administration sont basés sur l'emploi exclusif d'une seule langue et il est évident que la seule langue des Belges doit être le français. Pour arriver à ce résultat, il est nécessaire que toutes les fonctions civiles et militaires, soient confiées à des Wallons et à des Luxembourgeois; de cette façon, les Flamands, privés temporairement des avantages attachés à ces emplois, seront contraints d'apprendre le français et l'on détruira ainsi peu à peu l'élément germanique en Belgique.
> Letter of Charles Rogier to Minister of Justice Jean-Joseph Raikem, 1832, cited in E. Baudart, *L'avenir de la Wallonie* (Brussels, 1945), 38.

De Tael is gansch het Volk (Language is the whole people).
> Motto of a Flemish literature society founded at Gent in 1836.

Il est de notoriété que des comités flamingants existent, qui aspirent jusqu'à introduire l'usage du flamand dans les séances de l'Académie royale de Bruxelles, à le faire admettre dans les débats du Parlement belge, à titre de langue légale et officielle, en un mot à le faire monter au rang de langue nationale. Voilà des prétentions exorbitantes contres lesquelles nous voulons protester.
> C. S[oudain] de N[iederwerth], *Du flamand, du wallon et du français en Belgique* (Liège, 1857), 6.

Comme notre sol, formé des alluvions de fleuves venant de France et d'Allemagne, notre culture nationale est une sorte de syncrétisme où l'on retrouve, mêlés l'un à l'autre et modifiés l'un par l'autre, les génies de deux races.
> Henri Pirenne, Preface to *Histoire de Belgique* (Brussels, 1900), ix.

Les Belges ont un destin commun, parce qu'ils ont une manière commune de se comporter, de réagir et de se projeter: un même complexe caractérologique. Ce complexe explique qu'un Namurois se sente plus proche de chez lui à Bruges qu'à Reims, un Anversois moins étranger à Mons qu'à Groningen.
> R. Micha and A. De Waelhens, "Du caractère des Belges," *Les temps modernes* 4 (1949), 416.

... toute la mediocrité et tout ce "middelmatisme" bien belge, sont également imputable à ce trait caractéristique qui nous distingue d'autres petits pays: le mauvais jumelage.
> Lode Claes, "Flamands et Francophones," *Revue nouvelle* 17 (1961), 176.

. . . laissez-moi Vous dire la vérité, la grande et horrifiante vérité: il n'y a pas de Belges. . . . Non Sire, il n'y a pas d'âme belge. La fusion des Flamands et des Wallons n'est pas souhaitable; et la désirât-on, qu'il faut constater encore qu'elle n'est pas possible.

> Jules Destrée, *Lettre au Roi sur la séparation de la Wallonie et de la Flandre* (Brussels, 1912), 8, 11.

Mon pays, c'est la Wallonie. Il est politiquement incorporé dans un pays plus grand: la Belgique.

> Jules Destrée, *Wallons et flamands* (Paris, 1923), 11.

Les Flamands . . . ont modifié les fondements de notre droit public en y introduisant une notion nouvelle: ils ont substitué aux droits de l'homme et du citoyen un droit différent, fondé sur la communauté ethnique. Ce droit nouveau, ce droit communautaire, ils l'ont fait prévaloir en matière linguistique sur la liberté individuelle et sur l'autorité du père de famille.

> *La Wallonie en alerte* (Liège, 1949), 6.

Au principe si naturel et juste de la liberté et de l'égalité des Belges en matière linguistique, qui reconnaît à l'homme le droit de choisir la langue sans être influencé par la crainte de vexations quelconques, on a substitué le principe contradictoire de l'égalité des langues, qui assujettit l'homme à une langue imposée.

> N. Toussaint, *Bilinguisme et éducation* (Brussels, 1935), 44.

Car les Wallons acceptent en général comme un axiome qu'il est aussi difficile, pour ne pas dire impossible, et peu naturel aux Wallons d'apprendre le flamand qu'il est facile et naturel aux Flamands d'apprendre le français.

> C. H. Höjer, *Le régime parlementaire belge de 1918 à 1940* (Uppsala and Stockholm, 1946), 19.

Entre le fort et le faible c'est la liberté qui opprime, et la loi qui affranchit.

> J. B. H. Lacordaire (1802-1861), cited in E. Van Cauwelaert, *Taalvrijheid? Een kritische motivering van de taalwetgeving* (Antwerp, 1971), 224.

. . . la liberté linguistique de l'individu ne résulte pas du libre jeu des forces qui s'affrontent dans notre société: elle est le fruit d'un équilibre difficile entre la contrainte légale et la pression sociale.

> F. Maes, "La langue, la loi, la liberté," *Revue nouvelle* 17 (1953), 639.

. . . le cerveau de l'Administration doit penser aussi bien en flamand qu'en français.

> *La Réforme de l'Etat* (Brussels, 1937-38), 1: 326.

La capitale d'un pays bilingue doit être radicalement bilingue. Elle risque, sinon, de se voir contester son statut de capitale.

> L. L. Cappuyns, brief to the Meyers Commission, 1967, 27.

Comme l'a dit un humoriste, la Belgique est le seul Etat au monde où coexistent plusieurs majorités opprimées, trois groupes qui ont chacun une certaine suprématie et qui, tous trois, nourrissent un complexe d'infériorité.

> Pierre Wigny, *Comprendre la Belgique* (Verviers, 1969), 178.

Houdt middelmat—garde la moyenne mesure.

> Motto of the Flemish poet J. B. Houwaert (1533-1599), cited in H. Carton de Wiart, "Psychologie du peuple belge," *Revue des deux mondes* 103rd year, vol. 15 (1933), 535.

De soep wordt nimmer zo heet gegeten als zij opgediend wordt (Soup is never eaten as hot as it is served).

> Flemish proverb, cited in H. D. de Vries Reilingh, *België: lotgenoot in de Lage Landen* (Meppel, 1954), 56.

Chapter 1

Historical Introduction

Belgium shares with Switzerland the same basic language frontier between the Germanic and Romance languages, but it should be noted at the start that important differences arise in the geographical setting. While Switzerland is in many respects defined by its geography, the main feature of the Low Countries is a general openness of the terrain and therefore almost unlimited options in the drawing of political boundaries. Historically, this openness led to a bewildering series of political and dynastic changes, military invasions, imperialist adventures, and periods of dependency for the lands that now comprise the Belgian state. This again contrasts sharply with the almost seven centuries of substantial political independence of the Swiss Confederation. This complexity of the political history of the Belgian provinces left behind a highly diversified store of historical memories and traditions, and for generations it has served as a source of inspiration for those who become dissatisfied with the existing state and regime. The openness of the geographical setting and its political consequences have also left their imprint on the political culture, tempering stubbornness with political realism, and devotion to principle with willingness to compromise when circumstances require it.

Certain other basic differences between the Belgian and the Swiss experience should be remembered. Belgium has been a founding member of both the Benelux Treaty and the European Common Market, and postwar discontent with the form of the Belgian state has been expressed within the context of emerging supranational European institutions. Finally, while both Belgium and Switzerland have been extensively involved in international economic relations, the Belgian state and monarchy were also politically involved in Africa for about eight decades as a significant colonial power, ruling over an area some eighty times the size of Belgium itself. The abrupt termination of the colonial tie in 1960 necessitated painful economic and psychological adjustments for the Belgian population.

A The Late Emergence of a Belgian State

The modern Belgian state rests upon complex historical foundations. As early as the twelfth century the towns of Flanders experienced rapid economic development, expansion of trade, and a high level of cultural development. The Burgundian period, from 1382 to 1477, brought gradual political expansion until most of the provinces of modern Belgium and Holland were under a single ruler, with some degree of centralized administration. The Burgundian lands then came under the control of the German emperors, passing to Spain with the abdication of Charles V in 1556. The unity of the northern and southern Netherlands was shattered, however, by the successful revolt of the northern provinces and the restoration of Spanish authority in the south by the Duke of Parma in the 1580s. This cataclysmic event, reinforced by subsequent selective migration for religious and economic reasons, initiated the modern-day gulf between Catholic Belgium and Protestant Holland.

Subsequently, the southern provinces—excluding the ecclesiastical principality of Liège, which remained a member of the German Empire—were ruled successively by Spain and Austria until the late eighteenth century. During the French Revolution they were invaded by French armies and, together with Liège, were annexed to France for some twenty years. In modern times this occupation has been viewed very differently by Walloon and by Flemish historians. For the former Bishopric of Liège, and for Francophone Belgium generally, this is a period of liberation and prosperity. For many Flemings, it is remembered as a time of religious and linguistic constraint, and for them the real liberation came with the defeat of Napoleon and the departure of the French armies in 1814. By the Treaty of Vienna, the southern provinces were reunited with Holland as the Kingdom of the Netherlands, a union that lasted fifteen years before it was broken by the Belgian Revolution of 1830, in which the southern provinces reacted against northern hegemony and won their independence. In larger historical context, then, the life span of an independent Belgian state has been relatively short, and even this brief period has been disrupted by eight years of German occupation during two world wars. It is important to remember the political complexity of the history of the Low Countries, because if some of the more radical opponents of the Belgian regime in the twentieth century have called for a restructuring of political boundaries, with seemingly visionary links to Holland, or France, or even Germany, such linkages have significant antecedents in earlier history. The same can be said for the Benelux Treaty, and even those who see the vocation of present-day Brussels as capital of Europe are following closely in the footsteps of the Emperor Charles V, who once ruled the vast combined dominions of Spain and the Holy Roman Empire from the same city.

Before we examine these developments and particularly their linguistic aspects more closely, it is worth noting that they have given rise to an important historiographical debate, the significance of which transcends the immediate issues of Netherlandic history. On the one side we find the "Belgicist" views epitomized by Henri Pirenne (1862-1935), whose magisterial multivolume *Histoire de Belgique* presents Belgian history as a vast continuum from the earliest times to the twentieth century. According to Pirenne, the political unification of the Burgundian period was founded on the already flourishing common civilization of medieval Flanders and Brabant, and it foreshadowed the period of independence after 1830. Further, the distinguishing feature of Belgian civilization in Pirenne's view has been its syncretic quality, its blending of Latin and Germanic influences in peaceful coexistence. He finds abundant evidence for this thesis even in the earliest periods, and the whole work may be viewed as a continuous exercise in nation-building (Pirenne, 1948-52; 1900).

However, the Pirenne thesis has its problems. It does not account for Liège, which had little common political history with the other Belgian territories until after the French Revolution. More important, it ignores the many ties between the northern and southern Netherlands which existed until the revolt against Spain in the sixteenth century. This point has been elaborated by the Dutch historian Pieter Geyl (1887-1966), who, in a series of writings spanning more than four decades, argues for a more unified perspective on Dutch and Belgian history. The basic reason for the independence of the northern provinces, he contends, was Parma's inability to subdue the provinces protected by the major river systems. The religious divergence between north and south arose not from any cultural differences existing before the separation but from subsequent emigration of Protestants from the south and enforced Protestantization in the north (Geyl, 1964, chaps. 1, 2). More generally, he directs his attack against the Belgicist school and equally against its Dutch "little-Netherlands" counterparts for their "unhistorical" reading of the past through modern eyes, but he also finds an *explanation* for these historiographical tendencies in the bitterness engendered in both countries by the Belgian revolution of 1830 (Geyl, 1955, chap. 9).

The controversy also has aspects that are more specific and more relevant to our inquiry. Pirenne, whose first volume of the *Histoire de Belgique* appeared in 1900, represented not just a Belgian view, but a view of a specific Belgium. "Professor Pirenne," Geyl observes (1955, 190) "was a Walloon, teaching history, in French, to Flemish students at the only public university in the Dutch-speaking part of the country, at Ghent," and the bicultural model to which he subscribed was becoming less and less acceptable in Flanders even as the later parts of his seven-volume history were emerging from the press in the 1920s. Geyl, on the other hand, had come in contact with Flemish nationalism at a student congress as early as 1911, and his espousal of a Great Netherlandic historical framework was matched by a lifelong sympathy for the Flemish Movement. It was these early contacts, he recounts, that "led me to question the spirit in which the history of our common past was generally written; to question the Belgicist view which tried to imprison Flanders in a fundamentally anti-Dutch

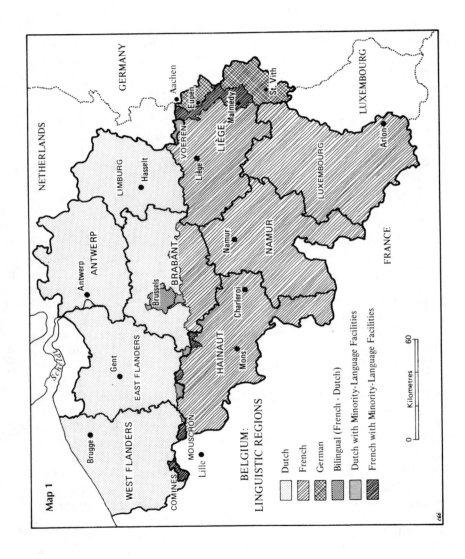

Map 1

BELGIUM:
LINGUISTIC REGIONS

Dutch

French

German

Bilingual (French - Dutch)

Dutch with Minority-Language Facilities

French with Minority-Language Facilities

conception; and to question the Little Netherlands, or Dutch State, view, which amounted to a denial of the Flemings . . . (1955, 194)." The full range of Geyl's discussion raises important general questions about the relationship between historiography and national political traditions, which will not be pursued here. The more specific point to be noted is that there is a respectable and interesting, though far from dominant, academic tradition giving credibility and legitimacy to forces in Belgian political life that question the foundations and claims of the Belgian state of 1830. At a narrower level, Pirenne's conclusions about the spread of bilingualism in the early period were immediately contested by Flemish writers who saw them as salvos in the ongoing language struggle in Flanders (Stracke, 1913; Vermeylen, 1918, chap. 2; Van de Perre, 1919).

Whereas linguistic diversity in Switzerland became politically significant only after the Old Confederation began to expand in the sixteenth century, it has been a characteristic of the Belgian lands from their earliest history. The most salient feature of this diversity is a sharply defined linguistic frontier that crosses present-day Belgium in an east-west direction from just north of Lille in France to Aachen in Germany (see Map 1). To the north of this line various Flemish dialects and standard Dutch are spoken; to the south standard French is found, as well as some elements of Walloon dialects, which are, however, considerably less prominent than the Flemish dialects to the north. Historically, this linguistic frontier has never had any significant connection with any political frontier, and only in recent years have the political boundaries of several Belgian provinces and administrative districts been adjusted to correspond to the linguistic frontier.

The linguistic frontier originated in Roman times and has varied only slightly since the eleventh century. Such a persistent sociological phenomenon has given rise to an extensive academic literature. Among broader speculative works that seek to explain the origins of the frontier, one may begin with Godefroid Kurth's immensely detailed study of the language frontier published in the 1890s, which attributes the frontier to a fortified Roman road that ran from Boulogne to Bavai to Cologne and that impeded further Frankish penetration southward. Another school sees the issue in terms of relative density of population, contending that the Frankish invaders penetrated much further south but were in turn assimilated in the more densely populated areas south of the frontier. The historian Jean Stengers argues that no hypothesis advanced so far is sustainable because of the almost total absence of reliable historical evidence for the critical formative period. But the question remains open as archaeological research on Frankish settlements continues (Kurth, 1896-98, 1: 544-48; Dhondt, 1947; Verlinden, 1955; Stengers, 1959; Petri, 1937; 1977). In addition to these historical aspects of the frontier, there is an extensive literature concerned with analyzing and documenting the present-day language boundary, often in painstaking detail, and especially in relation to certain contested areas where the linguistic situation is rather complex (Verdoodt, 1973, 123-33). The frontier acquired administrative significance for the first time in 1822 with the application of William I's legislation on the use of Dutch in Flemish communes (Legros, 1948, 14). As early as 1819, Levy notes (1954b, 388), the line on maps was carefully drawn through the midpoint of the uninhabited forest of Soignes.

It is significant that the language boundary never became a closed political frontier but remained a zone of trade and continuous interlinguistic contact. The feudal principalities of Flanders, Brabant, and Liège all included territories of both languages, and both French and Dutch are represented in the oldest surviving documents. Pirenne notes evidence of individual bilingualism in the monasteries of the Carolingian period. In Flanders proper the language of the populace was Germanic, that is, *dietsch* or *thiois*, while French came into vogue with the upper classes, becoming a language of culture and letters and also an administrative language in the twelfth and thirteenth centuries. Even at this date there was reaction. The Flemish poet Jacob van Maerlant (ca. 1235-1300) rejected the courtly French style for a simpler didacticism, and his dictum *Wat waelsch is valsch is* indicates an attitude of suspicion and antipathy that echoes strongly in Flemish thought seven centuries later. In the prosperous expansionary period of the fourteenth and fifteenth centuries, the use of Flemish appears to have increased, and it spread even into the Walloon regions (Pirenne, 1948-52, 1: 107-109, 203-208, 214-15, 483-85). In particular, the children of noble and mercantile families were taught both languages, since for Walloon merchants a knowledge of Flemish gave them access to the towns and trade of the Hanseatic League (Curtis, 1971, 137). Des Cressonnières (1919), who investigated far more intensively than Pirenne the pattern of language usage in public life from the fourteenth to the eighteenth centuries, finds abundant evidence of institutional bilingualism and respect for local linguistic liberties in all the territories concerned, even during the supposedly centralizing Burgundian period. While the Valois dukes of Burgundy at first tried to establish French as the sole language of administration, this led to inconvenience and delays in translating documents. As the complexity of government increased, it became more and more necessary to seek top officials with a knowledge of Latin, French, and Netherlandic. While French remained the language of the court and central government, the influence of Netherlandic tended to fluctuate according to the varying strength of particularism and town liberties (Armstrong, 1965).

With the successful revolt of the northern provinces in the sixteenth century and the closure of the Scheldt by the Dutch (Bindoff, 1945), the southern provinces and the port of Antwerp entered a long period of economic and cultural decline. Extensive emigration depopulated the towns of Flanders to the advantage of neighboring Dutch cities, and the departure of the commercially oriented middle class enlarged the social gulf between the ruling nobles and the Flemish-speaking masses (Wilmars, 1968, 25-30). Continuing pressure from Holland was a factor in this decline, and the Scheldt remained closed to the southern provinces until the French Revolution. As Geyl has noted (1920, 30), "there is no sadder spectacle than that of the relations between Holland and Belgium in the 18th century, the relation of oppressors and oppressed." The language of the Flemish population, which was sealed off by the Counter-Reformation from contact with the dynamic but Protestant northern provinces and impoverished further by middle-class emigration and by poor educational facilities, underwent a long period of stagnation during the seventeenth and eighteenth centuries while the Dutch language in Holland continued to develop. By cruel coincidence, the same period saw French reach its apogee as the preeminent language of European culture. Thus even before the outbreak of the French Revolution, French had become the dominant language of cultivated society in the Austrian Netherlands as elsewhere in Europe, and the rising status of French, which promoted linguistic equality and political stability in Switzerland, had just the opposite effect in Belgium.

The language usage of this period, a topic much debated in the polemical literature, has been analyzed with rare objectivity by Deneckere (1954). The picture he portrays is a mixed one. French was the dominant language of fashion, of several departments of the central government in Brussels, and of the highest court. Flemish was used in the Estates of Flanders, in local government, and by most of the clergy. Both French and Dutch, as well as Latin, appear in scientific presentations, and at the University of Louvain instruction in the humanities was in Latin. The quality of both French and Flemish was low, and Flemish was heavily contaminated by gallicisms. On balance, Deneckere finds no conscious policy of *francisation* but concludes that situational factors, including increasing centralization of government and the outlook of the elites, favored the continuing expansion of French (1954, part I; and cf. Des Cressonnières, 1919, chaps. 5, 6; Smeyers, 1959).

The period of French domination and annexation from 1795 to 1815 enhanced the position of the French language even more. Politically, the former Prince-Bishopric of Liège and the Austrian Netherlands were now under the same jurisdiction and reorganized as *départements* of France, with French citizens occupying most of the senior administrative posts. Economically, the Belgian provinces prospered within the Napoleonic continental system. With the rapid development of industry in the Walloon provinces, there emerged a strong bourgeoisie, secularly oriented, inspired by revolutionary ideals, and qualified to vote by a property franchise. Reforms swept away archaic provincial institutions and introduced a highly centralized administration and unified legal codes.

The first principle of governmental language usage in this period was to do everything in French, though in practice official texts were supplemented by Flemish translations to the extent necessary. Thus decisions of civil tribunals were published in French only, those of criminal tribunals in French and Flemish. Knowledge of French in the Flemish region became more explicitly a matter of social class and of urbanization, spreading downward from the top and from the towns into the villages and countryside. Deneckere, who examined court proceedings in West Flanders, concluded that French was known by the propertied class and officials, by a majority of merchants and some soldiers, by a minority of artisans and police, but not by workers, domestics, or country people. Of the educated classes, only the clergy were not subject to *francisation*, their exclusion arising from revolutionary measures directed against the Church (Deneckere, 1954, part II). In such a setting French continued to spread, with considerable support from the elites, until by 1814 Flemish was almost totally excluded from public life.

In 1815 the Congress of Vienna, in the course of its general adjustment of European diplomatic interests, detached the Belgian provinces from France and somewhat artificially reunited them—after more than two centuries of separation and accumulating resentment—with predominantly Protestant Holland as the United Kingdom of the Netherlands. King William I, descendant of the Stadholders of Orange-Nassau, a progressive monarch but stubborn and authoritarian in temperament, soon ran into difficulties with his Belgian subjects. His first move in language policy was basically a withdrawal of official support for French. This was followed in 1819 by an executive decree to make Dutch the sole official language beginning in 1823 in the four Flemish provinces of East and West Flanders, Antwerp, and Limburg, and later this was extended to include Flemish Brabant and Brussels. Such a policy clashed headlong with the entrenched career interests of established officials and lawyers who by now used French almost exclusively in public life. Ultimately, under growing pressure, it had to be modified by decrees in 1829 and 1830 that reinstated French as an optional language in the Flemish provinces for official documents and court proceedings, but by this time the attempt at Netherlandization had seriously alienated the governmental and professional elite of the Flemish provinces.

But language was not the only issue, nor even the dominant one. In some respects Belgium prospered under the union. The monarch's liberal reformist policy actively promoted the economic development of the southern provinces and began to overhaul and modernize the educational system. The Catholic University of Louvain, closed by the French in 1797, was reopened as a state university in 1817, along with two new state universities at Gent and Liège to match the three existing universities of the northern provinces. New state primary and secondary schools were established, and existing Catholic private schools were made subject to state inspection. However, the Catholic clergy, already deeply suspicious of Protestant Holland, were further antagonized by these educational measures and by other religious frictions (Delplace, 1899). The emerging Walloon industrial bourgeoisie, feeling insufficiently protected by the low Dutch tariff system, developed economic grievances. As the list of religious and economic grievances grew longer, some Flemish particularist scholars found further grounds for dispute in the different spelling systems currently in use in the northern and southern provinces, alleging that Dutch and Flemish were in fact separate languages (Clough, 1930, chap. 2; Curtis, 1971, 182-90; Vanhamme, 1968, 259-60; Deneckere, 1954, part III; De Jonghe, 1967).

In a more general sense, the Belgian provinces signally failed to achieve an equal partnership with the north during the union period. Despite having a larger population than the Dutch provinces, the Belgian provinces in 1827 had, by one estimate, 1 cabinet minister out of 7, 1 diplomat in 28, 17 high civil servants out of 300, and 6 generals out of 22 (Schreurs, 1948, 34; Delplace, 1899, 174). This level of representation helps explain the King's continuing insensitivity to Belgian grievances. In the end it was the combined opposition of a French-speaking liberal bourgeoisie and traditionalist Flemish Catholics that led to the Belgian Revolution of August 1830. It is important to recognize that this Revolution was the product not of any nationalist movement but of a combination of groups reacting against specific administrative measures. Its improbable success owed more to Orangist indecision and to the diplomacy of the great European powers than to the strength or cohesion of the insurgents. "If I may believe the representations which reached me from many quarters," reported the British writer Frances Trollope after an extended visit in 1833, "no country was ever revolutionized by a feeling so little general as that which severed Belgium from Holland" (1834, 1: 53). For some time the internal balance of forces remained in doubt (Stengers, 1950-51), but the one element of substantial consensus among the masses was an antipathy to everything Dutch, and this unhappy legacy of the union with Holland was to influence the language question in independent Belgium for a long time to come.

In its practical aspects the Revolution had been mainly the work of a determined bourgeoisie, and this bourgeoisie was overwhelmingly French-speaking, even in the Flemish provinces. Its political hegemony was established by a limited franchise which gave the vote to some 46,000 electors in a population of about four million (Gilissen, 1958, 84). As early as November 1830 a decree of the provisional government declared French the state language but called for translations of documents into Flemish or German dialects to be published wherever local conditions might require them. The preamble to this decree noted "that it would be impossible to publish an official text of laws and decrees in Flemish and German" because of variations in usage of these idioms from province to province and even from district to district (Recueil des lois, 1831, 1: 282-83; Herremans, 1965, 50-51). The German-speaking areas at this point included the whole of Luxembourg, most of which was detached from Belgium by the final settlement of 1839, which left King William as Grand Duke of Luxembourg. Notwithstanding the 1830 decree, the post-independence Recueil des lois et arrêtés royaux continued to be published in a bilingual edition, with French and Dutch on facing pages, until 1836, when it became unilingually French.

The Belgian Constitution of 1831 was a liberal but not a revolutionary document. Some 40 per cent of its clauses were carried over from the United Netherlands Constitution of 1815 and a further 45 per cent were taken from the French charters of 1830 and 1791 (Gilissen, 1968, 132). Its sole linguistic provision, Article 23, was an expression of linguistic freedom that was clearly a reaction against the attempted constraints of the previous regime, constraints imposed arbitrarily by executive decree without parliamentary approval (Maroy, 1966, 454). Appearing in a section of twenty-one articles focusing on classical civil liberties, this article states:

The use of the languages spoken in Belgium is optional (facultatif). It can be regulated only by law, and only concerning official acts and judicial matters.

The Belgian leaders of 1830, as Maurice Herremans notes, were content to record the decadence of the Flemish language on the statute book (1948, 82; 1965, 51). As Lord Durham was to do in Canada in 1839, they identified their own language with commerce, modernity, and progress, and they were confident that time alone would bring linguistic unity, though some leading figures like Charles Rogier were not above urging total exclusion of Flemings from public employment until they perceived the advantages of learning French (Baudart, 1945, 38).

B   The Flemish Movement and its Consequences

As matters turned out, the linguistic evolution of independent Belgium took an unpredictably different turn. Beginning shortly after independence, the Flemish-speaking part of the population experienced a long, slow, many-faceted improvement of their material and psychological position in Belgian society that in certain aspects continued well into the 1970s. In a century and a half of collective endeavor the Flemish "decadence" of the early nineteenth century has been substantially overcome, but the mentality of the struggle persists strongly, and the Flemish Movement in the broad sense remains a potent force in contemporary Belgian life. Its consequences not only for language policy but for the very structure of the state itself can hardly be underestimated.

This is not the place for a detailed historical analysis of the Flemish Movement. Its story has been told many times, in several languages, from diverse vantage points, and over several decades since the late nineteenth century.[1] The notion of a single "movement" may be deceptive. The term Flemish Movement refers to a wide range of cultural, educational, social, economic, and political activities and organizations, which have been linked primarily by their common aim of improving the position of the Flemish-speaking population and of the Dutch language in Belgian society. This action has been directed not only towards political and economic objectives but towards social and psychological ends as well. The full rationale for this complex social phenomenon will emerge only in later chapters as we analyze the socioeconomic structure and attitudinal patterns of Belgian society.

Yet the distinctive stages in the evolution of the Flemish Movement deserve careful attention, for they invite comparison with other nationalist movements, and specifically with the Finnish and French-Canadian cases, which will be examined in succeeding volumes. The first phase, commencing immediately after independence, was almost exclusively linguistic and literary. Its aim was to rekindle a sense of pride in Flemish history, culture, and language. The foremost figure of this period was the poet and philologist Jan Frans Willems (1793-1846), the "father of the Flemish Movement," whose literary career spanned three political regimes. After being deprived of his post as archivist of Antwerp for continuing Orangist sympathies after the 1830 Revolution, Willems turned to the study of old Flemish literature and worked for the revival of a neglected Netherlandic tradition. In turn, this scholarly tradition fostered a romantic popular literature, whose foremost exponent was the novelist Hendrik Conscience (1812-83). His historical novel, *The Lion of Flanders*, published in 1838 and commemorating the defeat of the French at the Battle of the Golden Spurs in 1302, provided a symbol and a rallying point for an emerging popular awakening. This first phase of the Flemish Movement also saw some unsuccessful petitioning to Parliament, but this campaign focused narrowly on language rights (Curtis, 1971, 210-11). Despite a severe economic

---

[1] As might be expected, most of the important recent studies are in Dutch, although several earlier ones appeared in French. Among many possible choices, one might select, in Dutch, Prayon-van Zuylen (1892); Fredericq (1906-1909); Basse (1930-33); Lamberty (1933); Willemsen (1954a, 1954b, 1969, 1974-75); Elias (1963-65; 1969); Van Haegendoren (1962); Picard (1963); Todts (1961-71); and a very useful reference work, the *Encyclopedie van de Vlaamse Beweging* (Deleu et al., 1973-75). In French there are Hamelius (1894); Vermeylen (1918); and Herremans (1948). In English there are important studies by Clough (1930) and Curtis (1971); a translation of an excellent journalistic overview by Ruys (1973); and a more popular treatment by Carson (1969). Many of these contain further bibliographies, but in addition one should consult the admirable specialized bibliographies of Verdoodt (1973) and Herremans (1965).

crisis in the textile towns of Flanders and the famine following the potato blight of the 1840s (Vermeylen, 1918, 30-31), the limited goals of this first phase were epitomized by the motto of one of the first literary societies formed at Gent in 1836 to promote Flemish interests: *De Tael is gansch het Volk* (Elias, 1963-65, 2: 45, 403).

Emphasis on the language and the literary tradition would remain a feature of the Flemish Movement, but a second phase, directed towards parliamentary redress of grievances and the winning of linguistic equality in a legal sense, began about 1860. The way was opened for this change of emphasis by the appointment in 1856 of an official commission on Flemish grievances which included in its membership several leading figures of the Flemish Movement. Its report, submitted a year later, is important as the first comprehensive statement of Flemish claims. In addition to an historical survey of the language question and a justification for improving the position of the Dutch language in Flanders, the commission produced a detailed program of reforms, including greater use of Dutch at several levels of regular and special education; the translation of official publications; administrative communications with Flemish provinces and communes in Dutch or in both languages; optional use of Dutch in the courts; a knowledge of Dutch in the diplomatic service; division of the army into Walloon and Flemish units, with each to be commanded in its own language; and establishment of a Flemish section of the Royal Academy. The commission also assembled some interesting documentation on contemporary plurilingual regimes elsewhere in Europe, including Switzerland, Austria, Sardinia, and the Duchy of Schleswig, as well as on the Belgian provinces before 1789 (*Commission flamande*, 1859; Clough, 1930, 88-90; Elias, 1963-65, 2: 287, 290). The report, however, met with strong governmental disapproval and had little immediate impact, even its publication being delayed for two years.

Gradually, and partly as a result of certain *causes célèbres* in the courts that served to mobilize Flemish opinion, the way was prepared for successful legislative initiatives in Parliament even though Parliament itself still rested on a narrow franchise. The most sombre and dramatic of these court cases (though not strictly relevant to Flanders since it unfolded entirely in Wallonie) was that of Jan Coucke and Pieter Goethals, two Flemish workmen who were tried for the murder and robbery of an elderly widow at Couillet near Charleroi in March 1860. Their trial was conducted entirely in French before the Assize Court of Hainaut at Mons, and even the defence attorney was unilingual. The evidence against them was circumstantial, turning primarily on a remark between the two men overheard by a jailer and allegedly mistranslated by the court interpreter. Nonetheless, both were found guilty and guillotined in November 1860.

Several months later, the case took a dramatic and unexpected turn when another suspect confessed to complicity in the murder and declared

Coucke and Goethals innocent. Almost overnight the fate of the two Flemings became a central symbol of the wider injustices suffered by all unilingual Flemings in a Belgian society dominated by Francophones, a powerful argument in the mounting campaign for legislative protection of Flemish rights. More than a century later, the case still emerges spontaneously in interviews with Flemish leaders as an instance of gross miscarriage of justice, a Belgian equivalent of the case of Sacco and Vanzetti, and an example of linguistic oppression. Recent studies have tended to demythologize the incident, suggesting not only that the degree to which the two Flemings were involved in the murder remains unclear but also that they were not so totally unilingual as later legend maintains (Prayon-van Zuylen, 1892, 207-15; Bossier, 1950; Laurent, 1971; Deleu et al., 1973-75, 1: 341-42).

Once mobilized for action by this case and by others less tragic but no less demeaning, Parliament produced a series of laws—which were usually weakened during their passage—to improve the legal status of *Nederlandsch* in the Flemish provinces. The most important of these measures concerned the use of languages in penal courts (1873 and 1889), in communications between the public and state—but not provincial or communal—authorities (1878), and in state-run secondary education (1883), where only modest successes were registered and where extension to the important Catholic private school sector was delayed until 1910 (Clough, 1930, 142-54). The culmination of this first series of language laws was the De Vriendt-Coremans law of 1898, which gave Netherlandic formal legal equality with French as an official language. This period also saw a considerable development of the symbols of official bilingualism, including bilingual coinage (1886), banknotes (1888), postage stamps (1891), King Leopold II's first public address in Flemish (1887), the first speech in Flemish in the lower house of Parliament (1888) and in the Senate (1900), and in 1895 full bilingualism of the official gazette, the *Moniteur* or *Staatsblad* (*Admission progressive*, 1969). In general, the most that could be achieved in practical terms through this first series of linguistic laws was the right of Dutch to coexist with French in the Flemish provinces, and some laws in their final version offered less than equality. Nevertheless, language practice in Flanders began to change. Prayon-van Zuylen notes that the proportion of cases pleaded in Dutch at Gent rose from 24 per cent in 1874 to 38 per cent in 1887-88 (1892, 327-28). In the Walloon provinces, official unilingualism was never questioned during this period.

With the achievement of formal legal equality by the end of the century, the way was opened for the Flemish Movement to enter a third and more complex phase that turned away from literary romanticism and stressed the primary importance of economic and social action. Manhood suffrage had been won in 1893, though its impact was lessened by the retention of plural voting based on economic and educational status. It was now possible for Flamingants, as the more activist leadership of the movement were called, to mobilize the general population and develop a greater consciousness of group identity. The most characteristic figure in this changing emphasis was Lodewijk De Raet (1870-1914), who wrote tirelessly of the need to improve the economic and educational position of the Flemish population, and who was active himself in organizing university extension classes in Brussels. More clearly than any of his predecessors, De Raet perceived the Flemish question as a matter of material interests: *Taalbelang is stoffelijk belang* (Lamberty, 1933, 127-28). The most salient issue of this period was a campaign for Netherlandization of the still mainly Francophone state university of Gent. Against more moderate proposals for a gradual transition, De Raet argued for an accelerated *vernederlandsing* with special emphasis on the technical programs (Curtis, 1971, 270-85; Clough, 1930, 159-69; Lamberty, 1951; 1968, 148-49; CRISP, 1974, no. 637:2-4). As with other measures of this kind, there were delays in Parliament and strong Francophone opposition, and the issue remained unresolved when Belgium was overrun by the German armies in 1914.

This third phase of the Flemish Movement began to have some impact on the Francophone population. The Walloon provinces had not been directly touched by the early language laws, but under the new wider franchise the Walloon masses could also be mobilized for political purposes. Faced with growing political demands of the Flemish Movement, the Francophone electorate gradually became more aware of its own distinctive cultural and economic interests. After some insignificant early activity by cultural organizations and sporadic political manifestations in the 1880s, more serious political action developed in the 1900s, reaching maturity with the first Assemblée wallonne in 1912.

Within a year this assembly adopted a distinctive set of symbols for Wallonie, including a national holiday (in late September to commemorate the 1830 uprising), a coat-of-arms, and a distinctive flag featuring the *coq wallon*. It also founded a periodical with the significant title *Défense wallonne* (Destrée, 1923, chap. 6). Such activities were scarcely an exact counterpart to the Flemish Movement. Instead, this first Walloon reaction appears to have been born of feelings of defensiveness and insecurity, as a response to an increasingly self-conscious Flemish population whose preponderance in numbers was becoming more significant in the new era of mass politics.

The Flemish Movement was catastrophically undermined and divided by the effects of the First World War. In August 1914 the German armies ignored Belgian neutrality and overran most of the country within a month. Flemish opinion, vaguely pro-German before the war, was profoundly shocked by the invasion, but gradually some of the more radical leaders began to see the possibility of winning certain long-denied Flemish objectives by cooperating with the occupying power. In their turn, the German military authorities saw diplomatic advantages in furthering Flemish aspirations and counteracting the influence of France in Belgian politics. In concrete terms this policy of Flemish "activism" or collaboration led to the reopening of Gent University as a Dutch-language institution in 1916, to administrative division of the Ministry of Arts and Sciences, and—in March 1917—to the administrative separation of Flanders and Wallonie with separate capitals in Brussels and Namur (Clough, 1930, 187-203). Nor was language neglected. In a series of orders carefully linked to existing—but largely neglected—prewar Belgian legislation, the German occupation authorities decreed the general use of Flemish in the Flemish provinces, French in the Walloon areas, and German exclusively in the German-speaking communes bordering the Grand Duchy of Luxembourg. This effort to reverse the process of *francisation* (or "Frenchification") extended even to Brussels, which was to use only its Flemish street-names (*Merkblatt*, 1916).

The institutional framework for Flemish activism was provided by the Council of Flanders, a group of intellectuals, teachers, and officials selected at an activist gathering in Brussels in February 1917 without popular mandate. This council, politically inexperienced, internally divided, and closely controlled by the German occupation authorities, tried to act as a provisional government and went so far as to declare the political independence of Flanders in December 1917. The proclamation remained without effect, but the chief legacy of activism was to put political independence on the agenda of the Flemish Movement for the first time. The Flemish activists, as Ruys notes (1973, 76), were comparable to the Czechs who rejected their Austrian fatherland, but their misfortune was in seeking aid from the losing side.

Despite its high visibility, activism represented only a minority opinion within the Flemish Movement. Many of its traditional political leaders remained loyal to the Belgian regime throughout the war, either remaining politically inactive under the occupation or in some cases escaping to neutral Holland, where they continued to work for the achievement of Flemish objectives within the framework of a Belgian state. Still another current of opinion developed among the Flemish rank and file of the Belgian army, which had been forced into the extreme corner of West Flanders by the German advance. During the long months of trench warfare these units formed study circles that addressed the question of postwar Flemish objectives through institutional and constitutional reforms. The Frontists, as they were known, already distrusted by the military authorities, became further suspect in April 1918 when they tried to establish contact with the activists. The ending of the war left the Flemish Movement divided over its objectives and largely discredited in the eyes of the restored political elite, which was all too ready to link the excesses of activism with the Movement as a whole.

The first decade after 1918 produced certain modest advances for the Flemish cause, but the results fell far short of the expectations aroused during the war. In 1921 a new law regulated internal language use in the administration for the first time. It also recognized the principle of separate linguistic regions for Flanders and Wallonie for all levels of government, but then allowed exceptions in internal or external language usage at the option of municipal councils or individual citizens. The Brussels area was given a bilingual regime, and higher civil servants in the central government were for the first time expected to be bilingual. However, efforts to put effective sanctions in this law met with Walloon opposition and were defeated. In 1923 the long, bitter struggle over the *vernederlandsing* of Gent University moved a step further with a bill allowing students to take either one third or two thirds of their program in Dutch and the rest in French, a compromise that satisfied neither side. These measures indicate a substantial gulf between the political elites and an increasingly self-aware Flemish electorate, which had increased its electoral potential in 1919 with the replacement of plural voting by simple manhood suffrage. The Walloon population, on the other hand, saw itself disadvantaged by increasing requirements for bilingualism and also reacted negatively (Clough, 1930, 232-34; Höjer, 1946, 18-19; Curtis, 1971, 312-13).

A decade of postwar complacency was shattered at a parliamentary by-election on December 9, 1928, when Dr. August Borms, the only wartime activist still in prison, whose activities on the Council of Flanders had caused him to be sentenced to death and—additionally—to a loss of political rights for ten years,[1] was put forward as a candidate by the tiny Flemish nationalist Front Party and overwhelmingly endorsed by the Antwerp electorate over a Liberal opponent. This thunderbolt, followed by sharp nationalist gains at the general election of 1929, made it unmistakably clear to the other parliamentary parties that it was time to take the claims of the Flemish Movement more seriously.

The positive effects of this increased concern appeared in the form of a second round of language laws formulated and passed between 1930 and 1938, in some cases after difficult interparty negotiations. The first, providing for the full Netherlandization of the University of Gent, passed without serious opposition in 1930, and this step soon led to the creation of further Dutch-language programs at the privately controlled universities of Louvain and Brussels. A second educational measure, concerning the language of primary and secondary education, was passed in July 1932. It reaffirmed the basic principle that the language of instruction in primary and secondary education was the language of the region—French, Dutch, or German, as the case might be—but it still left the door open at both levels

---

[1] The death sentence was not carried out, but in the Second World War Borms was less fortunate. After collaborating again with the German occupation, he was sentenced to death a second time and executed in April 1946.

for children whose mother tongue was other than the regional language to receive instruction in another official language. During the complex negotiations in Parliament many understood that these minority-language facilities would be transitional classes only, but the wording of the legislation itself is ambiguous on this point and leaves much to the discretion of local and national authorities. In the Brussels area and in bilingual communes along the language frontier, children were to be instructed in their mother tongue—French or Dutch—as declared by their father, and early compulsory study of the other official language was also required in these communes but not elsewhere (Rüling, 1939, 112-20; Curtis, 1971, 324-32).

Almost simultaneously, another law of June 1932 on the use of languages in administrative matters reaffirmed and strengthened the principle of Dutch as the administrative language of Flanders and French as that of Wallonie. It made various special arrangements for the communes of the Brussels area and the Brabant provincial administration, for communes speaking predominantly a language other than that of their region, and for communes with language minorities of more than 30 per cent as revealed by the latest census. A more interesting feature of this legislation is that it reduced the requirements of the 1921 law for individual bilingualism among employees of central state departments to a relatively few senior officials in each department, with services below the top levels being organized as far as possible in unilingual French and Dutch units. An important aspect of this change was that files were henceforth to be treated from start to finish in the language in which the matter originated; there would be no resort to translation for the convenience of public servants. This law found favor among both Walloons and Flemings, and it marks a first significant step on the road to administrative separation along linguistic lines (Curtis, 1971, 332-40; Maroy, 1966, 464-65).

This second series of language laws was rounded out by the law of June 1935 on the use of languages in judicial matters and that of July 1938 on languages in the army. The first of these provided that in courts of first instance the language used in civil and penal procedures should be the official language of the region concerned, with either French or Dutch being used in the Brussels area, and that the language of first instance should govern procedure in higher courts. The second law envisaged the establishment of unilingual army units up to battalion and regimental level, but its implementation was delayed by the outbreak of hostilities in 1939. Since both these laws, with certain amendments, are still in force, they will be examined further in chapter 4.

By 1939 the program of the "minimalists"—the part of the Flemish Movement that worked for basic language reforms within the existing Belgian state and through the traditional political parties—had been largely achieved. The organized political strength of the Flemish electorate had been demonstrated unmistakably, and the language legislation of the period assured the eventual predominance of the Dutch language in Flanders, even if various local exceptions and general problems of enforcement still remained to be resolved. The Walloon population, faced with an irresistible Flemish demand for full language equality and symmetry in its application, abandoned the cause of the Francophone minority in Flanders and the concept of a bilingual Flanders in order to avoid corresponding demands from the economically weaker Flemish minority in Wallonie. Meanwhile the more extreme strands of Flemish nationalism, untrammelled by the responsibilities of office, had begun to pursue more fanciful goals, which looked beyond language policy to the nature of the Belgian state itself.

The decade of the 1930s was a period of divisions and doctrinal confusion for the Flemish Movement and a period of severe strain for the Belgian economic and political system. The most prominent successors to the Front Party of the 1920s were the Vlaams Nationaal Verbond (or VNV) and Verdinaso. The VNV, a loose association of several tendencies, leaned to both a federalist Belgium and a Great Netherlands or "Dietschland" doctrine of uniting Flanders with Holland. It included partisans of both democratic and totalitarian persuasion. Verdinaso, which stood for Verbond van Dietsche Nationaal-solidaristen, more authoritarian in organization and openly Fascist in doctrine, developed the idea of a Dietsche Rijk that would include Holland, Flanders, Friesland, Wallonie, and Luxembourg, a modern incarnation of the Burgundian Empire. On the Francophone side, there emerged another strong authoritarian movement, Rex, headed by the Walloon Leon Degrelle. After the general election of 1936, it formed an alliance with the VNV that accounted for 37 out of 202 seats in the lower house. The formal text of this alliance explicitly recognized the federalist goals of the VNV (Etienne, 1968, 179-80), but the arrangement between the Flemish and Francophone right soon faltered and Rex lost ground heavily at the election of April 1939. By this time the Flemish nationalists, somewhat sobered by the fate of Austria and Czechoslovakia, were exploring with the Flemish wing of the Catholic party various approaches to greater administrative separation and especially to cultural autonomy within the existing Belgian state. These discussions were interrupted by the outbreak of the war.

In the summer of 1940, the mainstream of the Flemish Movement faced a second German occupation with the deliberate intention of avoiding the mistakes of the activists of the First World War. In practice, however, many individuals soon found it all too easy to slide gradually into collaboration. To all appearances Germany seemed to have won the war, and in contrast with 1914 the King and various leading figures of the political and economic elite led the way by adjusting pragmatically to what appeared to be inevitable. Moreover, German policy from the outset was more favorable to the Flemish than to the Walloon population, releasing

Flemish prisoners of war, applying existing language legislation rigorously, and rehabilitating former activists. Some VNV leaders and members of smaller pro-Nazi groups became zealous collaborators, as did some of the Francophone leadership of Rex. Other Flemish nationalists maintained a more cautious attitude to Germany and even drifted away from the ethnic nationalism of the Great Netherlands idea to return to the notion of a more decentralized Belgium (Ruys, 1973, 110-25; Gérard-Libois and Gotovitch, 1972, 142-44; CRISP, 1970, nos. 497-98; 1972, no. 581). The period is a complex one, especially when viewed from the calmer perspective of the 1980s, and generalizations about collective Flemish or Walloon responses to the occupation tend to blur the substantial variations among individuals, even among different members of the same organization.

The liberation of Belgium from German occupation in 1944 brought a return of the wartime government-in-exile from London and a vigorous pursuit of political and economic collaborators and those who had served in German military or police units. These included both Walloons and Flemings: one careful statistical analysis shows that the total number of convictions in all categories in proportion to the population was only slightly higher for Flemings than for Walloons—0.73 per cent in Flanders compared to 0.52 for Wallonie and 0.56 for Brussels (Gilissen, 1951). Nevertheless, the Flemish soon became convinced that this *répression de l'incivisme* was directed not only at collaborators in the legal sense but at Flemish nationalists in general, and that even the "Flemish idea itself" was being hunted down (Ruys, 1973, 128), as it had been all too successfully for a decade following the First World War. For several years after 1944 political manifestations of the Flemish Movement were virtually forced underground, but its doctrines were kept alive at the cultural level mainly through the activities of the major Flemish cultural foundations. In any case the repression period contributed a bitter supplement to the history of Flemish-Walloon relations. On the Flemish side, it led to strong recurring demands for a general amnesty for wartime offences, which were just as firmly opposed by Francophones.

The temporary silencing of Flemish nationalism after the liberation coincided with reawakened sensitivities in Wallonie. These feelings surfaced dramatically at the first postwar meeting of the Congrès national wallon held at Liège in October 1945, where a strong plurality of delegates voted in a first ballot—a so-called *vote de coeur*—for the reunion of Wallonie with France. In a second ballot—a calmer *vote de raison*—they opted overwhelmingly for an autonomous Wallonie within a federalized Belgium (Herremans, 1951, 228-30; Schreurs, 1960, 34-35). The issues that provoked this rather emotional protest against a unitary Belgium included a growing demographic imbalance between Wallonie and Flanders, economic stagnation, pent-up resentments against wartime collaboration and supposedly inadequate prosecution of *incivisme*, and the beginnings of the "royal question," that is, whether Leopold III should be restored to the throne in the light of his wartime collaboration. Taken together, these and other issues seemed to raise doubts about the future of Francophone Belgium, and the reawakening of Walloon sensitivity can be seen as an essentially defensive reaction against a loss of control over questions deemed vital to their own interests (*Wallonie en alerte*, 1949). To the extent that they leaned towards federalism, Walloons could find some common ground with Flemish federalists. It is important to note, however, that while Flemish nationalism had tended to be most strongly associated with the Flemish Catholic right, and even with the extreme or antiparliamentary right, the regionalism of Wallonie was just as markedly associated with the socialist left. This overlapping of cleavages, while far from total, was to add an extra element of tension to some of the struggles that lay ahead. The relatively late emergence of Walloon self-awareness is matched by a correspondingly slender literature on the question. Apart from the pioneering study of Maurice Herremans (1951), serious studies taking a specifically Walloon frame of reference began to appear only after the traumatic conflicts of the 1960s (Genicot, 1973; Hasquin, 1975-76).

The decade of the 1950s saw Flemings and Walloons divided over a whole series of issues, beginning with the passionate climax of the "royal question" in 1950, when continuing bitter divisions over King Leopold's wartime conduct forced him to abdicate in favor of his son. Not all of these issues had any direct or even indirect linguistic implications, and yet the cumulative effect was to widen further the gulf of mistrust between the two communities. As an example, the measures taken by the Socialist-Liberal coalition government against the Catholic secondary schools in 1954, which precipitated the "schools war" of 1954-58, were seen by Catholic Flemings as not only a socialist but also a Walloon initiative. Meanwhile, the Centre Harmel, a study commission established by Parliament in 1948, had initiated a major inquiry into all aspects of the *problème communautaire*; its results, including studies, interim reports, and a final report published in 1958, would provide an extensive basis for the highly intricate political debate that lay ahead (Centre de recherche, 1958; CRISP, 1961, no. 131).

As the Flemish Movement revived and gradually re-entered the political process, two broad political objectives became clear. First, a cumulation of grievances arising from the administration of the language laws led the Flemish Movement to call for what was confidently expected to be the "final chapter" in the hundred-year struggle for acceptable language legislation (Ruys, 1973, 152). This campaign led to a third round of language laws passed in 1962 and 1963 after gigantic mass demonstrations and exhausting parliamentary struggles. Second, the parliamentary elites, in the face of growing pressures from increasingly militant interest groups, began to tackle the infinitely more complex task of reforming the structures of the state itself. The object here was to find some satisfactory institutional form for the broad concept of "cultural autonomy," which had been an increasingly salient goal of Flemish nationalist policy since the 1930s and which was now proving increasingly attractive to many Walloons as well. Beginning in 1963, this second phase led to a major constitutional overhaul, completed in outline by December 1970, but the detailed legislative implementation of the principles enunciated in this reform was only partially achieved during the next decade.

Since many of these developments of the postwar period are discussed in other chapters, there is no need to trace their history in detail here. The political issues that have tended to divide Walloons and Flemings along linguistic lines will be analyzed more fully in Chapter 3. The language legislation of the early 1960s and the long road towards constitutional and institutional reform will be outlined in Chapter 4. Finally, in Chapter 5 special consideration will be given to the thorny problems of the Brussels capital area, a mainly Francophone urban enclave in a Flemish countryside. These problems have constituted a major obstacle to reform as well as a graveyard of ministerial reputations; even in the 1980s, they remain unresolved after years of effort to find a minimally acceptable solution.

There are also certain external perspectives that might be noted. In sharp contrast to the easily defended Alpine redoubt of Switzerland, the Belgian terrain is far more open to outside influences, and the evolution of the Flemish Movement is therefore linked more obviously to changes in wider European politics. The first legislative victories for the Flemish cause in the 1870s followed soon after the unification of Germany and that country's crushing military victory over France in the Franco-Prussian War. Early pan-Germanist thinkers were quick to take up the cause of Flemish nationalism, though at the diplomatic level relations between the two countries remained correct enough down to 1914 (Kohn, 1957; Gotovitch, 1967). After the First World War and the German occupation, which revealed the shortcomings of a foreign policy of neutrality jointly guaranteed by the three neighboring great powers, Belgium sought security through a military alliance with France. The accord of 1920, which immediately proved a source of Flemish discontent in domestic politics, came under increasing pressure in the 1930s with the rise of Flemish right-wing parties sympathetic to Germany. For a combination of domestic and external reasons it was abandoned in 1936, to be replaced by a policy of increased military preparedness and an independent foreign policy on the Dutch model (Van Cauwelaert, 1946; Laurent, 1969b). Formal dissociation from France did not spare Belgium a second German invasion and occupation from 1940 to 1944, and one major difference between Swiss and Belgian history is that in the Belgian case the occupation authorities were able, for some eight years in two world wars, to exploit linguistic divisions as they saw fit in pursuit of German national interests.

Chapter 2

Language Groups and Belgian Social Structure

A   Languages and Language Regions

Although Belgium was one of the first countries to organize census language statistics in a systematic way, it is somewhat paradoxical that attempts at precise comparisons over time have encountered significant technical difficulties. More serious problems arose after the language laws of the 1930s attached important political and administrative consequences to the census results. For a century, from 1846 to 1947, the Belgian census regularly recorded language data for individuals, except for the census of 1856. In 1846 respondents were asked for the single language usually spoken. From 1866 to 1900 the question focused on which of the national languages (French, Dutch, German) was *understood*, with the possibility of multiple responses. The four censuses from 1910 to 1947, while continuing to ask about the national languages known, also asked those who named more than one language a second question, namely, which one they "used most frequently." As in the Swiss case, no attempt was ever made in the Belgian census to distinguish between the standard languages and their corresponding Flemish, Walloon, and Germanic dialects. The publication of the linguistic results of the 1947 census led to intense political controversy concerning some communes along the linguistic border and in the Brussels metropolitan area. One consequence was the dropping of all language questions in the census from 1961 onward. The development of the Belgian language census and the increasingly charged political atmosphere surrounding it have been described in a number of publications by Paul Levy (1938; 1950; 1954a; 1954b; 1959; 1960a; 1960b; 1962; 1964; 1974), as well as by others (Galderoux, 1959; Jonckheere, 1970; Verdoodt, 1973, 120-23).

On the basis of the relatively rich data resulting from these census language questions, which are available down to communal level, we can construct two main tables for the country as a whole, one to show reported language knowledge (Table 1), the other to indicate the relative predomi-

Table 1

Belgium: Reported knowledge of national languages, 1866-1947 (percentages)

Year	Total population		French only	Dutch only	German only	French and Dutch	French and German	Dutch and German	French/ Dutch/ German	None of national languages
	000s	%								
1866	4,828	100	42.3	49.8	0.7	6.4	0.4	*	0.1	0.2
1880[a]	5,520	100	42.6	47.5	0.8	8.1	0.7	0.1	0.3	0.1
1890	6,069	100	40.9	45.2	0.5	11.6	0.9	0.1	0.6	0.1
1900	6,694	100	38.5	42.2	0.4	12.0	1.0	0.1	0.6	5.2
1910	7,424	100	38.2	43.4	0.4	11.7	1.0	0.1	0.7	4.5
1920	7,466	100	38.2	42.7	0.8	13.0	0.7	*	0.5	4.1
1930	8,092	100	37.6	42.9	0.8	12.9	0.8	0.1	0.7	4.1
1947	8,512	100	34.2	41.8	0.7	15.6	0.9	0.2	2.5	4.0

* Indicates .05 per cent or less.
a Percentages for 1880 based on total population less 283,000 infants not counted for language purposes.

Sources: 1866-1900: calculated from *Annuaire statistique*, 1901, 90-91; 1907, 92-93; *Recensement*, 1900, xlii; 1910-47: *Recensement, 1947* (supplement published in *Moniteur belge* of June 26, 1954), 152-55.

nance of one language or the other, as indicated by the language used "most frequently" by bilinguals combined with data for unilinguals (Table 2). The censuses from 1866 to 1900 do not provide the necessary information for Table 2, while the question asked in 1846 belongs more properly to Table 2 than to Table 1. In using both these tables for comparisons over time, however, a significant difficulty arises. In early censuses infants were either classified according to the language of the household or of the parents or not counted at all, but from 1900 onward they were included in the group speaking *none* of the national languages. In 1930 fully 82 per cent of this latter group were infants under two years of age. Therefore, in order to establish precise trends from the nineteenth century to the twentieth, one must make rather complicated adjustments concerning this changing category of "non-speakers," bearing in mind that the age distribution for Francophones has tended to differ from that for Flemings.

Table 2

Belgium: Language spoken most frequently, 1846-1947 (percentages)

Year	Total population		French	Dutch	German	Other and not declared
	000s	%				
1846	4,337	100	42.1	57.0	0.8	0.1
1910	7,424	100	42.9	51.6	1.0	4.5
1920	7,466	100	43.9	50.8	1.2	4.1
1930	8,092	100	43.4	51.1	1.2	4.2
1947	8,512	100	41.9	52.6	0.9	4.6

Sources: 1846: *Recensement*, 1846, xxxvii; 1910-47: *Recensement*, 1947 (supplement published in *Moniteur belge* of June 26, 1954), 152-55.

The most noticeable trend in Table 1 is the increase in French-Dutch bilingualism. If we include those speaking all three national languages, the proportion rises from 6.5 per cent when first reported in 1866 to 18.1 per cent in 1947. At some later censuses the level of bilingualism may even be slightly underreported, as was urged by Flemish nationalist organizations. More detailed inspection of figures over several censuses suggests that French-Dutch bilingualism, as might be expected, has been more widespread in larger, urban communes than in rural areas and more pronounced among the adult population than among young people. Bilingualism also has a regional focus, as we shall see shortly, being concentrated most strongly in the province of Brabant and the *arrondissement* of Brussels.

A second and perhaps more important feature to be noted from Table 2 is the remarkable overall stability of the two major linguistic groups. If we set aside the group speaking none of the national languages, it can be shown that in the century from 1846 to 1947 the Netherlandic-speaking proportion of the population declined by just under two percentage points to about 55 per cent, and the Francophone population rose by a similar margin to roughly 44 per cent. These changes are well within the ranges found in Switzerland over a similar period (see Volume 1, Table 6, 50). As we shall see shortly, however, this relative stability is the product of various demographic and linguistic factors that tend to counterbalance one another, but in such a way as to give rise to acute political tensions.

It is frequently said of Belgium that most bilingualism is found among the Flemings, but we cannot test this generalization statistically because for those reporting a knowledge of two or more national languages the census contains no indicator of mother tongue or home language, as distinct from the language "most frequently spoken," and this latter concept appears to be influenced more by the immediate social environment than by the individual's original linguistic background. We can, however, trace the incidence of bilingualism geographically. From Table 3 it can be seen that French-Dutch bilingualism has been more widespread in the Flemish than in the Walloon provinces, but highest of all in Brabant, which lies astride the linguistic frontier. Within Brabant the densely populated *arrondissement* of Brussels, which contains the metropolitan area of the capital, has shown a higher level of bilingualism than either the mainly Dutch-speaking *arrondissement* of Leuven (Louvain) or the mainly French-speaking *arrondissement* of Nivelles. The rate has been still higher in the capital itself, where some ten out of nineteen communes of the Brussels metropolitan area showed more than 50 per cent of the population in 1947 speaking both French and Dutch. Comparison over time shows increasing levels of personal bilingualism in all provinces, and this trend continues even after 1930 in spite of legislation favoring official institutional unilingualism.

The census data on languages by provinces and *arrondissements* allow us to clarify one other significant point, the size and location of the linguistic minorities in Flanders and Wallonie. As may be seen from Table 4, these minorities have been relatively small in percentage terms, both in recent times and earlier. Furthermore, they are not unduly concentrated along the east-west language frontier, which for much of its length constitutes a sharp line of separation between communes. One study based on 1930 census data found that of some 177 communes adjacent to the French-Dutch linguistic frontier, 130 had a linguistic majority of 90 per cent or higher and only 12 had a linguistic majority of less than 70 per cent (Levy, 1960a, 75-76). More complicated problems arise in the periphery around the Brussels metropolitan area, which constitutes a predominantly Francophone island in the Flemish-speaking part of Brabant province, but these will be considered in Chapter 5.

Table 3

Belgium: Incidence of French-Dutch bilingualism by provinces, 1866, 1930, and 1947 (percentages)

Area	Speaking French and Dutch			Speaking French, Dutch, and German		
	1866	1930	1947	1866	1930	1947
Flemish provinces						
Antwerp	6.1	11.8	13.8	0.2	1.6	4.4
West Flanders	7.6	15.2	19.8	*	0.5	2.4
East Flanders	6.4	11.5	14.7	0.1	0.5	2.3
Limburg	6.4	8.6	10.4	0.1	0.5	2.0
Walloon provinces						
Hainaut	2.1	5.6	6.7	*	0.1	0.7
Liège	2.9	4.8	5.8	0.1	0.4	1.9
Luxembourg	0.2	0.6	1.6	*	0.2	1.0
Namur	0.6	1.7	3.5	*	0.1	0.9
Province of Brabant	16.1	28.6	31.8	0.3	1.0	3.6
Arr. Brussels	23.1	35.6	38.4	0.4	1.3	4.3
Arr. Leuven	9.3	13.3	16.7	0.1	0.5	2.2
Arr. Nivelles	1.6	7.1	11.0	*	0.1	1.2
Whole country	6.4	12.9	15.6	0.1	0.7	2.5

* Indicates .05 per cent or less.

Sources: 1866: calculated from *Annuaire statistique*, 1901, 86-91; 1930, 1947: *Recensement*, 1947 (supplement published in *Moniteur belge* of June 26, 1954), 72-73, 152-53.

The language data of the Belgian census have never been cross-classified with economic indicators, and hence they cannot be used to tell us anything of the socioeconomic status of the linguistic groups concerned. Behind the very modest percentage figures in Table 4, the more impressionistic literature on Flanders describes a social and economic elite of Francophones, composed mainly of families rooted in Flanders for generations and hence fully Flemish in any "ethnic" sense, who comprised the old aristocracy, upper mercantile and business interests, and the liberal professions. Until the Second World War this Francophone bourgeoisie dominated the working world, but in the postwar period it has been increasingly replaced by a primarily Dutch-speaking elite as the first generations of university graduates to be educated wholly in Dutch have risen to senior positions. For several generations the linguistic frontier in Flanders was a double frontier based not only on geographical but also on social class boundaries, a situation that Maurits Van Haegendoren has not hesitated to label "domestic colonialism" (1970, 18). This socioeconomic dimension of the linguistic boundary *within* the Flemish region has incontestably heightened linguistic tensions. One of the primary concerns of this and succeeding chapters must be to document as carefully as possible the emergence of Dutch-speaking elites in various sectors of Belgian life and the reduction of this imbalance.

Table 4

Belgium: Linguistic minorities as a percentage of total population, Flanders and Wallonie, 1866, 1930, and 1947

Region	1866	1930	1947	1930	1947
A Flanders				Speaking French only or most frequently	
		Speaking French only			
Flemish provinces					
Antwerp	0.8	1.5	0.7	4.1	3.0
West Flanders	4.1	4.7	4.3	8.3	8.3
East Flanders	1.0	1.1	1.0	3.4	3.1
Limburg	4.5	3.2	2.0	4.6	3.4
Arr. Leuven					
(Brabant)	3.2	3.4	2.6	6.5	5.7
B Wallonie				Speaking Dutch only or most frequently	
		Speaking Dutch only			
French provinces					
Hainaut	1.8	0.8	0.5	2.6	1.9
Liège	3.9	1.4	1.2	2.7	2.6
Luxembourg	0.1	*	0.1	0.2	0.3
Namur	0.1	0.2	0.2	0.4	0.8
Arr. Nivelles					
(Brabant)	0.3	1.1	1.3	3.2	3.9

* Indicates .05 per cent or less.

Sources: 1866: *Annuaire statistique*, 1901; 1930, 1947: *Recensement*, 1947 (supplement published in *Moniteur belge* of June 26, 1954), 152-53.

If the Francophone minority in Flanders has been highly visible in a sociological sense, the Flemish minority in Wallonie has been almost invisible. To all appearances it has been composed mainly of Flemish immigrants of modest economic status who in most cases are in a process of linguistic transfer and cultural assimilation. Though the census gives no information on intergenerational changes, one anthropological study of a Walloon village near Liège found 12 per cent of the population to be of Flemish origin, and this group was concentrated mainly at the lower end of the social scale (Turney-High, 1953, 104-105).

    Up to a certain point one may also use the census data on languages to document the changing geography of the German-speaking minority. In the 1830s Belgium had a German-speaking population of roughly 250,000, but close to 80 per cent of this population was lost to Belgium with the cession of Dutch Limburg and the Grand Duchy of Luxembourg to the Netherlands in 1839 (Rüling, 1939, 8; Verdoodt, 1968, 8). Of a total of 34,000 German speakers recorded at the census of 1846, 26,000 were in the Belgian province of Luxembourg, mainly concentrated in the *arrondissement* of Arlon, while 4,000 were in Liège province, mainly in the northwest region around Montzen. In Luxembourg province the number declaring German as their only or most frequent language had shrunk to 19,000 by 1930 and then to less than 3,000 by 1947, when painful memories of wartime occupation were still fresh. In Liège province the German-speaking population increased sharply with the acquisition from Germany after the First World War of the so-called East Cantons, the districts of Eupen, Malmédy, and St. Vith, which boosted the number of German speakers in the enlarged province from 19,000 in 1910 to 62,000 in 1920. In these areas of "New Belgium" linguistic transfers have proceeded more slowly, and in 1947 Liège province accounted for 57,000 German speakers, or 72 per cent of those declaring German as their principal language in the country as a whole. The census data on the German-speaking minority, however, are not very satisfactory, and the 1947 data for Luxembourg province in particular serve as a reminder that the concept of the language used most frequently leaves much to the individual volition of bilingual respondents, especially in periods of political tension, and that more sensitive research methods may be necessary to arrive at reliable results.

On balance, one must evaluate the language questions in the Belgian census rather negatively. While they appear at first sight to be linguistically neutral and apparently admirably oriented towards measuring current language behavior, in practice they give rise to serious difficulties. The chief problem seems to be the absence of a concept of mother tongue or home language as a starting point from which to measure second-language knowledge or language shift, a problem which applies not only to Belgian bilinguals but also to aliens of other mother tongues, who are nowhere specifically identified in the census as non-native speakers. In part this absence of a clear point of departure may reflect government policy, which was preoccupied in the early census commentaries with emphasizing the spreading understanding of French as the major administrative language, even to the extent of obscuring the basic linguistic situation. Further, the concept of the language spoken most frequently, introduced in the 1910 census, while apparently intended as an indicator of the respondent's basic cultural affiliation, proved in practice to be dismayingly subject to environmental and social influences, to the detriment of its validity as linguistic evidence. As Levy notes, those who had demanded the new indicator, the Flemings, had wanted it to be based on mother tongue or *langue propre* (1962, 145-46; 1950, 519-20).

A crucial development occurred in the language legislation of 1932, when the language of communal administration was removed from the discretion of the communal councils and legally linked with the predominant local language as revealed by the latest census. This change, as numerous observers have stressed, gave the Belgian census the character of a referendum and weakened further the already frail linguistic objectivity of its questions. The next census, that of 1947, while undoubtedly broadly accurate in a global sense, produced bizarre results in certain communes along the linguistic frontier and in the Brussels area, where respondents were registering not their linguistic situation but their preferences as to the local administrative language (Levy, 1962, 147). The detailed results of the 1947 language census were not immediately released, and when they were eventually published—after a change of government—in 1954, they evoked a storm of angry protest on the Flemish side over "thefts of territory" in these border areas. The Flemish nationalist movement, already deeply suspicious of the subjectivity of the language census, was so embittered by the 1947 results that it mounted a massive campaign, through the coordinated efforts of some twenty-five major Flemish associations, to block the language census scheduled for 1960 (*Geen talentelling*, 1959). To this the Francophone side responded by demanding a language census as a basic democratic liberty. Despite the formation of an academic commission to reconsider the form of the census questions, objectivity soon became impossible and the regular 1960 language census was first postponed and then cancelled. Similarly, the 1970 and 1981 censuses contained no questions concerning language, and for the foreseeable future the ban seems likely to be continued. In the meantime the language law of 1962 has frozen the boundaries of the linguistic regions so as to make them independent of any future linguistic changes.

With the fixation of the linguistic frontier, the continuing existence of linguistic minorities in Flanders and Wallonie lost all direct political or legal significance and became a matter of sociological interest only. The disappearance of the language census meant that any new linguistic data had to be sought from surveys and other similar sources, which are in most cases not directly comparable with the census questions. Further, in the sensitive political climate of the 1960s, any inquiry touching explicitly on language evoked hostile responses that tended to distort the information being sought. Consequently the most reliable indicators of language use since 1947 are those where language data emerge unobtrusively or indirectly.

Perhaps the most obvious possibility is to study the evolution of the language groups through education statistics, which list the number of pupils by language of instruction but which do not give breakdowns by region in their published form. For this purpose we can select the elementary school population, covering the six years from the ages of about six to twelve, as the most uniform group for comparison. Table 5 shows the evolution of this group for the generation born since about 1945, and while this group represents only one selective age-specific section of the population it can also be considered to some degree indicative of the generations that will follow it. On balance, the dominant impression given by this table is one of continuing overall stability in linguistic proportions since the 1950s in spite of a considerable rise and fall in the school-age population. Even more striking, the linguistic proportions throughout this table remain reasonably close to the 57:42:1 ratio for the total population revealed by the first linguistic census of 1846 (see Table 2 above). The relatively minor shift of the last few years has been in favor of the Francophones.

Table 5

Belgium: Elementary school population by language of instruction, selected years (percentages)

| School year | Total | | Dutch | French | German |
	000s	%			
1956-57	866	100	57.2	42.3	0.5
1960-61	919	100	56.1	43.3	0.6
1965-66	980	100	57.3	42.1	0.6
1970-71	1,021	100	57.7	41.6	0.7
1975-76	956	100	57.6	41.7	0.7
1980-81	857	100	55.5	44.5	
1982-83	812	100	55.2	44.8	

Source: Calculated from *Annuaire statistique*, 1968, 123; 1979, 133; 1983, 166.

A second source of information is in the language of *miliciens*, the successive classes of nineteen-year-old males called up for military service, who may serve in the language of their choice provided they have the linguistic capability to do so. These data are less precisely representative than education data because of complicated and changing provisions for exemptions, postponements, and rejection of unfit candidates, provisions that can affect the language communities in slightly different ways because of differences in family size, educational levels, and occupational categories. However, they have certain advantages in being available for study over a longer period and by separate regions or military *arrondisse-ments*, as well as for the country as a whole. From unpublished data supplied by the Ministry of National Defence, it can be calculated that the proportion of Dutch speakers among those called for service averaged just fractionally under 60 per cent for the decade 1941 to 1950, rose to 62 per cent in the mid-1950s, and then fell back to 60 per cent in 1959-61. It stayed within the same general range at 61 per cent in 1963 and 1964, 58 per cent in 1965, 59 per cent in 1970, and 62 per cent in 1977. What seems clear is that in spite of short-term fluctuations the overall proportions have not visibly shifted from the 1950s to the late 1970s.

Table 6

Belgium: Use of mass media by language, by linguistic regions, 1969 (percentages)[a]

| Region and category of media | Language of mass media used by respondent | | | | |
	French only	Dutch only	Both French and Dutch	Neither French nor Dutch	Total
A Flanders (N = 5,938)					
Newspapers	2	65	2	31	100
Belgian broadcasting	3	70	8	20	101
Newspapers plus Belgian broadcasting	2	78	11	9	100
Newspapers plus Belgian and foreign broadcasting	2	65	26	7	100
B Wallonie (N = 3,718)					
Newspapers	68	1	—	31	100
Belgian broadcasting	72	1	3	24	100
Newspapers plus Belgian broadcasting	85	1	4	10	100
Newspapers plus Belgian and foreign broadcasting	66	2	24	8	100
C Brussels-Capital (N = 1,351)					
Newspapers	58	8	4	30	100
Belgian broadcasting	62	6	11	21	100
Newspapers plus Belgian broadcasting	70	6	16	8	100
Newspapers plus Belgian and foreign broadcasting	53	7	34	6	100

[a] In this table and some later ones, totals may not equal exactly 100 per cent because data are rounded to the nearest figure.

Source: Special computer runs from SOBEMAP survey, 1969.

A third approach is to examine the use of mass media as revealed by the extensive surveys of newspaper readership conducted for the advertising industry. Table 6 is based on one such study conducted in 1969, showing the language pattern indicated by reported use of mass media in each language region, as measured by four different media indexes: newspapers alone; Belgian radio and television alone; newspapers and Belgian broadcasting combined; and a broader index including newspapers plus both Belgian and foreign radio or television stations. It should of course be remembered that the electronic media are less "pure" as linguistic indicators than the newspaper press. One may listen to radio for its musical content or watch television for its visual appeal, and the rather elevated use of non-Belgian broadcasting media of the other language in both Flanders and Wallonie may be partially explained by these extralinguistic factors. One can interpret this table in various ways, but what stands out is the virtual absence in Wallonie and Flanders of "unilinguals" of the minority language of the region.

To enable us to analyze these same data further, another index of media use was calculated to show the preponderant language of each respondent as indicated by reported media use. This new index was established by calculating, for French and Dutch media separately, the sum of the *types* of broadcast media reported in the survey (Belgian radio, foreign radio, Belgian television, foreign television) plus the *sum* of newspapers read. Results were then categorized according to the total reported for each language as French only, mainly French, French and Dutch equally, mainly Dutch, and Dutch only. This technique led to a crude but nonetheless useful index of language preponderance for each respondent, which could then be compared against other variables in the SOBEMAP survey. Altogether fewer than 3 per cent of survey respondents reported no media use at all, but for technical reasons the language of periodicals read could not be retrieved and a few respondents who reported only German-language media are omitted from this calculation, leaving about 7 per cent of respondents who cannot be classified linguistically by this method.

Table 7 shows the profiles of media predominance for each of the major language regions, age groups, education levels, and social classes. The results by language region highlight the dominance of Dutch in Flanders and French in Wallonie, as might be expected, and they also provide a measure of French influence in Brussels. Results by language are also not too surprising in that greater bilingual usage among the young may simply reflect that group's greater use of electronic media. The remaining variables are more interesting, however, because they show quite clearly that at the date of this survey French usage was more extensive and Dutch usage less extensive at higher levels of education and social class. This skewed or unbalanced relationship between language usage and socio-economic status lies at the heart of the Belgian language conflict, and we shall encounter it in many different aspects in the course of this study.

If language statistics for individuals are no longer recorded by the census, it is because public policy in Belgium has taken a different direction with the language laws of the 1930s and 1960s. After 1932 data began to be kept on the basis of three major language regions—Flanders, Wallonie, and the old administrative *arrondissement* of Brussels—and after 1963 the predominantly German-speaking areas in the East Cantons ap-

Table 7

Belgium: Language predominance as indicated by overall media use by selected variables, 1969 (percentages)

Variable	French only	French > Dutch	French = Dutch	Dutch > French	Dutch only	No French or Dutch media	Total
A Language region							
Flanders (N = 5,938)	2	2	5	19	65	7	100
Wallonie (N = 3,718)	66	18	6	1	2	8	101
Brussels-Capital (N = 1,351)	53	21	8	5	7	6	100
Whole country (N = 11,007)	30	9	6	11	37	7	100
B Age							
15-24 (N = 1,696)	26	13	8	18	30	5	100
25-54 (N = 5,538)	29	9	6	12	38	6	100
55 plus (N = 3,773)	34	8	4	6	38	10	100
C Education							
Primary or less (N = 5,048)	26	7	5	10	43	9	100
Secondary (N = 4,988)	32	12	6	13	32	6	101
Post-secondary (N = 690)	40	15	9	11	22	4	101
D Social class							
Well-to-do (N = 427)	44	17	6	9	19	5	100
Middle (N = 2,663)	36	13	6	12	27	5	99
Skilled workers (N = 4,418)	29	9	6	12	38	6	100
Unskilled workers (N = 3,459)	25	6	5	9	44	11	100

Source: Special computer runs from SOBEMAP survey, 1969.

peared as a small fourth region for statistical purposes, though administratively they remained part of the *arrondissement* of Verviers in Liège province. The most important change of the 1963 legislation was the creation of a new administrative *arrondissement* of Brussels-Capital for the Brussels metropolitan area, leaving the remainder of the old *arrondissement* of Brussels to be added to the linguistic region of Flanders. Since 1963 Belgian statistics have been increasingly based on these four linguistic regions, as well as on the more traditional nine provinces and forty-three administrative *arrondissements*. Previous tables have shown that the two largest of these regions, Flanders and Wallonie, have been and undoubtedly remain highly homogeneous in a linguistic sense, probably more homogeneous than the Swiss cantonal groupings analyzed in Volume 1, though the different language census questions in the two countries make exact comparisons impossible. The more complex linguistic composition of the Brussels area will be examined more fully in Chapter 5.

Table 8 shows the basic population distribution by language regions, calculated on two distinct bases. Part A takes the whole of the old administrative *arrondissement* of Brussels as the centre or capital, and attributes the other two Brabant *arrondissements* of Leuven and Nivelles to Flanders and Wallonie respectively. As a point of departure for this table, we have taken data for 1831 and 1840 which were adjusted to the post-1839 boundaries and published in the population registers in 1842. Though these figures might seem open to challenge, they were based on both local records and central government inquiries and are similar to census data in terms of accuracy. Data in Part B are adjusted to the post-1962 boundaries from 1930 onward, but for earlier years they are calculated unofficially for the Brussels urban area on the basis of language census data. In 1831 the urbanization of the communes adjacent to Brussels had scarcely begun, and the population shown is that of the commune of Brussels itself. In two other respects the figures are not precisely comparable over time. Territorial acquisitions from Germany added a population of some 64,000 to Wallonie in 1920, and minor changes in provincial boundaries along the linguistic frontier in 1962 resulted in further population adjustments which gave Wallonie a further net advantage of 64,000. In global perspective these adjustments are relatively small, representing 0.9 per cent of the total population in 1920 and 0.7 per cent in 1962.

What emerges primarily from Table 8 is the relative growth of a centre in and around the capital, a centre which has left the rest of Belgium increasingly conscious of its peripheral status. Part B shows a proportionate freezing of that centre for administrative purposes at approximately the level attained in the 1920s; the relative expansion of the centre has in fact continued into the suburban area outside Brussels-Capital, primarily in Flanders but to some degree in Wallonie just south of the linguistic frontier. Flanders also has made tangible relative gains in the twentieth century, but

Table 8

**Belgium: Population by linguistic regions, selected
years, 1831-1981 (percentages)**

Year	Total population 000s	%	Flanders	Wallonie[a]	Arrondissement of Brussels
A Pre-1962 regions					
1831	3,786	100	53.2	39.2	7.6
1840	4,073	100	52.2	39.8	8.0
1846	4,337	100	50.8	40.5	8.7
1866	4,828	100	47.5	42.6	10.0
1880	5,520	100	46.5	42.2	11.3
1900	6,694	100	46.9	40.4	12.7
1920	7,466	100	46.9	38.7	14.4
1930	8,092	100	48.0	37.1	14.9
1947	8,512	100	50.2	34.5	15.3
1961	9,190	100	51.2	33.1	15.7
1970	9,651	100	51.2	32.7	16.1

Year	Total population 000s	%	Flanders	Wallonie	German region	Brussels agglo- meration
B Post-1962 regions						
1831	3,786	100	58.1	39.2	n.a.	2.6
1846	b	99+	54.2	40.3	n.a.	4.9
1866	b	99+	50.7	42.4	n.a.	6.4
1880	b	99+	49.4	42.1	n.a.	7.9
1900	b	99+	49.7	40.3	n.a.	9.4
1920	b	99+	50.5	38.0	n.a.	10.9
1930	8,092	100	51.1	37.2	0.7	11.0
1947	8,512	100	53.5	34.7	0.6	11.2
1961	9,190	100	55.1	33.2	0.6	11.1
1970	9,651	100	56.1	32.1	0.7	11.1
1981	9,849	100	57.2	32.0	0.7	10.1

[a] In Part A Wallonie includes German-speaking areas and from 1920 includes new territories
acquired from Germany after the First World War.
[b] In Part B figures for these years exclude a few mixed-language communes and also
German-speaking areas.

Sources: Part A: 1831-40: calculated from *Population: relevé décennal*, 1842, 46, 244;
1846-1947: *Recensement*, 1947, 1: 172; 1961: calculated from *Recensement*, 1961, 1: 33; 1970: estimated from *Recensement*, 1970, 1: 30, 48.
Part B: 1831: calculated from *Population: relevé décennal*, 1842, 21, 244; 1846-
1920: calculations of H. Picard in Cliquet, 1960, 80; 1930-70: *Recensement*, 1970, 1: 48; *Statistiques démographiques*, 1969, no. 3: 23; 1981:
Annuaire de statistiques régionales, 1981, 208.

it must be remembered that in relative terms it had lost ground in the middle decades of the nineteenth century as a result of the agricultural famine in the 1840s, depressed textile industries, and the development of a prosperous heavy industry in Wallonie (Kittell, 1967). It is very clear, however, that since the late nineteenth century Wallonie has been the chief loser both in population and in developmental terms, and this relative decline makes the question of Brussels that much more important to Francophones as a factor in preserving some kind of linguistic balance. Further analysis by provinces shows that while Brabant, Antwerp, and Limburg have increased their relative share of the population since 1880, all others, including Dutch-speaking East and West Flanders, have lost.

When viewed from the perspective of language regions, which is the way imposed by public policy since the language laws of 1962-63, the Belgian language situation looks somewhat less stable than the Swiss, and especially from the perspective of Wallonie. It also appears less stable from the standpoint of language regions (Table 8) than it does from the standpoint of linguistic predominance among individuals (Table 2), which changed relatively little between 1846 and 1947. It can be argued that this perceived instability heightens minority awareness and tends to increase linguistic tension and group hostility, but before accepting this argument uncritically we should examine the components of the changing population distribution between regions and—as far as the data allow—between languages.

In principle the basic components for this analysis are the same as those examined for Switzerland in Volume 1, namely, the rate of natural increase, patterns of internal and external migration, language acculturation and language transfer, and—if we wish to treat Belgian citizens separately—the naturalization of aliens. The available statistical series, however, force us to look for the main trends in somewhat different ways. To take the regional population figures first, we can say that changes are the result of figures for net natural increase, that is, births minus deaths, combined with a figure for net changes from internal and external migration, that is, immigration to the region concerned minus emigration from it.

The basic trends in terms of natural increase and net migration can be seen in Table 9. What stands out from these data and from other studies (Morsa, 1963, 21; 1964, 19) is the relatively higher birth rates and lower death rates in Flanders, which in combination have given Flanders a significantly higher rate of natural increase than either Wallonie or Brussels. In the past this has been offset by greater gains from internal plus external migration in Wallonie and Brussels—but offset only partially. During the third of a century following the census of 1947, the population of Flanders (in its post-1962 boundaries) increased more than three times faster than that of Wallonie or Brussels, and for the period from 1971 to December 1980 the combined population of Wallonie and Brussels remained almost stationary, while that of Flanders continued to increase. The indicated totals at the end of this period differ slightly from the first results of the 1981 census, held in March of that year.

Table 9

Belgium: Population changes by language regions, 1947-80 (thousands)

Period	Belgium	Flanders	Wallonie	German region	Brussels-Capital
A 1948-61					
Initial population					
(1947 census)	8,512.2	4,551.9	2,949.5	54.8	955.9
Net natural increase	612.2	(509.7)[a]	72.4		n.a.
Net migration	65.3	(−70.5)[a]	26.3		n.a.
Total change	677.5	512.1	95.8	2.9	66.9
Percentage change	8.0	11.3	3.3	5.2	7.0
B 1962-70					
Initial population					
(1961 census)	9,189.7	5,064.0	3,045.3	57.7	1,022.8
Net natural increase	307.9	287.0	16.3	4.1	0.5
Net migration	153.3	65.6	35.7	0.2	51.8
Total change	461.2	352.6	52.0	4.3	52.3
Percentage change	5.0	7.0	1.7	7.4	5.1
C 1971-80					
Initial population					
(1970 census)	9,691.0	5,432.8	3,124.9	62.1	1,071.2
Net natural increase	96.0	133.0	−25.2	0.5	−12.3
Net migration	116.4	84.6	92.3	2.2	−62.6
Total change	212.4	217.5	67.1	2.7	−74.9
Percentage change	2.2	4.0	2.1	4.3	−7.0
D 1947-80					
Percentage change	16.3	24.1	8.2	18.2	4.2

[a] Incomplete data excluding parts of old *arrondissement* of Brussels left outside Brussels-Capital in 1963.

Sources: *Recensement*, 1961, 1: 37; 1970, 1: 48; calculations from *Annuaire statistique*, 1972-81 (page 15 in each volume).

Demographic differences between Flanders and Wallonie have been a longstanding tendency in Belgium. In broad terms, birth rates in the Walloon provinces fell below 30 per 1,000 in the 1880s or earlier, but did not fall to that level in the Flemish provinces until the 1900s. Birth rates fell below 20 per 1,000 in the Walloon provinces around 1909, but in Flanders only in the 1930s (Tulippe, 1965, 6). By 1938, thirteen out of nineteen

Walloon *arrondissements* and also Brussels had more deaths than births, while every single Flemish *arrondissement* showed a net increase. The persistent pattern of low birth rates has given rise to serious concern in Wallonie and has led to a number of studies, including a much discussed report by the French demographer Alfred Sauvy (Sauvy, 1962; CRISP, 1962, no. 156), and to numerous other works listed in Verdoodt (1973, 37-41). This clear difference in demographic structure in turn has led Wallonie to take a greater interest in positive population and immigration policies than has been the case in Flanders, and it has also led to basic differences in mass attitudes. A Walloon public heavily conditioned for a generation or more by frequent references to "the lowest birth rate in the world" (Grégoire et al., 1958, 276) or to "the oldest population in the world" (du Roy, 1968, 128-29) has developed persistent feelings of defensiveness, insecurity, and pessimism about the future that have increased its sensitivity on other aspects of language policy. In the 1970s and 1980s these negative attitudes have been further reinforced by economic depression, even lower birth rates, and demographic projections of a severely depopulated Wallonie (André, 1983; André et al., 1984). Flanders, on the other hand, has shown no special concern for demographic insecurity despite its own falling birth rate, and indeed one of the central motifs of the Flemish Movement in the twentieth century has been the concept of *volkskracht*, a sort of collective strength of the Flemish population, of which one key component is demographic vitality (Cliquet, 1960, 84).

The pattern of interregional and external migration is difficult to describe in exact numbers because some "emigrants" move to unknown destinations and also because the boundaries for regional statistics were changed in 1962. In general it can be said that between 1947 and 1961 both Flanders and Wallonie lost population by net internal migration to the *arrondissement* of Brussels, but some of these losses or their equivalent reverted to Flanders in 1962 when the old *arrondissement* of Brussels was split into three new *arrondissements* of Brussels-Capital, its peripheral communes, and Halle-Vilvoorde, with the latter being included in the Dutch-language region. All three regions in this period had net gains from external migration, but almost three quarters of this flow went to Wallonie. For the period 1962-70, but calculating for the *new* boundaries, all linguistic regions show net gains from migration, Wallonie and Flanders by a modest 1.2 and 1.3 per cent respectively, and Brussels-Capital by a more significant 5.1 per cent.

There appear to be no statistics available on the language spoken by emigrants from Belgium, but one can estimate roughly the mother tongue of immigrants from census data on nationality, which show that citizens of France and the Netherlands resident in Belgium were approximately balanced at every census from 1890 to 1947, except for 1920 when nationals of France made up 45 per cent of the foreign population, compared with 26 per cent for the Netherlands (Morsa, 1966, 44). In 1970 the census showed

61,000 citizens of the Netherlands, of whom 75 per cent were living in Flanders, and 87,000 citizens of France, of whom 84 per cent were in Wallonie or Brussels. These two groups together, however, accounted for only 21 per cent of the non-Belgian population at that date, while Italians and Spaniards accounted for 45 per cent. During the next decade the non-Belgian proportion of the population rose from 7 per cent in 1970 to 9 per cent in 1980, but by regions the 1981 census figures showed 13 per cent for Wallonie and no less than 24 per cent for Brussels, compared with 4 per cent for Flanders (Van der Haegen, 1981, 4; *Annuaire de statistiques régionales*, 1977, 22; 1981, 209).

Although the tracing of actual migration flows is complicated and ultimately frustrating because of missing data and altered boundaries, we can represent the net results by taking a "snapshot" at any census point of place of residence compared with place of birth. This is done in Table 10, which shows the net effect of cross-regional internal migration and immigration from abroad for the three major language regions in 1970. This table shows that less than half the population of Brussels-Capital was actually born there; the rest were born in Flanders, Wallonie, or abroad in roughly equal proportions. While the other regions both have higher percentages born in the region, the relatively greater significance of immigrants in Wallonie emerges clearly. It must be remembered that these figures relate to birthplace and not to nationality. In 1970 some 35 per cent of the foreign-born population had Belgian citizenship, and conversely 31 per cent of the non-Belgian population were born in Belgium.

Table 10

Belgium: Region of residence by region of birth, 1970 (percentages)

Region of residence	Total population 000s	Total population %	Region of birth Brussels-Capital	Flanders	Wallonie[a]	Abroad	Unknown
Brussels-Capital	1,075	100	48.4	17.4	15.6	17.3	1.3
Flanders	5,417	100	2.0	92.4	1.4	3.9	*
Wallonie[a]	3,159	100	2.0	4.2	82.5	10.6	0.7
Belgium	9,651	100	7.2	55.2	29.5	7.6	0.5

* Means .05 per cent or less.
[a] Includes German-speaking areas.

Source: Calculated from *Recensement*, 1970, 3A: 18.

Of all the factors underlying changing linguistic proportions, the most difficult to describe in quantitative terms is undoubtedly the rate of language transfer for individuals or between generations. As was shown in Volume 1, this factor was difficult to estimate for Switzerland, and for

Belgium the additional difficulties in the census categories themselves have already been described. Among the rather imprecise generalizations that can be offered, it seems clear that the rate of language transfer is highest in the Brussels metropolitan area, where several generations of immigrants of Flemish stock have been subject to language shift from Dutch to French. Similarly, linguistic transfer among non-Francophones who migrate permanently to Wallonie appears to be almost total, and in 1970 the Walloon population included some 133,000 persons, or 4 per cent of the regional total, born in the Netherlandic linguistic region. For Flanders the linguistic and migratory evidence points to relatively little linguistic transfer in either direction, at least until 1947. After that date there are few relevant data of any kind, and it would seem that to go further one must proceed either by inference and estimation from other variables or by survey research. For Belgium as a whole there can be little doubt that the net long-term effect of language transfer has been to favor the French language or, more accurately, to offset the greater birth rates of the Dutch-speaking population. One estimate suggests that if migration and language shift had been absent during the preceding century, the Flemish proportion of the population would have been 65 per cent (Cliquet, 1960, 79).

Our point of departure was the question of relative stability or instability of language groups and language regions. Subsequent analysis suggests that the distribution of languages in Belgium has rested for more than a century upon a combination of differential birth rates, migration patterns, and language transfers, a combination that has operated asymmetrically but in an approximately counterbalanced fashion. Such a system, however, was based on premises that proved increasingly unacceptable to Flemish nationalism, premises that assumed a greater prestige for the French language and a tendency towards its adoption by the upwardly mobile middle classes, especially in the Brussels area. This meant that even if Wallonie itself was in decline as a region, Francophone Belgium in the wider sense, with its greater linguistic resources, could maintain some rough balance even in the face of greater demographic vitality in Flemish Belgium. The basis for this equilibrium, however, has been increasingly undermined in recent decades by certain policy measures—by the development of territorial unilingualism in the 1930s, and by the attempt to freeze the expansion of Brussels in the 1960s. The result was that public policy, even while responding to basic aspirations of the Flemish Movement, introduced new elements of instability between the linguistic communities.

B   Language, Dialect, and Language Contact

Before looking more closely at the languages and dialects of Belgium we should remember certain aspects of the wider linguistic context, which is less symmetrical than the Swiss case examined in Volume 1. While Switzerland is surrounded by—and participates in—three languages and cultures of major European significance, the comparative status of French and Dutch is far less balanced from either a European or a global perspective. The Netherlandic cultural tradition, even when fully reinforced by Flemish, South African, and former colonial contributions, falls short of its far-flung French counterpart by virtually any imaginable scale of measurement. Secondly, the Netherlandic language itself, which has emerged out of a situation of high dialectal variation in both the northern and southern Netherlands, is still less completely standardized than is standard French, especially in its written form. Finally, in a sociological sense, the Belgian language situation is basically bipartite rather than tripartite, because the small and relatively rural population of German Belgium is in no sense a counterweight to the far larger language communities of Flemish or Francophone Belgium, nor is it even comparable with the substantially larger and more urbanized population of Italian Switzerland.

To consider the case of Flemish Belgium first, high dialectal variation has been characteristic of both the northern and southern Netherlands from earliest times. For the southern provinces one can distinguish four major dialects that correspond approximately to provincial boundaries, namely West Flemish, East Flemish, Brabantic, and Limburgic, plus some smaller intermediate dialects between regions. Both Limburgic and Brabantic extend significantly into the southern provinces of the present Netherlands, while West Flemish extends across the border into the adjacent region of France between Dunkerque and Lille (Vanneste, 1974, 40 bis-40 ter; Pauwels, 1956, 116-18). Between the more distant of these dialects, such as West Flemish and Limburgic, comprehension is difficult, but this posed no problem as long as the elites communicated primarily in French. The rise of the Flemish Movement, however, meant among other things that Flemish had to become more than a collection of diversified patois, and thus was posed the problem of finding a standard or norm around which the various dialects might find common ground. There were also serious practical difficulties. In the 1830s the Flemish translations of legislation in the official gazette had been criticized as monumentally incompetent, and by 1844 a minister could point out that the spelling system had been changed five times in twelve years (Hamelius, 1894, 83-85).

The fundamental problem in the search for a standard language lay in the bitter legacy of the divorce between Belgium and Holland. A standard already existed in the cultivated Netherlandic of the northern provinces, but it was irretrievably associated with the Orangist monarchy and with Protestantism. If Henri Bourassa could later argue in Canada for the French language as "guardian of the faith" (Bourassa, 1919), the problem for the Flemish provinces was that the standard language represented antichrist, the materialist and Protestant values to which the rural and clerical traditions of Flanders were unalterably opposed. The appointment of a government commission in 1837 to consider the standardization of spelling became a signal for anti-Dutch forces to mobilize in defence of Flemish as a language distinct from the standard Nederlands of the north and in defence of the older orthographic system of Desroches as most appropriate for this distinctive Flemish idiom. In 1841 the commission recommended a system of orthography close to, but not identical with, that of Holland. Its adoption by the government in 1844 occasioned a sharp parliamentary debate in which the conservatives attacked the decision as unconstitutional and even treasonable, a form of moral reannexation to Holland. But their motion of censure was defeated, and despite further skirmishes in pamphlet literature, the first major engagement of the "spelling war" had been won by the proponents of a united Netherlandic language (Hamelius, 1894, 83-88). Arthur Curtis considers the outcome of this phase highly significant, for if conservative Catholic elements had prevailed, a prolonged conflict over the selection of a standard language might well have fatally weakened the Flemish cause in its uphill struggle with French (1971, 203-206).

The debate, however, was far from conclusive. In 1849 Belgian and Dutch philologists held the first of a series of joint language congresses which continued through the following decade. They worked together towards a major Netherlandic dictionary, publication of which began in 1864. The slightly modified De Vries-Te Winkel spelling system proposed for this dictionary found favor among philologists and was soon adopted in Belgium by a royal decree of November 21, 1864, but the Dutch government refused official sanction and adopted a policy of orthographic *laisser faire*. In Belgium these developments produced a new reaction, this time against the constraints of an overly rigid standard Nederlands in favor of a greater freedom to draw upon the resources of the regional dialects. The focal point of this dialectal particularism was West Flanders, but it found defenders elsewhere, including some in Holland. Its highest literary expression was in the poetry of Guido Gezelle, its philological support in De Bo's *Westvlaamsch Idioticon* (1873). Even the particularists, however, by now tended to acknowledge the utility of a unified Netherlandic language even while refusing it undivided allegiance (Hamelius, 1894, 93-95, 206-209; Curtis, 1971, 206-207; Geerts et al., 1977, 189-90).

There remained the question of a standard for the spoken language, which became the subject of a prolonged debate particularly after 1890. At one time an issue for a small Flamingant cultural elite only, the question acquired some urgency with the establishment of Netherlandic-speaking normal schools in the 1880s. There existed a ready model for emulation in the cultivated Netherlandic of Holland, but to many Flemish intellectuals this idiom sounded more "foreign" than the cultivated French in which they had been educated. In terms of the values and traditions of Flanders there seemed to be something inherently contradictory in trying to resurrect and revitalize the Flemish heritage through the medium of a standardized Dutch Netherlandic. For almost a generation scholars argued over how a cultivated Flemish could be built up, some calling for a slower and more deliberate pronunciation of the dialects, others for literal pronunciation of the written language. By 1914 the advice of a rising generation of trained linguists was no longer contested: cultivated Netherlandic in Flanders must be based upon the cultivated Netherlandic already developed and spoken by the educated elite of the Netherlands (Curtis, 1971, 252-62).

Some three generations after 1830, the Flemish Movement had arrived at something approaching a consensus concerning the standard language, which has become increasingly known as *algemeen beschaafd Nederlands*, or "common cultivated Netherlandic," often simply abbreviated as ABN. Van Loey (1945, 71) aptly summarizes the issue as viewed by the Flemish intellectual elite:

Netherlandic and Flemish are not two different languages. There is only one cultivated Netherlandic language, the correct and uniform usage of which may be studied and mastered down to the smallest details. Beyond that language, there are words, constructions and tendencies in pronunciation that are more common in the Netherlands in some cases, and in Flanders in others, a situation somewhat analogous to that of the French language in France and Belgium. In any case, the Flemings have no need to construct a cultivated language. They have one: Netherlandic.

We shall be happy if the reader has understood the various obstacles that the Flemish have had to overcome for more than a century in their struggle to purify and extend their common language. They have had to root out barbarisms, gallicisms, provincialisms; to free themselves from the tyranny of a stilted, bookish written language; to conquer apathy, laxity, ignorance, prejudice. And if "Flemish" appears to be changing, this is because it is becoming more correct.

The ideal in this respect would be a situation in which a subject speaking the cultivated language would never betray his origin in terms of region or social class.

Selecting a standard language is one thing, but winning mass acceptance for it is another. The earliest leaders of the Flemish Movement spoke only their respective dialects, but already by 1912 a linguist could point with some pride to the spread of correct Netherlandic among the younger Flemish elite (Curtis, 1971, 259-60). The promotion of standard ABN gradually became a generalized campaign, supported particularly by the major Flemish cultural foundations. By the 1950s a Flemish dialectologist could report a distinct advance in the use of ABN as compared with the 1930s, though virtually no families at that date had abandoned the use of dialect at home (Pauwels, 1956). More recently the spread of ABN has undoubtedly been aided by the rise of the electronic media and by increased geographical mobility of the population. In an interview with one young social scientist, he described to me how his experience of dialectal diversity during military service led him to make a deliberate decision to use only ABN—which he had been taught at school—for all occasions, and how this decision had created temporarily a certain social distance from his friends, who gradually adjusted to his decision and in some cases shifted to ABN themselves.

Although most recent sources agree that the knowledge and use of ABN are steadily increasing, it is not easy to describe this trend in quantitative terms. One study of Dutch-speaking Brussels school pupils in 1964 found that while ABN was scarcely used by primary pupils in situations outside the family, it was used by fully half the pupils at the secondary and normal school levels (Delfosse, 1964, 514). A more detailed sociolinguistic survey, conducted in 1972 by Baudewijn Meeus and based on a mixed sample drawn from the Brussels suburbs and rural Brabant, found that virtually all respondents had at least a passive or receptive knowledge of ABN, but that their own use of it varied widely according to the situation. For the whole sample 75 per cent or more of respondents reported greater use of ABN than dialect in talking with a priest, public servant, doctor, teacher, shop assistant, a "well-dressed stranger," or on the telephone. This proportion fell somewhat for conversation with a boss, subordinate, or colleague (64, 58, and 51 per cent, respectively), and still further with people of "lower social status" or country people. The lowest rates (15 per cent or less) were recorded for discussions with parents, spouse, neighbors, and friends at home, though it is noteworthy that 26 per cent reported speaking mainly ABN with their own children. Further analysis of the sample showed greater use of ABN among urban dwellers, younger age groups, the better educated, and those in higher-status occupations (Meeus, 1974a, 1974b). An earlier study of ten different spheres or domains of language use highlighted contact with governmental authorities as the only sphere in which ABN clearly predominated over dialect (Meeus, 1971). Another survey of Flemish immigrants to Brussels found that ABN was the language first learned in childhood for only 6 per cent of adult respondents, but for households with children 29 per cent used ABN as the childhood language (*Wetenschappelijk onderzoek*, 1975, Working Paper no. 2: 12).

These findings suggest that Flemish Belgium may be classified as a situation of generalized diglossia in which most people have at least some knowledge of standard Dutch in addition to their own regional dialect. In this respect Flanders may remind us of German Switzerland, but in the latter case the domains of dialect and standard language are relatively stabilized, whereas in Belgium the standard language has greater social prestige and is making continuing inroads on the dialects. So far the Flemish dialects are far from being ousted, but their formerly dominant position is at least threatened. Unlike the Swiss-German dialects, they enjoy no reserved domains, even at the intimate or familial level, where they would be immune from attack. As Flanders has moved from French-

Dutch bilingualism to Dutch unilingualism in public institutions, the standard language has gained a minor boost from the Francophone minority in Flanders, many of whom have switched to ABN for public purposes while continuing to speak French at home and bypassing dialect altogether. The transition to ABN has also won approval in Francophone Belgium, which has long found the diversity of Flemish dialects a serious obstacle to French-Dutch bilingualism. Across the border in the Netherlands itself, ABN, which evolved gradually from the cultivated language of the Amsterdam patriciate in the mid-seventeenth century, has similarly been spreading more widely from the bourgeoisie to other classes as Dutch society has become more integrated (Goudsblom, 1964).

The written Netherlandic language, standardized only in relatively recent times, has continued to develop, particularly from the standpoint of spelling. A movement to simplify and regularize the spelling of words arose in Holland in the 1890s and found adherents and opponents in both countries. In the 1930s the spelling debate became acute, but in spite of a joint Dutch-Belgian commission on the question nothing was settled and confusion remained general until the Second World War. In 1944 the Belgian and Dutch governments-in-exile in London decided to regulate the question through another joint commission, and in 1957 this procedure was formally institutionalized within the framework of the Dutch-Belgian cultural accord of 1946. By this 1957 agreement the two governments formally undertook to consult each other with respect to all spelling regulations so as to promote full orthographic uniformity of the Dutch language (CRISP, 1970, no. 494: 27). In 1980 a new treaty assigned the power to regulate the Dutch language to a supranational body, the Netherlandic Language Union (Ballegeer, 1984, 73-75). One may recall, however, that the normal diplomatic language between Holland and Belgium remained French until after the Second World War (van der Straten-Waillet, 1963-64, 17-18).

The establishment of institutional mechanisms was only a small part of the task. There remained larger questions of substantive decisions and public acceptance. Certain basic changes in spelling rules came into force for educational and official use in both countries in 1947, but several issues, including the complex problem of foreign loan words, were left to be settled later. A joint commission appointed to settle these issues produced in 1954 a compromise position on loan words whereby some were vernederlandst and others were not, while still others were given a double "preferred" and "optional" status. Dissatisfaction with this middle-ground position led to another joint commission on loan words in 1963, the Bastaardwoordencommissie, which issued two further reports in 1967 and 1969. These reports argued for a more radical vernederlandsing of the loan words in the interests of a more simplified, more phonetic spelling of the entire language. They evoked a sharp reaction in some circles and were ridiculed in the Dutch press as the "odeklonje spelling" (based on the proposed orthography for *eau de cologne*). Interestingly, some Dutch critics of the postwar reforms have seen them as too sweeping, too anti-French, and too Belgian, while some Belgian critics have seen them as too *Hollands* or Dutch (Geerts et al., 1977).

The full range of subtle variations in argument in the postwar spelling debate is admirably summarized by Geerts and his colleagues (1977). What they find is a basic division between educators, who largely favor reform on the grounds of simplification and democratization of instruction, and a conservative opposition comprised of academics, publishers, and others with linguistic "vested interests," who are concerned with wider cultural questions and relationships with other languages. But there are other variations. Spelling reform in Holland was most strongly associated with the political left, but in Belgium it was most strongly favored in Catholic circles. While they find a desire to preserve similarities with adjacent languages, as might be expected, they also note the existence of a desire to underline differences on political grounds. Thus in Belgium many Flemings prefer the form *kultuur* because c is too close to French, while in Holland many prefer *cultuur* because k is too close to German. In the wake of an intense debate, no official action was taken on the reports of 1967 and 1969. In the 1970s the spelling question remained far from settled in many details, but there was a clear determination, especially on the Belgian side, that uniformity of usage between the two countries must be maintained at all costs.

Like Flanders, Wallonie has also been characterized by a series of regional dialects, but its linguistic evolution has been considerably different. In popular usage all the dialects spoken in Wallonie are often loosely referred to as Wallon, but in a stricter sense one can identify some Picard dialect (in the Mons-Tournai area along the French border) and some Lorraine dialect (in the extreme south around Virton), as well as at least four major and several minor varieties of Wallon. One recent anthology of dialect literature recognizes no less than forty-seven regional variants (Piron, 1979, xiii). These dialects did not become a written language in any general sense, and apart from a limited range of literature that began in Liège around 1600, most other written functions were left to be exercised through standard French. For almost eight centuries the dialects and standard French have lived in peaceful coexistence, beginning with a situation in which dialect was the normal spoken idiom and French the written language. Bilingualism, based at first upon a passive knowledge only of standard French, made headway after the Renaissance, especially among the upper classes. Language shift became far more rapid in the nineteenth and twentieth centuries, during which period a substantial part of the population abandoned the dialect as mother tongue. Some scholars now foresee the eventual disappearance of the dialects, which will leave behind only regional traces in the French that replaces them.

It is difficult to assess the exact state of the dialects of Wallonie in the 1980s because the evidence is rather mixed. One frequently cited survey of some 900 communal councils in 1920 found that 43 per cent functioned exclusively in French, 33 per cent in French and Wallon, and 23 per cent in Wallon exclusively. Virtually all authorities agree that the usage of dialect has decreased markedly since 1920. Nevertheless a 1965 study of school children in ten villages in rural Hainaut showed between 20 and 90 per cent of the boys still to be *patoisants*, though almost all the girls spoke French even if they understood patois. There is also a class dimension: the dialects survive among manual workers and rural laborers as an idiom of the workplace even though the professional and white-collar workers speak almost exclusively French. While active usage thus appears to be dropping, passive or receptive knowledge of dialect still appears strong. A 1969 survey of school children in the city of Liège found that 64 per cent of the children reported they could not speak Wallon, but only 15 per cent said they could not understand it (Piron, 1970; 1975; Van Passel and Verdoodt, 1975).

Hand in hand with the decline of Wallon have come attitudinal changes. Once condemned as an obstacle to progress, the dialects have had fewer and fewer detractors as they have edged closer to disappearance. Recent writers have found new virtues in them because of their expressive functions, their intimacy, and their special value in a society characterized by depersonalization and alienation (Piron, 1975, 36-38). Hence in comparing the language situation in Flanders and Wallonie we are left with the paradox—which will appear less paradoxical after reflection—that in Flanders the regional dialects are still vigorous but widely disapproved of by the academic elites, while in Wallonie the dialects are endangered and debilitated but increasingly an object of elite solicitude.

Although the German-speaking areas account for only a tiny fraction of the total Belgian population, they are quite diversified in a linguistic sense. In the south, in the *arrondissement* of Arlon, where German is no longer a majority language, the local dialect is Letzeburgish or Luxemburgish. The communes of the St. Vith district and part of the Malmédy district in Liège province belong to the same dialect group, which is a form of Moselle Frankish or Middle German. Farther north, in Eupen district, the dialect is a Ripuarian Frankish, influenced by Aachen just across the West German border. To the northwest of this area, around Montzen, there is another change to Low Frankish, which in turn merges into Limburgic a little farther on. It is important to note that whereas this area has a sharp administrative frontier between standard German and standard Dutch, the related dialects merge into one another by a gradual transition. The six communes of the Voer or Fouron area, which became a focal point in the legislation of 1962 on the linguistic frontier and which have remained a major unresolved issue between Flemings and Walloons, belong to this transitional area where the dialect cannot be classified definitively as Germanic or Netherlandic (Verdoodt, 1968, 6, 23-24; 1976, 211-12).

Although older studies of the German areas are fairly numerous (Verdoodt, 1968, 177-81), more modern research was rather fragmentary until the late 1970s, when the Research Centre on Multilingualism in Brussels began more systematic studies on changing usage of dialects and standard languages in several sub-regions (Nelde, 1979a; 1979b; Nelde et al., 1981; Kern, 1983; Trim, 1983). Yet these areas are of considerable linguistic interest, having undergone severe linguistic and psychological stress in modern times. The so-called East Cantons or New Belgium (Eupen, Malmédy, and St. Vith), divided in medieval times between the Duchies of Limburg and Luxemburg, were annexed to France in 1795, awarded to Prussia in 1815, annexed to Belgium in 1919, re-annexed to Nazi Germany in 1940, and in 1944 finally returned to Belgium, which then instituted a thorough investigation and repression of all acts of *incivisme* during the Second World War. In the post-1945 period the status of German in Belgium generally has continued to be handicapped by the legacy of two wartime occupations. Nevertheless field research by Peter Nelde, which focused on selected localities of Old Belgium where institutional support in the public sector is largely lacking, found that German dialects still pre-dominated in family settings in roughly two households out of three in the Arlon district in the south and slightly above this level in the middle and northern areas, with considerable variations from one locality to another (Nelde, 1979b, 51, 73). Other voluntary domains of language usage, such as media consumption or the language of work or of leisure, showed levels of usage of dialect or standard language well below these levels of use within the family, however, and a major concomitant of high dialect usage appears to be rural isolation. The situation may well be different in New Belgium, where public institutional usage at least partially reinforces the private domains.

We consider next the question of contact between the official languages. Here it must be noted that the theoretical model or pattern for such contacts has undergone change since the mid-nineteenth century. The architects of Belgian independence in 1830 visualized a polity in which the various local dialects—Flemish, Walloon, and German—would continue to be used for regional purposes, but in which standard French would be the sole vehicle for wider public communication in administrative and judicial matters. The model is clearly articulated in Soudain de Nieder-werth (1857), who sharply opposed contemporary attempts to raise the status of Flemish as an unprogressive, backward-looking policy. Such a model could function smoothly as long as political life was in the hands of a mainly French-speaking elite, but it came under increasing challenge with the democratization of the political process and the rise of the Flemish

Movement. These developments necessitated the development of a new language model, in which cultivated Nederlands would assume the same position in relation to the Flemish dialects that standard French enjoyed in relation to the Walloon dialects. Further, because of past inequities and the long drawn out struggle to define and achieve this new model, the language issue acquired an explosive sensitivity to even the most trifling inequalities between Dutch and French.

In practice the quest for a meaningful language equality has encountered serious obstacles. In the face of a deeply entrenched opposition to any linguistic rights for the Flemish minority in Wallonie, the Flemish response has been to work towards a Flanders that is as fully unilingual in Dutch as Wallonie has been in French. Whereas language accommodation before the Second World War depended heavily upon a Flemish elite that had received its post-secondary education in French, the generation born after about 1910, which is still functionally bilingual but educated entirely in Dutch, is less fluent in French and has been less willing to assume the whole burden of bilingualism. In the face of a scarcity of Walloon bilinguals, the Flemish reaction has been to seek greater cultural and administrative autonomy so as to decrease the need for high levels of cross-linguistic contact.

Concerning the informal or social level, it is difficult and perhaps imprudent to generalize. In the mid-1950s a Netherlands linguist could write that "always and everywhere in Belgium, in a company consisting of Walloons and Flemings, French is the language of conversation" (van Haeringen, 1960, 54). Whether this situation has changed in any significant way since then is difficult to say, but the number of occasions where such language contacts might normally occur has almost certainly diminished since the 1950s. It can also be recorded that in the 1970s a Walloon cabinet minister could hold a press conference for the combined Belgian media entirely in French; the inverse situation for his Flemish colleagues would hardly have been conceivable.

Finally, as in the case of Switzerland, there is an interesting area for study in the effects of language contact upon the languages themselves, both in their standard and dialectal forms. Concerning the standard languages, the general impact of French on Dutch has been studied by the Netherlands linguist Salverda de Grave (1906; 1913) and by others whose work is listed in van Haeringen (1960, 69-70). A more sensitive question politically is the special impact of French influences on the standard Netherlandic of Belgium. The classic study of these influences is that of Willem De Vreese (1899), who deplored the mixture of influences in Flemish authors and called for a purification of the language (taalzuivering). The ABN movement has long displayed a certain wariness towards gallicisms. In interviews it is often remarked, rather impressionistically, that the standard ABN of Belgium shows less tolerance for foreign

borrowings—especially from French—than does the more relaxed Nederlands of Holland, and certain once-fashionable terms of French origin have
been losing ground to indigenous terms (Van Loey, 1954, 289-90). A less
sensitive concern, but still worth mentioning, has been the study of Germanic influences on Nederlands (Moortgat, 1925). Both gallicisms and
germanisms—but especially the former—figure prominently in the *Nederlandsche taalgids* of Constant Peeters (1930), a massive, authoritative work
dedicated to the identification of South-Netherlandic particularisms and to
their replacement by correct standard Netherlandic terms, which serves as
a source for several subsequent pocket language guides.

The inverse relationship, the impact of Dutch upon standard international French, has been relatively slight and of interest chiefly to linguists
(Valkhoff, 1931; 1944, chap. 3). More significant has been its impact upon
the French of Belgium and especially of Brussels. This impact has been
studied descriptively from a linguist's standpoint by Wind (1937; 1947;
1960), who finds that influences on vocabulary have been most marked in
the private and social sector, among the lower classes, and in the domain of
affective, and especially pejorative, language (1937, 165-67). In this narrower Belgian context, however, Netherlandic influences are usually
treated as one species of a larger category of *belgicismes*, which are
defined as any particularism that differentiates the French of Belgium from
the French of France. Apart from Netherlandic expressions or constructions or *flandricismes*, these also include *wallonismes* (i.e., influences of
the dialectal substrata), archaisms, and phonetic variations. The general
attitude of the Francophone cultural elite to these phenomena is typified by
the title of a recent study, *Chasse aux belgicismes* (Hanse et al., 1971).
Particularisms of all kinds are not to be cherished but simply rooted out.
Such an attitude can be traced back to the dawn of Belgian independence
and even earlier, when a work appeared under the title *Flandricismes,
Wallonismes et expressions impropres dans la langue française* (1830),
which was reprinted in revised and updated form as late as 1928. A century
and a half after independence, the open season on belgicisms continues
unabated, and there are no signs of a shortage of game.

As for influences on German in Belgium, Peter Nelde (1979c) has
analyzed the many ways in which the special linguistic situation of the East
Cantons or New Belgium has influenced the language of the only current
German-language daily newspaper, *Grenz-Echo*. An earlier study of several publications over a longer period, however, concluded that the German language was relatively well maintained in New Belgium but more
strongly influenced by French in the more marginal German-language
press of Old Belgium (Magenau, 1964, 147-48).

The question of external linguistic influences on the dialects has given
rise to a relatively rich scholarly literature. Among the more notable
examples, reciprocal exchanges of loan words between Walloon and

Flemish dialects were studied by Grootaers (1924), and a monumental study by Geschiere (1950) traces Netherlandic influences on the Walloon dialect of Liège, where language contact has been both intensive and prolonged. Similarly, Germanic influences on Walloon dialects have not been neglected, especially in the case of Malmédy, which was annexed to Prussia and Germany from 1815 to 1919, and where German replaced French in the schools in the 1870s (Warland, 1940; and cf. Haust, 1933a, 725-27; 1933b). One of the more comprehensive recent studies is an investigation of the regional French of Brussels, which has long existed in close proximity with Brabantic patois and has been much influenced by it, especially among lower socioeconomic groups (Baetens Beardsmore, 1971), and even systematically convergent with it according to some writers (De Coster et al., 1971, 81-82). The first of these two works has a useful and extensive general bibliography which can serve as a guide to more specialized regional and topical studies in dialectology.

C   Linguistic and Other Cleavages

It is a widely accepted view, emphasized by several authors, that Belgian politics since independence has been dominated by the three major cleavages of religion, class, and language (Lorwin, 1974; Dunn, 1970; Meynaud et al., 1965, 22-40; Urwin, 1970). Other authors retain these three cleavages but add a fourth, weaker, centre-periphery division (Heisler, 1974, 179; Quévit, 1978, 10-11). Our concern at this point is not to study each of these major cleavages as such, but rather to see how they intersect with one another. If the theory of cross-cutting cleavages in the political process is to be assessed in the Belgian context, it is important that the degree or angle of cross-cutting be carefully documented. We shall examine here the relationship of linguistic divisions with the other major divisions of religion and social class, as well as with other divisions in Belgian society that have been less politicized. Most of the available data for such comparisons are available only on a territorial basis, that is, by language regions or provinces rather than by the language of individuals.

In considering these relationships one must keep in mind two general features of the Belgian context that have already been mentioned. First, modern Belgium is itself the product of a major religious-cultural cleavage between the northern and southern Netherlands which proved too stressful to be bridged during the short period of union between 1815 and 1830. As noted in Chapter 1, the divorce of 1830 had a major impact on the subsequent history of the language question. Second, the language cleavage in Flanders was complicated by having both a territorial aspect—the geographical frontier with Wallonie—and a social class aspect—the gulf between the Flemish masses and the Flemish elites, who had become predominantly French-speaking.

To consider religious cleavage first, a superficial inspection might suggest its virtual absence in Belgian society, and one leading handbook of political data does indeed classify Belgium as religiously homogeneous (Banks and Textor, 1963, Table FC66). It is true that for centuries the non-Catholic population has been very small. Even in 1829, at the end of the union period, the population in the southern provinces was 99.6 per cent Roman Catholic, and by 1846 the small Protestant population had declined by almost half (*Statistique générale*, 1865, 2: 3). No census since then has asked for religious affiliation. However, the real religious cleavage in Belgian society, highly politicized at certain periods of Belgian history, has been within the Roman Catholic community in the form of profound disagreement over the appropriate relationship between church and state. Clearly, it is not easy to measure the intricacies of belief systems, yet differing views of the role of the Church in Belgian society give rise to behavioral manifestations that can be directly measured and compared from one language region to another. In the most general terms, the situation is often described as a Catholic Flanders facing an irreligious Wallonie and Brussels, but as we shall see this simplified picture requires certain qualifications.

Table 11 illustrates the relationship between language regions and religious practice using several categories of data on religious practice. The most obvious dimension for measurement in a Roman Catholic milieu is attendance at Mass, which has been studied in Belgium since the late 1940s and since 1962 systematically recorded twice a year by the diocesan authorities. Part A of the table shows results of these ecclesiastical censuses, calculated as a percentage of the age group that might be expected to attend, which is in turn about 84 per cent of total population (Mols, 1971, 394-95). These figures show a clear downward trend in all three language regions but also a tendency for the significant discrepancies between regions to be maintained. Closer analysis shows further variation within regions. The dioceses of Hasselt and Bruges, corresponding approximately to Limburg and West Flanders, are consistently above the average for Flanders as a whole, and the diocese of Namur, corresponding to the civil provinces of Namur and Luxembourg, is well above the average for Wallonie. From the standpoint of economic structure, the areas of lowest participation are the major cities, the industrial towns devoted to coal, steel, and textiles, and adjacent rural areas (Collard, 1952, 649). In terms of social class, studies of Brussels have shown that while more than 40 per cent of families in middle-class districts attend Mass, the rates for working-class districts range from 6 to 15 per cent (CRISP, 1963, no. 224: 16). These data from ecclesiastical sources may then be compared with self-reported attendance figures from surveys (Part B of the table), which indicate a slightly wider gap between Flanders and the other regions, and with survey questions asking respondents directly whether they are practising Catholics or not (Part C). These latter figures show a significant decline in those practising between 1968 and 1975, but once again the contrast between Flanders and the other regions remains striking.

Table 11

Belgium: Selected indicators of religious behavior, by language regions

	Belgium	Flanders	Wallonie	Brussels[a]
A Estimated attendance at Mass (as percentage of non-excused population[b])				
Circa 1950	49.6	60.2	40.7	34.9 (2)
1964 (October)	44.7	54.3	34.3	26.6 (1)
1972 (October)	34.2	40.9	28.2	17.2 (1)
B Self-reported attendance at Mass (percentage going "Every Sunday" or "Almost every Sunday")				
1975	36	49	21	20 (1)
C Self-reported religious practice				
1968 practising Catholics	58	72	43	34 (1)
1975 practising Catholics	47	60	32	26 (1)
non-practising Catholics	34	30	39	44 (1)
non-Catholics	16	8	26	25 (1)
D Baptisms, marriages, and funerals				
Baptisms (as percentage of total births)				
1967	93.6	95.9	92.7	89.8 (3)
1976	86.7	91.3	89.5	73.7 (3)
Religious marriages (as percentage of civil marriages)				
1967	86.1	91.5	83.3	77.9 (3)
1976	77.9	83.3	75.4	69.4 (3)
Religious funerals (as percentage of total deaths)				
1967	84.2	91.4	78.9	80.5 (3)
1976	83.7	90.7	79.0	78.9 (3)

Table 11—Continued

	Belgium	Flanders	Wallonie	Brussels[a]
E Divorced population (per 1,000 residents)				
1961	9.2	4.7	10.6	27.2 (1)
1970	10.4	5.6	12.7	28.9 (1)
1977	12.0	8.8	12.3	28.6 (1)

[a] Refers either to Brussels-Capital (1) or to old *arrondissement* of Brussels (2) or to ecclesiastical diocese of Mechelen-Brussels (3), with corresponding adjustments to other regions.
[b] The non-excused population is estimated on the basis of total population aged 5 to 69.

Sources: A: Collard, 1952, 649; Van den Bosch and Gouverneur, 1974, 17-32, 49-64; B: AGLOP, 1975, variable 275; C: Delruelle et al., 1970, 39; AGLOP, 1975, variable 29; D: CRISP, 1981, nos. 925-26: 5; E: *Recensement*, 1970, 5A: 131; *Annuaire de statistiques régionales*, 1981, 15.

For more formal occasions, such as baptisms, marriages, or funerals, the rate of religious observance is considerably higher, indicating that much of the Belgian population remains at least nominally Catholic, even if it is not attending Mass regularly or otherwise practising Catholicism on an everyday basis. Part D of Table 11 is based on data organized by ecclesiastical dioceses, which means that data for the Brussels agglomeration are partially obscured among results for the larger diocese of Mechelen-Brussels, corresponding roughly to the civil province of Brabant plus the *arrondissement* of Mechelen. Once again there are slight downward trends (except in funerals) during the period for which figures are available, and also continuing differences between language regions, but the most noteworthy point is that these data for solemn religious ceremonies coincide not with figures for practising Catholics but much more closely with the 1975 survey figures for practising and non-practising Catholics taken together. Finally, as seen in Part E of the table, the more active Catholicism of Flanders is reflected in an incidence of divorce that is less than half that found in Wallonie, while the considerably higher figures for Brussels appear to be a combined result of religious liberalism and urbanization. Differential divorce rates are of long standing and can be calculated at least as far back as 1920 (Zoller, 1963, 76).

Further evidence of regional differentials in religious behavior and attitudes may be found from a variety of sources. For the 1950s the rate of ordinations of priests was highest in Flanders, 12 for every 10,000 young people, compared with a rate of 10 for Wallonie and 8 for Brussels (CRISP, 1967, nos. 352-54: 15-16). Birth rates, as already noted, have been persistently higher in Flanders, and on average families are larger. Behind these demographic differences lie significant differences in attitudes. A 1951 survey found that in Flanders 31 per cent of respondents wanted to have four or more children, compared with 17 per cent in Wallonie and 4 per cent in Brussels. Correspondingly, in Flanders 31 per cent approved of limiting the number of children, compared with 48 per cent in Wallonie and 70 per cent in Brussels (INSOC, 1952, nos. 1-2: 67). More recent studies on demography and fertility have found interregional differences in the proportion of wanted and unwanted births (Emery-Hauzeur and Sand, 1974, 4-5) and in the practice and methods of contraception, as well as major differences in the use of various contraceptive techniques between Belgium as a whole, Great Britain, and the United States (Cliquet, 1968, 27-33; Morsa, 1970, 58-59; Morsa and Julémont, 1971, 147).

The general picture that emerges from this evidence and from other indicators is that in spite of significant variations within both regions and some changes over time, Flanders clearly still differs from Wallonie in the degree to which it adheres to traditional Catholic values, and this adherence has important institutional consequences beyond the immediate limits of parish and family life. It may be seen in more frequent parental preferences for the *écoles libres*, the Catholic school system organized by the Church but now partially subsidized by the state; in membership in Catholic trade unions rather than socialist or liberal unions; and in voting for Catholic political parties. Each of these institutional manifestations of the religious cleavage can be measured and compared by language regions.

Table 12

Belgium: State and private school enrolment by major language administrations, 1975-76 (percentages by cells)

Level and authority	Dutch system	French system[a]	Total
A Pre-school level			
Public	16.4	26.2	42.7
Private	41.8	15.5	57.3
Total (N = 438,000)	58.3	41.7	100
B Elementary level			
Public	22.5	26.1	48.6
Private	35.0	16.4	51.4
Total (N = 959,000)	57.5	42.5	100
C Secondary level			
Public	16.9	21.9	38.8
Private	41.9	19.3	61.2
Total (N = 810,000)	58.8	41.2	100

[a] In this table German-language enrolment is included in the French system.

Source: Calculated from *Annuaire de statistiques régionales*, 1978, 62.

The basic distribution of pupils between the state and the Catholic educational systems in the 1970s is indicated in Table 12, which gives figures by language regime rather than by region and thus incorporates results for Brussels within the French and Dutch totals. This table shows that Netherlandic education is primarily organized privately by the Church while Francophone education is predominantly directed by public authorities, but there are also significant minorities on both sides. Among other anomalies, it may be noted that while the system as a whole shows a preponderance of Dutch-speaking pupils, as might be expected, the public sector is preponderantly French-speaking at all three levels. German-language enrolment, which is available separately for some earlier years, is predominantly organized by public-sector schools. In the longer term the general trend has been towards growth of the Catholic sector, which rose from 28 per cent of total elementary enrolment in 1890 to 47 per cent in 1913 and to 52 per cent by 1960 (CRISP, 1971, nos. 542-43: 27).

A somewhat parallel development can be seen in the development of Catholic trade unionism. The Confédération des syndicats chrétiens (CSC) experienced a period of rapid growth after the Second World War and surpassed the socialist Fédération générale du travail de Belgique (FGTB) in total membership by 1959 (Lorwin, 1975, 250; Spitaels, 1967, 49). The membership pattern of these two principal federations by language region is given in Table 13, which shows a growing Catholic predominance in Flanders and continuing socialist predominance elsewhere. But once again significant minorities of the other federation are found in all three regions. Between 1947 and 1969 the Catholic unions made significant advances in all regions, and these advances continued in the 1970s. Membership in liberal trade unions is not shown in this table because it is not available on a regional basis. One can, however, estimate the relative strength of the three groups by regions by looking at the results of elections to works councils and to health and safety committees. Thus in 1979 liberal candidates won 8 per cent of the total vote for health and safety committees in the four Flemish provinces and 4 per cent in the four Walloon provinces—in both cases approximately twice the percentages obtained in 1958—as well as 10 per cent in Brussels, though overall they won only 4 per cent of the seats (CRISP, 1980, no. 888: 8-9, 13-14). The increase in liberal and Catholic union strength can be traced at least in part to the growing proportion of skilled, white-collar, and professional positions in the work force.

A third institutional consequence of the religious cleavage is the popular vote for Catholic parties. At the six general elections from 1946 to 1961 the Parti social chrétien (PSC) received between 41 and 48 per cent of the popular vote for the country as a whole, which made it the largest party both in votes and in seats throughout the period. For Flanders it had absolute majorities of 51 to 60 per cent, while for Wallonie the figures were 30 to 34 per cent and for Brussels 30 to 35 per cent. After 1961 this support was eroded by the growth of regional parties, but this development will be examined further in Chapter 3.

Table 13

Belgium: Relative strength of socialist and Catholic trade unions, by language regions, selected years (percentages by cells)

Year and organization	Flanders	Wallonie	Brussels	Whole country
1910				
Socialist unions	27.7	24.6	6.0	58.4
CSC (Catholic)	27.2	10.1	4.4	41.6
Total (N = 119.000)	54.9	34.8	10.4	100
1947				
FGTB (socialist)	27.1	24.9	5.7	57.8
CSC	33.7	6.1	2.4	42.2
Total (N = 1,037,000)	60.8	31.1	8.1	100
1969				
FGTB	21.4	19.6	6.2	47.3
CSC	38.7	9.4	4.6	52.7
Total (N = 1,741,000)	60.1	29.0	10.9	100

Sources: Calculated from Spitaels, 1967, 34, 52; CRISP, 1959, no. 18: 5; 1972, no. 572: 24.

We may summarize the institutional manifestations of this first basic cleavage in Belgian society by citing figures mainly for the mid-1960s assembled by CRISP (1967, nos. 352-54: 58). At that time the Catholic sector accounted for 63 per cent of preschool education, 61 per cent of secondary education, 53 per cent of primary education, 52 per cent of post-secondary education, 47 per cent of trade union membership, 46 per cent of hospital beds, 45 per cent of newspaper circulation, 44 per cent of members of social insurance plans, 44 per cent of members elected to works councils, and 41 per cent of votes at the 1961 general election. Not all of these data can be obtained by language regions, but it is a reasonable hypothesis that all of these sectors could be divided in approximately the same way as the examples that we have given, that is, with Flanders being preponderantly Catholic and Wallonie and Brussels preponderantly non-Catholic in every sector.

It is this pattern of *partial* cumulation of the ideological and linguistic cleavages—and not least the significant ideological minorities found in each language region—that is fundamental not only to Belgian social structure but also to the Belgian political process. Its recognition is a prerequisite to any institutional accommodation of the language question.

In this important respect the Belgian case differs from the Swiss case, where the religious majority has been the same in both major language groups and the linguistic majority has been the same in both major religious groups, whether estimated on a personal or a regional basis (see Volume 1, 74-78).

Table 14

Belgium: Economically active population, professional status by language regions, 1947 and 1970[a] (percentages)

Year and category	Whole country	Flanders	Wallonie	Brussels arrondissement
1947				
Employers, managers, self-employed	22.0	23.5	20.7	20.2
Employees	18.9	14.8	18.7	31.5
Workers	49.4	49.4	53.8	40.3
Family helpers	6.4	7.9	5.3	4.0
Unemployed, *miliciens*	3.3	4.4	1.5	4.0
Total	100	100	100	100

Year and category	Whole country	Flanders	Wallonie	Brussels-Capital	German region
1970					
Employers, managers, self-employed	15.6	16.1	15.3	13.1	24.0
Employees	34.7	31.2	34.7	50.6	26.4
Workers	43.3	46.6	42.2	31.0	43.1
Family helpers	3.2	3.1	3.7	2.6	4.6
Unemployed, *miliciens*, unknown	3.2	3.0	4.1	2.7	1.9
Total	100	100	100	100	100

[a] 1947 figures are for pre-1962 language regions.

Sources: *Recensement*, 1961, 8 Part 1: 29-30; 1970, 8A: 28-29.

If the religious cleavage can be amply documented in many sectors, data are less abundant for the study of social class. As in the Swiss case, one can seek for Belgium both objective data for occupational or social status and subjective data for the respondent's own identification with a particular class or group. For the former, one may obtain some help from one of the census variables that categorizes the economically active population as employers and self-employed, salaried employees, workers, and home helpers, thus providing a rough dividing line between manual and non-manual occupations. Table 14 shows the distribution of these categories in each language region for 1947 and 1970, though it must be remembered that the 1947 data refer to the old language regions and the former *arrondissement* of Brussels. Even after allowing for boundary changes, what stands out in this table is the distinctiveness of Brussels and the relatively similar profiles of Wallonie and Flanders, as well as the growth in all regions of white-collar employment at the expense of other categories.

Data on subjective identification with a specific social class may be found in two major surveys of the Belgian population conducted in 1968 and 1975. As shown in Table 15, the responses for Flanders and Wallonie proved quite similar on this dimension, especially in the 1968 survey, whereas Brussels differed by its markedly heavier orientation towards the two higher-status categories. Since both surveys focused on electoral behavior, only Belgian citizens are included. Data on class structure are often difficult to obtain and difficult to interpret, but in this case both the objective and subjective data point towards a rough similarity between Wallonie and Flanders, so that if there is any significant cumulation of cleavages in terms of social class and language region, the basic contrast is between a bourgeois-oriented centre and a working-class periphery that includes both Flanders and Wallonie. Other aspects of this centre-periphery opposition will emerge when we examine economic indicators in the next section.

Table 15

Belgium: Self-identification in terms of social class, by language regions, 1968 and 1975 (percentages)

Class	Whole country		Flanders		Wallonie		Brussels-Capital	
	1968	1975	1968	1975	1968	1975	1968	1975
"Working class"	54	44	57	47	55	49	33	19
"Middle class"	37	44	35	39	35	46	47	59
"Upper class"[a]	5	5	4	7	4	2	15	9
Other and no reply	5	7	4	7	6	4	5	13
Total	101	100	100	100	100	101	100	100

[a] Categorized as *bourgeoisie* in 1968, *classe supérieure* in 1975.

Sources: 1968: calculated from Delruelle et al., 1970, 39; 1975: AGLOP, 1975, variable 30.

Even though Flanders and Wallonie show broad similarities in class structure, certain qualifications and refinements may be noted. A separate study of intergenerational social mobility, based on the same 1968 survey data, concluded that in Wallonie there was greater social distance between manual and nonmanual occupations, and a smaller tendency to cross this line, than in the other regions (Delruelle, 1970, 42, 66, 84). This is consistent with various observers who find that in Wallonie the Socialist party is more radical, and the Catholic party more conservative, than in Flanders (Lorwin, 1975, 260-63; CRISP, 1963, no. 205: 4). For Flanders Delruelle found occupational stratification to be more rigid generally than in the other regions, a finding that she associated with greater traditionalism in Flemish society (Delruelle, 1970, 42, 67, 84, 101-102). In a later study of Belgian elites, which was based on language region rather than language spoken by the individual, the same author found substantial over-representation of Brussels in these elites, and a further slight advantage for Wallonie over Flanders if demographic factors are taken into account. The underrepresentation of the Flemish region was particularly marked in the age group over sixty, in the private sector, and to a lesser degree in the universities (Delruelle-Vosswinkel, 1972, 160-62, 188).

A further complication is that economic status and social status have not always coincided in Belgium. At independence there existed a landed nobility that for a time rivalled the bourgeoisie in power and influence, but in the longer run enmity faded into alliance and intermarriage as industrialism advanced and a politically organized working class emerged to challenge both groups (Bartier, 1968; Clark, 1984). In recent times the nobility, which numbered 788 families in 1957, has had little significance as a distinct interest group but is not quite so negligible from the standpoint of social status. Even in Flanders this group is thoroughly Francophone in lifestyle and considered impervious to Netherlandization (Wilmars, 1968, 188-90). One consequence is that some members of the Flemish economic and political elites have refused titles in order to keep their distance from a social establishment that they see as culturally alien (Claes, 1973, 224).

The main result of comparing class structure by language region is undoubtedly to highlight the contrast between Brussels and the other two regions. Yet it is important to remember also that Wallonie shows a sharper polarization between manual and nonmanual occupations than does Flanders, where both workers and middle classes alike faced a Francophone higher elite across a language barrier. We can discern here a pattern of mutually reinforcing institutions and attitudes that link the cleavages of religion, class, and language in a rather complex way. In a perceptive comparative analysis of the two regions, the Walloon Socialist leader André Renard argued that the class conflict in Flanders had been subordinated to the stronger imperative of Flemish emancipation as a people, and that the path to working-class emancipation in Flanders lay through fulfilment of the Flemish nationalist phase as a necessary precondition to social transformation (Renard, 1961, 228-29). From this standpoint it is not just coincidence but a consequence of the pattern of societal cleavages that in Wallonie the socialist unions (FGTB) are numerically stronger than the Catholic ones; that the former are more attuned to doctrines of class conflict; and that in daily life the distance between workers and bourgeoisie appears to be greater. In Flanders, by contrast, the greater strength of the Catholic unions coincides with greater doctrinal emphasis on interclass cooperation derived from Catholic social thought and with greater cohesion across class lines in everyday social relations. One tangible measure of sharper class polarization in Wallonie may be seen in the more confrontational style of industrial relations practised there. Although available figures are incomplete and not totally reliable, it can be estimated roughly that over the seven years from 1971 to 1977 the work force of Wallonie, numbering approximately half as many unionized workers as Flanders, lost more than 40 per cent more working days through strikes than did their Flemish counterparts (*Annuaire de statistiques régionales*, 1976, 143; 1978, 192).

A third and less important line of cleavage that can be compared by language regions is the urban-rural division. In a small country characterized by short distances, efficient transport, and extensive patterns of commuting to work, this question is more complicated than it looks. However, an official study using 1961 census data and rather simplified criteria of classification found that Flanders and Wallonie had approximately equal proportions of their total population living in rural communes (16 and 15 per cent), in "urbanized" small communes (43 and 46 per cent), and in towns and cities (41 and 39 per cent), while Brussels-Capital was by definition wholly urban (Van Waelvelde and Van der Haegen, 1967, 26-27). However, a major restructuring of municipalities has reduced the total number of communes from 2,663 when this study was made to 589 in 1983, with most of the changes becoming effective in 1977.

A simpler approach is to look at major metropolitan areas only, of which only five as currently defined exceed 200,000 in population. Apart from the nineteen communes of Brussels-Capital itself, which constituted a separate, officially bilingual language region of 997,000 residents at the 1981 census, two of these *agglomérations* are in Flanders and two in Wallonie. Antwerp and Gent, which had at the 1981 census 501,000 and 239,000 residents, respectively, together made up 13 per cent of the population of Flanders, while Liège and Charleroi, with 214,000 and 222,000, respectively, accounted for 14 per cent of the population of Wallonie (*Recensement*, 1981, 1: 75-79). Apart from the contentious question of Brussels itself, one can conclude that Flanders and Wallonie are reasonably balanced in terms of urban concentrations. It is also worth noting that in modern Belgian politics the urban-rural cleavage has never become politicized to the point that a separate farmers' party emerged, as happened in the case of Switzerland. One comparative study of these two political systems attributes this difference to the substantial coincidence in Belgium of the rural-urban cleavage with the Catholic-non-Catholic cleavage, and to the ideological sympathy of the Catholic party for rural values (Dunn, 1970, 88-90).

A fourth line of cleavage that rather unexpectedly varies by language region is the age distribution of the population. Because of demographic differentials discussed earlier in this chapter, the population of Flanders is younger than that of Wallonie or Brussels; in 1970 the difference in average age between Flanders and Brussels was a full four years (*Recensement, 1970*, 5A: 135). The distribution of young people, old people, and those of working age in each language region during the past century is illustrated in Table 16, which shows a continuing tendency for Flanders to have a higher proportion of young people even after birth rates began to decline. A closer study of all the census years shows that the largest discrepancies between Flanders and Wallonie occurred between 1910 and 1947, and that by 1961 the gap was somewhat narrower. As noted earlier, however, differences in age structures and in demographic trends have led to significant interregional differences both in general attitudes and on some specific issues of social policy, such as family allowances, immigration, and old-age pensions.

D Economic and Developmental Comparisons

As in the Swiss case, our next concern is with the comparative economic situation of the Belgian language groups. At the level of official data, this means essentially focusing on the different linguistic regions, because the census has never published a breakdown of any economic or social indicators by the language of individuals. One can, of course, go further by means of survey data. If we retain the same hypotheses that were adopted for Switzerland in Volume 1, our interest will centre upon current economic comparisons of regions, upon past economic relationships and comparative rates of change and development, and more marginally upon aspects of longer-run regional development that may have left an imprint upon collective attitudes. We surmise that all of these factors may have some relationship to the levels of tension or accommodation between regions and language communities.

Most recent data for Belgium are available on the basis of post-1963 language regions, but even older provincial data involve less laborious calculations than those necessary for Swiss cantonal data. For historical comparisons, however, it is often necessary to compare older data based on provinces or *arrondissements* with revised language regions of 1963 that are not strictly comparable. This means especially that data for the old mixed urban-rural administrative *arrondissement* of Brussels must be compared with data for the new wholly urban region of Brussels-Capital, which contained in 1961 some 71 per cent of the population of the former *arrondissement*. A more serious problem in comparing regions arises from the fact that because of the country's small size, highly developed rail and road networks, and low-cost commuter fares, a significant proportion of the work force lives in one region and works in another. A large proportion of the flow consists of commuters residing in Flanders or Wallonie and working in Brussels-Capital, and anyone watching the throngs that emerge from or converge upon Brussels Central Station during rush hours can only marvel at the scale of the operation.

Table 16

Belgium: Age structure by language regions, selected census years, 1880-1981 (percentages)

Year and age category	Flanders	Wallonie	Arrondissement of Brussels	
1880				
0-20	47.1	44.3	43.9	
21-64	45.9	49.4	51.2	
65 or over	7.0	6.3	4.9	
Total	100	100	100	
1910				
0-20	45.5	38.1	37.7	
21-64	48.1	55.1	57.0	
65 or over	6.4	6.8	5.3	
Total	100	100	100	
1947				
0-20	33.8	26.2	24.5	
21-64	56.8	61.5	64.2	
65 or over	9.4	12.3	11.3	
Total	100	100	100	
Year and age category	Flanders	Wallonie	Brussels-Capital	German region
1970[a]				
0-20	34.2	31.6	26.8	35.8
21-64	53.6	53.7	57.2	52.1
65 or over	12.2	14.7	16.0	12.1
Total	100	100	100	100
1981[a]				
0-20	30.4	29.7	25.6	31.6
21-64	56.0	55.5	56.9	55.5
65 or over	13.6	14.8	17.6	12.9
Total	100	100	100	100

[a] 1970 and 1981 data are by revised language regions.

Sources: *Recensement*, 1947, 5: 22; 1970, 5A: 53; 1981, Résultats généraux, 70-71.

At the 1970 census the number of commuters travelling to Brussels-Capital for work had grown to 246,000, which was equivalent to 38 per cent of the total labor force working in Brussels or 7 per cent of the entire Belgian labor force. They came from every *arrondissement* in the country and from 97 per cent of the 2,379 then existing communes, although approximately half of the total came from other nearby communes of Brabant province. Whereas in 1961 some 78 per cent of the commuter influx came from the Flemish language region, the greatest increase during the 1960s was experienced by Wallonie, whose share of the total increased from 22 per cent in 1961 to 29 per cent in 1970. Our main concern here is to note the impact of this population movement upon the regional economies. At the 1970 census Brussels-Capital, which had 11.1 per cent of the total Belgian population and 12.9 per cent of the total economically active population by place of residence, had no less than 18.6 per cent of the total active population by place of work as a result of the net imbalance in commuter movements (*Recensement*, 1970, 9: 45, 47, 50; Deblaere et al., 1974). These special structural factors must be remembered when we look at data on gross regional product or regional incomes.

The pattern of commuting may be viewed from two sharply different perspectives. One view, especially prevalent in Flemish circles, sees it as an outcome of limited employment opportunities in Flanders—and more recently in Wallonie—a factor which forces laborers to travel long distances in the absence of local job opportunities, a form of economic oppression or even "colonialism" (Van Haegendoren, 1978, 71). Another interpretation, however, is that the pattern of commuting represents the preferences of many members of the Brussels work force to live outside the capital area for either economic or non-economic reasons, and here it is possible that for some Flemings the strongly Francophone milieu of the capital may be one factor in the decision. Both perspectives may be partially valid, but to be more precise requires more detailed analysis of the commuters. We do know that in 1970 roughly half came from the adjacent *arrondissements* of Brabant province and half from more distant areas; that they were not mainly manual workers, as is sometimes suggested, but primarily white-collar employees, in roughly the same proportions as the work force resident in the capital; and that this preponderance of employees was found for every one of the nine provinces from which commuters came (Deblaere et al., 1974, 23, 35).

In comparing the economic levels of the language regions, it is convenient to begin with statistics on gross regional product, which are shown in Table 17. The first part of this table shows the regional product per capita as a percentage of the average for Belgium as a whole, based on the *total resident population* of each region. This section shows a steady improvement for Flanders and an equally persistent decline in Wallonie, with Flanders actually overtaking Wallonie in the mid-1960s. The trends are less consistent in Brussels and also partly obscured by the change in the territorial unit, but the relative advantage of Brussels over the other two regions stands out clearly. However, this is not the whole story. For the census years 1961 and 1970 we can calculate another set of indexes based on the active population actually *working in the region*, and these figures are shown in Part B, again as percentages of the average for Belgium as a whole. By this measurement of production per worker at the workplace, the superiority of Brussels almost disappears, but the relative improvement of Flanders in relation to Wallonie is again confirmed. Indeed the economic advancement of Flanders is somewhat understated by per capita data in both parts of this table, because total population and workforce have both increased faster in Flanders than in Wallonie. It should be noted that these series, drawn from several different sources, reveal minor discrepancies from one source to another, but the general trends are fairly clear.

A second approach to regional economic comparisons is to look at income levels, and for Belgium the most comprehensive way of doing this is by using data on taxable incomes, which exclude exempt income or incomes too low to incur tax. The first part of Table 18 shows the position of the three language regions as measured by average income per capita based on total resident population (that is, whether economically active or not). By this criterion Flanders overtook Wallonie around 1967, while Brussels was far ahead though losing relatively from year to year. The superiority of Brussels may be traced to three major factors. First, a higher proportion of its residents was economically active (42.4 per cent at the 1970 census compared to 37.7 for Flanders and 36.0 for Wallonie). Second, the structure of the Brussels economy is different, being more oriented towards tertiary-sector activities and nonmanual occupations. Finally, Brussels-Capital accounts for a disproportionate share of investment income, as is made clear by studies published by CRISP (1972, no. 561; 1976, no. 711), and approximately half of all investment income goes to the top 0.5 per cent of taxpayers.

One can largely compensate for differential rates of participation in the work force by looking at income levels per tax return, and the effect of a few very high incomes can be isolated by looking at the median rather than the arithmetic mean. This is done in the second part of Table 18, which on this basis shows Flanders overtaking Wallonie about 1970, and Brussels beginning only moderately ahead of the other regions and losing the whole of its advantage by about 1978. The earlier advantage of Brussels stems partly from structural factors, because industrial wages in Wallonie have been generally higher than in the other regions. One study of employment sectors and remuneration showed that in 1963 Flanders had almost half its work force in lower paid industries such as clothing, shoes, textiles, and woodworking, while Wallonie had only about one fifth in these sectors and almost three quarters of its work force in higher paid industries such as steel, coal, and metal working. At that time the average industrial wage in Flanders was only 81 per cent of the average for Wallonie, but roughly two thirds of this disparity would have disappeared if Flanders had had the same industrial structure as Wallonie (Van Campenhout et al., 1967, 20, 50-53).

Table 17

Belgium: Gross regional product per capita, by language regions, selected years, as percentages of national average

Year	Total GNP[a] (billion BF)	Flanders	Wallonie[b]	Brussels *arrondissement* (1) or Brussels-Capital (2)
A Based on total population by residence				
Old boundaries				
1948	306	100	85.6	103.4	139.5 (1)
1953	392	100	85.8	101.9	142.4 (1)
1955	n.a.	100	87.3	100.6	140.8 (1)
1959	n.a.	100	88.1	97.5	144.5 (1)
1963	n.a.	100	89.7	93.2	147.8 (1)
1966	794	100	92.1	90.5	145.5 (1)
1968	906	100	94.5	87.4	143.8 (1)
New boundaries				
1963	n.a.	100	90.0	93.2	169.7 (2)
1966	799	100	93.1	90.2	163.1 (2)
1968	914	100	94.7	87.6	163.2 (2)
1970	1,133	100	96.0	88.9	152.6 (2)
1973	1,600	100	98.2	87.4	146.6 (2)
1976	2,349	100	99.5	84.4	150.3 (2)
1979	2,929	100	99.6	84.1	153.1 (2)
B Based on active population by place of work				
1961	n.a.	100	96.3	102.5	104.7 (1)
1970	1,135	100	102.6	99.0	94.0 (2)

[a] Estimated in billions of Belgian francs at current prices.
[b] Includes German region.

Sources: A (old boundaries): 1948, 1953: Chaput-Auquier, 1962, 8-9; 1955-66: *Bulletin de statistique*, 1968, 275; 1968: *Etudes statistiques*, 1971, no. 23: 48; (new boundaries): 1963-79: *Etudes statistiques*, 1973, no. 32: 25; *Bulletin de statistique*, 1979, 125-27; 1982, 464-65; B: 1961: Dereymaeker, 1966, 5; 1970: calculated from *Etudes statistiques*, 1973, no. 32: 25; *Recensement*, 1970, 9: 17.

Table 18

Belgium: Taxable income of individuals by language regions, selected years,[a] as percentages of the national average

	Belgium (thousand BF)		Flanders	Wallonie	Brussels-Capital	German region
A	**Based on *average* income per capita (total population)**					
1964	27.7	100	90.8	95.3	159.9	n.a.
1968	40.0	100	94.4	93.2	148.5	n.a.
1972	54.7	100	95.7	94.1	139.2	n.a.
1976	107.9	100	98.2	93.8	128.0	82.0
1980	163.5	100	99.9	95.4	115.4	86.4
1984	226.6	100	99.5	98.0	109.0	89.4
B	**Based on *median* income per tax declaration**					
1964	68.1	100	94.0	104.2	123.7	n.a.
1968	97.5	100	96.9	100.0	116.4	n.a.
1972	130.3	100	99.1	98.2	111.4	n.a.
1976	240.8	100	100.9	96.7	105.4	89.8
1980	370.7	100	102.3	95.9	100.4	91.4
1984	490.9	100	101.4	97.7	99.8	91.7

[a] The years are those of tax returns and refer to incomes of the preceding year.

Sources: *Bulletin de statistique*, 1967, 147; 1971, 445; 1974, 958; *Annuaire de statistiques régionales*, 1978, 115; 1982, 120; unpublished data from Institut national de statistique.

In explanation of these data on production and income, it can be noted that the decade of the 1960s brought considerable changes to the Belgian economy. Flanders, with lower wages, excess labor, and easy access to the sea, attracted much new investment, including a new steel complex near Brugge (CRISP, 1961, nos. 124 and 127) and oil refining and chemicals around Antwerp. On the other hand, Wallonie, with declining coal fields and an aging steel industry that faced increasingly severe competition in the Common Market, underwent a severe economic crisis. As a result of these contrary tendencies Flanders outdistanced Wallonie both in regional product and in personal incomes during the latter part of the 1960s. In Walloon circles there were prolonged recriminations about the alleged role of Belgian public policy in deliberately channelling new investment to the Flemish provinces and refusing to acknowledge the economic problems of Wallonie, but the more important factor seems to be that the economy of Flanders offered locational advantages to the industries concerned. These economic advantages proved self-correcting as wage levels in Flanders caught up with those in Wallonie and as the economy of Wallonie slackened, with the result that by 1969 the bulk of new American investment had been diverted to Wallonie (CRISP, 1970, nos. 503-504).

Table 19

Belgium: Percentages of active population in major economic sectors, by language regions, selected census years, 1866-1970[a]

Year	Bel- gium	Flan- ders	Wal- lonie	Brussels *arron- dissement* (1) or Brussels- Capital (2) or Brabant (3)	German region
A Primary sector					
1866	32.7	37.2	26.2	34.9 (3)	—
1910	22.5	28.6	17.5	18.7 (3)	—
1947	12.1	14.8	11.8	5.2 (1)	b
1961	7.2	8.1	8.3	2.7 (1)	b
1970	4.6	5.2	5.1	0.2 (2)	14.8
B Secondary sector					
1866	38.2	35.9	42.5	33.6 (3)	—
1910	45.5	42.0	53.3	40.3 (3)	—
1947	47.3	36.2	53.1	38.4 (1)	b
1961	45.7	47.6	48.0	36.0 (1)	b
1970	43.7	47.3	44.2	26.4 (2)	41.2
C Tertiary sector					
1866	20.4	19.3	19.4	26.3 (3)	—
1910	30.0	28.0	27.8	38.9 (3)	—
1947	37.1	34.5	33.3	52.2 (1)	b
1961	43.0	39.7	40.5	57.3 (1)	b
1970	49.6	46.8	49.7	62.6 (2)	43.2

[a] The third region includes all of Brabant province in 1866 and 1910, the old *arrondissement* of Brussels in 1947 and 1961, and Brussels-Capital in 1970, with appropriate adjustments for Flanders and Wallonie.
[b] Included with Wallonie in 1947 and 1961; not applicable before 1920.

Sources: 1866, 1910: Karush, 1977, 41-42; 1947-70: calculated from *Recensement*, 1961, 8 Part 1: 21, 24; 1970, 8A: 40.

Apart from data on regional product and personal incomes, various other indicators can be used to illustrate the relative economic position of the language regions both in recent times and in the longer run. For the long run there are few data that are both easily available and informative, but the structure of the active population by economic activity can be traced by provinces from the earliest censuses, and this is shown in summary form for the three major economic sectors over more than a century in Table 19.

Since the definition of sectors changes considerably in earlier censuses, these data should be viewed more as interregional comparisons at given dates than as a uniform chronological series, especially since the regional boundaries also cannot be completely standardized. It may be noted that totals for the three sectors together do not add up to 100 per cent, since the data do not include *miliciens*, the unemployed, or persons in early censuses whose activities were either badly designated or simply not recorded. What stands out most prominently in this table and in the more detailed data underlying it is the greater emphasis on primary-sector agriculture in Flanders until the 1950s, the greater development of industry in Wallonie until the 1960s, and the relative strength of the Brussels area in the tertiary or services sector during the entire period. A more detailed analysis by individual industries for the period from 1846 to 1910 highlights the substantial lead of Flanders in textiles, and an even more commanding lead of Wallonie in mining and metal working, for every one of the seven censuses examined (Karush, 1977, 73-76).

For more recent economic indicators there are many possible choices, and Table 20 presents a selection of typical indicators of material wellbeing. In making a selection I have as far as possible sought out data that are reasonably uncontaminated by other considerations. Thus the table omits an index based on the age of housing, which is sometimes used, because it seems too closely bound up with demographic differences between regions. Many similar indexes of material wellbeing are explored by Deblaere and others (1967), but their concern is with individual *arrondissements* and hence their results are presented in such a way that broad comparisons by language regions are not possible. Results by *arrondissements* are nevertheless a useful reminder of the wide economic disparities that exist *within* both Flanders and Wallonie, just as in the case of French and German Switzerland, both of which were shown in Volume 1 to have wide intraregional disparities in spite of rather similar levels of economic wellbeing when considered as language regions.

Some of these indicators in Table 20 require additional explanation. Since the figures on unemployment (Part A) are not published elsewhere as a series, it should be noted that they represent data for male unemployment plus female unemployment as a percentage of the population covered by illness and invalidity insurance (INAMI) rather than those under social security (ONSS); that they refer to full-time rather than part-time unemployment; and that they represent monthly averages of unemployment throughout the year. Further analysis of these data shows that unemployment rates for women have been chronically higher than for men, reaching double and even triple the male rate when unemployment levels soared in the recession of the 1970s and 1980s. The data on savings (Part B), drawn from large-scale surveys of household budgets, show a relatively higher propensity to save in Flanders even in 1961 when average incomes were still lower than in other regions.

Table 20

Belgium: Indicators of economic wellbeing by language regions, selected years

Indicator and year	Whole country	Flanders	Wallonie	Brussels *arrondissement* (1) or Brussels-Capital (2) or Brabant (3)[a]
A Unemployment (as percentage of insured population)				
1958	3.8	4.8	2.5	3.0[b]
1960	5.9	7.0	4.7	4.4[b]
1962	3.5	4.0	3.1	2.7[b]
1964	2.4	2.6	2.5	1.8[b]
1966	2.8	2.8	3.7	1.7[b]
1968	4.8	4.5	6.5	2.7[b]
1970	3.2	2.6	5.0	1.8 (2)
1972	3.7	3.2	5.2	2.4 (2)
1974	4.4	3.7	6.0	3.1 (2)
1976	9.3	8.5	11.1	8.7 (2)
1978	11.4	10.5	13.3	10.5 (2)
1980	12.6	11.7	14.4	11.8 (2)
1982	17.7	16.8	19.5	18.0 (2)
1984	19.9	18.4	22.7	20.3 (2)
B. Savings (as percentage of disposable income)				
1961				
Workers	8.7	9.5	8.1	8.5 (1)
Employees	8.9	11.1	8.2	7.2 (1)
Inactive	7.4	8.1	5.9	9.4 (1)
1973-74				
Workers	n.a	14.1	12.6	10.8 (2)
Employees	n.a.	18.1	12.5	13.8 (2)
Inactive	n.a	9.8	8.2	10.0 (2)
C Private automobiles per 1,000 population				
1930	11	8	12	17 (3)
1939	17	12	20	25 (3)
1950	31	23	35	42 (3)
1960	82	68	88	103 (3)
1970	212	201	208	241 (3)
1980	321	313	311	349 (3)

Table 20—Continued

Indicator and year	Whole country	Flanders	Wallonie	Brussels *arrondissement* (1) or Brussels-Capital (2) or Brabant (3)[a]
D Percentage of dwellings with private bath				
1961	23.6	21.2	20.9	38.8 (2)
1970	49.1	49.5	45.2	57.0 (2)
1981	76.1	76.5	75.3	75.9 (2)
E Percentage of dwellings owner occupied				
1961	49.7	55.2	52.4	23.2 (2)
1970	54.8	59.9	57.0	27.0 (2)
1981	60.8	65.5	63.4	31.0 (2)
F Physicians per 10,000 population				
1938	7.7	5.8	8.4	16.2 (3)
1960	12.4	9.2	13.0	18.6 (3)
1980	22.4	17.2	22.5	33.0 (3)
G Consumption of electricity (KWH per capita per year)				
1958	1,314	1,032	1,942	980 (3)
1967	2,209	2,123	2,840	1,520 (3)
1978	4,335	4,757	4,693	3,368 (3)

[a] In each case the appropriate territorial adjustments are made for Flanders and Wallonie.
[b] Unemployment figures before 1970 refer to the area served by the Brussels regional office of the National Employment Office (ONEM).

Sources: A: Annual reports and unpublished data from ONEM; 1984 unemployment data use June 1983 insurance data as the base population; B: Dereymaeker, 1966, 13-14; *Etudes statistiques*, 1975, no. 41: 5; C: calculated from *Annuaire statistique*, 1931-32, 10, 212; 1940, 14 and 1951, 280; 1950, 30, 280; 1960, 26-27 and 1961, 319; 1971, 14-15, 352; 1980, 25-38, 372; D, E: *Annuaire de statistiques régionales*, 1977, 35-36; 1978, 39-40; 1982, 35, 38; F: Janne, 1964, 27; *Annuaire de statistiques régionales*, 1980, 11, 47; G: Romus, 1968, 160; *Annuaire de statistiques régionales*, 1980, 11, 80.

Other indicators in this table show Flanders closing the gap with Wallonie with respect to private automobiles by about 1975 (Part C), and remaining slightly ahead on bathtubs (Part D), no doubt because a more rapid population increase in Flanders has called for more construction of new housing. Owner-occupied housing figures (Part E) must be interpreted with caution. While affluence is increasing levels of ownership significantly in all regions, the highest levels of ownership are in the least urbanized provinces, namely Limburg, Luxembourg, and Namur, and in the German-speaking region. A more sizeable gap remains with respect to medical services (Part F), where it has taken much longer to change the educational infrastructure. Finally, the data on total consumption of electricity (Part G) represent primarily industrial uses of electrical energy, which may explain why Brabant remains well below the national average. Here it may be noted that in the two decades from 1958 to 1978 consumption in the four Flemish provinces rose from 79 per cent of the national average to 110 per cent, while in the four Walloon provinces it declined from 148 per cent of the national average to 108 per cent, a striking illustration of the changing industrial base.

Alongside these indicators of economic standing we may place certain indicators of communications development, which can also indicate broadly the levels of economic development and modernization of the respective language regions. These are set out in Table 21, which shows that Flanders overtook Wallonie in radio sets in the 1960s while enjoying a slight edge in television sets from the beginning. The apparent lag in telephones per 100 households must be adjusted by the fact that average family and household sizes are larger in Flanders, but the lag of Flanders in education was still visible though greatly reduced as late as the 1970 census. One other obvious communications index, newspaper circulation, is deliberately excluded from this table because of complexities in the data. Both circulation and readership data for the daily press will, however, be explored in Chapter 4 (see below, 251-53).

Among longer-run indexes of development, one fruitful source is census data on literacy and illiteracy. Illiteracy rates for three generations are calculated in Part D of Table 21, but it must be remembered that these rates are based on total population including young children, and that age structures have differed both by region and over time (see Table 16, above). A more finely tuned indicator, which avoids this difficulty and focuses upon a narrower age group, is the rate of illiteracy among young men called up for military service. The trend by individual provinces appears in Table 22, which shows steep declines in every province but also considerable variations both within and between regions. In Wallonie it is interesting to note that throughout this period illiteracy was highest in heavily industrialized Hainaut and lowest in the two southern provinces. The literacy gap between Francophone and Flemish recruits had shrunk to less than 1 per cent by 1952 and had totally disappeared by 1965, when illiteracy rates were 1.3 and 1.2 per cent respectively (Van Haegendoren et al., 1957, 14; *Analyse de la population*, 1965, 43-44). Shortly after 1900 the level of illiteracy among the working classes was more closely analyzed by age, sex, and urban-rural differences in the course of a survey directed by the British investigator Seebohm Rowntree, who found illiteracy to be higher among older persons, females, and in the smaller towns and villages of Flanders (1911, 263-68).

Table 21

Belgium: Indicators of communications development by language regions, selected years

Indicator and year	Whole country	Flanders	Wallonie	Brussels *arrondissement* (1) or Brussels-Capital (2) or Brabant (3)[a]	German region
A Telephones per 100 households					
1961	24.2	20.5	23.1	40.5 (2)	21.2
1970	36.1	33.0	35.2	51.2 (2)	30.9
1981	61.9	60.5	61.1	72.1 (2)	62.5
B Radio licences per 100 persons					
1934	7.2	5.7	8.2	9.5 (1)	b
1939	13.2	10.7	15.4	16.4 (1)	b
1949	16.1	14.1	18.5	17.3 (1)	b
1959	28.1	26.1	30.6	29.1 (3)	b
1969	34.2	34.2	33.5	36.7 (3)	b
1979	45.2	45.8	43.8	45.6 (3)	b
C Television licences per 100 persons					
1958	2.5	2.6	2.2	2.6 (3)	b
1963	12.9	14.0	11.5	12.6 (3)	b
1968	19.6	20.4	18.8	19.0 (3)	b
1973	24.3	25.0	23.7	23.6 (3)	b
1979	29.7	29.8	29.8	29.3 (3)	b
D Educational indicators					
(1) Illiteracy (percentage of total population unable to read and write)					
1866	52.7	55.9	50.1	50.8 (3)	—
1900	31.9	36.4	27.9	29.5 (3)	—
1930	15.7	18.0	13.9	13.6 (3)	b
1947	12.3	14.1	10.6	11.0 (3)	b
(2) Adult illiteracy (percentage of population 21 or over unable to read and write)					
1910	14.8	17.2	13.5	12.5 (3)	—
1930	6.6	7.5	6.0	5.6 (3)	b
1947	3.6	4.0	3.2	3.3 (3)	b
(3) Diplomas **Secondary diploma or higher (as percentage of total population)**					
1970	19.6	18.9	19.9	23.2 (2)	9.8

Table 21—Continued

Indicator and year	Whole country	Flanders	Wallonie	Brussels *arrondissement* (1) or Brussels-Capital (2) or Brabant (3)[a]	German region
University degree or equivalent (as percentage of population 25 or over)					
1961	1.8	1.4	1.6	4.0 (2)	0.8
1970	2.7	2.2	2.4	5.3 (2)	1.5
(4) Population attending school in 1970 (as percentage of age group)					
14-18 years	68.2	66.8	69.3	75.5 (2)	47.8
19-24 years	14.5	13.0	14.6	22.4 (2)	11.1

[a] In each case the appropriate territorial adjustments are made for Flanders and Wallonie.
[b] Included in data for Wallonie; not applicable before 1920.

Sources: A: *Annuaire de statistiques régionales*, 1977, 35; *Recensement*, 1961, 3 Part 1: 62-63; 1970, 2A: 52-53; 1981, Résultats généraux: logements, 227; B: calculated from *Annuaire statistique*, 1936, 12, 254; 1940, 14, 299; 1950, 30, 260; 1960, 26-27, 333; 1970, 32-33, 408; 1980, 24-38, 398; C: calculated from *Annuaire statistique*, 1958, 26-27, 326; 1963, 28-29, 373; 1968, 32-33, 399; 1974, 14-15, 422; 1980, 24-38, 398; D (1), (2): calculated from *Recensement*, 1900, xlvi; 1910, 2: 470-71; 1930, 3: 10-13; 1947, 4: 10-11; D (3), (4): *Recensement*, 1970, 10A: 17, 62, 102.

What general conclusions emerge from this economic comparison of regions? Because of space limitations, the data summarized above represent only a fraction of what is available, and in a situation where linguistic tensions are high one can obtain divergent results from different indexes and even from different presentations of the same basic data. Yet in broad outline the basic trends seem clear. The historical economic lag of Flanders that was visible for the first century of Belgian independence was still in evidence after the Second World War, but during the 1950s and 1960s the economy of Flanders developed more rapidly than that of Wallonie until the two regions were at roughly comparable economic levels by the later 1960s. During this period families in the Flemish region, in spite of lower personal incomes, showed a slightly higher propensity to save and to invest in major assets such as housing ("Situation économique," 1963, 5-6; and cf. Table 20, Part B).

Wallonie, facing major problems of declining economic structure as well as a prolonged demographic crisis during the same period, reveals more noticeably pessimistic attitudes concerning its economic future. Because of its greater polarization of social classes, its population has been less receptive to belt-tightening measures, and governmental efforts at economic restraint led to a prolonged general strike in the winter of 1960-61. As a result of its strong orientation to socialism, Walloon public opinion has looked mainly to state intervention for a solution to its economic crisis, and here the awareness of diminishing political influence resulting from negative demographic trends has intensified anxieties about the future. By the mid-1970s the economic "reconversion" of the former coal-mining areas of Wallonie was under way and the most acute phase of the structural crisis appeared to be receding, but the more general problems of slower economic growth and stationary population persisted.

Table 22

Belgium: Illiteracy among army recruits, by provinces, 1843-1900

Province or region	Percentage unable to read and write			
	1843	1860	1880	1900
Flemish provinces				
Antwerp	48	31	19	9
West Flanders	56	42	21	16
East Flanders	60	52	34	20
Limburg	48	38	18	9
Regional average	57	43	25	15
Walloon provinces				
Hainaut	53	47	28	14
Liège	44	33	14	8
Luxembourg	22	16	3	2
Namur	36	22	7	4
Regional average	44	36	18	9
Brabant	51	38	20	10
Whole country	51	39	22	12

Source: *Annuaire statistique*, 1901, 218-19.

In both Flanders and Wallonie one finds much criticism of the higher economic levels prevailing in Brussels, criticism that often does not recognize the structural differences and special conditions upon which these economic differentials are founded. Nor is this image of Brussels difficult to understand, for even the first-time visitor must be impressed by the visual evidence that bears witness to a prolonged policy of heavy investment in amenities for the centre at the expense of the periphery, a policy that has left Brussels more fitted to be a capital for a state of 50 million people—or perhaps for an integrated European Community—than for a country the size of Belgium. A century and a half of centralization has accumulated a rich legacy of palaces, parks, museums, physical monuments, and general infrastructure that can hardly fail to provide extra ammunition for those who see some form of federalism or decentralization as desirable for economic reasons. From this angle one can interpret the current regional malaise in Belgium as the reaction of a neglected periphery against a privileged centre, and even in the midst of the hottest language battles this aspect never quite disappears from view.

One special characteristic of recent interregional rivalry in Belgium has been the ready availability of large volumes of data broken down by language regions, particularly since the language legislation of 1962 and 1963. This makes it easier for public attention to focus on bare regional averages, with less awareness of intraregional variations or longer historical trends, the latter being difficult to establish because of altered regional boundaries. Regional comparisons became even easier in 1977 with the establishment of the *Annuaire de statistiques régionales*, an annual publication of diversified social, economic, and fiscal data arranged wherever possible according to the four language regions of the country. Once again we may compare Belgium with the Swiss case analyzed in Volume 1, where comparisons between French and German Switzerland typically involved tedious statistical calculation for twenty-six cantonal units, and even then produced only crude approximations to the language boundaries. These two cases suggest some reciprocal relationship between the form in which data are recorded and public perceptions of the structure of cleavages.

As in the Swiss case, the underlying attitudes towards economic issues in both Flanders and Wallonie appear to be influenced significantly by collective memories of economic development over a century or more. The recent prosperity of Flanders is still overshadowed by the long period of economic retardation and deprivation that preceded it, and especially by the simultaneous famine and industrial crisis of the 1840s that depopulated the provinces of East and West Flanders. As a result, Flemish leaders have been slow to display confidence in the economy of their region and even slower to show sympathy for the difficulties of once-prosperous Wallonie. If economic conditions on the Walloon side are still quite favorable from an objective standpoint, the problem is that they are a pale reflection of a still better past, especially in Liège, where economic readjustment has been aggravated in a psychological sense by the loss of an earlier privileged position (CRISP, 1972, nos. 548-49: 46-47). One result of these tendencies is that Wallonie acquired a new minority complex in economic matters before Flanders could lose its older one, and the existence of reciprocal minority sensitivities that go beyond economic questions to other policy issues has created a climate in which intergroup attitudes are noticeably ungenerous and negotiations difficult. This general attitudinal climate and its political context will be examined more closely in the next chapter.

Chapter 3

Group Images, Attitudes, and the Political System

This chapter will explore certain attitudinal dimensions of the Belgian language situation and their consequences for the political system. Its first concern is with perceptions of group characteristics, ranging from impressionistic studies of the Belgian "national character" early in the twentieth century down through more systematic recent research in social psychology. More than in the Swiss case, it is important to try to locate these images of Walloons and Flemings in an international context because of the complicated and fundamentally asymmetrical relationship between the Belgian language groups and their nearest neighbors. A second concern is to trace the main divergences and agreements between the language communities on specific policy issues and on political values, especially since the Second World War. A third section will explore how these divergent images and attitudes have been accommodated within the Belgian political parties, and a fourth will trace the impact upon the party system of a heightened emphasis on linguistic and "community" issues during the 1960s and 1970s.

A   Group Images and Stereotypes

A useful starting point for a survey of group images occurs early in the twentieth century, when the then current vogue for studies in the psychology of "peoples" or "races" led the jurist Edmond Picard to attempt a systematic essay on Belgian national character. In this study he identified five major characteristics of the Belgian: moderation, individualism, industriousness, an aptitude for association, and a penchant for living well. In spite of his professed aims, the differences between Flemings and Walloons keep breaking through, so that "living well" is manifested among the Flemings by household decoration, among Walloons by parades and feasting. In the end he takes refuge in Pirenne's notion of a syncretic culture receptive to the influences of two different races (Picard, 1906a; 1906b).

91

Another work of the same period, which takes as its canvas the whole of
Europe, lays more stress upon these divergences, portraying the Flemings
as more serious, tenacious, and heavy, and Walloons as more playful,
witty, active, bold, talkative, and also more militaristic (Fouillée, 1903,
391).

Since these early essays there has been a steady stream of impressionistic portrayals of Flemish and Walloon group characteristics, most of it
confirming earlier work and elaborating upon it. From this literature we
can construct a composite portrait that contrasts Flemish seriousness with
Walloon light-heartedness, caution with openness, sensuality and mysti-
cism with intellect and reason, creativity with a bent for critical analysis,
faith with rationalism, traditionalism with innovation, and collective orientation with a thoroughgoing individualism. Flemish society is seen as
essentially rural and agrarian in its value system as compared with the more
urban and industrial orientations of Wallonie. Further, Flemings are represented as persevering, slow, mistrustful, quick to take offence, organized,
gregarious, clean and orderly, while Walloons are more adaptable, viva-
cious, frivolous, teasing, somewhat undisciplined, and overly critical. The
Flemish temperament originates in the Baroque, the Walloon in the
French Revolution. These comparisons could be extended much further,
but for a more serious analysis it would be necessary to examine the
contexts and sources of these statements more closely than space allows
here (Rowntree, 1911, 18-19, 103; Jennissen and de Mont, 1911, 29-30;
Gillouin, 1930, 111; Marneffe, 1934-36; Goris, 1943; Haesaert, 1947;
Dupont, 1947; Larochette, 1947; de Vries Reilingh, 1954, 47-63; Desonay
and van Duinkerken, 1963-64; Meynaud et al., 1965, 39; Van Haegendoren, 1965, 10; Piron, 1970, 89; Molitor, 1974, 421-24). Stereotypes in
folklore are less balanced than those of intellectuals. Some of the more
pejorative and scatological aspects of the image of Flemings in Walloon
popular tradition, one article suggests, have their origins in the deplorable
social condition of Flemish migrant workers and their families in Wallonie
in the nineteenth century (Quairiaux and Pirotte, 1978).

There are also some interesting variations and nuances in this literature that draw attention to areas of common ground. Carton de Wiart
(1933), while admitting basic differences in temperament, insists in the
tradition of Pirenne and Picard that a thousand years of cultural co-
penetration have produced a common set of civic values. This view is
shared by Micha and De Waelhens (1949), whose portrait of Belgian
character reflects the traumas of wartime occupation in placing a strong
emphasis on concern for the immediate and the concrete, on resourceful-
ness in any situation, and on accommodative noncompliance under external pressures. Molitor sketches a common "cultural model" of Belgian
society that includes some of the same characteristics and adds among
others a mistrust of the state (1974, 421-24). Others have explained the

Belgians' pervasive image of themselves as *frondeurs* and disparagers of central governmental authority as a consequence of prolonged foreign domination (Lorwin, 1962, 25-26; Carson, 1969, 12-13).

The image of Brusselers in this impressionistic literature is neither sharp nor flattering. The tendency is to see them as a mixture, an alloy, a combination of the less desirable characteristics of both Flemings and Walloons. Thus one Flemish writer has referred to the offspring of the hybrid culture as "sterile mules" (Van de Perre, 1919, 255-56), while the Walloon socialist leader Jules Destrée called Brussels *la cité des métis*, criticizing especially its "mediocrity" (*in medio mediocritas*), its bilingualism, its insensitivity to ethnic appeals (1923, 117-33). Other writers have singled out its materialism and a temperament that is neither speculative nor artistic (Mols, 1960, 29; Des Ombiaux, 1921). In these sharply pejorative images one can perhaps detect a note of frustration and envy on the part of the more disadvantaged periphery in relation to a more favored centre.

If the image of Brusselers is somewhat clouded, those of Flemings and Walloons are sharply delineated and reasonably uniform from one observer to another. Our concern is not to ask how far there is an objective basis to these stereotypes, but simply to note their existence as an element in the belief systems of the population. But there are also other elements to be noted. Many observers have stressed an element of pragmatism, political realism, and willingness to compromise that is common to all groups, and this appears to be at least in part a legacy of Belgium's long-term international situation. The Southern Netherlands, both before and after 1830, has been a buffer state, highly vulnerable to the storms of European politics, and over the centuries its peoples have learned how to bend with the tempest rather than break. This tendency has been carried over into domestic politics and has become a noticeable feature of the political culture. Far from being considered a virtue, however, this pragmatic streak is deplored in some quarters and linked to the proverbial Belgian *mediocrité* or *middelmatisme*, which in turn is attributed by some to *mauvais jumelage*, the yoking together of two incompatible ethnic communities (Claes, 1961, 176). Thus where Pirenne could find positive elements in cultural contact, Lode Claes sees sociological barriers and intellectual sterility. On the other hand, one may tentatively identify this little-esteemed quality of *middelmatisme* as an important resource for conflict management in the political system.

While the quest for Walloon and Flemish characteristics suggests a recognition of both faults and virtues on either side, a more important and less symmetrical dimension is the existence of feelings of group superiority and inferiority, which have been noted by many observers and manifested in many ways. One central element of this superiority/inferiority relationship was Francophone disdain towards the other language itself, a prolonged insistence that "Flemish" was not a language but only a cluster of rural patois (Leclercq, 1930, 7-8). Such attitudes have been used to justify refusal to learn Dutch and to resist its recognition in the schools. Jan Grootaers refers to the "silent intolerance" of Francophones in Belgium as a pressure just as severe as the noisy countermeasures of Flemish activism, and he suggests that refusal to learn the second language—whether in Brussels or Montréal—is a refusal to accept its speakers on equal terms as persons (Telemachus, 1963, 306).

The focal point for much of this unequal contact is Brussels, where Flemish inferiority is to some degree institutionalized in the theatre. Wilmars (1971, 123-24) describes how the principal music hall of the capital, once a centre for locally produced revues in Brussels dialect, became transformed linguistically until it featured popular variety programs in French in which the Flemish were regularly patronized and ridiculed. In middle-class theatre, one of the legendary comedies of the Brussels stage is Le mariage de Mlle. Beulemans (Fonson and Wicheler, 1910). The central figure, Monsieur Beulemans, is a successful brewer of modest Flemish origins, wealthy, honored by his peers, a minor European version of the Horatio Alger tradition, but he remains a figure of ridicule for his coarse manners and most of all for his hopelessly unsuccessful attempts to speak a cultivated French, an ability possessed in full measure by his daughter and his Parisian-born future son-in-law. For Francophone Belgians, Beulemans remains to this day the archetype of the bumbling, semi-bilingual Fleming, materially successful but culturally ridiculous. For the social scientist, he is recognizable as a classic textbook case of status inconsistency. In such an attitudinal setting, the rather paradoxical persistence of a Flemish minority complex becomes easier to understand, and the reflexes of underdogs and of "overdogs," as Val Lorwin has termed them, have continued (1972, 409).

Amid so much unsystematic material on attitudes and images it is refreshing to turn to a large-scale systematic investigation directed by Professor Jozef Nuttin of the University of Leuven, the UNESCO Research Project on Ethnic Attitudes and Stereotypes in the Belgian Context, which has included a series of theses focused on three major topics. The most relevant for our purpose is a group of studies on student stereotypes of Flemings, Walloons, and Brusselers, which yield interesting empirical data (J. M. Nuttin, Jr., 1958; Uitterhaegen, 1963; Ledent, 1964; Cuypers, 1965; Van Slambrouck, 1967). A second group investigates the effects of personal contact and other variables on attitudes concerning other groups (Spoo, 1955; Brackelaire, 1958; J. M. Nuttin, Jr., 1959; Van den Hoof, 1965). A third group investigates small-group dynamics within linguistically homogeneous and mixed French-speaking and Dutch-speaking groups (Daenen, 1960; Lagrou, 1960; Van Elst, 1961; Orlemans, 1961; Van Horenbeeck, 1961; Rombauts, 1962; Bouwen, 1965; Van Lommel, 1965). Still others investigate related topics, such as changes in group attitudes over time (Kabugubugu, 1970), or the relations between intergroup attitudes and other control variables (Vermylen, 1966). Most of these studies have remained unpublished, but summaries or overviews have been published for the work on stereotypes by Jozef Nuttin (1976), on personal contact by J. M. Nuttin, Jr. (1959-60), on group dynamics by Jozef Nuttin (1970) and Rombauts (1962-63), and on attitudinal change over time by Kabugubugu and Nuttin (1971).

Unlike the Swiss studies on stereotypes conducted by Hardi Fischer and his colleagues, which used the Osgood semantic differential technique (see Volume 1, 94-95), the Nuttin studies on stereotypes followed methods first developed by Katz and Braly (1933; 1935; 1967). Work began with the collection of a list of characteristics of the other group suggested by Flemish student respondents, supplemented by consultation of the relevant literature. Preliminary characteristics were then refined to a list of fifty-four equally balanced positive and negative characteristics which were then translated into French. A similar list was developed from Francophone students and written sources, refined, and translated into Dutch. Experimentally it was found that some two thirds of the characteristics on the Flemish list could be used on the Francophone list, while one third were new items. Further, each item on each list of characteristics was also given a "social desirability" rating by averaging responses from test groups who rated the characteristics on a seven-point scale ranging from $+3$ to -3. Various groups of respondents were then shown one of the four lists of characteristics and asked to indicate the five most typical characteristics of the other group, of their own group, and in some cases how they thought the other group characterized their own group. Analysis then focused on those characteristics named by 10 per cent or more of each group of respondents, and by weighing response frequencies against the social desirability ratings an overall positive or negative rating could be calculated for each group profile as perceived by each group of respondents (Nuttin, 1976, 9-15).

From the total materials available from several theses devoted to this project one can assemble twelve matching sets of stereotypes, as shown in Table 23. These include four of Flemings, as seen by themselves (FF), by Walloons (WF), by Francophone Brusselers (BF) and a projective heterostereotype (FWF), that is, how Flemings *think* Walloons see Flemings; and similarly four corresponding sets for Walloons (WW, FW, WFW, and BW) and for Brusselers (BB, FB, BFB, and WB). For the sake of simplicity Table 23 lists only the top ten characteristics of each set (shown here in their French version only), although in the original experiments the analysis was done on all characteristics named by 10 per cent of respondents or more, ranging up to twenty or more characteristics. Some of these sets are available from two or more independent sources and for different dates,

Table 23

Stereotypes of Flemings, Walloons, and Brusselers held by university students at Leuven

A   Images of Flemings

(1) FF (N = 404)		(2) WF (N = 258)		(3) FWF (N = 404)		(4) BF (N = 176)	
travailleur	61	complex d'infériorité	61	lourd	69	travailleur	70
complexe d'infériorité	55	travailleur	59	primitif	63	complexe d'infériorité	60
épris de liberté	38	grégaire	49	grégaire	41	grégaire	38
tenace	28	obstiné	38	peu accomodant	36	susceptible	37
hospitalier	26	courageux	35	obstiné	32	lourd	33
franc	25	lourd	35	complexe d'infériorité	27	obstiné	31
grégaire	23	susceptible	30	impérialiste	18	courageux	30
esprit social	18	envahissant	24	travailleur	17	primitif	23
courageux	17	primitif	21	envahissant	15	tenace	16
obstiné	15	peu accomodant	17	rouspéteur	14	bon-vivant	15
(Cuypers, 1965, 35)		(Ledent, 1964, 73-74)		(Cuypers, 1965, 38)		(Ledent, 1964, 77-78)	

B   Images of Walloons

(1) WW (N = 258)		(2) FW (N = 404)		(3) WFW (N = 258)		(4) BW (N = 176)	
rouspéteur	45	poseur	42	indiscipliné	48	bon-vivant	35
indiscipliné	37	vantard	40	rouspéteur	33	indiscipliné	32
individualiste	34	prétentieux	39	profiteur	28	spontané	27
bon-vivant	32	spontané	31	prétentieux	26	rouspéteur	24
épris de liberté	29	bon-vivant	24	moqueur	24	hospitalier	24

Table 23—Continued

spontané	20	colérique	19	envahissant	23	épris de liberté	22

spontané 20
hospitalier 18
large d'esprit 16
moqueur 16
coeur sur la main 15

(Ledent, 1964, 99-100)

colérique 19
jovial 17
beau parleur 16
suffisant 15
courtois 14

(Cuypers, 1965, 32)

envahissant 23
peu accomodant 19
individualiste 19
bon-vivant 18
impérialiste 18

(Ledent, 1964, 104-105)

épris de liberté 22
jovial 20
individualiste 18
vantard 16
coeur sur la main 15

(Ledent, 1964, 92)

C Images of Brusselers

(1) BB (N = 176)

rouspéteur 40
individualiste 33
épris de liberté 26
large d'esprit 25
bon-vivant 22
cultivé 19
indiscipliné 18
profiteur 15
poseur 14
{ amateur d'art 13
beau parleur 13

(Ledent, 1964, 119)

(2) FB (N = 404)

vantard 47
prétentieux 43
profiteur 39
poseur 38
bon-vivant 31
suffisant 30
superficiel 25
obstiné 20
beau parleur 18
peu accomodant 16

(Cuypers, 1965, 41)

(3) BFB (N = 176)

prétentieux 62
profiteur 43
vantard 38
individualiste 27
hospitalier 23
impérialiste 22
poseur 22
beau parleur 20
indiscipliné 19
bon-vivant 18

(Ledent, 1964, 121)

(4) WB (N = 258)

vantard 62
poseur 39
prétentieux 37
beau parleur 36
superficiel 33
suffisant 30
rouspéteur 21
individualiste 19
profiteur 17
bon-vivant 13

(Ledent, 1964, 113)

but this table is based on two sources only because Ledent (1964) and Cuypers (1965) used the same set of characteristics—based on the Francophone list—while other studies based on the Flemish list are not easily comparable. What stands out in these lists of stereotypes is the degree of common content in different images of the same group, though the relative ranking and weighting of the profile are often different. Among the similarities, there is a strong overlap between the Walloon and Flemish images of Brusselers. Where the images do diverge, the autostereotype tends to be more positive (or less negative) than the others, which is not surprising. The differences in overall ratings of these images arise largely from different loadings or weightings of certain positive and negative characteristics. For example, Flemish students widely believed that Walloons saw the Fleming (FWF) as *lourd* and *primitif*. In fact, the Walloon image of the Fleming (WF) did include both these characteristics, but they were selected less often than the Flemish respondents supposed, while more positively rated characteristics (e.g., *travailleur*) were chosen more frequently than they imagined.

One simplified method for overall comparison of stereotypes may be seen through use of the "social desirability" scale, which was calculated separately for Francophone respondents by Ledent (1964, 47-52) and for Flemish respondents by Cuypers (1965, 28-30), on the basis of evaluations developed from their respective sample populations. The resulting values for each profile are shown in Table 24. As might be expected, the autostereotypes are the most favorable, though only moderately positive at best, and the projective heterostereotypes are all strongly negative. What is less expected is the even more negative heterostereotypes of Brusselers as seen by both Flemings and Walloons (FB and WB). Comparison of the values in Table 24 with those of other studies in the series shows few major discrepancies except in the autostereotype of Flemings (FF), for which Nuttin (Ledent, 1964, 84-86) and Van Slambrouck (1967, 81) found considerably more positive self-images of +1.68 and +1.49 respectively. This suggests that the original list of characteristics developed by Nuttin from and for Flemish respondents may have been more successful in tapping major dimensions of the Flemish self-image than the modified Nuttin list developed by Ledent from and for Walloon subjects and then used in translation by Cuypers for Fleming respondents. At a more general level, this in turn underlines the difficulty, inherent in the Katz and Braly method, of developing a list of characteristics that will be neutral or impartial in its application to two or more cultural groups.

Methodological considerations aside, it is instructive to examine these Belgian findings in relation to Hardi Fischer's hypothesis that for healthy intergroup relations the projective heterostereotype (for example, FWF) should be basically congruent with both the autostereotype (FF) and the heterostereotype (WF). Table 24 suggests that these conditions are not fulfilled among Belgian students, despite the fairly high degree of common content in the stereotypes revealed by Table 23. For both Flemings and Walloons there is a very wide gap between the autostereotype and the projective heterostereotype, and for Flemings it is even wider according to Van Slambrouck's figures: +1.49 compared with −1.34 (1967, 81). Similarly, for Brussels the gap between the autostereotype and the others is quite wide in spite of the sober neutrality of the self-image. But is the situation better in Switzerland? There appears to be no way of making direct comparisons between the Swiss findings of Fischer and his colleagues and the Belgian work of Nuttin and his students, because the methods used are too dissimilar. One of the rare Belgian studies to use the semantic differential method in studying stereotypes is that by Leniere (1966), and here also comparison is doubtful because the Belgian experiment used adult male respondents aged thirty-five to forty-five, a mailed questionnaire with a low (10 per cent) response rate, and apparently an eight-point scale (0 to 7 inclusive) instead of the usual seven-point scale. In its findings, this study reports that both Flemings and Walloons saw in their own group a number of positive qualities that they failed to discern in the other.

Table 24

Ratings of student stereotypes according to social desirability of most typical group characteristics

Images of Flemings	FF +0.88	WF −0.46	FWF −1.70	BF −0.27
Images of Walloons	WW +0.70	FW −0.92	WFW −1.39	BW +0.58
Images of Brusselers	BB −0.07	FB −1.80	BFB −1.54	WB −1.66

Sources: Same as for Table 23.

Other findings from the Nuttin project may be mentioned more briefly. J. M. Nuttin, Jr. selected from a large sample of Flemish students those with the most favorable and those with the least favorable attitudes towards Walloons, and in comparing these two groups he found that students with the least favorable attitudes had less personal contact with Walloons, held less favorable attitudes towards Belgium and Brussels, and were more positive towards Flanders. Their stereotypes of Walloons were composed predominantly of negative characteristics. Further, these students tended to come from larger families, from a lower occupational status, from a less urban milieu, from exclusively Dutch-speaking homes, and were themselves less competent in French; but they were also more active in Flemish youth movements and showed more interest in a solution for the "national question." While the general conclusion was that favorable attitudes and cross-linguistic contacts were mutually reinforcing, a closer analysis of a subgroup that had moved from no contact at all before reaching Leuven to high levels of contact at university led to the formulation of a new hypothesis: that for those with no previous contact the experience of personal contact has a leveling or moderating effect, improving the least favorable attitudes but also tempering the most favorable ones (J. M. Nuttin, Jr., 1959; 1959-60; J. Nuttin, 1970, 204-207; Spoo, 1955; Vermylen, 1966).

The late Amédée Kabugubugu, himself a victim of genocide in his native Burundi within months of completing his doctorate, compared the attitudes of Flemish students in science and medicine across a twelve-year interval between 1956 and 1968. Using Likert scales, he found that for the 1968 sample attitudes were significantly less pro-Belgian and more pro-Flemish, and that the various milieux of the students (youth movements, school, family) could also be rated less pro-Belgian in the second survey. Similarly, attitudes towards Brussels were significantly more negative, though attitudes to Walloons did not basically change. However, it was also noted that the social origins of the 1968 sample were considerably more diversified than those of the 1956 group, and the "Belgian problem" itself had also evolved considerably in the interval (Kabugubugu and Nuttin, 1971; Kabugubugu, 1970).

Kabugubugu's results are consistent with those of another study done independently of the Nuttin project, which attempted to measure distances between some twenty-six politically relevant concepts using semantic differential techniques (Servais, 1970). This study found that Walloon respondents felt close proximity between concepts such as *les Wallons* and *Belgique unitaire*, or between *nation wallonne* and *nation belge*, while they saw extreme distance between *nation flamande* and *Belgique*, or between *peuple flamand* and *unité belge*. Flemish respondents also felt extreme distance between *nation belge* and *Flandres*, or between *les Flamands* and *Belgique unitaire*. They did not share the Walloon perception of proximity between Wallonie and Belgium as a whole, but they did see close proximity between *nation flamande* and *fédéralisme* or *Belgique fédérée*. From this and from other data Servais concluded that there existed a more clearly defined sense of community on the Flemish side, with more extensive use of its own symbols, while the Walloon sense of community was less specific and more closely bound up with the concept of Belgium as a unitary state (1970, 143-44).

The importance of linguistic and cultural affiliation as an element of personal identity can be studied from questions asked in the 1975 Belgian electoral survey. Table 25 shows results from two different questions in this survey, the first asking respondents to compare their cultural or regional identity against certain other roles or characteristics, the second placing regional and cultural affiliations in the context of certain geographical options. Part A of the table shows that in all three regions individuals defined themselves most frequently in linguistic or cultural roles, followed by occupational and national roles, with religious characteristics quite far behind. While cultural responses in Flanders and Wallonie overwhelmingly coincided with the respective regional cultures, those in Brussels-Capital were quite mixed (17 per cent identified themselves as Brusselers, 8 per cent as Walloons, 6 per cent as Flemings). Interestingly, some 13 per cent of the sample placed other roles first as substitutes for the listed ones, including 4 per cent who named sex roles and another 4 per cent who picked ideological ones (AGLOP, 1975, variables 279-83). In comparative perspective, it is significant that in Switzerland unqualified "Swiss" identities outnumbered cantonal or linguistic group identities by significant margins (see Volume 1, Table 25, 109), whereas in Belgium primary identification by culture or region outnumbered national or "Belgian" identities by roughly two to one in the whole sample and by three to one in Flanders. However, the Belgian and Swiss response categories for these questions are too dissimilar for extensive comparison.

Part B of Table 25 appears to be somewhat at odds with Part A; in this new context pan-Belgian feelings appear more widespread than feelings for the three regions or the two language communities or even both in combination. At first glance this is rather baffling, particularly since the data came from the same survey. One possible explanation is that while individual Belgians may have strong images of *themselves* in terms of a personal cultural or linguistic identity, the concept of language region or linguistic community as a specific territorial or social unit may be more nebulous, especially in competition with the demonstrably very strong pull of local affiliations in this survey. A further point to be noted in this second part of the table is the altogether negligible role of the provinces as a focus of identity. All these questions can be pursued further by an analysis of respondents' second and even third choices, but the results become too complex for full treatment here.

The complexity of these questions of primary identity during the 1970s is further increased by an apparently strong element of volatility over time that coincides with institutional changes. By 1979 a new survey showed primary identification with Belgium as a whole at 41 per cent for the full sample (33 per cent in Flanders, 50 per cent in Wallonie), compared to 24 per cent in 1975. Annual repetitions with the same panel of respondents showed a tendency for these levels to increase slightly over the next three years, to the extent that from 1980 to 1982 pan-Belgian orientations slightly surpassed regional and cultural-linguistic orientations combined. On the other hand, primary identification with the respondent's town or commune fell precipitously in this second survey, to 13 per cent in 1979 and only 9 per cent in 1981. Here, however, it must be remembered that the entire system of municipal boundaries had been radically restructured and rationalized in 1976, with apparent negative effects for local orientations (CRISP, 1980, no. 880: 9-10; 1981, nos. 927-28: 23; 1982, no. 966: 11; 1983, nos. 991-92: 15-16).

Table 25

Belgium: Perceptions of primary identity by language regions, 1975 (percentages)

Type of characteristic	Flanders	Wallonie	Brussels-Capital	Whole country
A Primary perception of self[a]				
Linguistic/cultural (Fleming, Walloon, Brusseler)	38	29	31	34
Socioeconomic (professional/ managerial, employer, employee, worker, farmer, independent)	27	26	23	26
Religious (Catholic, non-believer)	9	6	7	8
National (Belgian)	12	21	23	16
No answer or other category named	14	18	15	16
Total	100	100	99	100
B Primary geographical/ cultural affiliation[b]				
Local (commune, its vicinity, town)	59	42	23	49
Province	2	4	0	2
Region (Flanders, Wallonie, Brussels)	10	21	12	14
Language community (French, Dutch)	6	4	17	7
Belgium	19	26	43	24
Other	4	3	5	4
Total	100	100	100	100

[a] The question was: "How do you see yourself first of all?" (12 listed characteristics).
[b] The question was: "To what do you feel you belong the most?" (nine geographical and cultural options). Nonrespondents excluded (21 per cent).

Source: Computer run from AGLOP, 1975, variables 257-58, 279-83.

Our examination of group images to this point has focused on internal reference groups only, that is, on how members of one Belgian subculture view their own group or another Belgian subculture. It is also possible to introduce external comparisons, and if we choose this larger frame of reference the clarity of images of Wallonie and Flanders begins to break down, even at the level of impressionistic sources, because of changes in the reference groups that serve as a background. In this larger context we may begin by hypothesizing a crude spectrum of group characteristics ranging from France to Wallonie to Flanders to the Netherlands. One dimension of this comparison has been aptly expressed by Val Lorwin: "To their Dutch neighbors, the Belgians appear too excitable for the rule of law. But to the French, they appear staid, mild, and constitutional" (1965, 10; and cited in Huyse, 1970, 186). The materials for a full examination of this hypothesis are rather fragmentary.[1] The question is also of some theoretical complexity. In addition to examining the context of stereotypes or images and whether they are basically negative or positive, we may ask further questions about which foreign country (if any) is seen as a cultural model, or even a political model, and how prevalent, how uniform, and how intense these feelings are.

At the impressionistic level there is ample material for a comparison of prevailing images of Flemings and Netherlanders, and the almost exclusively negative content on both sides is often explained by the legacy of hostility and lack of contact after the 1830 separation, by the divergence in religious traditions, and by a historical experience that ranged success and expansion in the north against stagnation and foreign rule in the south. Thus a composite picture based on several sources including interviews suggests that Netherlanders simply reject the notion of the hardworking and patient Fleming, as seen by Walloons, seeing him instead as "noisy, extravagant, indiscreet, naive, impulsive, and, above all, given to excess in eating and drinking" (Desonay and van Duinkerken, 1963-64, 40). Flemings are also seen by Netherlanders as undisciplined, easy-going, untrustworthy, improvising, unrefined, and given to religious festivals, carnivals, carousing, cafe life, and fantasy (Clough, 1930, 268-69; Jaspar, 1952; Van Haegendoren and de Vries Reilingh, 1959; Brugmans, 1972). Flemings, according to these same sources, tend to regard the Netherlander as the ultimate exemplar of the Protestant work ethic, hardworking, materialistic, practical, economically motivated, frugal, parsimonious, even greedy or cheating. He is also seen as a perfectionist, stiff, formal, austere,

---

[1] Some relevant data, focusing primarily on religious and moral values, appear in a recent study by Rezsohazy and Kerkhofs (1984), which may be compared with similar data for France and the Netherlands in Stoetzel (1983). Results vary considerably. While some variables highlight similarities of Flemings to Netherlanders and of Belgian Francophones to the French, others show both Belgian groups to be more traditionalist on moral issues than either of their immediate neighbors.

impatient, clean, orderly, self-confident, condescending, and plain in taste and dress. Much of this stereotype of the Netherlander is undoubtedly held by Walloons also, and a substantial part of it is a polar contrast to the Dutch image of the Fleming.

In a perceptive article, a former Belgian ambassador to the Netherlands extends these comparisons to describe contrasting climates of politics and administration, finding the Belgians more pragmatic, more ready to improvise, more emotional and impulsive, more willing to compromise, less tied to principles and to regulations than their Netherlands counterparts. The Belgian administrative style is less rigid, less technical, and more closely integrated with the political process. Parliamentary life is more casual, more impulsive, and less professorial, so that each country displays a political style reflecting the national temperament (van der Straten-Waillet, 1968).

With the formation of Benelux and the increase in contacts after the Second World War, the question of Dutch and Belgian attitudes towards each other became more significant. In 1948 Pierre de Bie conducted a small survey of attitudes towards Benelux and the Netherlands, as well as of stereotypes of the Dutch and the Belgians, among Belgian university and technical students. His findings on stereotypes were close to those of the impressionistic literature, but he also found that Flemish and Walloon respondents expressed sympathy towards Holland, and also perceived Dutch sympathy towards Belgium, in much the same proportions (55 to 61 per cent). However, Flemings were slightly more willing than Walloons to live in Holland (29 per cent against 20 per cent) or to marry a Dutch partner (88 per cent against 71 per cent). Further, the two groups viewed the Benelux arrangement differently. Among the Flemings, 55 per cent wished to see it extended in a cultural sense and 25 per cent wished further political ties, while 94 per cent of Walloons saw it as a purely economic arrangement (de Bie, 1951, 51-55). In its later, more developed form, the Benelux Economic Union has been regarded with deep suspicion by some Francophones who consider it a conspiracy to drown Wallonie in a Netherlandic ocean, a view presented forcefully in the anonymous tract *Benelux: 20 millions de Néerlandais?* (Gallus, 1969).

A special reason for pursuing these questions a little further is that from the standpoint of external orientations, the Belgian case is less symmetrical than the Swiss one outlined in Volume 1. In Switzerland the orientation of *political* values towards the common Swiss political culture and of *cultural* values towards the respective cultural kin in France, Italy, and Germany was clear enough and relatively similar for each of the three major groups, in spite of a reassessment of cultural ties between German Switzerland and Germany under Nazism. For Wallonie also the question seems clear cut. Beyond any doubt the primary cultural orientation of Wallonie is towards France, and Huggett (1969, 90-91) notes the long-standing drain of Belgian

Francophone writers and artists—including Flemish Francophones like Maeterlinck and Verhaeren—towards Paris. It is often suggested that France is the spiritual *patrie* of the Walloons and that Paris is nearer than Brussels. If France is not held up as a political model as well, this may stem more from a sense of political and economic realism than from positive orientations towards the Belgian political culture. In noticeable contrast with the Swiss case, one seldom encounters expressions of pride in Belgian political institutions of the sort that are almost daily fare in the Swiss press, at least in the Belgian press of the troubled 1960s and 1970s.

For Flemings there is no obvious predominance of any single foreign model, because the "natural" cultural orientation towards Holland was blocked by historical circumstances. For several decades after 1830 France was the predominant cultural model for all cultivated Belgians (Hamelius, 1921, 4), but the rise of the Flemish Movement challenged this predominance. Some Flemish intellectuals turned to Holland in spite of the formidable barriers to cultural contact, others to Germany, and more recently increasing numbers of academics have been more influenced by the United States or Britain. But none of these influences has become dominant, and for many Flemings the influence of Paris has remained paramount, not so much in a linguistic sense as in general culture and lifestyles. This diversity of foreign models, and the limited influence of any one of them, accompanied by a measurable decline in pro-Belgian feelings (Kabugubugu and Nuttin, 1971), help to explain the growing intensity of orientations towards Flanders itself as a compensatory mechanism in recent decades. It is sometimes suggested that the Flemish are inward-looking and show little interest in Belgian external relations (Grammens, 1961, 1084-85), but against this must be set survey results that show public support for a European political federation to be as high in Flanders as in Wallonie, or even slightly higher (Doucy et al., 1971, 105). This apparent anomaly could be explained by the possibility that some Flemings would prefer to see Flanders involved directly in Europe as a region rather than through the intermediation of the Belgian state.

Some more general empirical data may help set this rather special Belgian-Dutch relationship in perspective and also indicate the degree of overlapping of Flemish and Walloon perceptions. In 1953 a survey of some 300 elementary school teachers—a group important for the formation of values among the population at large—asked Francophone and Flemish respondents about perceived similarities between their own group and certain foreign nationalities, and also about friendliness or hostility of their governments towards Belgium. Results are shown in Table 26, which indicates significant group differences but also quite favorable attitudes among both groups to *both* France and the Netherlands as compared to the other countries tested. Among other results in this table, the sharp intergroup divergence over West Germany may be noted.

Table 26

Perceptions of international social distance and foreign governments' attitudes towards Belgium, 1953

	Language of respondents	
	French	Dutch
A Social distance of population from own group (percentage replying "similar in most points")		
France	88	66
Netherlands	69	89
Great Britain	51	54
West Germany	25	60
United States	35	44
U.S.S.R.	6	1
B Attitude of governments towards Belgium (percentage replying "friendly")		
France	90	81
Netherlands	76	93
Great Britain	76	82
United States	69	83
West Germany	26	48
U.S.S.R.	1	1

Source: Leplae, 1955, 744-48.

From the Dutch standpoint also, it can be shown that Belgium was seen as the "best friend" of the Netherlands by 30 per cent of the population in 1968 (35 per cent in 1965), leading the United States (20 per cent), Great Britain (11 per cent), and West Germany (8 per cent) by considerable margins. Further, in 1971 Dutch sympathies *towards* the Belgian people were the most favorable of several nations listed, though closely followed by very positive feelings towards the British, the French, Germans, and Americans (NIPO, 1968, no. 1223; 1971, no. 1407). We might tentatively explain these generally favorable attitudes between Belgium and the Netherlands, despite relatively negative stereotypes of the typical citizen, in terms of a recognition of their common interests as adjacent small states surrounded by more powerful neighbors.

It should be noted that the very positive Dutch sympathies for Belgium do not imply special concern for the language issue or for the Flemish cause. Another Dutch opinion poll ranked "Flemish-Walloon questions in Belgium" as the lowest—by a considerable margin—in a list of some twelve possible concerns of Dutch foreign policy (NIPO, 1977, no. 1834). The early decades of Belgian independence saw little direct contact between the two countries and several areas of unresolved friction (de Bie, 1951, 5-15; van Raalte, 1948). Later, as relations gradually improved, the primary consideration was commercial advantage rather than cultural kinship. Clough, who describes in detail the pro-Flemish and pan-Netherlandic elements in Holland in the 1920s, nevertheless makes it clear that the prevailing public attitude towards the Flemish Movement was one of "general and official indifference" (Clough, 1930, 266-76), and a Dutch parliamentarian of the same period emphasizes Dutch neutrality on the Flemish question and Dutch diplomatic interest in a unified Belgium as a buffer against France (ter Spill, 1924, 164-70). The ensuing half century of increasing contact appears to have brought little basic change in Dutch attitudes towards the Flemish cause.

Social psychologists warn us that there is no predictable link between attitudes and behavior, yet it is not inappropriate to investigate whether the respective orientations of Flemings and Walloons to the outside world produce different behavioral results. In short, to what extent are there differences in such matters as reading habits, the use of broadcasting, travel patterns, or even in the products they buy? Table 27 shows for each language region which authors are read, where vacations are spent, and which motor vehicles are sold in greatest numbers. Broadcasting patterns are more complicated and will be examined in a later section (see below, 245-48). Though the reading and holiday figures are by now outdated, they both show clearly the strong orientation of Wallonie to France as well as the more pluralist orientation of Flanders. The data on reading patterns also highlight the extremely weak position of Belgian authors, with the exception of Dutch-speaking authors in Flanders. The data on automobiles suggest that even in a changing market French-made vehicles have had a modest sales advantage in Wallonie, and German-made ones a corresponding advantage in Flanders. Differences also appear in the pattern of visits to some pavilions at the 1958 Brussels World's Fair. Walloons concentrated more on the pavilions of France, Britain, Japan, Luxembourg, Morocco, and Tunisia; Flemings preferred those of the Netherlands, Austria, Switzerland, and the Vatican. Among domestic pavilions, Walloons showed greater interest than Flemings in civil engineering, urbanism, and transport, while just the opposite happened in the case of agriculture, the food industries, savings, and Catholic missions (INSOC, 1959, nos. 1-2: 50, 56, 58).

Because of the overall complexity of the relationship between Belgium and the Netherlands, any conclusions concerning external images and attitudes must be considered highly tentative at this stage. While the data that bear on this relationship are quite abundant, their quality is rather fragmentary. In particular, there appears to be an absence of survey data providing any kind of direct comparison between the internal and external groups, such as is available for Switzerland through the use of sympathy

Table 27

Belgium: Selected behavioral differences by language regions, various years

Indicator and date	Flanders	Wallonie	Brussels arron- dissement	Whole country
A Book currently read by na- tionality/language of au- thor, 1951 (percentages)[a]				
Belgian (French-speaking)	2	8	1	4
Belgian (Dutch-speaking)	23	3	7	14
French	25	53	36	37
Dutch	8	*	*	4
British, American	26	28	32	27
German	2	1	3	1
Other	14	7	21	13
Total	100	100	100	100
B Country of holidays, 1956 (as percentage of those going abroad)				
France	26	57	37	41
Switzerland	12	9	11	11
Austria	16	6	7	10
Italy	5	9	12	8
Luxembourg	7	5	5	6
Netherlands	4	2	2	3
Britain	3	1	2	2
Scandinavia	2	1	1	1
Other countries	24	10	22	18
Total	99	100	99	100

Indicator and date		Flanders	Wallonie	Brussels- Capital	Whole country
C Registrations of new autos by country of origin (as per- centage of total regional registrations)					
West Germany	1969	44.9	39.4	40.9	42.0
	1981	36.1	31.3	38.2	34.8
France	1969	23.2	28.5	29.6	25.9
	1981	21.2	24.9	25.4	23.1

* Less than 0.5 per cent.
[a] Figures include both original texts plus works read in translation. For the *language* in which the book was read, see Table 51 (below, 262).

Sources: A: INSOC, 1951, no. 4: 28-30; B: INSOC, 1956, nos. 5-6: 39-41; C: *Vehicules à moteur neufs*, 1969, 82-83; 1981, 76-79.

scales in the 1972 survey of Swiss voters. In that survey all Swiss language groups in general showed higher sympathy scores for other Swiss sub-cultures than for their cultural kin in neighboring countries (see Volume 1, Table 23, 96). In the absence of such data we can only guess at whether, for example, Walloons feel closer to the French in France than to the Flemish, whether Flemings feel they have more in common with Netherlanders than with Walloons, and whether or not these relationships are symmetrical. We can, however, find some scales measuring sympathy for regions and for nineteen other social groups *within* Belgium in the 1975 AGLOP study. Table 28 contains a selection of these that gives, for respondents in each language region, the average sympathy levels that they showed for their own and other regions, for religious groups, and for some occupational groups.

Table 28

Belgium: Sympathy scores towards selected social groups, by language regions, 1975 (averages, on a scale from 0 to 100)

| | Region of respondent | | | |
Listed social group	Flanders	Wallonie	Brussels-Capital	Whole country
Flemings	76	42	48	61
Walloons	49	77	63	60
Brusselers	35	54	72	46
Catholics	60	51	49	55
Nonbelievers	48	44	50	47
Managers	49	46	51	48
Workers	70	75	65	71
Foreign workers	45	45	42	45
Farmers	67	63	59	65

Source: Computer run on survey data of AGLOP, 1975, variables 122-43.

What stands out first from Table 28 is that the interregional comparisons are much sharper than those in Switzerland, where the maximum range was 19 percentage points as compared to 41 for respondents in Flanders and 35 in Wallonie. Second, the Swiss ratings are in general strikingly higher or more positive than their Belgian equivalents, averaging 80 for five internal linguistic and religious subcultures against only 54 for the five corresponding Belgian groups. This could stem in part from differences in survey methods but it also suggests a lower level of integration at the affective level in Belgian society. The only obvious foreign comparison here is the category of foreign workers, who were rated 26 percentage points below workers generally but slightly above the unemployed or the rich, and just marginally below Brusselers. This rating, however, is not directly comparable with the ratings for neighboring nationalities available in the Swiss survey, and similar data for Belgium would be of great interest.

B Language Groups, Political Issues, and Political Values

In this section we consider a question posed earlier in the Swiss context, namely, what issues and what *kinds* of issues tend to divide the language groups in Belgium? In this connection it is useful to go back to the General Introduction to this inquiry to remind ourselves that a specific disagreement over a policy issue need not be considered a cleavage in the strict sense unless it persists or becomes institutionalized in the structure of parties or other social institutions (see Volume 1, 16-19). The Belgian case will show, however, that some specific issues may become greatly intensified if they tend to divide the country along the lines of its existing social and political cleavages. When this happens, such issues create new burdens for the institutions intended to regulate existing conflicts. Lode Claes, writing from a Flemish nationalist standpoint, has suggested that "one of the first things to be noted by anyone who probes beyond the usual commonplaces is the different reactions of the two parts of Belgium to all the great political issues and crises which have faced the land since the end of the Second World War" (1963-64, 43; cf. 1973, 232-33). Though others might qualify this hypothesis, it has sufficient validity to merit more detailed consideration in relation to several of the most critical political issues that have faced postwar Belgian governments. In this category one can include the issues of *incivisme*, the royal question, the "schools war," the general strike of 1960-61, the division of Louvain University and expulsion of the Francophone section from Flemish territory, and in a more general sense the entire *question communautaire* as it has unfolded in the language legislation of 1962-63 and in subsequent moves towards constitutional reform.

The post-liberation prosecution of wartime collaborators and of acts of *incivisme* has already been mentioned briefly in Chapter 1 (above, 30-31). Its legacy was to prove an enduring one. One special problem was that although statistical evidence of prosecutions and convictions suggests little indication of discrimination against Flemings, both sides were already highly sensitized by wartime passions and by the stormy history of the question following the First World War. The machinery of justice functioned hastily and not always evenhandedly. Many Flemings became convinced that the courts operated with particular severity against the political right and against Flemish nationalism. A decree of September 1945 provided for the loss of political and civil rights for many minor collaborators whose offences were not severe enough to warrant legal charges, and tens of thousands of people in this category found themselves permanently excluded under subsequent legislation from social benefits, war damage claims, and even the right to exercise a profession. As early as 1948 the influential Catholic journal *Revue nouvelle* called for modifications of the penalties prescribing loss of political and civil rights, but in 1959 it could point out that these disabilities still continued for minor offenders and that 140 were still in prison for more serious wartime offences ("Incivisme devant nous," 1948; "Liquider la répression," 1959). In the face of this immobilism, the Flemish Movement gradually returned to its post-1918 objective of total amnesty. But the question of a general amnesty has remained beyond the political capacity of any postwar ministry, and the issue has virtually taken on a life of its own as a permanent symbol of Flemish grievances within the Belgian state. Even as late as 1976 a series of articles on the question in *Le Soir* produced a wave of sharply negative letters from readers who urged that wartime acts of collaboration were basically unforgivable, and that their perpetrators must never be restored to full rights of citizenship. In the 1980s the issue has resurfaced periodically and remains unresolved.

The "royal question" fed upon the same passions as the issue of *incivisme*. King Leopold III, whose personality contained anachronistic touches of James I and Louis XIV, was already on a potential collision course with his ministers in the years before the war. But the crucial moment came when the King, in the face of hopeless military odds, refused to accompany his ministers into exile and instead surrendered himself and the Belgian army, without ministerial advice, to the invading German forces on May 28, 1940. This action, together with his subsequent actions during the war, led the Socialists, Communists, and eventually the Liberal party to oppose his return to the throne in 1945. After a prolonged stalemate, the question of Leopold's resumption of his office was put to the electorate in a "consultation" or referendum in March 1950, the results of which show how the language regions and provinces were divided over the question. The proportion of valid votes in favor of his return was 58 per cent for the country as a whole, but this figure was composed of a yes vote of 72 per cent in Flanders (with all four provinces strongly in favor) and a more marginal no vote in Wallonie and Brussels of 58 and 52 per cent respectively. The province of Brabant as a whole was almost evenly divided, and the two smaller provinces of Wallonie also voted yes, though not so strongly as the Flemish ones (Arango, 1961, 187-90; Van Molle, 1972, 443-44). These results did nothing to diminish Socialist determination to prevent Leopold's return. When, after new elections in June, a new Catholic single-party ministry with a narrow parliamentary majority moved to restore Leopold, the industrial towns of Hainaut and Liège erupted in mass demonstrations and riots inspired by the Fédération générale du travail de Belgique (FGTB). Under the shadow of escalating demonstrations that rapidly brought the country to the threshold of civil war, the leaders of the three major parties reached agreement that

Leopold's abdication in favor of his son was the only possible solution, and this was announced on August 1 (Arango, 1961, 199-204; CRISP, 1974, no. 646; Duvieusart, 1975).

Two aspects of the crisis over the throne deserve emphasis. First, the issue revolved almost entirely upon Leopold's wartime conduct, and the institution of the monarchy itself was never seriously in question. Divisive as the issue was for a full decade, Leopold's predecessor, Albert I, had become a strong symbol of Belgian unity during the First World War. This integrating role of the monarch has been restored, though only gradually, under Leopold's successor, to the extent that the Belgian monarchy can again be viewed as both a symbol of unity and a mediator of conflicts (Lorwin, 1966, 177). Second, and perhaps more important in context here, the Flemish were keenly aware that the outcome represented not the will of the electoral majority but the success of extraparliamentary action and the threat of civil strife. It was an example that they were prepared to follow in their turn.

The royal question was barely out of the way before a third major issue surfaced. In 1951 the single-party Christian Social ministry began to improve the conditions of support for Catholic secondary education against vigorous opposition from the Socialists and Liberals. When the government changed in 1954 the new Socialist-Liberal coalition tried to reduce this support and take a position favoring the state schools, a policy that provoked mass Catholic—and predominantly Flemish—demonstrations in Brussels. The new education law became a major issue in the 1958 election. Both sides campaigned for effective freedom of choice in education: the Catholics saw this in terms of equal treatment for those in the private sector, while the government saw it as a question of providing more schools in the public sector. When the Socialist-Liberal coalition narrowly lost the 1958 election, both sides were prepared to depoliticize the issue, and this was accomplished by interparty negotiation of a complex package deal to resolve outstanding issues. Interestingly, the resulting *Pacte scolaire* was negotiated privately by an interparty committee of twelve, approved by congresses of the three major parties, and formally signed by their representatives before being presented to Parliament (Meynaud et al., 1965, 150-176).

While the 1950 vote on the royal question tended to divide Wallonie and Flanders somewhat more sharply than would have been expected from the division between parties of the left and right at the election of 1949 (Arango, 1961, 189), the "schools war" of the 1950s remained essentially a division based on parties. Its greatest significance lay in its negotiated settlement, for the *pacte scolaire* removed important confessional issues from the political agenda and thereby opened the way to the expression of new demands based on class and language. It also removed a major force for cohesion in the Christian Social party and facilitated the emergence of more explicit linguistic and regional demands both within and outside the party.

A fourth major crisis, the general strike of 1960-61, arose from economic difficulties. Faced simultaneously with the loss of the Congo, economic crisis in the coal-mining areas, and a growing budgetary deficits, the ruling Catholic-Liberal coalition developed a mixed package of austerity measures in a single draft bill, the so-called *loi unique*, in the autumn of 1960. Though unpleasant for all groups, it was least palatable to organized labor, which found itself badly divided over how to express its opposition. The Catholic trade union federation (CSC) pressed for amendments through discussion with ministers, while the Socialist federation (FGTB)—whose counterpart political party was in opposition—was internally divided, with the more militant elements under the charismatic Liégeois leader André Renard pressing for a general strike. On December 16, a Renard motion for a general strike was narrowly defeated in the central committee, and a few days later, in the midst of spreading wildcat walkouts across the country, the national office of the FGTB left the decision to strike to its various regional committees. For the next four weeks the economy of Wallonie was brought to a standstill by mass demonstrations in the streets, but the strikers received only partial support in Flanders even from FGTB unions. Meanwhile the *loi unique* was passed in the lower house on January 13, and the strike petered out a week later (Féaux, 1963; Meynaud et al., 1965, chap. 4; du Roy, 1968, 116-27; Curtis, 1971, 494-502; Hasquin, 1975-76, 2: 335-39; CRISP, 1961, nos. 91, 113; Brazeau, 1966, Annex IV-B-2).

The general strike left a lasting legacy of bitterness in Walloon labor circles, whose leadership tried to mobilize the working class against the Belgian bourgeoisie only to find that they had created a costly and ultimately unsuccessful regional protest. Out of this disillusionment among Walloon socialists came a serious rift in the FGTB, the resignation of Renard as associate secretary-general, and the formation a month later of the first significant Walloon regional political party, the Mouvement populaire wallon. Perhaps more than any other single event of the postwar period, the general strike helped to crystallize feelings in Wallonie of helplessness and of the minority status of the region in the Belgian political system.

A fifth major political upheaval surrounded the passage of the three major language laws of 1962 and 1963, and this legislation in turn ties in with the subsequent long search for constitutional reform, whose full realization remains incomplete in the 1980s. The substance of these major institutional changes will be dealt with in Chapter 4, but here we are concerned to note that Flemings and Francophones approached the question of language legislation with fundamentally different perspectives. Walloons and Francophones of Brussels have shown a voluntarist or even a *laisser faire* attitude towards language, while the Flemings have been strong partisans of regulation through public policy, seeing the need to protect one's territory against linguistic infiltration as no less appropriate and necessary than the building of dikes against the sea. This difference in attitudes between voluntarism and territorialism was noted long ago by the Walloon leader Jules Destrée (1923, 186) and is sometimes linked to wider cultural comparisons between the Renanian conception of nationalism in France and Germanic theories of nationalism emphasizing soil and terri- tory. It seems more logical, however, to explain these radically different perspectives in terms not of national or cultural characteristics but of the relative positions of the languages in question. In the Belgian context the Dutch language is clearly on the defensive and stands to benefit from linguistic regulation, while French is clearly much stronger and less in need of legislative protection.

Once the language laws were passed, similarly divergent perspectives were carried over to the quest for constitutional reform. The Flemish goal was a sufficient degree of cultural autonomy to allow for a full develop- ment of Netherlandic culture independent of the older and stronger influ- ences of French. Walloons, secure in their culture but demographically a minority, sought institutional protection against possible domination by a Flemish majority. In Brussels the situation was partially reversed. There the Flemish were a minority both in numbers and in a cultural sense, but the majority of Netherlandic speakers in the country as a whole offered the means to protect the doubly disadvantaged Flemish minority in Brussels. All in all, the setting for constitutional reform was both complex and asymmetrical, but its structural elements were such that each of the inter- ests concerned had some bargaining leverage.

A sixth major issue, the *splitsing* of Louvain University into two autonomous, territorially separated institutions, was essentially a product of two other developments: the drive for the complete linguistic homogeneity of Flanders in the wake of the 1962-63 language legislation and the need for university expansion in the 1960s. The Catholic University of Louvain, the largest university in Belgium and the best known interna- tionally, had been basically Francophone from its re-establishment in 1833, but after the *vernederlandsing* of Gent University in 1930 it had become increasingly bilingual in its course offerings and programs. The town of Leuven—as Leuven/Louvain became in its unilingual Dutch designation—had developed various administrative and educational facilities for Francophone students, faculty, and their families, and the first round of conflict was generated by an attempt in 1962 to have these services recognized on the same legal basis as the facilities for linguistic minorities in communes along the linguistic frontier and around Brussels. The attempt was unsuccessful, but it generated reactions on the Flemish side that included the first demands for a transfer of the French section to

Wallonie. It is relevant that the town centre of Leuven is a mere eight kilometers from the linguistic frontier and about seventeen kilometers from the nearest boundary of Brussels-Capital.

The conflict became serious following passage in April 1965 of a first law on university expansion, which authorized the university to expand into the nearby Walloon district of Wavre and also into the eastern section of Brussels-Capital for its medical faculty. In November of that year a senior university administrator gave an interview to the student newspaper to explain the expansion plans, pointing out that the three sites could be seen in long-run perspective as three points of a triangle representing a much-expanded Brussels urban area. This statement galvanized the Flemish student body and the Flemish press. The Francophone administrator had been thinking of urbanization, but the Flemish readership saw his remark only in terms of *francisation*. The traditional image of the Brussels "oil stain" (*olievlek*) had become a more ominous triangle (*driehoek*), with its projecting point menacing the town of Leuven itself and the heart of Flemish Brabant. The incident precipitated a new round of demonstrations against the Francophone presence in Leuven, as did a formal declaration of policy by the bishops of Belgium in May 1966 stating that the Francophone and Flemish sections would remain unified in one university, situated in Leuven.

The full storm broke in mid-January 1968 with the publication of expansion plans which envisaged new investments and increased enrolments for the Francophone section in the town of Leuven itself. Since these plans were tied to projected legislation, Flemish Christian Social parliamentarians reacted directly by withdrawing their support from the government and bringing down the Vanden Boeynants ministry on February 7. There followed a bitter election that focused sharply on the Leuven issue and badly split the Christian Social party. After the election the Flemish Christian Social representatives made the transfer of the French section to Wallonie a condition of their participation in any new government, and after lengthy negotiations, this condition was met by a governmental declaration on June 25 announcing that the transfer would be effected by faculties and units as facilities were constructed at the new sites. The next few years saw the establishment of two legally distinct Francophone and Flemish universities, the division of the common *patrimonium*, and the first stages of construction of a new campus for Louvain-la-Neuve in open farmland at Ottignies, about twenty-five kilometers from Leuven on the other side of the language frontier. By early 1978 the two new campuses at Ottignies and Brussels were serving some 13,000 students, and the transfer—more diplomatically referred to in Flemish circles as a "siphoning off" (*overheveling*)—of the last Francophone faculties from Leuven was completed in 1979. One of the most painful features of the entire transaction was the fate of the central university library. After failure to find agreement on any principle of division by the language or origin of the items, it was decided to divide the entire collection according to odd and even shelf numbers, with the respective recipients of the two halves to be decided by lot (Leirman et al., 1968; Jonckheere and Todts, 1979; CRISP, 1962, nos. 173, 178; 1966, nos. 333-34; 1967, nos. 358, 364-65; 1968, nos. 394, 398; *Feiten en meningen*, 1966, no. 1; Goffart, 1969; Verdoodt, 1973, 134-44).

The Leuven issue illustrates how, in the Belgian context, an issue whose origin is of mainly local importance can ramify progressively until it assumes national importance and even shakes the foundations of the party system. In the process of escalation, academic considerations were progressively superseded by wider political considerations for the linguistic integrity of the Flemish region. A survey conducted in the autumn of 1966 indicates that virtually all of those who favored the transfer, and even a clear majority of those who opposed it, did so for political rather than academic or scientific reasons, and that a clear majority of all respondents perceived the transfer issue as one based on wider political considerations. Nevertheless, a majority of Flemish respondents saw the transfer as beneficial for both linguistic sections of the university itself, while a majority of respondents in Wallonie and Brussels saw primarily disadvantages for both sections (*Opinion publique belge*, 1967, 50-58; cf. Vlaemynck and Fauconnier, 1974).

Apart from these six major issues where intergroup conflicts have given rise to political crises of the first order, Flemish-Walloon differences have emerged on many other issues of Belgian politics during the postwar period. In earlier sections we have already noted the struggle in 1960 and 1961 to suppress the linguistic census, and more general disagreements over social welfare issues that have arisen from the differing demographic tendencies of Wallonie and Flanders. The point is that in Belgium every question on the political agenda has been scrutinized closely from a linguistic and regional standpoint, and appropriate balances have been sought. Lode Claes has noted the political tendency in this period to demand an equilibrium between Flanders and Wallonie in all policy decisions, whether concerned with mine closures, rail abandonments, economic expansion, new industrial plants, public works, or autoroutes (1963-64, 46). The principle has been applied even when no obvious balance has existed, so that when harbor improvements have been undertaken in Flanders, public works on an equivalent scale have been requested and obtained for Wallonie.

Even in foreign policy issues the same tendencies may be observed. Flemish-Walloon differences that are doubtless rooted in the differing external orientations of the language regions have surfaced over the questions of German rearmament and British entry into the European Common Market, where the Flemish have tended to see Britain as a useful counterweight to a Gaullist France (CRISP, 1969, no. 433: 4-5). Outside the Common Market, the more strongly leftist orientation of Wallonie has been manifested in more open attitudes towards the U.S.S.R. and China. Regional divergence over Chile was revealed in a parliamentary vote to suspend a program of professorial exchanges after the takeover by the junta in 1973. Although the proposal was sponsored by the Socialists, the vote came closer to an overall alignment of Flanders against Wallonie and Brussels than party representation would indicate (CRISP, 1975, no. 674). Even the choice of a fighter plane for the Belgian armed forces divided the country along community lines, and the choice of an American over a competing French model in 1975 put a severe strain upon the political system. The Belgian government at first leaned towards the French model for a combination of military and political reasons, but in the face of deep linguistic divisions in the government, in the relevant parliamentary committees, and in the press, it was forced to postpone a decision until the choice of the American model by its NATO partners forced the Belgian Cabinet to follow suit to ensure standardization of equipment (CEPESS, 1975, no. 851: 6-8; CRISP, 1975, no. 690).

Alongside this gallery of major and minor divisions over specific issues, it is necessary to point out that many other issues do not give rise to significant regional divisions, and that outside the areas of linguistic-regional conflict there exist important elements of consensus on political values and the rules of the political game. We can find evidence of considerable levels of satisfaction with Belgian life in general, as data in Table 29 indicate. There is acceptance of the parliamentary regime and of many of its specific features. There is widespread consensus on non-violence, or more specifically, on the acceptable limits to violence. Thus mass demonstrations and extraparliamentary action are accepted, but an electoral incident in 1970 that resulted in a fatality, the *affaire Georgin*, was strongly condemned on all sides (CRISP, 1970, no. 496: 10-12; Lorwin, 1965). As long as the Congo remained under Belgian control, there was substantial agreement in all language regions on the legitimacy of Belgian rule there. Concerning economic and social values, there are substantial areas of agreement on the general outlines of the welfare state, though here the differing ideological complexion of the regions produces significant interregional divisions over many specific issues. Finally, a study of the *affaire Merckx*, which found almost identical reactions concerning the Flemish cyclist in Antwerp and Liège (Bonis, 1969), suggests that sports may be an area of substantially shared interests and a factor for integration.

Many of the specific issues and values discussed above can be illustrated with empirical data of varying quality drawn from national opinion surveys over three decades, as illustrated in Table 29. In this table it is important to note the dates of the surveys, because some of the earlier data may indicate traditionalist attitudes that have changed considerably over time. In general terms it can be seen from Part A of this table that Flanders has been more anti-communist and less anti-German in foreign affairs, more conservative and noninterventionist in domestic issues, and more traditionalist on religious and moral questions. On European unification both groups have been more or less equally in favor, but the 1975 survey suggests that Flemings view the issue as less important and are less attracted to unification at the political level. No region is much inclined to make economic sacrifices for European unity.

Table 29

Belgium: Opinion data on select political issues and values, by language regions, various dates (percentages)

	Flanders	Wallonie	Brussels *arrondissement* (1) or Brussels-Capital (2)	Whole country
A Domestic and foreign issues				
1. Favors return of King Leopold (1950 referendum)	72	42	48 (1)	58
2. Family allowances (1952)				
− approves in principle	79	75	61 (1)	75
− higher for fourth child and beyond	52	32	11 (1)	39
3. Opposes West German rearmament (1955)	34	41	49 (1)	38
4. Opposes negotiations between West and U.S.S.R. (1955)	26	16	13 (1)	21
5. Opposes recognition of Communist China (1955)	38	31	22 (1)	33
6. Favors British entry to Common Market (1963)	66	50	57 (1)	58
7. Approval of governmental language policies (1963)				
− fully or partly	48	18	19 (1)	32
− not at all	33	65	67 (1)	50
8. Second-language goals for own children (1966)				
− learn more than one language	98	98	99 (2)	98
− learn second national language	96	70	83 (2)	84
− learn second national language *before* other languages	82	44	56 (2)	66
− not learn second national language	4	30	17 (2)	16
9. Opposes transfer of Louvain University to Wallonie (1966)	27	53	67 (2)	40
10. European unification				
− favors union/unification				
1956-57	61	70	n.a.	66
1962	68	60	n.a.	65
1975	54	59	65 (2)	57

Table 29—Continued

	Flan-ders	Wal-lonie	Brussels *arron-dissement* (1) or Brussels-Capital (2)	Whole coun-try
— considers unification "important" or "very important" (1975)	51	64	69 (2)	57
— favors political unification (1975)	46	57	62 (2)	52
— will accept economic sacrifices for unification (1975)	18	16	22 (2)	18
11. Favors major reform of management of Belgian industry (1975)	61	78	70 (2)	68
12. Methods of system change (1975)				
— global economic planning	39	47	54 (2)	43
— employer-union agreements	51	42	37 (2)	47
13. Favors worker self-management in industry (1975)	21	43	35 (2)	30
14. Favors dropping penal sanctions for abortion (1975)	32	52	61 (2)	42
15. Regionalization: favors same status for Brussels as for Flanders and Wallonie				
1975	19	39	57 (2)	30
1980	10	32	50 (2)	22
B Democratic values and the political system in general				
16. Prefers parliamentary regime (1954)	81	83	83 (1)	82
17. Legitimacy of Belgian presence in Congo (1956)	84	79	72 (1)	80
18. Individual liberties necessary to Belgian political system (1975)	72	71	78 (2)	72
19. Rights of the opposition necessary (1975)	62	64	70 (2)	64
20. Elections necessary (1975)	66	60	69 (2)	64
21. Parliament necessary (1975)	63	55	59 (2)	60
22. Monarchy (1975)				
— necessary	31	25	32 (2)	29
— not important or hindrance	47	47	49 (2)	48
23. Belgian unity (1975)				
— necessary	62	59	69 (2)	62
— not important or hindrance	18	15	11 (2)	16
24. Political regime preference				
— keep unitary state (1975)	46	54	51 (2)	49
(1982)	32	52	50 (2)	41
— establish federalism (1975)	35	36	34 (2)	35
(1982)	42	30	32 (2)	37
25. Economic regime preference (1975)				
— state control	30	42	21 (2)	33
— free competition	50	45	62 (2)	50

Table 29—Continued

	Flan-ders	Wal-lonie	Brussels arron-dissement (1) or Brussels-Capital (2)	Whole coun-try
26. Church in politics (1975)				
− favors intervention	21	17	12 (2)	19
− favors nonintervention	63	73	74 (2)	68
27. Satisfaction with life in Belgium (1975)				
− satisfied	63	54	59 (2)	60
− dissatisfied	15	25	25 (2)	19
28. Satisfaction with Belgian political system (1975)				
− satisfied	46	28	31 (2)	38
− dissatisfied	33	45	49 (2)	39
29. Attitude to the future (1975)				
− things will get worse	48	63	54 (2)	53

Sources: 1: Duvieusart, 1975, 54; 2: INSOC, 1952, no. 3: 10-11, 26-27; 3: INSOC, 1955, no. 1: 19-21; 4, 5: INSOC, 1955, nos. 2-3: 10-11, 37-38; 6: INSOC, 1963, nos. 2-3: 35; 7: INSOC, 1963, no. 1: 30-31; 8, 9: *Opinion publique belge*, 1967, 15-16, 47; 10: Doucy et al., 1971, 105-106; AGLOP, 1975, variables 213, 214, 219, 220; 11, 12: *Soir*, 1975, June 18, November 18; 13-15: AGLOP, 1975, variables 222, 227, 239; CRISP, 1981, nos. 927-28: 9; 16: INSOC, 1954, nos. 5-6: 9-11; 17: IN-SOC, 1956, nos. 2-3: 63-65; 18-28: AGLOP, 1975, variables 188-90, 337, 396, 398-403; CRISP, 1983, nos. 991-92: 23; 29: *Soir*, 1975, November 18.

The two items on language in Part A deserve a brief additional comment. The question on governmental language policy (item 7) was asked in April 1963, after the passage of the law of November 1962 on the linguistic frontier but during discussion of two further major language bills of 1963. The figures and the extensive commentaries published with this survey highlight the sharp disapproval of the electorate in Wallonie and Brussels for the language projects of the Lefèvre ministry, compared with only mixed support from Flanders, and further data in this survey show that the government's language policy was far more unpopular than its fiscal, economic, or social policies (INSOC, 1963, no. 1; F.T., 1963).

The 1966 question on which languages respondents wished their children to learn at school (item 8) can be classified as a specific policy issue, but it may also be viewed in a wider sense as an indicator of attitudes towards the outside world and towards Belgian society in general. The differential esteem for French and Dutch as second languages shows up clearly in these figures, and the point is emphasized by the sobering fact that attitudes towards Dutch as a second language were less favorable among intellectuals than among nonintellectuals in both Wallonie and Brussels. While those in Wallonie might plead that Dutch was unnecessary in some situations, the figures for Brussels suggest that one respondent out of six (and one out of four among intellectuals) considered the European role of Brussels as a multilingual international metropolis to be more important than its role as the national capital of a bilingual country (*Opinion publique belge*, 1967, 14-19, 68-69). While various later surveys do not permit direct comparisons with these figures, a comprehensive study of modern-language needs carried out by Baeten and Verdoodt in the early 1980s suggests, among its many findings, continuing differentials between Francophone and Flemish students in their esteem for Dutch and French as second languages and in their perceived need for them for their own careers. However, both groups showed strong and almost equal support for generalized passive bilingualism, that is, an ability to *understand* the second official language (CRISP, 1976, no. 742; 1984, nos. 1026-27).

Part B of this table contains data on attitudes towards democracy and the political system in general. Here it can be seen that in spite of some wide divergence over specific issues there is considerable consensus across the three regions over the basic rules of democracy and of Belgian politics. Explicit rejection of basic democratic values (items 18-21) is quite limited because typically 20 to 30 per cent of respondents offered no opinion on these questions. While respondents were more divided over the need for the monarchy, the three regional profiles on this item were quite similar. There was wide consensus on the need to preserve Belgian unity and on nonintervention in politics by the Church (items 23 and 26). Responses indicating basic political and economic preferences were more divergent, but in 1975 all three regions nonetheless leaned in varying degrees towards a unitary political regime and a free-enterprise economy (items 24-25). By 1982, however, the federal idea had become the stronger in Flanders. Finally, respondents in all three regions revealed considerable satisfaction with life in Belgium generally but then diverged rather sharply in their assessments of the Belgian political system and in expectations for the future (items 27-29), though on this last item the greater pessimism expressed in Wallonie may be not just an attitude but a realistic appraisal of the severe structural difficulties then facing the Walloon economy.

One further dimension in the list of political values is how inhabitants of the three regions rated themselves on a left-right scale. In the 1975 survey respondents were asked to situate themselves on a left-right scale of ten compartments which were then coded from 1 to 10. From this coding one can then calculate average or mean ratings for each region, which may then be compared with the ratings seen earlier for Switzerland (see Volume 1, 97) by multiplying by ten for conversion to a percentage scale. On this basis we can compare how respondents in the Belgian regions see themselves as compared to the respective language communities in Switzerland, and this is shown in Figure 1, with adjusted scores for Belgium.[1]

---

[1] The adjustment is necessary because Belgian scores were scaled from 1 to 10 (which then converts to 10 to 100), while the Swiss scale ran from 0 to 100. More comparable results are obtained if one scales the ten boxes or compartments used in the Belgian scale at the

Whether one uses adjusted figures or not, it is clear from Figure 1 that the interregional difference between Wallonie and Flanders of 19 percentage points is almost three times as great as the seven-point difference between French and German Switzerland, a finding that will have tangible consequences when we compare patterns of party support in the three Belgian regions. As in the Swiss case, these averages exclude the 46 per cent of Belgian respondents who did not or could not respond to this question.

Figure 1

Intergroup variations in self-placement on a left/right scale, Belgium and Switzerland (averages)

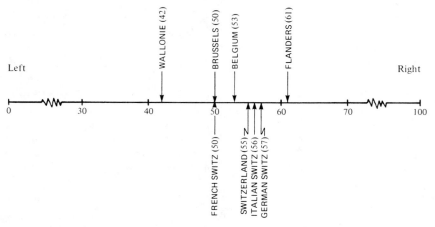

Sources: Belgium: Frognier, 1975, 473; AGLOP, 1975, variable 357; Switzerland: Kerr, Sidjanski and Schmidtchen, 1972, variable 217 (see Volume 1, 97).

So far the discussion has focused on issues that tend to divide the linguistic regions, but what is the overall situation if we look at *all* the issues in Belgian politics? Many studies on electoral behavior have suggested that for most voters issues of a cultural or symbolic nature tend to be seen as less important than "bread-and-butter" economic issues, and there is considerable evidence that this holds true for Belgium also, though various aspects of the *question communautaire* show up strongly during the 1960s as the dominant noneconomic issue. A survey among young people in 1961 showed that both Flemings and Walloons placed greater emphasis upon economic and social problems, though linguistic questions were closer behind in Wallonie and Brussels than in Flanders (D'Hoogh and Mayer,

mid-points of each box, that is, 0.5, 1.5, 2.5, etc., and hence the Belgian results as published should be reduced by 0.5 (or 5 percentage points) in each case. This has been done in Figure 1.

1964, 65). A small survey of electors in seven communes in 1964 showed that 28 per cent of respondents chose "prices and taxes" as the most important in a given list of ten political problems, but 21 per cent picked "Flemish-Walloon relations" as most important (Huyse, 1969, 105, 183). In 1966 another survey ranked "linguistic problems" sixth in importance in a list of eighteen problems, behind prices, taxes, physicians, and pensions, but well ahead of many social and environmental issues. By region, this issue was ranked sixth in Flanders, eighth in Wallonie, but third in Brussels, closely behind prices and taxes (Delruelle et al., 1966, 304, 313). Two years later a larger electoral survey asked respondents which of five categories of arguments they had been most sensitive to during the 1968 campaign, and on this question "linguistic problems" was most frequently ranked first in all three regions, followed by "the organization of Belgium" in both Wallonie and Brussels, with "social," "economic," and "professional" problems trailing except in Flanders (Delruelle et al., 1970, 133, 135; CRISP, 1976, no. 742: 2-4). Here, however, one should probably distinguish between the voters' awareness of campaign arguments and their own perception of the issues, which might well differ.

In the 1970s the salience of linguistic issues appears to have diminished slightly. Evidence for this change may be seen from a question in the 1975 AGLOP survey that asked respondents to rate the importance of some twenty-two different divisions or cleavages in Belgian society on a scale from 0 to 100. The mean scores were then ranked, and by this measure the "Flemings-Francophones" division was ranked fifth, three out of the top four being more clearly class-oriented ("employers-workers," "powerful-powerless," "rich-poor"). But interregional cleavages were also listed separately, and here it is interesting but not surprising that the cleavages "Flanders-Wallonie" and "Brussels-Flanders" were seen as considerably more salient than "Wallonie-Brussels," which ranked near the bottom of the list (Dewachter, 1975b, 546), a finding which tends to confirm the findings of Servais (1970) discussed earlier (above, 100). We can also examine the rankings by respondents in each region, as shown in Table 30. Here it is interesting to note that Brusselers ranked the three cleavages in which they are directly involved significantly higher than their counterparts in other regions.

One further comment is necessary on the relative salience of linguistic and nonlinguistic issues. Because the Belgian language cleavage is institutionalized almost exclusively on the basis of language regions, it follows that any nonlinguistic differences between regions will tend to be cumulated on top of the linguistic cleavage in quite visible terms. In the preceding sections we have noted a number of structural and attitudinal interregional differences on such diverse dimensions as demographic structure, industrial structure, incomes, religious traditionalism, and ideological orientations. This means in effect that many issue differences that are basically nonlinguistic in origin acquire an additional interregional and linguistic dimension, and also that conflicts over nonlinguistic issues acquire an extra edge of hostility or suspicion arising from the insecurities felt in each of the three main regions. Therefore, it is not enough to assess the salience of "linguistic problems" or the *question communautaire* as such; one must also allow for the contaminating effect of differences between regions that surface in the context of other conflicts.

Table 30

Belgium: Relative importance of selected cleavages in Belgian society, by language regions, 1975 (rank order out of 22)

Cleavage	Whole country	Flanders	Wallonie	Brussels-Capital
Flemings-Francophones	5	8	6	1
Flanders-Wallonie	8	9	4	8
Brussels-Flanders	9	6	19	4
Brussels-Wallonie	19	22	18	9

Source: Computer run from AGLOP, 1975, variables 78-99.

This is not the place for an extended comparison of the Swiss and Belgian political systems, but two observations virtually impose themselves at this point. First, the relatively high coincidence between language community and language region in Belgium facilitates the mobilization of political forces along linguistic lines and contrasts sharply with the more complex and diffuse relationship between language groups and cantons in Switzerland. In the next section we shall see some of the consequences of this difference in the interaction of political parties. Second, one characteristic of the Swiss scene stands out by its absence in contemporary Belgium: the tendency to see cultural diversity and linguistic pluralism as a positive value. Although the historian Henri Pirenne could praise the syncretism of Germanic and Latin temperaments early in the twentieth century, such positive views have seldom been advanced in the literature of the past six decades by either Walloons or Flemings. Even if positive evaluations of cultural pluralism in Switzerland are largely confined to the political and cultural elites—as they probably are—their importance for the development of more tolerant mass attitudes should not be underestimated.

C   The Pattern of Cleavages and the Political System

The balance of this chapter will examine how divisions between language groups and regions have found expression within the Belgian political system. To do this, however, we must first scrutinize that system in a broad context, because the linguistic/regional cleavage is bound up with the other major cleavages of religion and class in a complex and dynamic pattern. From the start, two features of the Belgian system must be kept in mind. First, and unlike the Swiss case, it is highly centralized, in the sense that all major issues have tended to converge into one major arena for discussion and decision-making, the national Parliament. Second, of the three major lines of cleavage, the religious division was the first to become politically significant, followed by the class division when organized labor turned to political action. This meant that by the time the linguistic cleavage assumed a new political dimension during and after the First World War, the other two major cleavages were already institutionalized not only in the party system but in the fabric of day-to-day social organization.

From the mid-1960s Belgian society has frequently been described as culturally segmented or *verzuild* (literally, "pillarized") into three distinctive ideological worlds or *familles spirituelles* according to the model developed for the Netherlands by Arend Lijphart (1968) and by earlier Dutch sociologists (Kruijt, 1959; Kruijt and Goddijn, 1968). In Belgium the basic structures of this social segmentation were complete before the First World War, as we may see from the vivid testimony of Seebohm Rowntree:

... it is the exception, rather than the rule, for persons holding different political opinions to co-operate in any other matter. Thus, in one town there will be a Catholic, a Liberal, and a Socialist trade union, a Catholic, a Liberal, and a Socialist co-operative bakery, a Catholic, a Liberal, and a Socialist thrift society all catering for similar people, but each confining its attentions to members of its own political party. The separation extends to cafés, gymnasia, choral, temperance, and literary societies, indeed it cuts right through life (Rowntree, 1911, 24).

Continuing segmentation in the 1920s is confirmed by an American observer who stresses the superiority of the Socialists over their Catholic and Liberal rivals in terms of organizational thoroughness and unity of purpose (Reed, 1924, 158-79). More recently the Walloon political scientist-politician François Perin has traced the three broad ideological streams underlying this tripartite segmentation of Belgian social structure and has linked them to three wider traditions that have shaped the European mind: traditionalist authoritarianism, classical liberalism, and nineteenth-century socialism (1968, 78-83).

In the seven decades since Rowntree's research in Belgium, the phenomenon of cultural segmentation on ideological lines, or *verzuiling*, has persisted and in some respects has become even more institutionalized. It has also become more formalized in that many of the privately organized activities of the early twentieth century have become incorporated—still in segmented form—into the structures of a modern welfare state, a notable example being the coverage of compulsory health insurance through ideologically oriented health insurance societies or *mutualités*. Segmentation has also extended to seemingly improbable areas, such as the organization of medical and scientific research, to the puzzlement of some non-Belgian observers (Fox, 1965). Its extension in the Congo after 1954 has been identified as one of the factors that destabilized the colonial regime (Young, 1965, 141-45). It has remained, pervasive but subtle, in the social, professional, and even the commercial life of Brussels, where the Catholic aristocracy developed its Quartier Léopold at some distance from the Liberal bourgeoisie of the Avenue Louise and its extensions (Mols, 1961, 17-19). One of the more curious examples of *verzuiling* was a bank owned by a socialist cooperative society, founded "to beat capitalism on its own terrain," which went bankrupt in 1934 (Claeys, 1973, 96).

The system of *verzuiling* also produces a cumulation of influences and affiliations. Thus at the extreme one can find a constituency federation of the Socialist party that requires of its parliamentary candidates that they belong to the party itself for at least five years, to a socialist trade union, a socialist *mutualité*, and a socialist cooperative (with a specified minimum volume of purchases per year), that they read two socialist newspapers, that their wives belong to the party and to its women's organization, that their children be enrolled in the party youth organization and in state schools, and that they reside in the *arrondissement* (Hill, 1974, 55-56; cf. Seiler, 1975, 370-71). This cumulation of memberships in the same ideological bloc has a double reinforcement effect. It fortifies the belief system of the middle-level elites and tends towards an interlocking network among executive members of the party and its supporting associations even where formal affiliations are lacking.

There is no need to describe the specific structures of segmented pluralism in detail here. They have been described elsewhere by several authors, both for the period before the Second World War (Höjer, 1946, chap. 2; Lijphart, 1981, 127-29) and more extensively for the postwar period (Meynaud et al., 1965, Part I, chap. 1; Lorwin, 1966; 1971; 1974; Van den Brande, 1967; Debuyst, 1967, 10-17; De Clercq, 1968; Huyse, 1970; CRISP, 1967, nos. 372-73). Analyses of each of the "three worlds" individually have appeared in several issues of the *Courrier hebdomadaire* of CRISP. Among the more important of these are an overview of the Catholic "world" (1967, nos. 352-54), followed by similar studies for the liberals (1971, nos. 522-24) and the socialists (1972, nos. 570, 572, 577, 582). The socialist subculture has also been analyzed by De Bakker and Claeys-Van Haegendoren (1973), who stress the structural ties arising from interlocking elites of the four major components (party, trade unions, cooperatives, and *mutualités*) and the resulting capacity for common action in times of crisis.

However, our concern here is less with the structure or the working of this system of segmented pluralism in general than with its implications for linguistic cleavage as the language question became more acute in the

1960s. In tracing these relationships it is more convenient analytically to consider political parties and other associations separately because the impact of intensified linguistic conflict has affected the party system in rather special ways, as the following pages will show. One may also observe here that traditional ideological *verzuiling* could hardly fail to serve as an illustration and model for Flemish nationalist aspirations for greater cultural and linguistic autonomy from the 1920s onward.

To consider first the case of associations and interest groups, one may say that ideologically segmented organization is in some sense the norm or model. As one outside student of the Belgian labor movement has re-marked: "In a fragmented political culture interest groups, especially those which are also large mass organizations, exist largely *within* a culture; seldom do they exist *across* cultural boundaries" (Barnes, 1964, 376). The rationale for this system in the trade union sector is that it permits the Catholic and socialist unions, which are divided on all major political questions, to participate fully in their respective political subcultures and yet to cooperate, especially at the higher levels, in questions of industrial relations. As already indicated, ideological segmentation in labor organi-zation has produced two major federations of Catholic and socialist unions, a third but smaller organization oriented towards liberalism, plus a few smaller unions independent of the three *zuilen* (above, 69-70).

Perhaps the most comprehensive data on segmentation are those for the *mutualités*, because compulsory health and disability insurance has been gradually extended until it covers virtually the entire Belgian popula-tion, and mainly through private societies or federations that grew from individual societies into ideologically oriented federations between 1906 and 1920 (CRISP, 1964, no. 258: 2). The relative distribution between the different cultural segments is shown in Table 31, which reveals that in contrast with the two major *zuilen*, the liberal sector is numerically rather weak and somewhat overshadowed by societies that are formally "neu-tral" or independent of ideological orientation. This table covers only workers and employees, however, and in the smaller voluntary sector for the self-employed the Catholic societies account for more than 50 per cent of the membership (CRISP, 1967, nos. 352-54: 31-32). This pattern is also typical of other types of associations, where it is usual to find segmented associations in the Catholic and socialist sectors but not necessarily for the liberal *zuil*, which is organizationally weaker. One significant exception occurs for farmers' associations, the two largest of which are both Catholic-oriented because of the predominance of practising Catholics among the rural population (CRISP, 1963, no. 183; 1968, no. 422).

In some cases, however, important associations do not coincide neatly with *zuil* boundaries, and here it is often the linguistic or regional factor that explains the discrepancy. Thus the three major Flemish cultural foundations, the Willemsfonds (founded in 1851), the Davidsfonds

(founded in 1875), and the Vermeylenfonds (founded in 1945)—
organizations that played a major part in the evolution of the Flemish
Movement and the mobilization of the Flemish masses—remained within
the boundaries of the liberal, Catholic, and socialist subcultures respectively, but concerned themselves only with the Flemish component of each
(CRISP, 1966, no. 342). Two postwar cultural foundations, the Flemish De
Raet Stichting, which is active in adult education, and the Francophone
Fondation Charles Plisnier, are pluralist umbrella organizations in ideological terms but also linguistically homogeneous, as is the Institut Jules
Destrée, which concerns itself more narrowly with the cultural and scientific interests of Wallonie. In spite of apparently conflicting objectives,
relations between the De Raet and Plisnier foundations developed cor-
dially, and in 1959 they sponsored a joint colloquium to discuss Walloon
and Flemish views on cultural questions (CRISP, 1962, no. 146; Brazeau,
1966, 3: Annex V-H). In wider perspective, these organizations can be seen
as an extension of the *verzuild* model to the linguistic cleavage as it
became more salient and ideological cleavage diminished.

Table 31

**Belgium: Population covered by compulsory
health and disability insurance, by
ideological orientation of insurance
societies, 1963 and 1971 (percentages)**

Insurer	1963	1971
Total population covered (000s)	5,478	7,832
Catholic societies	43.6	44.4
Socialist societies	31.0	29.1
Liberal societies	5.5	6.1
Neutral societies	8.9	9.7
Professional associations	9.7	9.7
Direct enrolment	1.3	1.0
Total	100	100

Sources: CRISP, 1964, no. 258: 14; 1972, no. 577: 14.

In economic matters, the most important organizations have focused
on the language regions. The Conseil économique wallon (founded in
1945) and its Flemish counterpart, the Economische Raad voor Vlaanderen
(founded in 1952), were established as broad associations for promoting
the economic development of their respective regions, though they differ
in organization and activities. While trade unionism has been segmented
on ideological lines, the chief division among employers' associations has
been regional, with the Flemish organization—the Vlaams Economisch
Verbond or VEV, founded in 1926—playing a major part in the economic
development of Flanders, the social emancipation of the Flemish popula-

tion, and the Netherlandization of Flemish industry (CRISP, 1974, no. 637; 1983, nos. 1003-1004). Corresponding regional organizations for Wallonie and Brussels were established only in 1968 and 1971 as the country moved towards regionalization of economic policy and planning (CRISP, 1972, no. 571). Considerable documentation on these cultural and economic interest groups is assembled in the study of Jacques Brazeau (1966), and further details for the Flemish side appear in Rock and Schevenhels (1968, 40-59) and Van Haegendoren (1968). One may view this territorial decentralization in the organization and activities of interest groups as a partial surrogate for federalism in a highly centralized political system that provided too little scope for the articulation of regional or linguistic interests before the reforms of the 1960s.

Some interest groups have developed primarily or solely around a Flemish clientele. Among these one may cite organizations such as the Vlaamse Toeristenbond, founded in 1922, which has functioned mainly as an automobile club and travel service, but also as a general instrument for enlarging Flemish horizons in a cultural sense. Another example is België in de Wereld, an association founded in 1963 to promote the interests of Flemings living overseas and to stimulate Flemish cultural activities abroad, objectives which it felt were being inadequately served by French-oriented official institutions. Some observers have explained the proliferation of homogeneous Flemish organizations by suggesting that the Flemings are more gregarious and more "associationist" by temperament, and some have pointed to the greater population density of the Flemish countryside. But another possible reason may lie in the vast effort of social mobilization engendered by the Flemish Movement. Just as ideological interests could be strengthened through the combined action of associations within the same *zuil*, so linguistic and regional interests could be reinforced—and indeed have been reinforced—on the Flemish side by the integrated action of a strong network of associations oriented towards the Flemish cause. Additionally, the relative neglect of Flemish interests in the public sector undoubtedly served as a stimulus to extra efforts at the level of interest groups and associations.

In recent years Flemish associational tendencies have received additional institutional support as a result of a 1976 decree of the Flemish Cultural Council, which provided for the creation of umbrella organizations or "domes" (*koepels*), that is, conglomerates of associations of the same philosophical-ideological orientation. Five such organizations were formed, representing traditional Catholics, progressive Catholics, liberals, socialists, and neutral associations, and these meet regularly to do preliminary work on cultural policies. As one observer has noted, this formal structuring of associations represents "the permanent and total organization of *verzuiling*" on the Flemish side ("Flandre et les Flamands," 1980, 371).

With respect to the system of political parties, it has been customary in Belgian political life to draw distinctions between the three traditional parties and all others. The traditional parties represent the three great ideological families, Catholic, liberal, and socialist. All three have origins in the nineteenth century and have comprehensive support from the above-mentioned networks of affiliated associations of the same ideological tendency. The traditions are not entirely continuous. After 1945 the prewar Belgian Workers' Party was refounded as the Belgian Socialist Party and the prewar Catholic Party as the Christian Social Party, both of them developing a somewhat modified organizational base and the latter also acquiring a more socially oriented program. The Liberal Party was more thoroughly transformed in 1961, dropping its traditional anticlericalism and reappearing as the Party of Liberty and Progress, or PLP, a move that was followed by sharp electoral gains at the next election. Notwithstanding these changes, however, the elements of continuity in the three "traditional" parties are clearly predominant (Lorwin, 1974, 182-88). One interpretation suggests that these changes reflect a change in emphasis for all three of the traditional parties from the church-state issue to a greater interest in economic and social questions (Bartier, 1968, 104-105).

The other parties on the Belgian scene may be grouped roughly into four categories. First, there is the Communist Party, founded in 1921, which may be viewed either as a fourth ideological or *Weltanschauung* party or as a second party within the socialist *zuil*. Except for a few years after 1945, it has had neither the electoral support nor the associational base to compete with the Socialist party. Second, there are the regional parties, formed around the *question communautaire*, which will be examined more closely in the next section. In Flanders regionalist tendencies have been electorally significant since the first Front Party victories in 1919, but in the other regions they became so only in the 1960s. A third category consists of dissident lists and offshoots from the major parties, secessionist movements that in most cases disappear after one or two elections. Finally, there has been a variety of other shortlived tendencies and movements, both Flemish and Francophone, including a few antidemocratic movements of the extreme right that attained significant followings during the 1930s—as the transient electoral success of Rex in 1936 testifies. All groups of the antiparliamentary right, however, were thoroughly discredited by the events of the occupation, and their cause has remained electorally insignificant since 1945 (Géoris-Reitshof, 1962; Stengers, 1965; CRISP, 1962, nos. 140-42; 1974, nos. 642-43; 1975, nos. 675-76). Within this fourth miscellaneous group one may note two emerging pro-environment parties, Ecolo on the Francophone side and Agalev on the Flemish, both of which won seats in Parliament for the first time in the 1981 election and increased their combined strength in the lower house from four seats to nine in 1985.

Apart from their historical primacy and supportive associational networks, the traditional parties have been regarded as such because together they have always accounted for a high proportion of the popular vote in parliamentary elections. This can be seen in Table 32, which compares the percentages of the total valid votes obtained by the various parties and categories of parties at elections to the Chamber of Representatives or lower house. Because of interparty cartels in certain provinces, it is impossible to establish exact figures for the Liberals and Socialists at some elections, and this table has been simplified by the inclusion of votes for dissident lists within the broad *zuil* totals. These dissident lists never exceeded 1 per cent of the total popular vote except briefly in the Catholic party, where they fluctuated between 2 and 4 per cent between 1919 and 1929. Further, the residual category "all others" contains a few lists that could more properly be classified as regional or separatist parties, but without extensive research any reclassification would be rather arbitrary. For 1974 and 1977 the continuity of earlier elections was broken by various party splits and new alliances that cannot be fully represented in this table, and a further difficulty is that the electoral *arrondissement* of Brussels still includes both Brussels-Capital and Halle-Vilvoorde, so that in practice the "regional" parties for Flanders and Brussels overlap territorially in this constituency. Finally, linguistic splits in the traditional parties are ignored in Table 32.

As may be seen from this table, the combined vote for the three traditional or *zuil* parties fell below 90 per cent of the total only four times between the extension of the franchise to adult male suffrage in 1893 and the 1960s, and all four of these results could be considered anomalies, those of 1936 and 1939 because of the crisis of the regime and the challenge of the Fascist-oriented Rex, those of 1946 and 1949 because of the temporary strength of communism. Nor was Flemish nationalism by itself a serious threat in this period. Only with the appearance of a significant vote for regional parties in Brussels and Wallonie in the 1960s did it become clear that a more fundamental challenge to the traditional party system was emerging. The combined vote for regional parties climbed from 9 per cent of the total valid vote in 1965 to 15 per cent in 1968 and 22 per cent in 1971, bringing deep repercussions for the party system, which will be examined more closely in the next section. The 1981 election was marked by a steep decline in the Christian Social vote and a lowest-ever total for the traditional parties, but the gains from this erosion went partly to the Volksunie and partly to three newer, "nonregional" parties that campaigned on antistatist and ecological issues.

Table 32 does not give indications of variations in party strength in the three main regions, but some differences could be predicted on the basis of attitudinal differences already recorded, and these are illustrated in Table 33. For each region this table gives the highest and lowest vote, and the unweighted average, for the six parliamentary elections from 1946 to 1961, which are reasonably typical of the period before the regional

Table 32

Belgium: Lower house election results by parties, 1894-1985 (as percentages of total valid votes)

Year	Traditional parties[a]				Regional parties			Com-munists	All others
	Catholics/Chr. Soc.	Liberals/PLP	Socialists	Total traditional parties	Flanders[b]	Wallonie[c]	Brussels[d]		
1894	51.6	29*	17*	97.5					2.5
1896-98	50.7	22*	24*	96.5					3.5
1900	48.5	24.3	22.5	95.3					4.7
1902-1904	49.8	25.3	20.6	95.7					4.3
1906-1908	48.6	27*	21*	96.9					3.1
1912	51.0	25*	22*	98.1					1.8
1919	38.8	17.6	36.9	93.3	2.6				4.1
1921	41.3	18.1	35.3	94.7	3.0			0.1	2.2
1925	38.6	14.6	39.5	92.7	3.9			1.6	1.9
1929	38.5	16.6	36.4	91.5	6.3			1.9	0.3
1932	38.8	14.3	37.3	90.4	5.9			2.8	1.0
1936	28.8	12.4	32.5	73.7	7.1			6.1	13.1[e]
1939	32.7	17.4	30.5	80.6	8.3			5.4	5.8[e]
1946	42.6	10*	32*	84.7	—			12.7	2.6
1949	43.6	15.2	29.8	88.6	2.1			7.5	1.8
1950	47.7	12*	36*	95.3	—			4.7	0.0
1954	42.0	13*	38*	93.6	2.2			3.6	0.5
1958	46.5	12*	37*	95.4	2.0			1.9	0.7

Table 32—Continued

| | Traditional parties[a] | | | | Regional parties | | | | |
Year	Catholics/ Chr. Soc.	Liberals/ PLP	Socialists	Total traditional parties	Flanders[b]	Wallonie[c]	Brussels[d]	Com- munists	All others
1961	41.5	12.4	36.7	90.6	3.5			3.1	2.9
1965	34.4	21.6	28.3	84.3	6.7	1.0	1.3	4.6	2.0
1968	31.7	20.9	28.0	80.6	9.8	3.4	2.5	3.3	0.4
1971	30.1	16.4	27.3	73.8	11.1	6.7	4.5	3.1	0.8
1974	32.3	15.2	26.7	74.2	10.2	5.9	5.1	3.2	1.4
1977	35.9	15.6	27*	77*	9.8	3*	4.3	2.7	1.6
1978	36.3	16.3	25.4	78.1	8.4[f]	2.9	4.2	3.3	3.3
1981	26.5	21.5	25.1	73.0	10.9[f]	1.7	2.5	2.3	9.6
1985	29.3	20.9	28.3	78.5	9.3[f]	n.a.	1.2	1.2	9.8

* Partially estimated because of electoral cartels in some constituencies.
a Traditional party figures include respective dissident lists.
b Includes Frontists, VNV, Volksunie, and minor Flemish nationalist lists.
c Includes Rassemblement Wallon and its predecessors.
d Includes Front Démocratique des Francophones (FDF), but not votes for Flemish regional parties in the electoral *arrondissement* of Brussels, which are in column for Flanders.
e Includes 11.5 per cent for Rex in 1936 and 4.4 per cent in 1939.
f Includes 1.4 per cent in 1978 and 1985 and 1.1 per cent in 1981 for dissident nationalist lists of Vlaams Blok.

Sources: 1894-1912: Hill, 1974, 101; 1919-61: Meynaud et al., 1965, 83; De Smet et al., 1958, Annex, 10-11; 1965-77: CRISP, 1968, no. 402: 4; 1971, no. 544: 3-4; 1977, no. 763: 4-5; 1978: CRISP, 1979, no. 828: 9-10, 37; *Annuaire de statistiques régionales*, 1978, 202; 1981: CRISP, 1981, no. 944: 13-14; Fraeys, 1982; 1985: *Standaard*, October 15.

Table 33

Belgium: Variations in party strength by regions, selected years (as percentages of total valid votes)

Region and year	Traditional parties			Communists	Regional parties[a]	All others
	Christian Social	Liberals/ PLP	Socialists			
A Flanders						
1946-61						
– range	50.9-60.4	8*-13.3	24.3-30*	0.1-5.5	0-6.0	0.1-1.7
– average	55.1	11.0*	28.0*	2.4	2.8	0.7
1971	37.8	16.4	24.5	1.6	18.8	0.9
B Wallonie						
1946-61						
– range	27.0-35.1	10*-14.7	37.8-49*	4.5-21.4	—	0-4.5
– average	31.6	12.2*	44.2*	9.9	—	1.6
1971	20.2	17.3	35.0	5.9	21.2	0.4
C Brussels-Capital						
1946-61						
– range	24.6-34.7	13.4-24.9	29.4-45.1	2.7-17.4	0-1.6	0-8.1
– average	30.3	18.6	39.3	7.1	0.8	3.9
1971	20.1	16.2	20.6	2.8	40.1	0.2

* Partially estimated because of electoral cartels in some constituencies.

[a] In Flanders: Volksunie and minor Flemish nationalist lists; in Wallonie: primarily Rassemblement Wallon; in Brussels: includes both Front Démocratique des Francophones and Flemish regional lists.

Sources: 1946-61: calculated from data and estimations in Hill, 1974, 101-102; 1971: CRISP, 1977, no. 763: 7-12.

challenge, and compares these with results for the 1971 election, which marks the strongest overall support to date for regional parties. What stands out in the period before the regional challenge is the clear Christian Social majority in Flanders and an equally clear leftist majority in Wallonie, where the combined Socialist and Communist vote fluctuated between 50 and 59 per cent. The dramatic gains for the various regional parties by 1971 appeared to come mainly at the expense of the Christian Social party in Flanders, of the combined left in Wallonie, and of all parties in Brussels, where the Brussels-based Front Démocratique des Francophones (FDF) alone obtained 34 per cent of the vote to become the largest party by a considerable margin. The dimensions of the regional challenge stand out clearly: by 1971 one voter in five in Flanders and Wallonie, and two out of five in Brussels, had deserted the traditional *zuil* parties for regional parties. During the 1970s this wave of support for regional parties gradually receded from 22 per cent of the total vote in 1971 to less than 16 per cent in 1978 and 1981, but not without leaving a significant imprint on the major parties, as will be seen in the next section.

Until the 1890s, the number of seats won by each party bore little relation to its percentage of the popular vote, and single-party governments were the rule from 1846 to 1916. Change began when the adoption of adult male suffrage in 1893 was followed by proportional representation within each electoral *arrondissement* in 1899, and this representation became more exact in 1919 with the introduction of transfers of votes at the provincial level (Hill, 1974, 52-54; Gilissen, 1958). The system is still considered to have a slight bias in favor of the larger parties, however, and one study of the four elections from 1954 to 1965 found that the discrepancy between the popular vote and the percentage of seats won averaged 5 per cent for the lower house and 8 per cent in the Senate (Dewachter, 1967, 404-405; Moureau and Goossens, 1958, 388, 391).

Since the reform of the electoral system in 1919, homogeneous one-party government has become the exception rather than the rule, the only durable example being the one-party Christian Social ministries from 1950 to 1954. We must make a clear distinction, however, between the Belgian system and the Swiss model of all-party government, which assumes an executive representative of all significant political interests. The normal Belgian pattern is closer to the model of a minimum winning coalition, or more specifically, of a minimum winning coalition that can be formed from the three traditional parties. While tripartite—and even rarely quadripartite—governments are not unknown, they tend to be regarded as exceptional responses to abnormal situations. The more usual practice, especially after 1945, has been a coalition of two of the three traditional parties that shares an agreed legislative program and a clear but not necessarily large parliamentary majority, an arrangement that characteristically leaves the third traditional party in vigorous opposition and sharpens interparty conflict.[1] One must bear in mind here that for constitutional revision or for legislation to implement the regionalization plans of 1970, some governments have had to command a minimum two-thirds majority in each house and coalitions have had to be constructed accordingly.

For half a century after 1919 the only other parliamentary group to participate in a coalition was the Communist party, which was briefly represented in several shortlived tripartite or quadripartite ministries between 1944 and 1947. One authoritative study summarizes the conventional wisdom of the 1960s by listing seven "possible" types of government: three homogeneous regimes, three bipartite coalitions, and the tripartite formula (Meynaud et al., 1965, 66-67). Even as late as 1969 the constitutional scholar Pierre Wigny could remark that "three so-called national or traditional parties have long been responsible for political life" and exclude other parties from consideration (1969, 58).

Closer analysis of the five decades from 1918 to 1967 shows that the tripartite formula (Catholics–Liberals–Socialists) prevailed for ten of these years but nine were in the prewar period. Virtually all the rest of this period before 1940 saw Catholic-Liberal, or bourgeois-oriented, coalitions. In the post-1945 period the pattern became more varied, and in addition to the homogeneous Catholic ministries of 1950-54 each of the possible bipartite combinations accounted for five years or more (Claeys, 1973, 99; and cf. Van Impe, 1968, 258-59; Perin, 1960, 251-52). The next decade, from 1967 to 1977, saw all the usual combinations except the Socialist-Liberal formula, as well as new departures that will be discussed in the next section. There are also some survey data to indicate that the public is divided in its ministerial preferences. A national survey at the time of the Catholic-Liberal ministerial shuffle in September 1960 found that 29 per cent favored a tripartite government but 48 per cent opposed one at that point (INSOC, 1960, no. 2: 23-24). A 1964 survey, based on a limited sample of respondents, found that 36 per cent expressed a general preference for the tripartite formula, 33 per cent preferred various two-party coalitions, and 12 per cent opted for homogeneous ministries of one party or another (Huyse, 1969, 122, 186).

In a wider sense, general acceptance of coalition ministries and of consensual decision-making can be seen as an important element of Belgian political culture. Val Lorwin suggests (1966, 177) that politicians learn accommodative behavior early as a result of various coalition formulas in municipal politics, a frequent route to the national Parliament. Debuyst's study of the members of the 1961 Parliament showed that some

---

[1] There is a problem of terminology here. As a result of linguistic splits in all three traditional parties, which will be described in the next section, the bipartite and tripartite formulas should now be viewed as four-party and six-party combinations respectively. So far (to 1985) no traditional party has entered or left a coalition without its ideological counterpart in the other language group.

72 per cent had had experience in communal politics and that 86 per cent of this latter group were holding communal and national mandates concurrently (1967, 129-30). This acceptance of consensual practices is not confined to elites. A recent opinion survey indicates that while the public is sharply divided over the future status of Brussels, as indicated in Table 29, item 15 (above, 119), there was substantial consensus in all regions that a solution should be worked out conjointly by Brusselers, Walloons, and Flemings (CRISP, 1981, nos. 927-28: 9-10).

Considered in broad perspective, the pattern of Belgian politics since 1945 can be seen as a succession of major issues or conflicts that have placed severe strains on the political system, and in most instances on one or more of the fundamental cleavages of religion, class, or language. Each of these crises requires for its resolution a particular arrangement of the forces and interests active on the political scene, and this in turn has involved in most cases a specially tailored coalition of these forces in a new ministry formed to tackle a selected set of immediate problems. The formation of such a ministry having the requisite balance of interests can be one of the most complex and delicate processes in the entire Belgian political system and may require weeks or even months of negotiation. If a ministry proves unable to meet its objectives, or if unforeseen developments emerge to upset its internal balance, the government will fall. Success is measured by the ability of a ministry to regulate a conflict at least to the extent of relegating it to a lower position on the political agenda. When a major conflict is successfully regulated, whether by interparty pact or otherwise, the way is cleared for priority to pass to other issues, which may in turn revolve around other cleavages and require a different constellation of forces for their solution. A notable example of this was the signing of the *Pacte scolaire* of 1958, which removed the most important religious issue from the top of the political agenda and thus opened the way for increased attention to the class division (retrenchment program and general strike of 1960-61) and the linguistic/regional division (debates and demonstrations leading to the language laws of 1962 and 1963). While outside observers have tended to see this pattern of conflicts as a simple succession of one salient cleavage after another across the political stage, more sensitive models of conflict analysis developed by Belgian scholars tend to present the changing salience of conflicts as a continuous dialectic in which the three basic cleavages are always present—though in varying intensity—in the political process (CRISP, 1967, nos. 372-73; 1970, no. 500; 1981, no. 916: 26; Van den Brande, 1967). Others have attempted to measure empirically the relative salience of issues as seen by parliamentarians. One 1975 survey found that the linguistic/regional division was perceived as being clearly predominant at that date but that it was expected to decline in importance within five years (Dierickx and Frognier, 1980, 169).

The contrast between this Belgian system of conflict resolution by a succession of changing coalitions and the more stable Swiss system of all-party government is instructive. What can explain this difference? The Swiss system is no doubt unusual in the resiliency and durability of its executive, and it also benefits from a strong consensus on political values among the citizens. But one crucial difference seems to be that in Switzerland many potentially conflictual issues are decentralized to the cantons and to the electorate, while the Belgian system has been so highly centralized as to impose an enormous load upon the central government. Because of centralization, more is at stake in the parliamentary arena. Because the stakes are higher, the political game is played more intensely and with less generosity. Further, the Belgian system and especially the party system were built primarily around religious and class divisions. They were less well adapted and structured to cope with linguistic and regional strains. When these strains built up to unprecedented levels in the 1960s, they created a total load too heavy for the existing system to sustain. This overload led to changes in the party system that will be discussed in the next section, as well as to fundamental constitutional and institutional reforms that will be outlined in Chapter 4.

D   Linguistic Conflict and the Party System

The impact of a heightened emphasis on linguistic and regional issues can be traced in three principal areas: first, the emergence of one significant regional party out of smaller marginal groups in each of the Belgian regions; second, the impact of these successful regional parties on the organization and activities of the traditional parties; and finally, the functioning of the party system as a whole under the more complex conditions of the 1970s. As may be seen from Table 32, electoral support for regional parties rose from less than 4 per cent of total valid votes in 1961, when only Flanders was involved, to 9 per cent in 1965, 15 per cent in 1968, and 22 per cent in 1971, falling back somewhat after that date. As Table 33 indicates, by 1971 the regional parties were, respectively, the largest party by far in Brussels, the second largest in Wallonie, and in third place in Flanders. In terms of parliamentary representation, Table 34 shows the increase in seats in the lower house from 1954 onwards in absolute and percentage terms, the total number of seats in the Chamber being 212 throughout this period. By 1971 regional parties also held 38 out of 178 seats in the Senate, or 21 per cent in each house. Such a tidal wave was bound to have repercussions on the traditional parties and on the party system as a whole, but before tracing this impact one should note that these new parties differ considerably among themselves in background and style.

Table 34

Belgium: Seats held by regional parties, Chamber of Representatives, 1954-85

Year	Volksunie[a]	Rassemblement Wallon[a]	FDF	Total regional parties	Percentage of total seats
1954	1	—	—	1	0.5
1958	1	—	—	1	0.5
1961	5	—	—	5	2.4
1965	12	2	3	17	8.0
1968	20	7	5	32	15.1
1971	21	14	10	45	21.2
1974	22	13	10	45	21.2
1977	20	5	10	35	16.5
1978	15[b]	4	11	30	14.2
1981	21[b]	2	6	29	13.7
1985	17[b]	0	3	20	9.4

[a] Including predecessor parties.
[b] Total includes one seat for Vlaams Blok.

Sources: 1954-65: Vidick, 1967, 361; 1968-78: CRISP, 1979, no. 828: 17; 1981: CRISP, 1982, no. 955: 3; 1985: *Standaard*, October 15.

The Volksunie, founded in 1954 out of a union of smaller Flemish groups, is a direct intellectual heir to the Flemish nationalist parties of the interwar period. As the original name (Christelijke Vlaamse Volksunie) suggests, it grew out of the Flemish Catholic right, and some of its early leaders were linked with the VNV and with those imprisoned after 1945 for collaboration during the occupation. Up to the early 1960s it was usually viewed as an extremist party, but at this point it severed formal connections with more militant Flemish organizations, largely over the issue of legality and extraparliamentary tactics, and gradually developed a more moderate image as its electoral support expanded and new leadership emerged. In its program, the Volksunie has embraced all the main tenets of Flemish nationalism: fixation of the linguistic frontier, territorial limitation and special status for Brussels, bipartite federalism, industrialization of Flanders, and amnesty for wartime offenders. Beyond these "community" concerns, however, it has gone on to develop a centre-left economic and social program in order to reinforce its existing strength among farmers, independent workers, and young people. Ideologically, it has become something of a catch-all party, rejecting the notion of class conflict, avoiding any special stance on religious issues, and surrounding its antidemocratic nationalist wing with a majority that leans to pluralist democracy (CRISP, 1962, nos. 148, 169; 1964, no. 230; 1966, nos. 336, 345; 1973, nos. 604, 606; Van der Elst, 1968).

Regional parties in Wallonie have shown less stability and continuity, and their antecedents have been less visible in electoral terms. The first electoral breakthrough came in 1965, when two small Walloon parties each won a seat in the lower house. In 1968, in the midst of the University of Louvain crisis, the new Rassemblement Wallon (founded in 1967), downplaying its socialist antecedents and appealing to the Walloons as a threatened community, made a dramatic gain by winning seven seats and 11 per cent of the regional vote. The immediate antecedents of Walloon regionalism may be traced to Walloon socialist disillusionment after the failure of the 1961 general strike, to the deteriorating economic structures of Wallonie, and to fears of declining political influence in the face of a declining regional population. Unlike its Flemish counterpart, the Rassemblement Wallon faced no linguistic issue in Wallonie itself. Its main concern was "reconversion" of the regional economy to stem the decline in resources and population, and the necessary means to this economic goal was seen as a federal form of government in which the interests of Wallonie could be safeguarded. Unlike the Flemish federalists, Walloon regionalists have favored a tripartite federalism in which Brussels Francophones would become a valuable ally against the numerical preponderance of Flanders, and in fact the Rassemblement Wallon has functioned in close alliance with the Brussels regional party, the Front Démocratique des Francophones (FDF), both at elections and in Parliament (CRISP, 1967, no. 367; 1971, nos. 516-17; Hasquin, 1975-76, 2: 343-62).

Both the Volksunie and to a lesser degree the Rassemblement Wallon have profited from the activities of networks of linguistic/cultural and regional organizations directed towards objectives similar to their own. Two mass movements, the Vlaamse Volksbeweging, or VVB (founded in 1954), and the Mouvement Populaire Wallon, or MPW (founded in 1961), were developed as pressure groups to sensitize the electorate to regional issues (CRISP, 1961, no. 130; 1965, no. 275; 1966, no. 319; Renard, 1961). In longer perspective there is a background of more specifically cultural organizations dating back in Wallonie to the period before 1914, and in Flanders to the nineteenth century. Although the Volksunie appears to be more thoroughly surrounded by a supporting network of social and professional organizations sharing the same Flemish nationalist goals (CRISP, 1966, no. 345; 1973, no. 604), both of these regional parties can be seen as the political expression of tendencies and movements that have been incubating in the respective language regions for some time.

By contrast, the appearance of a regional party in Brussels may be seen as a more spontaneous reaction against the linguistic laws of 1962 and 1963, a protest against the language policies of all three traditional parties. The Front Démocratique des Francophones, founded in 1964 to contest the 1965 elections, was immediately successful in capturing 11 per cent of the vote in Brussels-Capital in 1965, 19 per cent in 1968, and 33 per cent in

1971. At the start it favored no specific socioeconomic option but was careful to balance ideological tendencies on its executive. Its 1965 program focused sharply on the defence of Francophone rights in the capital and its suburban communes, calling for the repeal of the language laws of 1962-63, linguistic freedom in education, territorial expansion of the Brussels-Capital *arrondissement*, emphasis on the European vocation of Brussels, and—interestingly—an electoral reform to compel parties to present only unilingual lists of candidates in Brussels, rather than mixed lists, so that Francophone voters might choose exclusively Francophone representatives. Beyond this, the FDF in Parliament has pursued a policy of solidarity between Wallonie and Brussels, resistance to Flemish hegemony, and opposition to any form of Flemish-Walloon accord at the expense of Brussels. In organizational terms, it has remained carefully structured to preserve the delicate ideological pluralism on which it was founded (CRISP, 1965, no. 299; 1971, nos. 516-17; Lefèvre, 1980).

The trend to regional parties appeared even in the tiny German-speaking region with the formation in 1972 of a Partei der Deutsch-sprächigen Belgiër (PDB), an offshoot of a Christian Social dissident list at the 1971 election, which was committed to obtaining greater autonomy for the German areas. Although it could hardly aspire to immediate parliamentary representation given the miniscule population of the region, it captured 24 per cent of the total valid vote in the region in 1974 and remained at that level over the next three elections. With the appearance of the PDB, the trend set in motion at the 1965 election—the first after the passage of the new language laws—had run its full course: every region had developed a significant party specifically to promote regional interests. Among other consequences, these parties and their allied associations left their mark on the style and tone of Belgian political debate. An observer once remarked that the language of socialism is largely borrowed from the world of the military; in Belgium the same comment could be applied with equal justice to the verbal battles waged over the *question communautaire*, where Flemish objectives and tactics are regularly compared to the horrors of the German occupation and Flemish partisans reply in kind.

The unexpected success of the regional parties in the 1960s and 1970s has evoked various attempts to explain their electoral support. Thus Inglehart finds supporters of the Volksunie and the Rassemblement Wallon to be disproportionately representative of post-bourgeois values (1971, 1011-12), while Mughan looks for their voting strength in electoral districts having high industrialization or tertiary development (1979, 32-34). Similarly, Nielsen (1980) finds support for the Volksunie linked with the tertiary sector, commerce, and higher income areas. Other studies portray the FDF electorate as post-industrial (Van Malderghem, 1981) or as defenders of traditional individual liberties against an interfering bureaucratic state

(Deschouwer, 1982). The problem with these and other similar studies is that the available data are seldom conclusive.

A more practical approach is that of Delruelle and colleagues, who constructed an extensive social and behavioral profile of voters for each of the three traditional and three regional parties after the general election of 1968 (Delruelle et al., 1970). A more recent but less utilized source for the same purpose is the AGLOP survey of March-April 1975, the data from which permit a direct comparison between supporters of traditional parties and supporters of regional parties, either as two simple blocs or on an individual party-by-party basis. From computer runs based on this source we can say that in 1975 regional party supporters were significantly over-represented among voters under forty, among the middle and upper class, and in the top half of the income distribution. They were more likely to own a car. They were dramatically underrepresented among respondents who had primary education or less. Among the attitudinal variables, Volksunie and FDF supporters were more likely to put their regional identity ahead of any economic or religious characteristic, to place their language community or region ahead of any other geographic identification, and to rank intercommunity and interregional conflicts at or near the top of the scale of some twenty-two cleavages in Belgian society. On sympathy scales, supporters of all three regional parties show more extreme differentials in their sympathies for Flemings, Walloons, and Brusselers than do supporters of traditional parties (AGLOP, 1975). On some of these characteristics the Rassemblement Wallon stands out less sharply than the other two regional parties, but it must be remembered that at the date of the survey the Rassemblement was facing serious internal difficulties and an uncertain future.

Perhaps the greatest significance of the regional parties lies in the impact that they have had upon the traditional or *zuil* parties. The immediate background for this impact was the heightened linguistic tensions of the early 1960s surrounding the debates on the new language legislation, and the simultaneous waning of confessional issues, which had hitherto promoted traditional-party unity, as a result of the *Pacte scolaire* of 1958. This shift in priorities resulted in sharp losses of seats for both partners in the governing Catholic-Socialist coalition in 1965. While the reorganized and broadened Liberal party, the Party of Liberty and Progress (PLP), made substantial gains in this election as an opposition party, all three traditional parties came under increasing pressure to pay more attention to the regional issue. The impact of these centrifugal tendencies may be seen in party organization, in electoral campaigns, and in party behavior in coalition ministries, but there are variations in the timing and degree of this impact from one party to another.

In terms of party organization and activities, all parties have experienced the emergence of distinct Flemish and Francophone ''wings.''

This tendency appeared first in the Christian Social party, in which formally autonomous "wings" were created in 1965, followed by a divergence or "distancing" of the wings after the Louvain crisis of 1968. This led in turn to the creation of separate structures, separate programs, separate congresses, and separate "national presidents" for the two sections. In spite of all this, however, the party managed to preserve in the 1970s a coordinating committee between the wings, a common headquarters, and a common research organization (CRISP, 1970, no. 484; 1972, no. 565).

For the Socialist party, the tendency towards separate wings emerged first on a *de facto* basis when divergences at the 1966 party congress over conflicting objectives in the debate on constitutional reform were followed by separate congresses of Flemish and Walloon socialists in 1967 to discuss these issues further. In 1971, after Walloon objections to the election of a Fleming as president, the party established Walloon and Flemish copresidents (CRISP, 1966, no. 308; 1967, no. 387; 1968, no. 391; 1972, no. 570). In this form the Belgian Socialist Party continued for several years as the most unified of the traditional parties, until a widening gulf between the two leaders in 1978 led to acrimonious discussions of different "forms of socialism" based on Mediterranean and Scandinavian models. Since this date, Francophone and Flemish socialists have functioned as separate parliamentary parties, with separate party congresses, separate executives, and even a divided research institute. Finally, both parties emphasized the break by dropping the appellation "Belgian" from their names, the Parti socialiste (PS) in 1978, the Socialistische Partij (SP) in 1980 (Ceuleers, 1980). They have, however, established one joint committee: to prepare for the centennial in 1985 of a once-united socialist party, the Parti ouvrier belge.

The PLP was the last of the three traditional parties to come under centrifugal pressures. This might be explained by its striking electoral success in 1965, its relatively moderate position on the *question communautaire*, and its minority position in all three regions, which made it a smaller target for losses to regional parties. Nevertheless, increased polarization of positions concerning the future of Brussels following the 1968 elections put severe strains on party unity, and in 1971 the Flemish district and provincial federations decided to constitute a partially autonomous Flemish wing within the general framework of the party. In 1972 the Flemish wing became fully autonomous, but the next three general elections saw the Brussels Liberals maintaining their own separate organization and in 1974 even joining in an electoral cartel with the FDF. In 1979 Francophone Liberals of Brussels and Wallonie were reunited to form a "community" party, the Parti réformateur libéral or PRL (CRISP, 1969, nos. 434-35; 1971, nos. 522-24; 1979, no. 864).

As might be expected, the most severe organizational tensions arose in the electoral *arrondissement* of Brussels, which still corresponds to the post-1963 administrative *arrondissements* of Brussels-Capital and Halle-Vilvoorde combined, and thus still includes electoral subdivisions and local party associations from both Flanders and Brussels-Capital. In the Socialist party, most Flemish members withdrew from the bilingual Brussels federation in 1968 and formed their own separate federation of Flemish local sections. For the Christian Social party, whose supporters of both languages are more interspersed geographically, local associations could be either linguistically mixed or duplicated in the same commune. In 1968 the split in the national party led to the formal creation of separate Flemish and Francophone federations in Brussels, but under the influence of Prime Minister Vanden Boeynants these were still able to present a joint bilingual list at the 1968 elections. For the Liberal *zuil*, the PLP presented a bilingual list in Brussels at the 1968 election, but soon afterwards growing tensions between radical Francophones and moderates in the regional federation led to the creation of an unofficial Flemish federation alongside the official bilingual one (CRISP, 1970, nos. 473, 484). Thus for all three major parties the situational pressures led to some form of organizational schism in the Brussels electoral *arrondissement*, despite efforts of moderates to preserve structural unity.

A second manifestation of regionalism in the older parties may be seen in national and communal elections, especially in the preparation of party lists of candidates. Under more decentralized organization, the different wings were able to develop their own electoral programs, and even to present their respective lists under different numbers on the ballot, as the Christian Social party did in 1968. The wings came in direct contact only in Brussels, where practices have differed between parties and from one election to another. Thus in Brussels *arrondissement* the Flemish socialists ran their own "Red Lions" list in 1968, 1971, and 1974, winning roughly 10 to 11 per cent of the local Socialist vote. The Christian Social vote was divided between a bilingual cartel representing both wings and a dissident Francophone list in 1968, as was the Liberal or PLP vote in 1971. The Belgian system of proportional representation allows this proliferation of party lists without serious electoral disadvantage, and by 1974 the trend was for each wing of the traditional parties to present a separate list in Brussels *arrondissement*.

One major consequence of this trend towards separate lists for each wing appears to be the demise of bilingual lists based on linguistic alternation of candidates on the ballot or on some other formula prearranged by the party elites. Thus in 1977 the linguistic wings of the three traditional parties presented six separate lists in Brussels (CRISP, 1977, nos. 761-62), and the declared goal of the Front Démocratique des Francophones of unilingual electoral lists and strict proportional representation by language seems to have been attained for the traditional parties through the working of the political process. At the 1978 national election all major lists except that of the Communists were linguistically homogeneous. For the 1979 and 1984 elections to the European Parliament, which were organized by a special statute, Belgian voters were divided into two separate electoral colleges and could vote only for Flemish lists in Flanders and only for Francophone lists in Wallonie, while those in Brussels had the choice of both.

A third result of stronger regional parties has been increasing difficulty in forming and maintaining stable ministerial coalitions. With the three traditional parties all following to a greater or lesser degree a general trend towards autonomy of their linguistic wings and a "distancing" of these wings in terms of activities and program, it was natural for each wing to develop separate program objectives as conditions for joining a ministry. This has given the parliamentary arena some of the characteristics of a more extreme multiparty system and has increased the difficulty of forming and maintaining a government. Thus in 1968, when the Vanden Boeynants government fell over the Louvain issue, there was a 132-day hiatus before a new coalition could be formed. The period from 1971 to 1974 was one of considerable ministerial instability, with four different coalition formulas being tried in rapid succession (CRISP, 1974, no. 648). The formation of a ministry following the 1977 elections was delayed briefly by a last-minute rebellion of Walloon Christian Social ministers protesting the posts allocated to them by a Flemish Christian Social premier. The year 1980 alone saw no fewer than four distinct ministries, involving three different coalition formulas, though all were headed by the same prime minister. These examples and others suggest that the political system has become significantly less integrated under the impact of regional strains and splits in the traditional parties. On the other hand, it needs to be emphasized again that the six subdivided "traditional" parties have so far (1985) continued to negotiate and enter ministerial coalitions only in pairs, and in this respect the traditional ideological bases are still significant.

It might also be noted that major associations came under regionalist and linguistic pressures akin to those experienced by the political parties. One of the most publicized examples is that of the socialist trade union federation, the FGTB, which split almost exactly along linguistic lines over the general strike in 1960 and afterwards underwent severe strains when disillusioned Walloon leaders drifted away to form the Mouvement Populaire Wallon. After two years of negotiation and reconstruction, this split was partially healed by a special agreement that established linguistic parity on the central executive structure and special voting procedures requiring motions in the national committee to obtain either a two-thirds majority or majorities from both linguistic groups. By 1963 each wing had an effective veto over FGTB policies, and in 1967 it was further decided that the economic policies of the federation as a whole should be a synthesis of positions prepared by each linguistic community (Meynaud et

al., 1965, 101-108; Verdoodt, 1977, 32-33). After 1968 broad policy questions were increasingly handled by separate regional groupings for Flanders and Wallonie, and in 1978 the FGTB statutes were formally amended
to recognize and establish alongside the national secretariat three regional
bodies for Flanders, Wallonie, and Brussels to handle those economic
problems that were being shifted to the regional level by the ongoing
reform of political institutions. The Catholic federation, the Confédération
des syndicats chrétiens (CSC), whose statutes already guaranteed to Francophones two out of five seats on its executive committee (*Bureau jour-
nalier*) and seven out of twenty-four seats on its *bureau* or board, responded to similar pressures by establishing three regional committees
with powers of decision in matters of regional competence (Kendall, 1975,
231-32; CRISP, 1980, no. 866). These developments can be seen as responses to the increasing thrust of Walloon locals in both federations for
greater decisional autonomy and to the growing agenda of questions being
channelled to the emerging institutions of regional government.

Beyond the rise of the regional parties and the tensions in the traditional or *zuil* parties that were first reflected in the election of 1965, one
further development deserves attention. In the instability and confusion of
the early 1970s, the distinctions between traditional and nontraditional
parties began to fade. The three regional parties, at first treated as transient
movements of protest on the political scene, began to be accepted as more
permanent and to play a more complete role in the parliamentary process.
In the end they acquired what Val Lorwin has somewhat jocularly called
Allgemeinkoalitionsfähigkeit (1966, 178), that is, the capability, credibility,
and legitimacy to be considered as possible partners in the formation of a
government. We need not trace in detail the rather complex circumstances
that led to this level of acceptance. It is sufficient to record that the
Rassemblement Wallon joined the minority Catholic-Liberal coalition in
June 1974, and in so doing it parted company with its electoral ally, the
FDF, whose conditions for participation were unacceptable. The other two
regional parties, the FDF and the Volksunie, participated in interparty
negotiations following the 1977 election and both entered a four-party
coalition ministry with the Catholics and Socialists in June 1977 (CRISP,
1977, no. 754; 1978, no. 786; Lefèvre, 1977; Ceuleers, 1978; Mabille,
1978). These arrangements opened up a whole new range of coalition
possibilities, and they also reflect the continuing high priority for institutional reform and other regional issues on the political agenda during the
later 1970s.

From the standpoint of the regional parties themselves, however, the
experience of office did not prove a happy one. The Rassemblement
Wallon in office was plagued by left-right dissensions, by intraparty in-
trigue, and finally by the departure of a large center-right group—a group
that included three of its four ministerial representatives—to join a restruc-

tured Walloon Liberal party. At the 1977 election its representation in the Chamber dropped precipitously from thirteen seats to five. The Volksunie, as a coalition partner after 1977, had to face a rising tide of Flemish resentment against the new interparty agreement on the *question communautaire*, the so-called Egmont Pact, and the subsequent formation of two new Flemish nationalist anti-Egmont parties, which ran a joint list of candidates in the 1978 election as the Vlaams Blok. At that election the sharp drop in Volksunie representation in the lower house—from twenty seats to fourteen—and the winning of a seat by the Vlaams Blok were a clear message that the Egmont agreement was unacceptable to Flemish nationalist voters. While the Volksunie elected to go into opposition at this point, the FDF continued on as the only regional party in the first Martens government, only to see its three ministers forced out as a result of deep disagreements over the regionalization issue in January 1980. It in turn fell from eleven seats to five in the Chamber of Representatives at the 1981 election (Lefèvre, 1977; Platel, 1980; CRISP, 1978, no. 786; 1980, nos. 874-75; 1981, no. 916).

The experience of the 1970s suggests very clearly that no regional party has escaped electorally unscathed from a period of participation in office. The general problem seems to be that in the Belgian system the sharing of power as a partner in a governing coalition pays off only if a party can achieve some visible portion of its program objectives by doing so. Regional parties have found this difficult because they are small and relatively weak, while their general objectives are large and difficult, demanding major reforms of the system. In effect, they have lacked the force to impose their will except with the assistance and cooperation of the larger parties. Further, they appear to be more open to desertion by the voters for failing to produce results, because they lack the long-term ideological loyalties that sustain the *zuil* parties. In the light of their less than successful ministerial experiments in the 1970s, the long-run role of these parties as possible coalition partners is not easy to predict.

From a longer historical perspective, the Belgian party system before the 1960s substantially cross-cut the linguistic and regional cleavages in Belgian society as well as the numerous specific issues that found expression in regional terms. In the six national elections from 1965 to 1978 one can trace the transformation of that system, first through the establishment of new parties that gave priority to regional and linguistic interests in each of the four regions (including the German-speaking area), then through the coexistence of these new parties alongside the traditional parties and the growing acceptance of them as legitimate participants in the political system. The three main regional parties, though radically different from one another in objectives and ideologies, rather paradoxically found much common ground in Parliament in promoting linguistic and regional issues against the concerns and priorities of the traditional parties, and in pressing the case for institutional reforms. Their challenge to the system reached its peak in the early 1970s and then slowly receded as the traditional parties fought back with superior resources. But the price to be paid for meeting this challenge was a high one, for it involved the splitting of all three traditional parties along ethno-regional lines to an extent undreamed of a decade earlier. In brief, the regional parties succeeded in changing not only the agenda of Belgian politics but also the structure of the other parties in the political arena.[1]

The period from 1965 to 1980 was also marked by political crises, instability of governments, and at times a seemingly hopeless immobilism in the face of multiple conflicting political forces. In retrospect, however, it was also a period of visible progress towards major constitutional reforms and—even more difficult—towards the institutional implementation of political compromises embodied in the constitutional revisions of 1970. The establishment of cultural councils for each language community in 1971 and the decade-long search for an acceptable formula for regionalization, culminating in new legislation for Flanders and Wallonie in August 1980, are a testimony to the distance already covered. In an essay written in May 1980, at the height of parliamentary controversy over regionalization, André Molitor captured admirably both the predisposition to conflict and the conflict-regulating capacity of the Belgian political system:

In sum, although Belgium is not a nest of civil wars, by temperament and by tradition we Belgians are inclined toward internal quarrels; however, we recoil before spilt blood, and we hate authoritarianism and police regimes. Furthermore, over a long period of time we have developed a remarkable aptitude for negotiation, which contributes to solutions which never satisfy everybody but which are generally accepted (Lijphart, 1981, 153)

The exclusion of the Brussels question from the 1980 laws is a reminder that the reform process at this point was far from complete. From a longer-term perspective, it is quite possible that the changes effected in the party system during the 1970s will be seen later on as only one phase of a larger and more prolonged transformation of the Belgian political system as a whole, a transformation that some see extending to 1990 or beyond ("Réforme de l'Etat," 1984). In the midst of ongoing institutional changes, it would be foolish to speculate on the permanence or impermanence of the current party structures. One can, however, examine the incomplete process of constitutional and institutional reform with a view to understanding the framework within which any future party system is likely to operate, and this will be done in Chapter 4.

---

[1] Even the Belgian Communist Party was split linguistically in February 1984. It lost all its seats in Parliament—two in the Chamber, one in the Senate—at the election of October 1985.

Chapter 4

The Constitutional and Institutional Framework

In sharp contrast with the Swiss case, the Belgian political system stands out for its comprehensive network of language legislation, which specifies many features of language usage, both in a functional and a territorial sense, down to the level of the most minute details. But language legislation as such is only one part of the story; even more important in the 1960s and 1970s was the protracted search for an acceptable restructuring of the Belgian constitution and the Belgian state itself to meet demands for greater cultural and regional autonomy that surfaced in the course of heightened intergroup conflict after 1960. Even after the legislation of 1980 on regionalization, that search remained unfinished. Since more definitive institutionalization may still require years of difficult negotiations, the institutional reforms achieved up to 1980 will be outlined here only in very general terms. Within this general framework of language legislation and constitutional change, the rest of this chapter will then examine specific linguistic arrangements in Belgian institutions; for despite the intrinsic interest of the constitutional reform process as an illustration of the Belgian political system, our primary concern in this chapter must be to clarify the relationship between language practices in institutions and intergroup hostility or accommodation.

A   The Language Legislation of the 1960s

The language practices of independent Belgium since 1830 have evolved gradually from freedom to constraint, from *laisser faire* to language planning. The main linguistic provision of the 1831 constitution, Article 23 (see above, 22), was essentially a declaration of linguistic liberty, and it worked to the advantage of a middle class that was almost exclusively Francophone. This linguistic regime may be seen as a direct reaction to the largely unsuccessful constraints attempted by William I in favor of Dutch in Flanders between 1823 and 1829, and these in turn may be seen as a

149

reaction to even harsher constraints in favor of French imposed under the French occupation between 1795 and 1814. The first language laws in independent Belgium in the later nineteenth century, which sought to establish equal rights for Flemish alongside of French, implied obligations of bilingualism for public officials in Flanders but did not otherwise interfere with a noninterventionist linguistic regime. Only with the political mobilization of the Flemish masses after 1900 and the abolition in 1919 of the plural franchise—which by favoring the educated and well-to-do also favored Francophones—did there emerge a sufficient political base for stronger measures.

Even at this point, however, constraint continued to be tempered by exceptions forged during intricate parliamentary negotiations. The principle of territoriality of languages in the administration, including Dutch unilingualism in Flanders, was first enunciated in legislation in 1921, but this law permitted provincial and communal administrations to opt for bilingualism, and it also allowed communes along the linguistic frontier the choice of administrative languages if the census showed a linguistic majority different from that of the region (Curtis, 1971, 312-13). The more rigorous legislation of 1932, which is identified by most commentators as the real watershed between the personality and the territoriality principles in Flanders, removed the element of choice by municipal councils in the selection of local language regimes and tied it to the language situation indicated by the census. This change, as already noted, had the side-effect of politicizing census responses and also led to charges of manipulation of census returns in certain communes along the linguistic frontier. Similarly, the education legislation of the same year contained rather imprecise provisions for minority-language education that left to the communes and school authorities considerable discretion in applying them (Rüling, 1939, 112, 114-15). After Flemish parliamentarians had reluctantly agreed to what they believed to be transitional or "transmutation" classes for Francophone children in Flanders, they were disillusioned to find that some jurisdictions continued to offer an entire primary and secondary curriculum in French on the strength of this concession. The third round of language laws of the 1960s was born of a mounting determination on the Flemish side that such exceptions must be stopped and loopholes closed, but the basic principles underlying the legislation of the 1960s were, in most essential respects, those forged in critical interparty negotiations between 1929 and 1932 and embodied in the five main language laws of 1930 (University of Gent), 1932 (administration, education), 1935 (judicial matters), and 1938 (armed forces).

The general thrust of all this language legislation since 1930 can be reduced to three major principles. First, Flanders and Wallonie are officially unilingual language regions, functioning in Dutch and French respectively, and with certain limitations the same rule applies to the much smaller German-speaking area in Liège province. Second, the general rule for the national public service is bilingualism of services but unilingualism of employees, a formula adopted at Walloon insistence as a protection against the superior competence of Flemings in the official languages. Third, Brussels is envisaged as a capital befitting an officially bilingual country, at once symbolizing and accommodating both principal language groups but not impinging on their distinctive cultural identities. Beneath these three principles one can discern a fourth assumption, founded on earlier legislation, of absolute equality of the two official languages. Here it should be noted that in linguistic matters the mainstream of the Flemish Movement has never asked for more than legal equality between French and Dutch, despite some recent tendencies on issues involving material resources to seek a distribution proportionate to population rather than simple parity. Taken together, these four principles aim at policy symmetry through language planning and legislation in a situation that is fundamentally asymmetrical in sociological and linguistic terms.

The legislative implementation of these principles in their most recent form is found primarily in four laws passed in 1962 and 1963. The first of these, the Gilson law of November 8, 1962, attempted to settle outstanding frictions concerning the French-Dutch linguistic frontier, making special arrangements for certain border communes independently of and prior to other language legislation. A second Gilson bill, which became the law of August 2, 1963, sought to regulate language usage in government departments, in Brussels, and in the suburbs around Brussels. A third law, that of July 30, 1963, adapted the education system to the new territorial arrangements and at the same time sought to tighten dramatically the provisions of the 1932 legislation on minority-language or "transmutation" classes and on the language of instruction in Brussels. A fourth measure, the law of August 9, 1963, modified judicial districts to match the new territorial arrangements and was scarcely contested in Parliament. Of the major linguistic measures of the 1930s, only the law of July 30, 1938, on language usage in the army remained without significant change.

As had been the case in 1932, the political context for the passage of these new language laws was a complex and lengthy negotiation among the political parties in Parliament, with an intense involvement of their respective regional groupings. Beyond this there were mass demonstrations at the extraparliamentary level, notably two massive marches on Brussels organized by the Flemish Action Committee in October 1961 and October 1962. A prolonged deadlock over Brussels was finally broken at a marathon all-night bargaining session of the coalition leadership, the celebrated "conclave" of Val Duchesse. Further, the tensions did not stop with the passage of the legislation, because its legal implementation required approximately fifty royal decrees of execution, which were gradually elaborated, though not always on schedule, over the next few years.

The earliest of these decrees concerned the exact demarcation of the linguistic frontier, the establishment of control agencies, and a coordinated version of the laws of November 8, 1962, and August 2, 1963. A further series of seventeen decrees published simultaneously in November 1966 provided detailed regulations for many aspects of language usage in the administrative and educational sectors (CRISP, 1967, nos. 347-48). Many of the detailed provisions of the new language legislation can be more appropriately described in the relevant institutional sections later in this chapter, but the territorial arrangements, which constitute a common basis for the administrative, judicial, and educational statutes, may be outlined briefly here.

The notion of a fixed linguistic frontier was not new in the postwar period, but it received influential support when it was recommended formally in 1958 by the Centre Harmel. The principle of the law of November 8, 1962, was simple: to modify provincial and communal boundaries so as to coincide as closely as possible with the existing language frontier and then to freeze these boundaries permanently through administrative unilingualism. Such a policy would remove the need to rely on doubtful census data and would put an end to recurrent Flemish grievances over "theft of territory" (gebiedsroof). Though passed as ordinary legislation only, it can be viewed as politically irreversible in the light of the Flemish majority in Parliament. This fixing of the linguistic frontier by law marks the one significant change of principle between the legislation of the 1930s and that of the 1960s: a transition from flexible territoriality to fixed territoriality. By this change the Belgian system came closer to the Swiss model, though in the Swiss case the principle is enshrined in custom and jurisprudence rather than in general legislation.

The realization of this principle involved the transfer of certain communes which differed in language from the rest of their arrondissement or province to another province and language region (or from Flemish Brabant to Francophone Brabant and vice versa). In the final version twenty-five communes were transferred from the Flemish region to Wallonie and twenty-four others from Wallonie to Flanders. In population figures, however, Wallonie gained an estimated 87,000 new inhabitants compared with 23,000 for Flanders, for a net gain to Wallonie of some 64,000 (Martens, 1970, 159; Hasquin, 1975-76, 2: 372-73). At an even more microscopic level, some twenty-two villages and slivers of territory were transferred from one commune to another for the same reason. Many of these hamlets had fewer than 100 inhabitants, and one tract transferred to Flanders was later revealed to have no residents at all (Herremans, 1965, 29). The frontier between the French-speaking and German-speaking areas was untouched by this law, as was the sensitive question of Brussels and its suburban periphery.

In spite of the extreme sensitivity of the issue, most of the areas selected for transfer caused little dissension in Parliament, but there were two significant exceptions at the extreme western and eastern limits of the frontier, comprising nine Francophone communes of West Flanders clustered around Comines and Mouscron in the west, and six communes in and around the Voer valley of Liège province (known in French as the Fourons) in the east along the border with the Netherlands. The Centre Harmel had been deadlocked over the issue of the Fourons, where the vernacular, as we have noted above, was a transitional dialect between Dutch and German, and where French was the predominant language of administration. The Gilson bill as first drafted left both areas in their original provinces, as apparent exceptions to the rule of linguistic homogeneity, no doubt partly because their transfer would create geographic enclaves. This proved unacceptable to the parliamentary committee that examined the bill, which amended it to give Mouscron-Comines to the province of Hainaut and the Voer to Limburg. Local opinion in Mouscron-Comines was divided on the transfer, but in the Fourons the communal councils protested, though at first ineffectually because the combined population of these six communes was just over 4,000. Between November 1961 and November 1962 the bill as a whole underwent a long and precarious passage through Parliament (Curtis, 1971, 503-52; CRISP, 1979, no. 859: 11-17; Meynaud et al., 1965, 108-13). Its path was marked by two Flemish marches on Brussels and Walloon counter-demonstrations in Liège, and matters were not eased when the Liège provincial authorities held a local referendum in the Fourons in October 1962 that produced a 93 per cent vote in favor of remaining in Liège (Herremans, 1965, 34-36). In the escalation of feelings and rhetoric the Fourons became, for an aroused Wallonie, a central symbol of Flemish imperialism triumphant over the wishes of the local population. Meanwhile, the much more populous Mouscron-Comines area, with a population of about 71,000, was transferred from West Flanders to Hainaut without serious protest in recognition of the principle of linguistic homogeneity.

The debate of 1961-62 on the language frontier represents a typical Belgian approach to the settlement of a complex problem. Basically, it led to an interparty package deal worked out in the parliamentary arena, a deal that took into account the various interests of the coalition partners but showed little concern for the local interests being used as counters in the bargaining. Against those who proposed a local referendum to ascertain popular wishes, Minister Gilson insisted on the prerogative of Parliament to determine provincial boundaries (Curtis, 1971, 534). This particular package, however, whatever its relative fairness from a global perspective, did not become a settlement. By voting persistently for special lists representing "Return to Liège" at subsequent communal and national elections, the local population of the Voer has kept the issue alive, like a wound that cannot heal, into the 1980s. Because the Voer question has links with the wider linguistic conflict in Belgium as a whole, it will be examined more closely in Chapter 5.

The remaining territorial arrangements were included in the much more complex law of August 2, 1963, which regulated the use of languages in the administration. Primarily, these involved the geographical delimitation of Brussels and the listing of communes that must offer specified minority-language facilities to local minorities speaking French or Dutch or German. Intrinsically, the Brussels question was even more explosive than that of the linguistic frontier, because it brought two opposing concepts of language policy into head-on conflict. The Flemish saw the spread of Francophone metropolitan Brussels into Flemish rural communes as a cultural and ecological disaster, an "oil stain" (olievlek) to be contained at all costs by legislative measures. Francophones saw urban expansion and its accompanying linguistic transfer as natural sociological processes that must be allowed to continue and not strangled by an "iron collar" (carcan) of legislation. These fundamentally different perceptions of the situation, buttressed by colorful imagery and copious rhetoric, made the search for a compromise especially difficult.

Like its predecessor, the second Gilson bill had a difficult passage through Parliament, undergoing several basic modifications and bringing the government to the point of resignation. A proposal to annex six new communes to the existing nineteen communes of the metropolitan area provoked a strong Flemish reaction. An alternative plan to extend minority-language facilities to some twelve or fourteen suburban communes, including three just south of the language frontier in Wallonie, met insurmountable resistance from Walloon leaders, who remained largely indifferent to the fate of Brussels. An acceptable compromise was found only in the context of wider bargaining at the special "conclave" of Val Duchesse, after the government's resignation had been refused by the King (Meynaud et al., 1965, 114-20; Herremans, 1965, 93-94; Ruys, 1973, 165-68).

The final text of the legislation gives little indication of the passions that accompanied its passage. Basically, the old administrative arrondissement of Brussels was divided in three parts. The nineteen communes of the Brussels agglomeration became the new administrative arrondissement of Brussels-Capital, which remained officially bilingual. Six communes of the immediate periphery with large Francophone populations became a small administrative district on their own, known as the "arrondissement of the law of 2-8-1963." By Article 7 of the law these six communes were given very detailed and slightly varied language regimes that essentially called for services to individuals in French or Dutch at their option, for educational facilities at preschool and elementary levels in French at the request of sixteen or more families, but for Dutch to be the only internal working language for administrative purposes. Finally, all the remainder of the old arrondissement of Brussels became a new arrondissement of Halle-Vilvoorde, which formally became part of the unilingual

Dutch-speaking region. The new district comprising the six peripheral communes was not assigned to any language region by this legislation, an arrangement that left the two sides free to nourish differing expectations about its future. As already noted in Chapter 3, the electoral *arrondissement* of Brussels, corresponding to the old, undivided administrative *arrondissement*, remained unchanged. On this basis the "Brussels problem" was resolved for the near term, but for the longer run the costs of these unresolved ambiguities were to prove substantially higher.

Apart from Brussels and its suburban periphery, the two laws of November 8, 1962, and August 2, 1963, recognized five further groups of communes for which special minority-language facilities were to be provided. These included: (1) twelve communes of the Netherlandic region along the French-Dutch language frontier (including the six contentious Voer communes); (2) thirteen communes of the French region along the same frontier (including the Mouscron-Comines area); (3) all of the twenty-five communes of the German-speaking region, which retained facilities for Francophone minorities; (4) the six Malmédy communes of the French-speaking region, which retained facilities for German-language minorities; and (5) nine communes of the Welkenraedt-Montzen area of Liège province, lying between the Voer and the German-speaking region, for which the law of 1963 simply promised later regulation by royal decree. There is a distinct tendency in the Belgian literature to regard the communes with minority facilities as exceptions to the general rules, and indeed they are not very significant in terms of population. At the 1961 census the 71 communes with facilities, including the Brussels suburbs but excluding Brussels-Capital itself, accounted for just 2.7 per cent of Belgium's 2,663 then existing communes and also for 2.7 per cent of the total population.

Since the 1932 language legislation had been deemed unsatisfactory because of its failure to secure compliance from recalcitrant communes and other agencies, the legislation of 1963 paid special attention to enforcement mechanisms. Article 50 of the 1963 text gave the central government itself the power to discipline employees of communes, provinces, and other agencies for infractions if these bodies failed to do so. Article 51 provided procedures for the nullification of administrative acts and regulations not in conformity with the law. Articles 53 to 55 provided for a Commission permanente de contrôle linguistique (CPCL) of eleven members (five Flemings, five Francophones, one German speaker) with broad powers of surveillance, inquiry, and the right to be consulted by the government on all matters of general application of the law. Among other responsibilities the CPCL was called upon to oversee language tests for public servants, to institute nullity proceedings for nonconforming acts of the administration, to protect the linguistic minorities in communes with special linguistic facilities, and to report in detail on its activities each year to the government and to Parliament. If the CPCL failed to take certain actions within prescribed periods, the matter was to revert to the minister of the interior (*Emploi des langues*, 1963, 50-59).

For special problems there were special institutions. The formidable task of implementing the new laws in Brussels and the new suburban *arrondissement* was entrusted to an office specially created for the purpose, that of vice-governor of Brabant. More specifically, the incumbent of this new post was given a mandate to watch over all laws and regulations on language usage in the administrative and educational spheres in Brussels-Capital and in the six suburban communes with facilities, and to work more widely towards the harmonious development of the French and Netherlandic cultures in the capital. In addition, he was to coordinate the physical planning of Brussels and its development as a European and international metropolis (*Emploi des langues*, 1963, 8-11, 16-17). The 1962 legislation also provided for a commissioner for the *arrondissement* of Mouscron and a deputy-commissioner for the Voer communes, both of whom were given specific responsibilities for overseeing application of the legislation locally. These arrangements emerged during the political bargaining phase of the legislation, and may be seen as part of the process of reaching an overall agreement.

One American scholar has concluded that the Belgian legislation of 1962 and 1963 pushed the regulatory powers of government to their virtual limits insofar as they could be used to promote a specific pattern of language usage (Curtis, 1971, 557). Indeed some provisions of the law of August 2, 1963, appear to be so detailed or so far-reaching as to make effective enforcement impractical. Illustrations of this tendency will appear in later sections of this chapter, but first it is necessary to outline how the implementation of the third round of language laws was soon overtaken by a larger and more complex issue, the opening phases of the lengthy quest for major constitutional revisions and a radical restructuring of Belgian political institutions.

B   The Struggle to Reform the Belgian State

While the Swiss system of decentralized federalism is intrinsically well suited to the accommodation of religious and linguistic divisions that have a clear territorial dimension, the Belgian political system established in 1830 was highly centralized, a unitary state that retained most of the important and sensitive powers in the hands of the central government. Since 1830 the nine provinces have acquired a modest range of specific, relatively noncontroversial responsibilities, which include such typical items as provincial roads, non-navigable waterways, public health measures, technical education, cultural and youth centres, and other similar topics, though even in these areas their competence is often shared with other levels of government (Orianne, 1967; Declerck, 1961; CRISP, 1972, no. 547: 2-3). In a political sense the Belgian provinces have always had a very low profile, and this has been deliberate. Indeed one article of the *loi provinciale* of 1836 specifically forbids the provincial councils to corre- spond with one another on matters under their jurisdiction (CRISP, 1974, no. 628: 3). The communes, at first sight, are much more active. If we eliminate transfer payments from the central government to other govern- ments as an expenditure, it can be calculated that in 1966, before any form of decentralization had become a serious issue, the communes accounted for about 32 per cent, and the provinces for less than 3 per cent, of total government expenditures for all three levels (*Annuaire statistique*, 1968, 408, 414, 417).

Much of this activity of local government, however, is carried out to implement national legislation and is financed by transfer payments. In spite of older traditions of communal independence, effective communal autonomy has been greatly diminished in the twentieth century. Even the territorial boundaries of local government have undergone a major over- haul in recent years, a radical change that reduced the total number of communes from 2,359 to 596 as of January 1977, with some further amalgamations in urban areas to follow. It is characteristic of the Belgian political system that the ultimate political decisions concerning these wholesale fusions of communes, with their far-reaching implications for every aspect of local government, were made in the central political arena, on the basis of plans prepared by the Ministry of the Interior, and without formal consultation with the communal councils or the local populations concerned (CRISP, 1971, nos. 540-41; 1975, nos. 679, 697-98; 1976, nos. 736-37: 3). The parliamentary debate in the lower house, as the minister responsible admitted, was "tempestuous and difficult," and the bill passed by a narrow majority (Michel, 1976, 10-11).

The unitary state has not gone unchallenged, but until the twentieth century its detractors were scattered and without influence. In the years immediately preceding the First World War more influential voices were heard in favor of administrative separation of Flanders and Wallonie. This idea lost its respectability when it was partially instituted by the German occupying authorities during the war, but it was never wholly forgotten in Flemish nationalist circles. With the passage of the language laws of the 1930s, emphasis shifted to the notion of cultural autonomy of the two communities as a moderate alternative to more extreme nationalist posi- tions that leaned towards creation of a Great Netherlandic or neo- Burgundian state. The concept of cultural autonomy apparently first reached Belgium in 1913 through the Flemish Socialist leader Kamiel Huysmans, whose friendship with the Austrian Socialist leader Otto Bauer made him aware of Austro-Marxist attempts to balance the national and the social questions in the Habsburg monarchy through an imaginative scheme for dual parliamentary institutions to allow each nationality self-rule in educational and cultural matters (Deleu et al., 1973-75, 1: 696; Witte et al., 1978, 1:253-54). After 1945 cultural autonomy became a re-newed concern of the reviving Flemish Movement and a logical comple-ment of the linguistic frontier legislation of 1962. In the early 1960s it began to take tangible form through the gradual twinning or *dédoublement* of central government ministries responsible for education and culture, a development that will be examined more fully in a later section of this chapter (see below, 186-87).

Concurrently with these tendencies towards partial or full adminis-trative division, several proposals emerged for a more thoroughgoing federalization of the Belgian state. Between 1931 and 1962 no fewer than nine separate bills were introduced in Parliament to this effect, and still others were developed but not formally introduced. The first of those actually introduced, the Vos bill of 1931, was a measure developed by the Flemish nationalist Frontist party in consultation with certain scholars in the Netherlands, including the historian Pieter Geyl. The question surfaced again in the studies of the privately organized Centre d'études pour la ré-forme de l'Etat (CERE, 1937-38, 1: 309-92; CRISP, 1962, no. 135: 6-7). The next seven of these bills, introduced from 1938 to 1961, all originated from Walloon socialist or communist circles, and even the last one, a Volksunie initiative of 1962, was based on earlier work by a committee of Flemish and Walloon federalists. Most of these early federalist initiatives had been the product of relatively small groups of intellectuals. By 1961 the founding of the Mouvement Populaire Wallon under the leadership of André Renard and the continuing growth of the Volksunie meant that federalist ideas were making progress among the electorate through mass political movements. The literature on the question of federalism in Bel-gium is quite extensive, as may be seen from the bibliography of Verdoodt (1973, 188-99), but it is not always grounded on a firm knowledge of federal systems. For present purposes we need mention only a few selected items that provide an overview of the evolution of federalist ideas and especially of proposals for institutional reform (De Nolf, 1968a; 1968b; 1968c; Houtman, 1963; Daelemans, 1963; 1966; CRISP, 1961, no. 129; 1962, no. 135; Dehousse, 1961; CERE, 1937-38).

In spite of the proliferation of literature and the intensity of debate, it must be remembered that open or avowed partisans of federalism have remained a minority among the political elites, though of course tenden-cies differ markedly from one party to another. Paradoxically, if Belgian unitarism has weakened, antifederalism remains strong. For many intellec-tuals and politicians alike both the word and the concept of "federalism" have a distinctly pejorative ring. In some settings, notes the Walloon federalist Lucien Outers, certain terms become synonymous with chaos or decadence, and in Belgium the term "federalism" became an object of such "ritual denunciation" (1968, 195). At least three apparent reasons may be discerned for these negative attitudes. First, the Belgian political culture, to the extent that it has been shaped by external models, was most strongly influenced by France, the Netherlands, and possibly Great Britain, all of which have had strongly unitary regimes. Second, and more specifically, for many Belgians federalism acquired unpleasant if rather intangible associations with pre-1939 extremist Flemish nationalism and with wartime German occupation, and so acquired an image of incompatibility with loyalty to the Belgian state. Finally, there is a persistent conviction, even among scholars, that federalism is somehow more appropriate for situations where integration is on the increase than for processes of decentralization, and many who hold this view see no contradiction in supporting European federation while opposing a federalized Belgium. An outsider schooled in a federal system may find an element of simple irrationality in these attitudes, but they are nevertheless sufficiently strong that what passes elsewhere under the label of federalism may have to be called by another name in Belgium.

Beyond these attitudinal barriers, Flemish and Walloon federalists have tended to differ sharply over approaches, objectives, and priorities. While Flemish federalism has long been inspired primarily by the vision of cultural autonomy for Flanders and for Flemings in Brussels, Walloon federalism after 1945 was fueled by the increasingly urgent economic problems of Wallonie and by Walloon socialist demands for economic renovation through state action. In the light of these different objectives, Flemings incline towards a bipartite federation of two major cultural groups, Walloons towards a tripartite one of three distinct regions. The alternative of a federation based on the existing nine provinces or on modified provincial boundaries, so plausible to the outside observer, finds no significant support within Belgium itself, and indeed some recent reform proposals have tended either to reduce provincial powers or to eliminate them entirely.

The essential background to the argument over bipartite and tripartite models is that Wallonie and Brussels have very different and even conflicting economic interests, but for demographic reasons Walloons desperately need the support of Brussels Francophones to claim approximate parity in cultural matters. In return for this support, Brussels Francophones demand full regional status and autonomy for the capital. As a result the various federalist projects introduced in Parliament have differed widely in the status they accord to Brussels, from independent province of the federation to full integration in Flanders, with most projects giving it the status of an independent region or territory. As one federalist realistically remarked early in the debate, the situation virtually imposes some intermediate type of solution, a *fédéralisme à deux et demi* (Dehousse, 1961, 303-304). In the context of emerging decentralization, Brussels presents almost a classic example of the conflicts between local and national interests that occur regularly in the governing of federal capitals (Rowat, 1973).

The search for an acceptable reform of institutions has been a prolonged one, and some of the problems to be resolved have been enormously complex. Yet the point to be emphasized is that major institutional reforms have been initiated and far-reaching changes have already been achieved through prolonged bargaining and interparty consensus. For convenience of analysis, the process may be divided into two periods. The first, which was virtually completed by December 1970, saw the development and enactment of an important package of constitutional amendments that set out broad principles of decentralization and of certain other reforms. The second, which began just after these constitutional amendments, was intended to develop new institutions and mechanisms to implement these principles, a task that proved even more complex than the original amendments and remained incomplete a full decade later. A full-scale description of these institutional reforms would be so intricate as to have little appeal for non-Belgian readers. Our overview here must be greatly condensed and limited to certain aspects only.

If we focus on the post-1945 period, the path towards institutional reform begins with the work of the so-called Centre Harmel, a large mixed committee of parliamentarians and other prominent figures established by statute in 1948 to examine the outstanding problems of Flanders and Wallonie. After delays, its final report was deposited in 1958, together with some 5,000 pages of background studies and documents. The recommendations of its political section included proposals for stabilization of the linguistic frontier, decentralization in the public service, a doubling of the education ministry, regional advisory councils for economic and social questions, and reforms in local government (Centre de recherche, 1958; CRISP, 1961, no. 131). These proposals became a starting point for preparation of the language laws of 1962 and 1963 and also for a ministerial study group set up in 1962 to prepare the first steps towards constitutional reform, an ambitious project that was directed not only towards a solution to the burning *question communautaire* but also towards the adjustment of Belgian institutions to the demands of twentieth-century welfare politics in the widest sense.

Under the Belgian constitution, however, the revision procedure is complicated. According to Article 131 it requires as a first step a parliamentary declaration of the specific articles to be amended; this is followed by a dissolution of both houses and the election of a new parliament with constituent powers. The actual amendments must then be passed in each chamber with at least two thirds of the members present and at least two thirds of these voting for the amendment. In this instance the Social Christian and Socialist coalition partners reached agreement by 1965 on a list of constitutional articles to be amended, but in the ensuing election required by the amending procedure they lost the two-thirds majority necessary to implement their plans. As a result plans for amendment were largely sidetracked during the next three years except for a few noncontroversial measures, including a new Article 140 passed in 1967 to establish the text of the constitution itself in both French and Dutch. As for more sensitive issues, the Vanden Boeynants government declared a "linguistic truce" in 1966 and entrusted the search for solutions to another study commission, the Commission permanente pour l'amélioration des relations entre les communautés linguistiques belges (CPARCLB), also known as the Meyers Commission. This body, based on a careful balance of the two language groups, three regions, and three traditional parties, heard proposals from many interest groups and also gave special attention to the problems of Brussels and the German areas, but its work was cut short by the eruption of the Louvain crisis in 1968 and the downfall of the government (Meyers, 1968; CRISP, 1967, no. 381).

The new parliament that emerged from the elections of 1968 also had constituent powers, and the new prime minister, Gaston Eyskens, was more reform-minded than the Brussels-oriented Vanden Boeynants. There followed a two-year period of patient negotiations and hard bargaining, in which all parties participated for a time, to put together a mixed package of reforms that would win the approval of the necessary special majorities in both houses. Though some of the revisions were aimed only at the modernization of institutions and had little or nothing to do with the *question communautaire*, the latter was the storm centre of controversy. Broadly, three general problems were simultaneously at issue: the cultural autonomy of the linguistic communities, the regionalization of certain areas of economic policy, and appropriate guarantees for minorities. Some acceptable form of minority protection would be needed not only for Francophones in national politics and for Flemings in Brussels but also for the ideological minorities within each linguistic community when cultural autonomy began to function. Finally, after Herculean efforts, texts were elaborated even for the most sensitive issues, passed by both houses, given royal assent, and published by the last day of December 1970.

In all, some twenty-five constitutional articles were introduced or amended and four obsolete articles were abrogated by the two constituent parliaments between 1967 and 1971, comprising by far the most important body of revisions since 1831. About half of the changes have little or no direct bearing on intergroup relations and need not be pursued further here. Of those that do, we may single out the following provisions as the most important:

1. The recognition of four distinct linguistic regions—French, Dutch, German, and bilingual Brussels-Capital (Article 3 *bis*);

2. The recognition of three distinct cultural communities—French, Dutch, and German (3 *ter*);

3. The division of members of Parliament into two language groups and the establishment of these groups as cultural councils for their respec-

tive communities with full legislative powers over specified areas (32 *bis*, 59 *bis*);

4. Similar cultural committees in the Brussels agglomeration (108 *ter*);

5. The creation of a German cultural council (59 *ter*);

6. Alarm procedures in Parliament and in the Brussels Agglomeration Council to delay legislation seen as threatening to one or the other linguistic group (38 *bis*, 108 *ter*);

7. A guarantee for ideological and philosophical minorities (6 *bis*);

8. Linguistic parity in the national Cabinet (86 *bis*) and in the Brussels agglomeration executive (108 *ter*);

9. The recognition of three regions—Flanders, Wallonie, Brussels—to be endowed later by special law with legislative powers over specified social and economic matters (107 *quater*).

It may be noted that the first five of these changes relate to the realization of cultural autonomy, the next three to minority guarantees, and only the last, which is far from specific as to details, to the question of economic regionalization. Three further provisions concerned greater linguistic homogeneity in judicial districts (Article 104), special legal status for certain communes as a means to resolve the Voer problem (Article 1, subsection 4), and a temporary guarantee for the Francophone University of Louvain until its transfer to Wallonie (Article 132).

We may also note in passing that a considerable list of articles had been designated for amendment and then bypassed in the amending process. Most of these articles were of lower priority and unrelated to the *question communautaire*, but they included the original Article 23 on linguistic liberty and also Article 126, which designates the city (*ville*) of Brussels as the capital of Belgium and the seat of government (Senelle, 1972, 170-73). It had been intended to bring these two clauses into line with the new institutional arrangements, and how this was envisaged in early parliamentary drafts may be seen in a pamphlet explaining the reforms that was published by the minister responsible, Leo Tindemans (1969, 47-48, 50-51).

As soon as the constitutional amendments were passed, attention shifted to problems of implementation. Some of the changes required special legislation to give them effect, and some of these laws in turn required special parliamentary majorities. Once again hard bargaining was required, and each party had its own set of conditions as the price for its consent. Under these circumstances three important laws were passed in July 1971. The first provided for the division of Parliament into two linguistic groups and the establishment of these groups as cultural councils for their respective linguistic communities. The second specified the powers and mode of operation of these councils. The third established a new level of local government for metropolitan areas and federations of communes, with special arrangements for the Brussels agglomeration and for five new federations of communes on the periphery of Brussels (Senelle, 1972, 195-235).

But Flemish Socialists, Walloon Catholics, and Liberals on both sides were still fearful about their minority position in the new cultural councils. The price for their agreement was a new cultural accord to be signed by the three traditional parties, a *Pacte culturel* analogous to the *Pacte scolaire*, as an additional guarantee against ideological discrimination in the functioning of the new councils themselves and of the various cultural associations within their jurisdiction. A preliminary agreement of July 1971 led to a definitive text, formally signed in February 1972 by all parliamentary parties except the Volksunie, and to the expression of its principles in legislation in July 1973. This law is of more than passing interest, because in introducing it the minister of Netherlandic culture described it as an "improvement in democratic procedures," a renunciation of the majoritarian principle in favor of the "cooperation, participation, co-decision and co-management" of the entire population of all shades of opinion (Daubie, 1975, 178-79; and cf. "Pacte culturel," 1971; Daubie, 1972). The legislation makes a serious effort to spell out these concepts in highly elaborate principles and formulae involving both proportionate representation of the political-ideological tendencies and *cogestion* of cultural associations by a mixture of political and consumer representatives. A permanent monitoring agency, the Commission nationale permanente du pacte culturel, was established to oversee the application of the law (CRISP, 1974, no. 647; Daubie, 1975).

After a slow start, this body has been working unobtrusively since 1975 by hearing complaints against ideological imbalances in administrative and policy-making bodies and in grants programs at all levels of government, but primarily at the level of communal councils and local advisory committees. An analysis of its record to the end of 1981 shows a total of 358 formal complaints introduced in this period, with almost three quarters of these having originated from Flemish sources (CRISP, 1983, nos. 986-87: 35-36). Nevertheless the general impact of the *Pacte culturel* on Belgian society appears to have been more pervasive than these figures would indicate, because the educative activity of the commission and press publicity given to infractions have led to the prevention or settlement of many grievances before the formal complaint stage is reached.

The French and Netherlandic Cultural Councils were formally installed late in 1971 and began to function almost at once. Because Flemish cultural aspirations had not been satisfied by previous institutions, the Netherlandic council proved more active than its French counterpart. A comparison of the first seven sessions of activity shows that the Netherlandic council enacted twice the number of legislative decrees (*décrets normatifs*) and dealt with several times the number of oral and written questions, though the number of budgetary decrees was roughly the same for both (Brassinne, 1977, 185). The most spectacular act of the Netherlandic council was adoption of the so-called "Décret de septembre," a sweeping and controversial measure governing language relations between employers and workers in Flanders, which will be examined more fully in a later section of this chapter (below, 264-69). For both councils the general problem during this initial period was to find a way to function effectively in a political system where ministerial responsibility and administrative resources were still adjusted to a highly centralized parliamentary system (Gérain, 1975; Brassinne, 1977; CRISP, 1973, nos. 624-25; 1975, nos. 685-86).

A third cultural council, to serve the German community in the East Cantons, was created by a special law of July 1973 in execution of the new Article 59 *ter* of the constitution. Because of the small size of its constituency, it was given only advisory and limited regulatory powers at this stage, compared to the power of the other two councils to pass *décrets* having the full force of laws. Its twenty-five members were to be chosen in a special election held simultaneously with parliamentary elections (Senelle, 1978, 170-72, 232-42).

If the obstacles to implementing cultural autonomy were tackled by legislating intricate principles of the *Pacte culturel*, the road to regionalization was far more complex. For one thing, the ministries that succeeded the Eyskens government could not marshal the special majorities needed to implement regionalization as specified by the new Article 107 *quater* of the constitution. As a result a law on provisional regionalization, to be passed by ordinary majorities, was prepared first. A second difficulty arose from the fact that the terrain was already heavily overgrown with existing organizations active in the general area of economic development and planning.

The foremost of these bodies were the three regional economic councils, first founded as unofficial advisory bodies but given statutory recognition and definition in 1970 with a broad mandate as advisory bodies for regional planning and development. These councils served as points of contact between the major organized interest groups (employers, labor, independents, farmers) and the political elites (members of Parliament and provincial councillors). In addition to the councils for Wallonie and Flanders, there existed a third for the entire province of Brabant. This made for complicated overlapping jurisdictions over both Flemish and Walloon Brabant, with each falling under two councils simultaneously. All three councils were based on parity between the political and interest-group sectors, but the council for Brabant combined this with linguistic parity as well (CRISP, 1970, nos. 481-82; 1972, no. 584; 1973, no. 587). For those interested in forms of economic organization and decision-making, it might be noted that the student of economic structures soon becomes aware of substantial elements of corporatism (or, more precisely, what recent social science literature has labelled neo-corporatism or liberal corporatism) in the making of Belgian economic policy. From this standpoint one can view regionalization as the end result of a phased transfer of certain types of economic decisions from private bodies to quasi-public bodies to a decentralized governmental level, or—from a slightly different perspective—from one arena outside the central governmental arena to another.

A second type of organization created by the same legislation of 1970 was the société de développement régional (SDR). These were operational bodies of a technical character concerned with studies, economic planning, and other technical tasks delegated to them. Here the unit of organization could be either the province or the region, and some seven SDRs were in fact established, five for the four Flemish provinces and Flemish Brabant, one for the whole of Wallonie, and one for Brussels-Capital (CRISP, 1973, nos. 616-17; 1974, nos. 632-33). By the same legislation still more agencies were created at national level for planning and industrial promotion, so that the implementation of Article 107 *quater* had to proceed in a context of extreme institutional complexity (Beaufays, 1973; *Institutions politiques*, 1973). The non-Belgian observer is soon lost amid the terminology of regional economic councils, regional development societies, "preparatory" regional councils, successive blueprints for the permanent regional councils—not to mention still other bodies at the subregional and local levels—and a lengthy list of acronyms for all these organizations in both languages.

"Preparatory" regionalization was established by a law of August 1, 1974, passed under pressure from the Francophone regional parties but without the special majorities required by Article 107 *quater*. In the absence of the required majority, this law set up consultative councils only, without legislative or regulatory powers, though these powers were envisaged for the later, definitive stage. For the regional councils of Flanders and Wallonie, the members were to be simply the senators domiciled in each of these regions, while for Brussels the council was to be composed of senators domiciled in Brussels-Capital plus members elected by the Brussels Agglomeration Council on the basis of linguistic proportionality. Similarly, at the executive level, three ministerial committees of the national government were established to oversee regional activities and recommend allocation of regional budgets. All in all, the 1974 law constituted a first halting, experimental step in the direction of regionalization, and it still left decision-making in the hands of the same parliamentary elite, playing slightly modified roles but in different arenas with different combinations of players. The regional councils, accepted reluctantly by Flemish members and strongly opposed by the Socialist opposition as an inadequate step towards full regionalization, had a short and troubled existence. By an amendment in July 1977 the three councils were abolished, leaving the ministerial committees as the principal channel for formulating regional policy (CRISP, 1974, no. 665; 1975, nos. 667-68; Senelle, 1978, 249-70).

At this stage the reform process was far from complete. The new institutions were cumbersome, and they lacked an overall sense of direction. After further setbacks and postponements, the *dialogue communautaire* was resumed among the parties after the first elections for the reformed communes in 1976. Once again the bargaining was long and arduous, but from it emerged—after the 1977 parliamentary election—the essential outlines of a possible rationalization of the institutions that had blossomed in such profusion since 1970. Once again the agreement took the form of an interparty treaty or pact among the four parties forming the incoming government. Known as the *Pacte communautaire*, or Egmont Pact (from the palace in which it was negotiated), it was announced and approved by Parliament in June 1977. This text in turn was elaborated in further discussions held over several months at the Château of Stuyvenberg, and the Egmont-Stuyvenberg accord, announced by the prime minister in February 1978, provided a blueprint for a regionalized Belgium with detailed institutional plans for two cultural communities, three regions, a new level of subregions, and a phasing out of existing provincial functions. The cultural communities and the regions were to have their own legislative competence, their own executives, and elected councils, but some economy of representation was to be achieved by having elected members of the three regional councils recombine to sit as the two community councils and then combine again to sit as the upper house of the central legislature. The most innovative feature of the pact was a plan to ease the Brussels problem by allowing residents of the six peripheral communes with facilities, and of designated parts of other peripheral communes, to elect a fictitious domicile within any commune of Brussels-Capital for electoral, administrative, judicial, and educational purposes (CRISP, 1977, nos. 767, 772, 783-84; Senelle, 1978, 290-325; *Pacte communautaire*, 1978; Zakalnyckyj, 1978).

As matters turned out, the Egmont-Stuyvenberg proposals encountered both legal and political obstacles. On the legal side, the Conseil d'Etat, which serves as guardian of the rule of law in Belgium, ruled that the proposals required additional constitutional amendments to give them effect, and this in turn required the usual lengthy procedure of a declaration of articles to be amended, a dissolution of Parliament and new elections, the formation of a new government, and finally the passage of the amendments themselves by special majorities. When the government named some sixty constitutional articles for revision and appealed to the electorate in December 1978, it discovered the extent of Flemish displeasure at the concessions proposed for the Brussels periphery. The most vulnerable of the coalition partners, the Volksunie, lost heavily and went into opposition after this election. The lengthy ministerial crisis that followed was complicated by the need to find both revised institutional arrangements and the special majorities in Parliament for constitutional amendments to carry them out (CRISP, 1978, nos. 817, 819; 1979, nos. 847-50).

The following eighteen months were a period of great complexity in institutional reform, but only the broad outlines need concern us here. The first Martens ministry, formed after 103 days of tough bargaining, was founded upon an elaborate plan to bring about a new regime of communities and regions in three successive phases. The "immediate" phase was achieved by an ordinary law of July 1979. The next phase, "transitional but irreversible," requiring constitutional amendments, was jeopardized by the departure of the FDF from the government coalition in January 1980. The second Martens government, a Catholic-Socialist coalition, tried to continue with less ambitious reform plans in the Senate, where it still had a slim two-thirds majority, but it fell as a result of backbench defections among its own supporters. A third Martens government was then formed on the basis of a traditional tripartite coalition—Catholics, Socialists, and Liberals—with a new agreement to proceed with institutional reforms except for postponement of the Brussels question, on which no consensus could be found. On this basis the government then obtained the necessary majorities for a new round of constitutional amendments passed in July 1980 and two laws on institutional reforms in August. It remained formally committed to finding a solution for Brussels before the next communal elections in 1982, but the tripartite coalition fell in October 1980 over economic issues and the Catholic-Socialist government that succeeded it once again lacked the necessary votes for measures requiring passage by special majorities.

The legislation and constitutional amendments of 1980 brought several important changes to the institutions for decentralization developed during the 1970s. First, the former Cultural Councils became Community Councils, acquiring important new areas of legislative competence and independent executive bodies to manage their affairs. Second, Parliament acknowledged the fundamental asymmetry of Flemish and Francophone structures and aspirations by establishing a single executive and a single council for the Flemish community and the Flanders region, the Vlaamse Raad, while it established separate executives and separate councils for the French community and for the Walloon region. The three councils, composed initially of all parliamentarians of the corresponding language group or region (like the post-1971 Cultural Councils), were ultimately, after Senate reform, to be composed of elected senators only from the relevant language group or region, an idea developed in the Egmont-Stuyvenberg Pact. Members from Brussels-Capital on the Vlaamse Raad were to have advisory powers only when discussing matters relating to the Flanders region. The three executives, at first sitting as ministerial committees of the national government, were eventually to be separated and even barred from overlapping membership in the central ministry, thus evolving into miniature governments responsible to their respective councils for areas within their jurisdiction. One subsection of the act gave the two Francophone councils and executives the power to merge on the same basis as the Vlaamse Raad. However, from a political standpoint this is unlikely to happen, because Walloon socialists view the institutions of the Walloon region as an apanage of their own and an instrument for rebuilding the economy of Wallonie. The region of Brussels, not covered by the 1980 legislation, remained under provisional regionalization legislation as revised and coordinated in 1979, with an executive for regional matters within the national government but no regional council. Among other consequences, this meant that the Brussels executive would reflect the political forces present in the national government rather than those predominant locally.

The powers of the Community Councils, as enunciated by the 1980 amendment of Article 59 *bis* of the constitution and by the special law on institutional reforms, include both the powers of the former Cultural Councils and certain new responsibilities. First among the former are "cultural matters," which are specifically listed to include not only the more obvious activities concerning language and literature, fine arts, museums, and libraries but also broadcasting, youth policy, preschool and adult education, artistic and research training, sports, tourism, leisure activities, and several similar categories. Second, the new councils, like the Cultural Councils, have control over education, apart from certain basic provisions regarding the *Pacte scolaire*, educational structures, diplomas, salaries, and other general norms that remain under the central government. Third, they are responsible for cooperation between cultural communities and for international cultural relations. Fourth, they can pass decrees on language usage in administrative matters, in public and private education, and on some aspects of language usage in the private sector, but unlike the councils' other powers this last provision is limited in a territorial sense to the unilingual regions and does not extend even to communes with minority-language facilities. Finally, the two Community Councils were given responsibility over a new category of activities that emerged during the Egmont-Stuyvenberg discussions, the *matières personnalisables*, or services that could be divided according to the linguistic or cultural affiliation of the individual receiving them. In the 1980 law these are listed in some detail so as to include, broadly speaking, health care services, social welfare services, and applied scientific research in areas under the competence of the councils (Senelle, 1980, 188-90, 249-52; CRISP, 1980, no. 889).

The transition from Cultural Councils to Community Councils with expanded powers is undoubtedly a result of growing Flemish intransigence and of harder bargaining positions adopted by the Flemish political parties. The main effects of the shift have occurred in Brussels-Capital, where Flemish interest groups grew increasingly pessimistic through the 1970s about prospects for stable power-sharing arrangements between Flemings and Francophones in the projected Brussels Region. As a more promising alternative they leaned increasingly towards an option of separation and autonomy in the capital, with each side having a wide range of social institutions backed up by and tied in with those of the wider cultural community.

The powers of the regional councils, first enunciated in the provisional regionalization law of August 1974, have tended to grow in extent and complexity in later formulations, though some of the original regional powers that were considered more social than economic have ended up among the *matières personnalisables* assigned to the Community Councils. The competence of the new Regional Councils, as listed in the special law on institutional reforms of August 8, 1980, include: (1) land-use planning and urban renewal; (2) protection of the environment and disposal of wastes; (3) nature conservation, forests, hunting and fishing; (4) housing and sanitary inspection; (5) certain aspects of water resources and sewage; (6) regional economic development; (7) certain aspects of energy policy; and (8) certain financial and legal controls over local governments in the region concerned. The legislation lists these powers in considerable detail, along with explicit exceptions reserved for the central government and other matters where interregional or regional-national joint consultation is prescribed (Senelle, 1980, 190-95). Even a cursory reading of this list suggests a high potential for future conflicts of the sort well known to other divided jurisdictions.

In the remainder of the special law on institutional reforms, the composition, selection procedures, and operating rules of the three councils and their corresponding executives are spelled out in painstaking detail. Its counterpart "ordinary law" of August 9, 1980, enacted by ordinary majority and amendable in the same way, provides much further detail on the financing of the new institutions, the prevention and resolution of conflicts between jurisdictions, the rules of language usage in the new agencies, and legal consequences for provincial and local governments of the new institutions superimposed above them. On the financial side the new Community Councils, unlike their predecessors the Cultural Councils, which depended solely on central government allocations, are given the same financial resources as the Regional Councils. These include, at least in theory, revenues from fees, annual grants from the central government, rebates to the regions or communities of certain centrally imposed taxes, the possibility of additional regional or community levies on these same taxes, and the power to borrow. On the whole, however, the power to levy taxes independently of the central government is rather narrowly circumscribed, and the Ministry of Finance of the central government remains the sole collection agent for taxes. For at least the initial phase of the new institutions, the predominant source of funds appears inescapably to be direct grants from the central government, and in 1980 the total available from this source to the community and regional authorities combined amounted to 86 billion Belgian francs, or a mere 7 per cent of the central government budget, an amount considered totally insufficient and out of proportion to the powers and responsibilities transferred (Dersin, 1981, 216-21).

There remain some perplexing wider questions concerning the classification and evaluation of the new Belgian institutions. The task of classification is made more difficult by the curiously Byzantine (and still unfinished) compromise between bipartite and tripartite decentralization, a "solution sui generis" that Aristide Zolberg has cited as one more example of the Belgian practice of "splitting the difference" as a formula for conflict resolution (1977, 141). On the other hand, formal classification has gradually become easier as the original quest for a modest redistribution of rule-making or legislative competence in the early 1970s gradually led by logical stages to plans for parallel executives and administrative bodies by the end of the decade.

Is the new Belgian system to be classified as a form of federalism? One American observer labelled the 1970 version "an exotic hybrid . . . neither truly federalist nor as ferociously unitarist as before" and noted that Belgian scholars have tended to use neologisms to describe a situation that they consider to be unique in the world (Dunn, 1974, 163; cf. Mast, 1972, 879). The future Prime Minister Tindemans, in a politically adroit phrase, described the blueprint for reform in 1970 as "federalization without federalism" (Zolberg, 1977, 127-28), but here one must remember the general public aversion to federalism as a concept in Belgium, and also the very evident confusion among some Belgian writers as to what federalism essentially is (Maystadt, 1972, 137-40). A more serious analysis of the 1970 changes by a Belgian academic concluded cautiously that the new system was an "amalgam" combining some features of federalism with others characteristic of a decentralized but formally unitary state (Delpérée, 1972, 641-42, 660).

As institutional concepts evolved during the later 1970s, however, the system began to look less like an "exotic hybrid." The mass-circulation weekly Pourquoi pas?, which seemed to consider federalism simply a matter of degree, somewhat hastily labelled the August 1980 reforms as une décentralisation teintée de fédéralisme (1980, August 14). It is true that the new councils and executives were given little or no control over their own size or composition. One central point to be noted, however, is that both communities and regions have acquired far from negligible areas of legislative competence through formal constitutional amendments and special legislation, and only further formal constitutional amendments or laws passed by special majorities can undo or alter these grants of rule-making authority. Prime Minister Wilfried Martens, the principal architect of the reform package, was hardly less adroit than his predecessor Tindemans when he declared that the 1980 changes contained the "essential characteristics" of a federal state ("Réforme de l'Etat belge," 1980, 10). Not all Belgian scholars have agreed. In a careful analytical assessment, André Molitor has characterized the reforms and plans of the 1970s as a "system of regionalization or . . . very elaborate decentralization," and the 1980 proposals as not "a true federal system" though they were "a step in that direction" (Lijphart, 1980, 150-51). But the question, as he emphasizes in another study, is very much one of academic definitions, and he himself explicitly follows a definition and criteria of federalism developed by the French scholar Georges Burdeau, who defines federalism in terms of its point of departure, as an association of constituent units to form a new political entity (Molitor, 1981, 211-14).

From a different analytical perspective, the question is perhaps better understood if we first recall Carl Friedrich's reminder that the concept of federalism can sometimes take nonterritorial forms, as it did in Austria-Hungary and in Estonia (1975). If we then define federalism in terms of entrenched, independent levels of legislative authority, the Belgian political system, as set out in the 1980 reforms, can be categorized as a unique combination of territorial and nonterritorial federalism, each with its own assigned list of legislative powers. This combination is further characterized politically by continuing tensions between its bipartite and tripartite jurisdictions, by divergent Flemish and Francophone perceptions of priorities, and by a continuing need for a central government strong enough to keep these conflicting tendencies in balance. It is also, however, a weak and cautious federalism, enacted by the traditional parties and still entrammelled by a century and a half of unitary habits of mind. Thus in the blueprint the legislators of the communities and the regions are also expected to do double—or triple—duty as members of the central Parliament, and the communities and regions, in the initial stages at least, are far from having any effective financial independence. Of course these restrictions may change as the system evolves, but paradoxically, as a consequence of current rivalries over fiscal resources, Belgium seems fated to remain for some time to come a polity integrated by the very intensity of distrust across its regional and linguistic boundaries.

The new institutional reforms became operative in a legal sense on October 1, 1980, but their full implementation was to be phased in over several years. In practice, this process has gone more slowly than expected as a result of the economic and fiscal crisis that faced the Martens government as soon as the 1980 legislation was passed. Nevertheless, the three executives of the new councils were established as planned outside the national government after the 1981 parliamentary election (CRISP, 1981, no. 937), and by September of the same year more than 8,000 public service positions had been designated for transfer from thirteen different central government departments to the new jurisdictions, to reflect the programs and functions being given to the regions and communities (CRISP, 1981, no. 940; 1982, no. 967: 10). Actual transfers of personnel have gone more slowly, and not without some friction. In spite of earlier governmental commitments, the status of Brussels remained unchanged at the communal elections of October 1982, and a much-discussed Arbitration Court—called for by Article 107 *ter* of the 1980 constitutional amendments to settle jurisdictional conflicts between central, regional, and community legislation—was installed only in October 1984. Its carefully balanced membership of twelve was based on French-Dutch linguistic parity, proportionality by parties, and a statutory equal representation of jurists and parliamentarians from each language community. The new regime of communities was institutionalized for the German-speaking population of New Belgium by a constitutional amendment and a law of December 1983, which replaced the German Cultural Council with a new, separately elected community council and an executive analogous to—but not identical with—those created in 1980 for the French and Flemish communities (CRISP, 1984, nos. 1028-29).

More interesting than these new structures are the consequences of the new institutions for Belgian political life. In particular the new councils and executives have created additional political arenas where the priorities, pressure groups, and political forces in contention differ from those represented in the central Parliament. This development has been of special interest for the Francophone socialists, who have found in the two Francophone councils and executives an opportunity for an active and even a predominant socialist presence at a time when the party is in opposition in the central Parliament and when the general economic climate is far from favorable to them. Despite greater disparities in party strength in the councils than in the central Parliament, the new executive bodies have followed the Belgian norm of more or less proportional multiparty representation and consensual politics, with the two Francophone executives initially representing three parties and the Flemish representing four. In relations *among* governments, however, the participants in the revised system have rapidly discovered hitherto unsuspected possibilities for obstruction, delay, and frustration of the plans of other jurisdictions, and this in turn enhances the importance of the *comité de concertation*, a coordinating committee drawn from all four governments to regulate conflicts between them.

Even before the new councils have begun to function fully, all three have heard calls to extend their sphere of legislative authority. From a regional standpoint, both sides would like a larger say in the central government's policy towards the ailing Belgian steel industry and other industries still included within the national sector. From a cultural standpoint, both communities have sought an expanded independent role in international relations, and both have found a willing partner for this purpose in the government of Québec. The president of the Flemish executive was first in the field when he led a delegation on a well-publicized official visit to Québec in the spring of 1982, but the executive of the French community more than made up for this in November of that year by signing a comprehensive agreement for cultural cooperation and by establishing a Délégation Wallonie-Bruxelles in the city of Québec. General public reaction to the new system is still difficult to gauge, but there is some indication from the 1981 election and from surveys that the push for federalism or radical decentralization is still gaining ground in Flanders but may be stationary or receding among voters in Wallonie and Brussels (see above, Table 29, item 24, 119).

Cautious though it may be as an experiment in federalism, the new system marks a sharp break from pre-1970 Belgian political traditions. From the vantage point of the mid-1980s, any attempt at evaluation would clearly be premature, like a drama review written in midplay. The system itself will remain incomplete as long as the Brussels question is unresolved, and there is a strong possibility of further major institutional changes in the course of finding an accommodation over Brussels. Fortunately, it is not necessary here to evaluate the results of the long and arduous journey towards reform of the state that began under the Lefèvre government in 1962. Our immediate task is a simpler one: to take note of this revised but still evolving institutional structure of Belgium as a necessary background to the study of language arrangements in specific institutions, which will be examined one by one in the rest of this chapter.

C   Languages in Parliament

Unlike the case of Switzerland, where the principle of a plurilingual legislature was firmly established at the founding of the federal state in 1848, the Belgian case must be considered in evolutionary terms. As we have seen, the Belgian Revolution of 1830 was founded on a general repudiation of Orangist traditions, including some experience with a plurilingual parliament in the United Kingdom of the Netherlands before 1830. The post-1830 parliaments of Belgium were exclusively French-speaking for all official purposes, and only with the rise of the Flemish Movement was this supremacy challenged. In this section two questions call for special attention: first, the relative representation of language groups, and more recently of regions, in Parliament; and second, the formal status and informal usage of languages in the parliamentary process. Both question have important historical dimensions, and both reveal some differences between the two houses, the Chamber of Representatives and the Senate.

Both the representation of language groups and the evolution of language usage in Parliament are closely linked to the franchise. The *régime censitaire* of the 1831 constitution gave power almost exclusively to a Francophone bourgeoisie, even in Flanders. "From 1831 to 1893," one Belgian scholar notes, "our Houses of Parliament were just as French-speaking as the various Assemblies that succeeded one another in Paris" (Doms, 1965, 126). As a result of property qualifications that varied between town and country and from province to province, only 46,000 electors, about 1 per cent of the total population, or perhaps 5 per cent of adult males, could vote in the 1830s. In 1848, under the shadow of revolution, the government liberalized the requirements and extended the franchise to some 79,000 electors, a figure that subsequently grew to 97,000 in 1860 and 136,000 in 1892. A major reform in 1893 bringing in adult male suffrage increased the total number of voters to 1,371,000, but this was still tempered by a system of plural voting for property owners, the educated, and heads of families. In 1894 there were an estimated 850,000 electors with one vote, 290,000 with two, and 220,000 with three, so that it can be calculated that the 63 per cent of the voters with one vote had only 41 per cent of the total available votes. The system of plural voting lasted until 1919, when it was replaced by simple adult male suffrage. Meanwhile, proportional representation for elections to both houses had been introduced in 1899, and the 1919 reforms extended it by providing for *apparentement*, the pooling of the unused votes by provinces, so that the distribution of seats became closer to, though still not identical with, the distribution of valid votes cast (Gilissen, 1958; Hill, 1974, 52-55).

Since the 1921 constitutional reforms the Belgian Senate has had four categories of members, those elected directly, those elected by provincial councils (added in 1893), those elected by cooption by the Senate itself (added in 1921), and princes in line for the throne. The largest group are those elected directly, by proportional representation, on the same franchise as that for the lower house. Provincial councils elect one senator for every 200,000 inhabitants, with a minimum, however, of three for every province. These two groups in turn elect a third group, a device that enables each party to adjust the claims of discontented wings or factions after the normal elections. Thus after the 1981 election the Senate had 182 members, 106 by direct election (half the number of seats in the lower house), 50 elected by provincial councils, 25 by cooption (half the number of provincially elected senators), and 1 nonelected senator by right (Prince Albert, brother of the King). This triple electoral process has very intricate political and parliamentary consequences, as may be seen in several detailed electoral studies produced by CRISP (1968, nos. 409-10; 1972, nos. 557-58; 1974, nos. 650-51; 1979, nos. 830, 833, 842, 852; 1982, nos. 969-70). After the 1981 parliamentary election these categories continued but only directly elected senators could serve simultaneously on the community or regional councils of their respective language groups. For the longer run it is envisaged that the Senate will be reformed so as to reflect more directly its emerging role as the sole chamber of the communities and regions.

Although both houses are based on election by proportional representation, differences in selection methods and constituencies make for slight variations in party strength from one house to the other. The Senate has also differed from the Chamber of Representatives, however, in having had from the beginning a stiff property qualification for membership. In 1840 the list of those eligible for election to the Senate totalled only 668, and by 1890 the number of eligibles was still only 996 (Reed, 1924, 75). In 1840 61 per cent of senators belonged to the titled nobility (Bartier, 1968, 49), and the list of Senate presidents from 1831 to 1928 shows only one out of fourteen presidents without a title (Luykx, 1969, 560). The reforms of 1893 admitted a new category of senators elected by provincial councils but retained a high property qualification for those directly elected. Eligibility was considerably broadened during the constitutional revisions of 1920-21, but even after these reforms elected senators still had to satisfy one of a specific list of political, administrative, industrial, professional, or property qualifications, a reflection of a sector of opinion that wished the Senate to represent organized interest groups (Gilissen, 1958, 125-26, 139-40; Senelle, 1974, 138-49).

The evolving pattern of representation of languages in Parliament is closely linked with these changes in the franchise and qualifications for membership. Before 1893, all parliamentarians and also the great majority of their constituents had been educated in French at the secondary level. A unilingual speaker of Flemish or Dutch could scarcely have been elected to either house, and even for bilinguals the neglected and unstandardized state of the Flemish dialects posed barriers to their use for legislative purposes. Hence both houses remained resolutely unilingual themselves even while passing the first language laws for the use of Dutch in Flanders in the 1870s and 1880s.

The election of 1894, the first under manhood suffrage, saw the return of nine *flamingant* members who committed themselves to use Dutch in the lower house, not from personal necessity but as a reflection of their responsibility to their working-class constituents. With a few rare exceptions, parliamentary representatives from Flanders remained fluent in French until after the Second World War, by which time the generation educated wholly in Dutch was entering public life and finding it more natural to use Dutch on all public occasions. The veteran Socialist Kamiel Huysmans noted that by 1953 a "good half" of Flemish members spoke a correct Netherlandic, as compared to a mere handful at the time of his entry to the House in 1910 (Bracops, 1960, 32). From the standpoint of linguistic representation, then, one cannot measure the changing proportions of "French-speaking" and "Dutch-speaking" members in exact terms.

Historically, the more meaningful distinctions have been between unilingual Francophones, a large group of bilingual Flemings, and a scant handful of unilingual Flemings, and for most members from Flanders the factors determining language usage in Parliament appear to have been relative fluency, individual attitudes, party policy, and public pressure from Flemish nationalist movements. On balance, the decisive factor appears to have been mobilized public opinion in Flanders, and the 1919 Chamber, the first to be elected without plural voting, saw 82 out of 186 members take the oath in Dutch (Larochette, 1947, 456). By 1946, of all the members returned from Flemish districts, only four members from East and West Flanders took the oath in French, and by 1954 all those elected from Flemish districts took the member's oath in Dutch (*Annales parlementaires*, 1946, March 8, 4-12; 1954, April 27, 5-13).

From the standpoint of representation by regions, exact comparisons are easier. Here the problem has been a steadily widening gap between Flanders and Wallonie since 1900 as a result of the demographic and economic decline of Wallonie and the rather sporadic adjustments of seats to reflect changes in population. After an adjustment in 1949, the redistribution issue reached a stalemate again in the 1950s and was only resolved in 1965 when its solution was linked to a promise of special minority guarantees for Wallonie in the plans then under consideration for constitutional reform. By Article 49 of the constitution as amended in 1971, future redistributions were to be carried out automatically by royal decree after each census. Table 35 shows the distribution of seats by regions since 1892. The totals shown here for Brussels refer to the electoral *arrondissement* of Brussels, which corresponds to the new administrative *arrondissements* of Brussels-Capital and Halle-Vilvoorde. After the constitutional revisions of 1970 the linguistic distribution of members of both houses became important in a legal sense as the basis for membership in one or the other of the new Cultural Councils, as noted in the previous section. For this purpose all members from Flanders and Wallonie were automatically considered members of the Netherlandic and French Councils respectively, and the only factor subject to electoral variation was the proportion of Francophone and Flemish members returned in Brussels.

One further aspect of representation in recent years has been the question of linguistic balance on parliamentary committees and other similar bodies. For standing committees the basic distribution between parties is made according to a formula based on the D'Hondt system of proportional representation. Here it is interesting to note that the three traditional parties, in spite of splits, tensions, and "distancing" between the linguistic wings in electoral politics, were still acting as undivided units in terms of the committee formula in the late 1970s and still arranging appropriate Francophone and Flemish representation on parliamentary committees through internal consultation and agreement. The most sensitive and far-reaching examples of linguistic parity are those concerning various special committees and study groups dealing with the *question communautaire* itself and the reform of institutions generally, from the formation of the Centre Harmel in 1948 to the establishment of the Centre d'études pour la réforme de l'Etat in 1983. There is no need to rehearse examples in detail, but it may be noted that the formula of linguistic parity is often complicated by the need to balance pressing claims of the political parties involved, the three regions, and both houses of the legislature. The result is a tendency towards very large committees on issues of this kind in order to give at least one voice to each of the combinations of interests in question.

Table 35

Belgium: Distribution of seats by regions, Chamber of Representatives, since 1892 (percentages)

| | Total seats | | | | Brussels (electoral |
Year	N	%	Flanders	Wallonie	arrondissement)
1892	152	100	47.4	40.8	11.8
1902	166	100	47.0	40.4	12.6
1912	186	100	47.3	38.7	14.0
1925[a]	187	100	47.1	39.0	13.9
1936	202	100	47.5	37.6	14.9
1949	212	100	49.1	35.8	15.1
1965	212	100	50.5	34.0	15.6
1974	212	100	50.9	33.0	16.0
1984	212	100	51.9	32.5	15.6

[a] One seat added in Liège for territory annexed from Germany in 1920.

Sources: Calculated from De Smet et al., 1958, annex, 14-15; CRISP, 1971, no. 545; 1977, no. 763; *Annuaire de statistiques régionales*, 1976, 149; *Moniteur belge*, 1984, 3441; and unpublished data.

The evolution of language status and usage in the two houses has been traced in masterful fashion by Philippe Doms (1965), and our brief summary here will be drawn mainly from this source. Until the 1893 suffrage reform, French was the sole official language of documents and the only working language of Parliament, despite the preparation of Flemish and German translations for local use. The only exceptions in this period were symbolic rather than substantive. The member's oath was taken in Netherlandic for the first time in 1863, and this practice was regularized by a law of 1894 (*Règlement*, 1975, 118).

The 1894 elections marked an important turning point, and the handful of *flamingant* members lost no time in asking for bilingual stenographers to enable more generalized use of Dutch. Walloon members reacted strongly, seeking to restrict the use of Dutch to unilingual Flemings, and threatening to revert to Walloon dialects if bilingual Flemings spoke in Dutch. The 1894-95 session was a tumultuous one. Attempts to use Dutch met with systematic ridicule, interruption, and general disorder, and the press of both language groups became similarly inflamed. The most important language issue in this parliament was the struggle for the De Vriendt-Coremans bill to provide legal equality for French and Dutch, a bill that passed easily in the Chamber in 1896 but was totally emasculated by the more aristocratically based Senate. The Chamber refused the modifications, and after another year of public controversy and renewed parliamentary debate the original text was passed by both houses in the spring of 1898. By December of the same year its principles were incorporated in the rules of both houses, and gradually all current parliamentary documents began to be translated into Dutch. Formal equality, however, had little immediate impact on language usage. Members who spoke in Dutch continued to be met with inattention, noisy conversation, or departures from the Chamber, especially if they were bilingual, and the majority of Flemish members continued to use French. The Senate proved even more impenetrable, and only in April 1913 did a unilingual senator from Flanders venture to address the upper house, for the first time, in Dutch (Doms, 1965, 127-35).

The period following the First World War was marked by universal equal manhood suffrage in 1919, the first appearance of a Flemish nationalist party in the Chamber, and reform of the Senate in 1921. The Flemish nationalists quickly made their presence felt by protesting delays in translation of documents, the poor quality of translations, unilingual French declarations of governmental policy, and other linguistic deficiencies in parliamentary practice. As Dutch usage increased, Walloon members clamored more and more insistently for translation of every word spoken in Dutch. The atmosphere became even more tempestuous in the mid-1930s, when every minor lapse became an incident, and ministers were shouted down by one side or the other no matter which language they spoke. At this point it was proposed that the Chamber install simultaneous translation, already in use at the League of Nations, and this was done for the session of 1936-37, with almost immediate improvement in the parliamentary atmosphere. The Senate during this period continued to function predominantly in French, despite the appearance of a few Flemish nationalists, but in 1936 the upper house also installed simultaneous translation, and this led to a sharp increase in the use of Dutch (Doms, 1965, 136-38).

The period since 1945 has been relatively peaceful. Equal status of French and Dutch in Parliament has been fully recognized in a formal sense, and simultaneous translation has reduced practical difficulties to a minimum. The evolution of parliamentary usage of Dutch from occasional speeches in 1900 to normal daily practice in the 1960s is indicated in Table 36, which among other things shows the lag between the Chamber and the Senate. This table also shows that the use of Dutch in the lower house in 1960 was still slightly below the level that might have been expected from Flemish representation, that is, about 55 per cent (Table 35). While this might be due to lower participation of Flemish members in debates, it seems also to stem from a factor of asymmetry pointed out by Doms: that even in the 1960s French was still being used significantly by members from Flanders, while Walloon parliamentarians virtually never spoke in Dutch (1965, 139). One study of private member bills (propositions de loi) for two legislative periods from 1961 to 1968 found that 44 per cent were drawn up in Dutch, 54 per cent in French, and the rest without priority as to languages. However, in the second of these periods (1965-68) the numbers presented in Dutch and in French were virtually equal owing to a preponderance of motions in Dutch in the Senate (CRISP, 1974, no. 658: 18-19).

Table 36

Belgium: Percentage of parliamentary speeches given in Dutch, selected sessions, 1900-60

| Session | Chamber | | Senate | |
	Total	Percentage in Dutch	Total	Percentage in Dutch
1899-1900	652	2.5	n.a.	0
1909-10	728	10.2	n.a.	0
1919-20	525	31.4	n.a.	0
1929-30	1,398	22.0	719	11.7
1939-40	506	47.6	499	41.9
1949-50	324	33.6	264	31.1
1959-60	1,114	47.6	n.a.	41.6

Source: Doms, 1968.

The general practice through the 1970s, as revealed by interviews, was for both Francophone and Flemish members to speak their own language in Parliament and in committees. There were certain recognized exceptions. Party leaders of the mixed-language parties might speak in both languages to emphasize this fact, and some but not all ministers replied to questions in the language in which the question was asked. On occasion a speaker would emphasize a point directed to members of the other language group by switching to their language. The unilingual regional parties were generally the most consistent on language usage, and Volksunie members in particular were expected to use only Dutch in public. In private contacts there was more give and take in both directions,

though always in the context of differences in second-language competence between Walloons and Flemings. Unlike the Swiss case, where
Francophones and Italophones of all parties sit in a bloc on the left of the
lower house (see Volume 1, 129), seating arrangements in the Belgian
Parliament do not primarily reflect the linguistic division. In the later 1970s
each of the ideological families occupied its appropriate place from left to
right around the hemicycle, and within the three traditional-party groupings Socialists and Liberals were still linguistically intermingled while
Francophone and Flemish Social Christians were tending to sit as separate
groups. By 1984 members of the traditional parties were sitting as six
distinct groups.

Simultaneous interpretation is available in both houses and in all
parliamentary committees, though it is used by a handful of members only,
and generally on the Francophone side. There is an increasing tendency
towards passive bilingualism in Parliament, in that members use their
mother tongue but comprehend the other official language. On occasion
the ever-present interpreter will stop speaking if no one is listening to his or
her rendition. On the other hand, Walloon members on occasion call a halt
to committee proceedings if an interpreter is not present. A translation
service was established after the passage of the equality law of 1898, and all
parliamentary documents are translated except the stenographic record of
debates. Down to the 1930s, legislation was conceived and drafted in
French, then translated into Dutch. Since 1945 drafting has been done
increasingly in either language, reflecting the changing language patterns
of the public service. Draft bills are translated into the second language
before they leave the minister's office. Parliamentary staff are not part of the
public service, and they have their own distinct language requirements,
with examinations organized separately. Senior officials of Parliament are
required to have a knowledge in depth (*connaissance approfondie*) of both
official languages, and for lower levels there are compulsory language
courses to prepare junior staff for more senior positions.

With one exception, the printed documents of Parliament appear in
both languages, but the form varies according to the series. The *Annales
parlementaires/Parlementaire handelingen*, the official transcript of each
house, records debates only in the original language but headings and
lists of contents are in both languages. An edited and abridged record of
proceedings, the *Compte rendu analytique/Beknopt verslag*, appears in
separate French and Dutch versions. Until 1971 draft bills (*projets de loi* or
wetsontwerpen) and other parliamentary working documents were printed
with two versions in parallel columns on the page, French on the left and
Dutch on the right, and neither was considered to have priority or superior
validity. Since then, Dutch and French have occupied the left hand column
in alternate sessions. The same change took place in 1975 for the official
gazette (*Moniteur belge/Belgisch staatsblad*). By contrast, private member

bills (*propositions de loi* or *wetsvoorstellen*) are printed in parallel columns with the original (French or Dutch) on the left and a translation on the right. Still other documents, including the bound *Recueil des lois, décrets et arrêtés/Verzameling der wetten, decreten en besluiten* and individual statutes reprinted from the *Moniteur*, are printed with French and Dutch texts on facing pages, again with Dutch and French alternating on the left from year to year since 1975.

Although German has no official recognition in the parliamentary process, there is no legal barrier to its use in either house. If it is used, the text appears in the record in German and in French or Dutch translation at the option of the member concerned. In practice, German is virtually never used in either house, even for symbolic purposes, and the few members of German mother tongue—typically one or two members in each house—use French or Dutch in Parliament depending on whom they are addressing. In explanation of this practice one must recall the small size of the German-speaking community, its economic integration in Wallonie, and two wartime occupations that left an atmosphere unreceptive to the use of German in Parliament.

On the other hand, the German-speaking community received more explicit recognition in the constitutional revisions of 1970 (Article 3 *ter*), as did the German linguistic region (Article 3 *bis*). The law of July 1973 establishing the Council of the German Cultural Community provided that any member of either house from the Verviers district of Liège province who takes the constitutional oath in German may attend council meetings ex officio (Senelle, 1978, 232). Therefore, while German seems likely to remain excluded from Parliament as a working language, it has gained greater symbolic recognition as a result of the reform of institutions. The German-speaking community, as Prime Minister Tindemans noted in the mid-1970s, had been transformed from a protected minority into a separate cultural community in its own right (CPCL, 1976, 270), and this new status was enhanced by the institutional reforms of 1983. One harbinger of further symbolic change is found in the government's declaration of intended constitutional revisions prior to the 1978 election, which included Article 140 (on the French and Dutch texts of the constitution) so as to enable adoption of an official version in German. The 1973 legislation on the German Cultural Council also established a small committee of the council to make official translations of laws and regulations into German (Senelle, 1978, 233-34), but little was achieved in this area during the 1970s.

To be complete, this section should also examine and compare attitudinal and behavioral characteristics of Flemish and Francophone parliamentarians, but this approach soon runs into difficulties for lack of data. The Belgian Parliament has been widely studied from many standpoints, and the resulting literature has been systematically listed in an admirable bibliography by Willems (1980), but few of the items published so far are usable for this purpose. Direct comparisons of social backgrounds, career patterns, behavior, attitudes, or other characteristics of Flemish and Francophone members appear not to have been attempted, though limited results may be extracted indirectly from data arranged by parties. The comprehensive analysis of parliamentary membership undertaken by Debuyst (1967) focuses on those elected in 1961, before regional parties became prominent, and touches on Flemish-Francophone comparisons only marginally. A recent study of the legislative activity of senators reports no significant differences between Francophones and Flemings (Hocepied, 1984, 645-55).

More emphasis has been given to cross-national comparisons or to studies of the Belgian system as a whole. Thus Dierickx and Frognier (1980) have examined ideological perceptions of parliamentarians in Belgium, Switzerland, and Italy, but for each country their analysis focuses on the ideological dimensions of the political system as a whole. Dierickx (1978) examines Belgian parliamentarians for accommodative or consociational attitudes, and finds the evidence for such attitudes to be rather weak and inconclusive, even in the case of party leaders. From this he tentatively concludes that Belgian political stability is better explained by the multiple dimensions of ideologies in Parliament and the kind of coalition politics that these engender than by consociational attitudes of parliamentarians.

Another relevant cross-national study is David Rayside's comparison of Flemish and Francophone Social Christian parliamentarians in Belgium with Francophone and Anglophone federal Liberal members in Canada (1976; 1978), which found that the Belgians were far more sharply divided across language lines than the Canadians over a series of language-related issues. The Belgian members also revealed attitudes closer to those of party activists of their respective language groups than did their Canadian counterparts. Among the suggested explanations for these more divergent attitudes in Brussels were: the more even balance between language groups in Belgium; the greater burden of issues that arises under a centralized form of government; less effective control by party leaders; and less personal socialization among Belgian members, most of whom "almost invariably commute to the capital each working day" (Rayside, 1978, 79). The essential difference suggested by this study is that in Canada federal parliamentarians of both language groups hold similar attitudes but this consensus does not extend to party activists on either side, while in Belgium parliamentarians and party activists remain close together but intergroup differences extend directly and without mediation onto the floor of Parliament.

At a more impressionistic level, Francophone parliamentarians in Belgium appear to be more cohesive across party lines, which may simply reflect an awareness of their minority status in Parliament. The three

Francophone parties in the six-party government coalition drew up a joint declaration of objectives prior to the general election of 1978, and the same three parties arrived at another "secret accord" of Francophone solidarity in January 1980 to protect the interests of Brussels Francophones during the negotiations on constitutional reform. A declaration with similar objectives was issued by an interparty group of twenty-nine Brussels parliamentarians—twenty-eight of them Francophones—during the negotiations of 1968 (CRISP, 1969, nos. 444-45; 1979, nos. 847-48; 1980, nos. 874-75). In the Senate a "Francophone language group" was established formally in 1979, with an executive drawn from four Francophone parties, ostensibly to deal with measures requiring passage by special majorities or those threatening the rights of the Francophone community and calling for use of "alarm-bell" procedures for minority protection (*Soir*, 1979, June 9). While these developments are amply documented, the attitudinal dimensions underlying them do not seem to have been studied systematically.

The "alarm-bell" procedures themselves deserve special mention as a form of institutionalized minority protection. As a linguistic protection they were enacted in the 1970 constitutional amendments primarily to protect the Francophone minority in Parliament (Article 38 *bis*) and the Flemish minority in the Brussels Agglomeration Council (Article 108 *ter*, section 3). In both cases a motion of concern, signed by three quarters of the members of either linguistic group and introduced before the final vote on any nonbudgetary legislative measure, interrupts the proceedings and returns the measure to the executive level—which is composed on a parity basis in both cases—for reconsideration. The executive then reports back, with its recommendations, within thirty days. Similar but not identical "alarm-bell" procedures were then developed to protect ideological minorities against discrimination in the two main cultural councils and their successors, the community councils, but here the final decision was left to Parliament (Senelle, 1980, 178-79). The value of these guarantees so far has been more as a deterrent than as a weapon actually used. Up to 1984 the procedure had never been used between linguistic communities in Parliament and there has been an obvious reluctance to resort to it, [1] though it has been invoked a few times in the councils to protect ideological minorities.

The central Parliament is not the only legislative body in Belgium. One may also count in this category the nine provincial councils and the three community and regional councils created by the institutional reforms of 1980. Eleven of these twelve councils operate unilingually, five in Dutch

---

[1] It was invoked for the first time by the Francophone parties in Parliament, against a relatively modest project to subsidize a school of commerce in Limburg, on July 4, 1985. The government, overtaken a few days later by a second, more serious ministerial crisis, quietly withdrew the contested measure within the prescribed thirty-day period (*Soir*, 1985, July 6-7).

and six in French, but the Provincial Council of Brabant is an interesting exception. Consisting of ninety members elected at the same time as the central Parliament, it was composed in 1970 of fifty-two Francophones and thirty-eight Dutch speakers. By 1979 this proportion had changed to forty-nine Francophones and forty-one Dutch speakers, representing a partial correction of Francophone overrepresentation in relation to a provincial population estimated to be about 55 per cent Francophone (CRISP, 1970, no. 473: 2-7; 1979, no. 830: 5-9). Its executive, a body of six members in addition to the provincial governor, comprised three Francophones and three Dutch speakers, and also represented a coalition of six different political parties. The Brabant Provincial Council has long had simultaneous translation in its sessions and bilingual working documents, but its committees operate without interpretation with a little explanatory help as necessary from committee chairmen or secretaries.

The point to note is that the provincial institutions of Brabant, although situated geographically precisely at the storm centre of intergroup conflict, have operated peacefully and without significant language friction throughout a period notable for intense language conflict at national level. In particular, the six-party executive, a classic "tripartite" coalition with each of the traditional parties now split in two, has held firm in the early 1980s against attempts by the FDF in opposition to enlarge Brussels urban interests and Francophone rights in the periphery. This relative stability and tranquillity can probably be traced to a combination of several factors, including smaller institutions with more opportunities for cross-linguistic contact, an active concern to maintain the linguistic balance, moderation and flexibility at the administrative level, a modest budget, a relatively uncontroversial list of legislative responsibilities, and perhaps also a perception of common economic interests in maintaining an undivided province. Notwithstanding this record, however, most proposals for institutional reform have envisaged a division of Brabant province as well as a diminution or even a phasing out of provincial powers generally.

D   The Executive

As in other areas of Belgian life, the Flemish Movement made its presence felt even at the central decision-making level, the Cabinet. One full-length doctoral study of the postwar Belgian political elite from 1944 to 1970 reports that 40 per cent of all ministers appointed in this period were primarily Dutch-speaking, compared to 27 per cent for the period from 1918 to 1944. When the postwar figures were weighted according to duration of service, the Dutch-speaking proportion rose to 47 per cent, and within the postwar period itself there is a clear progression of Flemish ministers from 40 per cent or less in the several short-lived postwar cabinets to about 55 per cent during the 1960s. Among other changes, the representation of Brussels in the postwar period has tended to diminish slightly in favor of both Flanders and Wallonie, and in the 1960s this representation was also more balanced linguistically (Hodges, 1972, 175-80, 268-70, 276-77). The German-speaking community has apparently never been represented at Cabinet level, though one German-speaking member served briefly as a secretary of state, or junior minister, in 1973.

Behind this statistical evidence of increasing Flemish influence one can also trace the emergence of certain norms of representation in the Cabinet. As early as 1840 there was a tendency to representation of the more important provinces. In the twentieth century and especially after 1919 this regional demand became increasingly a direct linguistic-cultural rivalry between Flemings and Francophones. After the Second World War the convention of linguistic equilibrium grew strong enough that from 1950 to 1970 the maximum variation between the two groups was two ministers (Boeynaems, 1967, 480, 506; CRISP, 1968, nos. 414-15: 37). In 1970 the principle of parity in the Cabinet was entrenched in the constitution as one of the minority guarantees designed to protect the Francophone community after redistribution had given Flanders an absolute majority of parliamentary seats. The text of this amendment provided that "with the possible exception of the Prime Minister, the Cabinet (*Conseil des Ministres*) will have as many French-speaking as Dutch-speaking ministers" (Article 86 *bis*). It did not refer to secretaries of state, who hold ministerial rank but do not sit in the Cabinet, nor to the possibility of a German-speaking Cabinet minister, who would presumably be outside the formula.

The implementation of the new Article 86 *bis* begins properly with the formation of the Eyskens-Cools cabinet of 1972. Since then Gaston Eyskens, Tindemans, Martens, and Mark Eyskens—all Flemish prime ministers—have been left outside the parity formula, whereas the two short-lived ministries formed by the Walloon Socialist Leburton in 1973, and also the caretaker administration of 1978 headed by the Brusseler Paul Vanden Boeynants of the Francophone wing of the Catholic party (PSC), have all counted the prime minister *within* the parity formula (CRISP, 1974, no. 648; 1980, no. 895: 5). Counting changes in coalition partners, these cases represent fifteen different governments in a decade, and from these precedents one can see practice hardening into a clear convention that Flemish prime ministers remain outside the parity formula while a Francophone prime minister will find it difficult to do so.

Apart from the prime minister, the requirements of parity are rigorous, and they surface primarily as a consequence of resignations. When a Rassemblement Wallon minister changed parties and resigned in December 1976, the ministry was immediately recast with the same linguistic proportions. When the Rassemblement Wallon ministers were asked to resign on March 4, 1977, the prime minister requested two Dutch-speaking colleagues not to attend that day's Cabinet meeting so as to preserve the linguistic balance. Two days later, two Francophones from other parties were appointed to restore parity. The problem arose again when FDF ministers were dismissed on January 16, 1980. This time the government followed a ruling of the Conseil d'Etat that it could legally meet without balanced representation but announced that for political reasons it would not deliberate on sensitive political questions or answer to Parliament on such matters in the interval. Parity was restored eight days later by the formation of a new government (CRISP, 1977, no. 754: 13-16; 1980, nos. 874-75: 44-53).

Although linguistic balance is prescribed by the constitution, it is of course not the only factor that must be considered in cabinet formation. Luc Rowies has made interesting estimates of the representation of other major societal cleavages in the governments of this period, on the basis of which it can be calculated that the proportion of practising Catholics has ranged between 44 and 72 per cent, while the proportion of leftists or *progressistes* has varied more widely between 24 and 79 per cent, mainly because of the alternation between Socialists and Liberals as coalition partners (CRISP, 1980, no. 895: 33-35). From 1950 to 1984 the Social Christian party was included in every government except the Liberal-Socialist coalition of Van Acker from 1954 to 1958 and claimed the prime ministership for thirty out of thirty-five years. Since 1968, when the party first faced a significant "distancing" of its Flemish (CVP) and Francophone (PSC) wings, the prime minister has come from CVP ranks for fourteen out of sixteen years.

The sharpening of linguistic conflict over the past two decades has had other consequences for ministerial organization. Because of their responsibilities for the application of the language laws or for regional development, certain portfolios assumed a critical importance for both language groups in the 1960s, among them the Ministry of the Interior, of Economic Affairs, of Public Works, and of National Education. As frictions increased solutions were devised through various methods of twinning the portfolios concerned. Thus in 1961 the Ministry of National Education, which was the object of both linguistic and ideological rivalries simultaneously, was entrusted jointly to a Francophone Socialist minister and a Flemish Catholic deputy minister by an interparty agreement. In 1965 no fewer than four ministers or secretaries of state were named for this department, two Socialists for French and Dutch Education, two Christian Socials for French and Dutch Culture. In 1968 planning for constitutional reform was entrusted jointly to Flemish and Walloon ministers of community relations, who then found it logical to specialize on the cultural autonomy aspects and economic regionalization aspects respectively. By 1972, in addition to four separate cabinet ministers for French and Dutch education and French and Dutch culture, there were Flemish and Walloon secretaries of state for housing and regional planning to assist the minister of public works, and also Flemish and Walloon secretaries of state for regional economy to assist the minister of economic affairs. By 1973, a higher priority for economic regionalization led to the appointment of *three* separate ministers of regional affairs, for Flanders, Wallonie, and Brussels respectively. In June 1974, increasing pressures for regionalization and the admission of a regional party into the government led to the appointment of a Fleming and a Walloon to two newly established posts of ministers of institutional reform (Boeynaems, 1967, 480-81, 502-503; CRISP, 1974, no. 648; De Croo, 1965, 98-99).

Since 1960 the Belgian executive has also undergone significant changes in size and organization that may be attributed partly to linguistic conflict and partly to other influences. The first governments of Leopold I in the 1830s had five or six ministers. Post-1944 governments down to 1960 never exceeded twenty members, with an average of only sixteen during the 1950s. The figure rose to twenty-five in 1960 (including for the first time four junior ministers, or secretaries of state), and then climbed, with occasional cutbacks, to twenty-nine in 1968 and to an all-time high of thirty-six in the tripartite Leburton ministry of January 1973. The unweighted average for the ten ministries from 1960 to 1974 was twenty-seven members.

Much of this increase is accounted for by the secretaries of state, who do not sit in meetings of Cabinet and who are attached to a specific minister or ministers. Their legal status was regularized in the constitutional reforms of 1970 (Article 91 *bis*) and their powers defined in an *arrêté* of March 1972. Politically speaking, they appear to have eased the problems of cabinet formation, in a period when complex new pressures have had to be accommodated, by providing new channels for the representation of interests. Since they do not count technically as members of Cabinet, they provide a way to compensate the Flemish parliamentary majority for strict Flemish-Walloon parity in Cabinet. The most common pattern in the 1970s was to have a slight preponderance at this level of Flemings over Francophones—usually two—but Prime Minister Martens departed from this formula in 1979 by appointing four from each group (Waleffe, 1968, 99-104; Senelle, 1978, 176-77; CRISP, 1972, no. 578; 1974, no. 648; 1980, no. 895: 5). Insofar as the inflated size of the ministry in the 1970s was partly attributable to the development of regional institutions, some of the recent growth may prove reversible after the completion of regionalization and the separation of all regional executives.

Concerning language usage in Cabinet meetings, little can be documented with precision. Still, it is reliably reported from interviews and other sources (du Roy, 1968, 74) that every Belgian ministry conducted its meetings in French down to the late 1950s. In May 1961 simultaneous interpretation was introduced at the instigation of Prime Minister Lefèvre, and its use has since become standard in the Cabinet and its committees. In the late 1970s the listening devices were being used by about half of the

Francophone members but by none of the Flemings. The record of Cabinet proceedings, which is prepared in a few copies only and communicated to the King and the prime minister but to other ministers only as far as it concerns them individually, is kept in French or Dutch according to the language of the secretary currently responsible for its preparation. It is never made public.

Notwithstanding the interpretation facilities, a unilingual prime minister in Belgium labors under an increasingly serious handicap. Between 1944 and 1952, when Cabinet business was conducted exclusively in French, four out of seven prime ministers were unilingual Francophones. Since the ministry of Joseph Pholien (1950-52), however, bilingualism has tended increasingly to become the norm for the post, though not in any sense a formal requirement. Of the nine prime ministers who have served from 1952 to 1980, five were Flemings with at least a workable level of bilingualism, one (Lefèvre) was a bilingual Francophone from Flanders, and one (Vanden Boeynants) was a bilingual Brusseler of Flemish background. The other two (Harmel and Leburton) were native Francophones with an imperfect knowledge of Dutch. Harmel made great efforts to become bilingual and succeeded acceptably, but Leburton's inability to speak Dutch, as Zolberg notes (1977, 134), was used as a bargaining counter against him, among other things to obtain the appointment of two Flemish deputy prime ministers in his tripartite ministry of 1973. The evolution of Belgian politics strongly suggests that the Flemings, backed by greater linguistic resources and a larger political base, have a large and growing advantage in the contest for the prime ministership. In the thirty-two years from 1952 to 1984, Harmel and Leburton, the only "pure" Walloon incumbents, occupied the office for just under two years, in 1965-66 and 1973-74.

One final consideration is to recall that the Belgian executive includes the monarchy. Although the constitution holds that the King's actions are the responsibility of his ministers, this relationship was less than clear in the early years of Belgian independence, and even Leopold III held views that were difficult to reconcile completely with parliamentary democracy. Moreover, the frequency of ministerial crises has given the Belgian monarch a degree of initiative and discretion not usually found in parliamentary systems. Although the post-1960 linguistic tensions produced prolonged crises of 65 days in 1965, 132 days in 1968, and 99 days in 1979, political deadlocks during the formation of a ministry are not a new phenomenon. Similar crises over other issues have occurred before, including gaps of 45 days in 1949, 75 days in 1925, and 129 days in 1864 (Urbain, 1958, 70; Waleffe, 1971, 159-65; CRISP, 1979, nos. 847-50). As a result of these recurring difficulties the Belgian political system has evolved well-defined methods of reducing the political exposure of the monarch during crises in cabinet formation by delegating the preliminary tasks of investigation and negotiation with party leaders to an *informateur* and a *formateur* respectively, neither of whom will necessarily be the next prime minister.

In linguistic matters, the monarch has often set an example for the rest of Belgian society, and on occasion that example has proved more progressive than the attitudes of the upper echelons of Belgian society. Thus Leopold II gave the first royal speech in Dutch at the Royal Flemish Theatre on October 13, 1887, before Dutch was used in either house of Parliament, and one Flemish author, writing shortly after the event, testifies to the wave of excitement and joy that ran through the Flemish provinces after this event: *de Koning die Vlaamsch leert, de Koning die Vlaamsch spreekt!* (Prayon-van Zuylen, 1892, 439-43). In 1917, when the nationalist Front Movement had been banned by the army authorities and had appealed directly to the throne for a recognition of Flemish rights, King Albert contacted the leadership indirectly and offered encouragement. His sympathy was expressed more openly in a throne speech to Parliament in November 1918 that promised linguistic equality (Ruys, 1973, 79, 82-83). In wider perspective the Flemish masses, strongly royalist by temperament, have seen the monarchy as a linguistic ally against the Francophone bourgeoisie and have identified with the monarchy even when alienated from the government and administration.

E   The Public Service

Since no other aspect of language practice is more minutely regulated by legislation and executive decrees than language use in administration, it is appropriate to outline these legislative norms carefully before examining the public service in its daily practice. As embodied in their latest form in the law of August 2, 1963, and its subsequent decrees of execution, these norms or principles are wide-ranging in their application. The law extends to the services of the central government, the provinces, and the communes, and to both centralized and decentralized services. It applies to the administrative services and personnel of certain other bodies, for example, judicial bodies or school authorities, and to the electoral process. It specifies in detail differing rules for different regions, and for various groups of communes and special situations. Finally, it sets certain requirements for firms and enterprises in the private sector, which will be discussed in a later section of this chapter (below, 263-64).

Historically, language use in the administration evolved in five stages. For almost half a century after independence, in the absence of specific legislation, French was the sole official language, even in Flanders, and any use of Flemish by officials was unofficial and unregulated. The first law on administrative language in 1878 obliged central government officials in the

Flemish provinces and in Flemish Brabant to use Flemish in communicating with individuals and communes, unless the latter preferred to use French. Public notices were to be in Flemish or in both languages, but the internal language remained French. The legislation of 1921 went further, recognizing Dutch as the official language of the Flemish region and extending the obligation to use Dutch to the provincial and communal levels while leaving optional the simultaneous use of French in public notices. More important, this law also called for officials of the central government, the Brabant provincial administration, and communes of the Brussels area to demonstrate an elementary knowledge of the second official language, a requirement that immediately aroused Walloon sensitivities (Rüling, 1939, 10, 14-15; Van der Molen, 1951; Clough, 1930, 232-34). Moreover, officialdom during the first century of independence remained overwhelmingly Francophone. Out of 380 officials in the central administration in 1831, Lamberty (1933, 72) finds only 22 of Flemish origin. Two generations later, Prayon-van Zuylen cites a contemporary newspaper estimate for the central ministries of 80 per cent Walloons and Luxemburgers, 14 per cent "mostly francicized" Brusselers, and 6 per cent Flemings (1892, 459).

The law of 1932 on language usage in the administration is sometimes described as the major watershed in Belgian language policy (Molitor, 1974, 31), but in some basic respects it merely continued and strengthened the major tendencies of the 1921 legislation: administrative unilingualism in Flanders and Wallonie; compulsory bilingualism of services in Brussels, in Brabant, and in communes with official-language minorities of 30 per cent or more. Where it did break new ground was in reducing the requirements of personal bilingualism for officials in central departments and in reorganizing their work according to linguistic criteria. The essential features were spelled out in an important decree of execution dated January 6, 1933, which sketched out a blueprint for a central public service divided wherever possible into French and Flemish sections, with separate linguistic registers for existing and future personnel in each department and recruitment adjusted to maintain a "just equilibrium" between language groups. Unilingualism would be the rule, and matters would be handled in the language in which they originated, without translation. Even senior administrators could remain unilingual, in which case they would have a bilingual associate from the other language group to facilitate coordination between linguistic sections (Rüling, 1939, 104-11, 120-22; *Emploi des langues*, 1959, 22-33; Van der Molen, 1959).

Virtually all of the main features of the 1932 legislation were to be reflected in the 1963 law and its decrees of implementation, but this later measure sought to apply the principles more stringently, to close loopholes, to strengthen the mechanisms for application and surveillance, and to remedy the absence of sanctions in the earlier law. It was also far longer and more complex. While the 1932 law occupies six printed pages of text in each language, the 1963 law in coordinated form requires forty, plus thirty-four more for the ten decrees of execution of November 1966. All references in this section will be to this coordinated version (*Emploi des langues*, 1966a), which rearranged the rather disorganized text of 1963 and incorporated provisions still in force from earlier legislation.

After opening with sections that define the areas of application, the four language regions, and the four categories of protected linguistic minorities, the 1963 law continues with a long chapter on the provision of services at the local level by all levels of government (Articles 9 to 31). As a useful synoptic table drawn up by Maurice Henrard makes clear (1964, 40-41), these articles deal with six different categories of commune (unilingual regions, Brussels-Capital, Brussels periphery, language frontier areas, German areas, and the Malmédy communes), and with a dozen different sectors of language usage (internal language, relations with higher levels, with other services in the same region, in another region, in Brussels, with the public as individuals, public notices and forms, decisions in individual cases, certificates, public registers, and language requirements for officials both with and without public contact). The overall result of these combinations is a complex table with some seventy-two different cells, but we may summarize the major tendencies by saying that most internal language usage is in the language of the region if a unilingual region is involved, and most communication with the public in communes without minority protections is also in the language of the region. Under certain conditions, however, decisions concerning individual cases and formal documents or certificates may be translated without charge into French, Dutch, or German for those who can establish the need for a translation. In Brussels-Capital and the peripheral communes, relations with private individuals are in French or Dutch at the option of the latter. Finally, the language requirement for public servants is generally the language of the region only, but in Brussels-Capital and for those in public contact in communes with protected minorities a knowledge of the appropriate second language is indicated.

A similar set of provisions is developed for regional services (Articles 32 to 38), which are defined as services extending to more than one commune but not the country as a whole, such as those offered at the level of provinces or *arrondissements*. Here the possible combinations of communes and language regimes are truly bewildering, but the basic principles appear to be that external language usage is governed by the linguistic status of the commune concerned, and the internal language of the service itself by the location of the office. Thus regional services operating within a single language region use the language of that region as internal language and deal with the public as the respective communal governments would. Regional services involving both the French and Dutch regions and/or Brussels-Capital follow the rules of local services in Brussels-Capital. The really complicated cases are left for subsequent regulation by executive decree (Henrard, 1964, 47-51; Herremans, 1965, 103-104).

The language usage of services extending across the entire country is specified in equivalent detail (Articles 39 to 47). To attempt a bare summary once again, central offices are to deal with other levels of service in the language (or languages) of the region concerned. They are also to deal with enterprises, and with the public indirectly through regional offices, in the language of the region. When they deal with the public *directly,* public notices are to be in French and Dutch, and relations with individuals as well as certificates and documents for individuals may be in French, Dutch, or German at the option of the latter.

The staffing of central departments is to follow the principle of separate French and Dutch linguistic registers, and each department or service is to have separate linguistic sections wherever the nature of the work warrants it. Unlike the 1932 legislation, however, the 1963 law visualizes *three* linguistic cadres of senior officials, one French-speaking, another Dutch-speaking of equal size, and a third bilingual group drawn in equal numbers from the other two and comprising 20 per cent of those with the rank of director or above, a group estimated to number about 1,200 at the time (Herremans, 1965, 109). All officials below this level are to be placed on the French or the Dutch register respectively. The language register of employees is determined by the language of their recruitment examination or of their educational diplomas, and once settled transfers from one register to the other are prohibited. Those educated abroad or in the German region are allotted to the French or Dutch register by passing a special examination in the language concerned. In spite of the plan for a bilingual cadre of top officials, the 1963 law continued the earlier practice of providing a bilingual associate for unilingual senior administrators, but only for the official responsible for overseeing the unity of administrative regulations in each agency or division (Article 43; *Emploi des langues,* 1966b, 12-17).

The concept of services extended on a countrywide basis applies not only to central administrative departments and agencies but to other establishments serving the public at large, including about seventy located outside the Brussels area in unilingual regions. One of the most sensitive examples of these is the Brussels airport at Zaventem, in Flemish territory just outside the boundaries of Brussels-Capital. Others include state prisons, hospitals, research stations, scientific laboratories, railway workshops, and similar facilities (Herremans, 1965, 111-14). For these establishments most of the same rules of language usage are to apply, but in unilingual regions all staff are to have an elementary knowledge of the language of the region if they are in contact with the local work force or the public (Article 46). A third category of "countrywide" services is those offered outside Belgium, most notably diplomatic and consular functions. Here again public notices are to be prepared in French, Dutch, and "if the occasion demands" in German also, while correspondence and documents are at the option of the citizen. All posts abroad are to be divided between the French and Dutch registers on a strict parity basis at all levels, and in contrast with services in Belgium all holders of these posts are to demonstrate by examination an appropriate knowledge of the other official language (Article 47).

Various miscellaneous provisions of the law are a testimony to its thoroughness. Article 48 extends the law to international air transport, where the principal firm involved, Sabena, is technically a private enterprise in which the Belgian state is the majority shareholder. Other provisions concern electoral officers, private consultants engaged by government, and special facilities for Francophone staff and students at the University of Louvain (Articles 49 to 51). The final sections of the coordinated law, together with several decrees of execution of 1966, provide for protection of the employment rights of incumbent public servants at various levels who would have been eligible for promotions but for the application of various provisions of the law. These benefits, added at the insistence of the Francophone sector, in most cases take the form of supernumerary promotions or transfers to equivalent posts for which they are linguistically qualified (Articles 66 to 68; *Emploi des langues*, 1966b, 18-43).

The great problem of the 1932 legislation, and indeed of all earlier language laws on administrative matters, was an absence of effective sanctions and enforcement. The 1963 law provides two kinds of sanctions. First, officials who contravene the act are subject to disciplinary measures, and if their immediate superiors fail to impose a suitable penalty, as might well happen in communes where the legislation is widely disapproved, the governors of provinces and the central government are authorized to intervene directly. Second, administrative acts that are linguistically defective may be legally nullified by a higher level of government, or by the courts, or by the Conseil d'Etat, in which case they must be replaced in correct form by the authority that originally enacted them (Articles 57, 58).

The primary responsibility for general surveillance is entrusted to a Commission permanente de contrôle linguistique (CPCL), a body of eleven members (five Francophones, five Flemings, one German speaker) that replaced a rather ineffective body of the same name but lesser powers established under the 1932 act (Herremans, 1965, 311). The new CPCL was given broad investigative and advisory powers, including a right to be consulted by ministers on any matter of general application of the 1963 legislation. It can initiate nullity proceedings before the appropriate authority for any administrative act that is linguistically defective, and it must submit a detailed annual report on its activities to the government and to Parliament. If the CPCL fails to pronounce on a complaint within a specified period, the matter reverts to the minister of the interior for decision (Articles 60 to 62; Legris, 1965). Additional, geographically restricted surveillance powers are given to the vice-governor of Brabant, who oversees application of the legislation in Brussels-Capital and the six peripheral communes, and to two other commissioners given special responsibilities for the Mouscron district and the Voer communes respectively (Articles 63 to 65; CRISP, 1967, no. 374).

It is one thing to describe the legislative norms or models that govern language use in the administration, but considerably more difficult to obtain a balanced view of the situation in practice. For certain aspects information is sketchy and serious research appears to be lacking. One of the sensitive and crucially important questions over a long period has been the representation of the language groups in the departments and "parastatals," or quasi-public agencies, and especially in their upper ranks. On this question the establishment of separate linguistic registers during the 1930s led to some dogged parliamentary questioning in the late 1940s by Gerard Van den Daele, who became the chief spokesman for Flemish grievances in administrative matters (Ruys, 1973, 137; Herremans, 1951, 94-97). The results enable us to document the evolution of Flemish representation in the senior public service from a position of serious imbalance just after 1945 to something approaching equality by the late 1960s. Table 37 shows the linguistic situation in the departments and in the parastatals at certain dates for which data are available. It will be noted that the figures assembled by Van den Daele refer to several of the most senior ranks at a time when the operative formula was a "fair balance" (*juste équilibre*) between language groups with no special reference to rank (*Emploi des langues*, 1959, 10, 24); those of the Verbond van het Vlaams Overheidspersoneel (VVO) refer to the smaller number of posts from director upwards that are explicitly designated in the 1963 legislation for *equal* division between the two linguistic registers (*Emploi des langues*, 1966a, 42). That the parastatals were slightly more balanced than the regular departments in the 1940s is perhaps due to their more recent establishment, in many cases after 1945 (Lorwin, 1962, 19-20). It must be noted that the data in Table 37 are unofficial, based mainly on ministerial replies to parliamentary questions and assembled by Flemish activist sources, but they are comparable with official figures for category 1 personnel in central offices, which indicate a Dutch-speaking proportion of 39 per cent in 1939, the same in 1949, and 43 per cent in 1953 (Brazeau, 1966, Appendix III-A-1-5).

In 1949 and 1950 Van den Daele found a predominance of Francophones at the upper levels of every regular department, though a few parastatals were balanced or even slightly favorable to the Dutch register (1950, 8-25). He also noted that short-term changes from year to year often coincided with a change of minister from one language group to the other.

His figures for 1965 showed eleven departments as predominantly Dutch-speaking and six as predominantly French-speaking (Brazeau, 1966, Appendix III-B-2). By 1968 the more selective VVO data for directors and above show eight departments evenly balanced (apart from odd-numbered totals), eight with a slight to significant preponderance of officials on the French register, and three (Finance, Transport, and Culture) with a slight to significant preponderance of those on the Dutch register. Departments still preponderantly Francophone at the upper levels in 1968 included National Education, Agriculture, Justice, Economic Affairs, and the headquarters section of External Affairs. The better balance in most departments reflected the working of the 1963 law on language usage in administrative matters.

Table 37

Belgium: Higher public servants by language register, selected dates

Year and group	Total		Dutch register	French register
	N	%		
Departments				
1948	2,168	100	37.8	62.2
1950	2,086	100	40.1	59.9
1960	2,502	100	43.2	56.8
1962	2,475	100	46.7	53.3
1965	3,271	100	48.8	51.2
1968 (levels 13-17)	1,210	100	49.5	50.5
Parastatals				
1948-49	1,394	100	42.3	57.7
1950	1,668	100	43.3	56.7

Sources: 1948-50: Van den Daele, 1950, 18, 25; 1960: Van Haegendoren, 1962, 2: 226-27 (citing Van den Daele); 1962, 1965: Brazeau, 1966, Appendix III-B-2 (citing Van den Daele); 1968: VVO, 1967-68, 23.

The Ministry of External Affairs remained a special case. Before the Second World War, Val Lorwin observes (1962, 22), this department, together with the magistracy, had been the most aristocratic sector of the public service. As a result of legal precedents, it considered itself outside the scope of the 1932 language legislation (Herremans, 1965, 115). Entrance examinations were given in French only until 1937, then in both languages, and separate language registers begin from that year. Of 162 entrants by examination from 1937 to 1947, 22 per cent took the Dutch version (Van Bogaert, 1968, 681-82). Van den Daele's figures for senior officials in 1949 show Flemish representation at 16 per cent, the lowest of all the regular departments. At the same time the veteran Foreign Minister

Paul-Henri Spaak, a Francophone reputed to know no Dutch, asked Parliament to consider his department as a special case on the ground that diplomatic matters, as distinct from commercial relations, are normally handled in French and that a firm grasp of French from the time of recruitment is essential to any diplomatic career (Van den Daele, 1950, 13, 119-27). A revealing article documents the situation a decade later on the eve of the new language laws. Not one ambassador was on the Dutch language register, though two out of thirteen officials in the highest category were Flemings on the French register or on special appointment. Only two embassies (The Hague and Bonn) and two commercial offices (The Hague and Washington) were reporting to Brussels in Dutch, and these reports were then summarized in French for higher officials (Grammens, 1961). By this date, however, recruitment into the lower ranks had become more balanced, and by 1962 the language figures showed a proportion of 56 per cent Dutch speakers for *stagiaires* or trainees, 50 per cent for the fifth and sixth classes, 29 per cent for the third and fourth classes, and still only 17 per cent for the two top classes (Van Bogaert, 1968, 682). Balance at the lower levels had done little to change the predominantly Francophone atmosphere at the top.

The situation in External Affairs, long a matter of concern in Flemish circles, gave rise to two special remedial laws in April 1962. The first of these brought the department under the operation of the 1932 legislation and regulated the application of the language registers. The second sought to correct the linguistic imbalance at the top by a special direct recruitment of about fifty Flemish officials to the upper administrative levels, an operation dubbed *parachutage* by its critics. These recruits were to be drawn from the senior levels of other departments, from the magistracy or the Conseil d'Etat, from the universities or upper secondary education, from the former colonial service, or with special Cabinet authorization from other occupations. A further decree of 1965 tied promotions to the language registers, so as to balance numbers at each rank (Herremans, 1965, 115-21; De Groeve et al., 1968ff., 1:91-94). The avowed goal was *taal-evenwicht*, linguistic balance in the fullest sense, both in the department as a whole and for each administrative class.

Thanks to the close surveillance of the department by the Commission permanente de contrôle linguistique (CPCL), the effects of those measures may be traced in detail over the next decade. For posts in the diplomatic service the proportion of officials on the Dutch register rose from levels of 15 per cent in 1951 and 28 per cent in 1961 to 45 per cent in 1971 and 49 per cent in 1973, by which date the department was headed by its first Dutch-speaking minister, Renaat Van Elslande. On the Francophone side there were corresponding costs, in terms of delayed promotions and about fifty early retirements. By 1976 Dutch speakers represented 52 per cent of the diplomatic service and 54 per cent of upper-level staff at headquarters, and the CPCL in its annual reports was urging a careful planning of the intake at recruitment level to preserve an exact 50-50 ratio not only in the formal cadre but in the numbers actually serving in each rank (CPCL, 1974, 19-32; 1978, 93-113; Van Bellinghen, 1978, 693; Wilwerth, 1980, 92-109).

The distribution of junior public service positions—that is, appointments below the level of director—is based on the relative importance of the French and Dutch language regions for the work load of each department. By law, a linguistic ratio must be proposed by the agency itself, approved by the CPCL, and established by royal decree (*Emploi des langues*, 1966a, 42). In practice, the process involves extensive negotiation and consultation with the public sector trade unions and the two major linguistic associations of public servants, the VVO and its Walloon counterpart, the APWFSP. In some agencies this procedure has given rise to acrimonious conflicts extending over several years.

An illustration is the case of the Caisse générale d'épargne et de retraite (CGER), a parastatal concerned with savings, loan, and mortgage operations throughout Belgium, which had some 7,500 employees in 1978. Initially, an internal committee of the agency had arrived in 1971 at a norm of 53.6 per cent for Dutch-speaking employees, but the CPCL proposed raising this to 57.9 per cent. In issuing the formal decree in 1973, the then minister of finance, a Fleming, adjusted this to 56.9 per cent, which was then appealed by the CGER's association of Francophone personnel. In 1975 the Conseil d'Etat nullified the minister's decision for failing to take into account the volume of business generated in Brussels. This action was in turn protested by the CGER's association of Dutch-speaking personnel (*Soir*, 1975, July 20-22). At this point the process had to begin again, and a new proposal, more favorable to the Francophone side, was gradually elaborated through a new internal study group, approved by the minister and by the CPCL. In June 1976 the government adopted the formula of 52.5 per cent Dutch speakers for a three-year period, with the relative volume of business to be reviewed every three years.

The new formula brought only temporary peace. In 1980 the agency's mortgage loan records were reclassified according to the place of domicile, rather than the language, of the client, which led to the transfer of some 50,000 files of clients in the Brussels periphery to the Flemish section. The Francophone employees' association appealed this decision to the Conseil d'Etat, while their Flemish counterpart organization then presented a brief claiming 60 per cent of the activities and staff positions (*Soir*, 1980, July 19, September 26). In 1981 the CGER was reorganized as a public bank and an insurance fund, and in the following summer the Francophone employees launched a month-long strike against Flemish preponderance on the two new boards of directors. The Flemish employees in their turn tried to block a CGER loan to the floundering Walloon steel complex, Cockerill-Sambre (*Soir*, 1981, April 11, June 20-22, 27-29,

July 7, 17, August 14, 18). In such an atmosphere many aspects of daily operations fall under suspicion as part of a wider power struggle.

During the 1970s similar conflicts persisted around a few other agencies, most notably Sabena, the national airline, the Air Transport Administration, the Office of Foreign Commerce, and the Office for Cooperation in Development. One special problem for agencies operating outside Belgium was that an appropriate formula for a division of staff according to the volume of work handled in French or Dutch was seldom obvious and invariably open to argument. Moreover, in the work of these agencies important economic interests were often at stake and settlements were bound to be difficult. Nevertheless, the relatively few cases of prolonged conflict should not obscure the fact that by the late 1970s virtually all ministries and the great majority of employees of public corporations were functioning within legally established linguistic cadres accepted by both groups. A good many of these cadres were divided on a 50-50 ratio or close to it, but in a few cases the proportion ranged up to 75 per cent or even 90 to 100 per cent according to the location of the establishment and the nature of its work (CPCL, 1978, 22-27). These cadres, although legally fixed by royal decree, can be amended as work patterns change provided that the agency can document the need for change before the CPCL.

One noteworthy policy feature of linguistic representation in the Belgian public service is the differential basis for allocating upper-level and lower-level positions. Senior posts, highly visible and politically sensitive, are divided strictly on the basis of parity, though some divergences in practice occasionally arise between an agency's theoretical cadre and its actual personnel in service. The parity principle has the effect of giving the Francophone community a representation in the higher bureaucracy more than proportionate to its numbers. At the lower levels, which are less sensitive and less visible, representation is determined by a negotiated ratio for each agency based on the volume of work handled in each language. Despite the few exceptions that have attracted high-profile press coverage, the result of these two principles has been to depoliticize and to decentralize a highly controversial issue within a political system that is in other respects notable for both centralization and politicization of language issues. Indeed the overall linguistic division of the public service as a whole appears to be neither recorded by any governmental agency nor sought after by any activist group.

While the question of linguistic representation can be traced in some detail, the pattern of actual language usage in the public service is more difficult to document. One can find a few polemics and unsubstantiated generalizations, but serious research appears to be lacking. Molitor (1974, 248-49) emphasizes that the 1932 requirement of direct treatment of files in their original language, together with the 1963 provision for the organization of linguistic sections and divisions wherever conditions so warrant, have resulted in profound changes in the internal structures of departments and agencies, though only one—the Ministry of National Education and Culture—had been completely split prior to the reforms of 1980. In general terms, these changes appear to have reduced the volume of cross-linguistic contact and to have shifted it towards more senior levels of the bureaucracy and to employees in contact with the public in Brussels-Capital and certain other communes. Yet the need for intergroup communication continues, and one development of the late 1960s was an increased interest in developing "passive bilingualism," that is, encouraging employees to speak their own mother tongue but to understand the other language at a receptive level. The concept won support among the elites of both the public and private sectors on account of its symbolic neutrality and its feasibility in terms of linguistic capacity ("Bilinguisme passif," 1967; Laurent, 1969a). In practical terms, communication through passive bilingualism has become more feasible in recent years as a consequence of increasing use of standard Dutch or ABN by younger employees.

While individual cases and files are handled in their original languages, all public notices and public documents in Brussels and in services extending to Belgium as a whole must be published in both languages. Translation therefore remains a major task of the administration, but there is no central agency or office for this purpose. Each department or agency, and each ministerial staff, has a translation section to prepare texts in Dutch or French. In theory at least a similar arrangement applies to German. Each ministerial staff or cabinet has at least one German-speaking official to deal with German-speaking citizens in their own language.

This overview of the implementation of the 1963 legislation on language in administrative matters would be incomplete without some assessment of the part played by the main surveillance agency, the CPCL. In addition to its legal right to be consulted by governmental agencies on all significant linguistic matters—including the establishment of a formal hierarchy of ranks and a linguistic cadre in each agency—the CPCL monitors all public service examinations for proficiency in the second official language, receives complaints from the public about violations of the legislation, pays special attention to agencies, regions, and communes where implementation of the law has proved difficult, and initiates some studies of its own. One major weakness is its dependence on the Ministry of the Interior. At certain points since its inception the presence of an unsympathetic minister has spelled a critical lack of resources, and in 1968-69, under a Walloon minister, all work was suspended for a year and a half owing to the nonrenewal of commissioners' appointments. One can detect in the annual reports and other commission documents a continuing uneasy relationship between the ministry and the CPCL, and a recurrent claim on the part of the latter for greater independence.

An analysis of the first thirteen annual reports shows that the CPCL dealt with some 3,438 matters over the twelve-and-a-half-year period from mid-1964 to the end of 1976, for an average of about 275 cases per year. Of the total some 64 per cent began as complaints and 33 per cent arose as requests for opinions, while the remaining 3 per cent were studies initiated by the commission. In terms of language of origin, 72 per cent originated in Dutch, 26 per cent in French, and 2 per cent in German. Some 70 per cent of these cases went before both sections of the commission sitting in joint session; the remainder went to the Dutch section (24 per cent) or the French section (6 per cent) as affecting one region only. For the next four years, from 1977 to 1980, the number of cases increased slightly to an average of 316 per year and the proportion arising as complaints from the public increased to 83 per cent, but the proportion originating in Dutch and the distribution of cases between sections remained stable (CPCL, 1964-80). For the whole period both the language of origin statistics and the distribution by linguistic sections tend to confirm the view that language grievances still loom larger in the Dutch-speaking region and the Flemish community than they do in Wallonie or among Francophones.

The cases handled by the CPCL have covered a wide range of topics, from pronouncements against ambassadorial nominations that contravened the language law to the most minor administrative details. There were complaints about the absence of bilingual signs and services in the Brussels area, but also numerous complaints about the use of both official languages—or the wrong language—in unilingual regions. As examples, the following practices, all drawn from early annual reports, were found illegal: a bilingual postmark used at Tongeren in Flanders; a sleeve badge marked "Nederlands" to indicate a bilingual policeman in Wallonie; a railway station door in Flanders marked "Entrée—Ingang"; a bilingual telex message sent from Brussels to Wallonie; bilingual notices of general meetings in the *Moniteur* by firms located in Flanders; and a road sign in Wallonie marked "Leuven" (instead of "Louvain"). Several complaints concerned the use of the bilingual sign "Danger de mort—Doodsgevaar" in both unilingual regions, a practice which the CPCL found to be against the linguistic law but possibly sanctioned by conflicting legislation on worker safety. A reading of the CPCL reports suggests that its early work contributed to a climate of extreme pettiness in minor linguistic matters, but in justification the commission itself points out that it is bound by law to pronounce upon any complaint falling within its area of jurisdiction.

Against the rather negative public image of the CPCL—which is more pronounced in Francophone than in Flemish circles—it must be remembered that the legitimacy of the 1963 legislation was not accepted by significant elements of the Francophone population and deliberate non-compliance was widespread, even at the ministerial level. The commission's initial task was to win observance of legislation that had low levels of public support at the time of its passage (see above, Table 29, item 7, 118). Its achievement has been to win at least formal compliance with the 1963 law even from the most recalcitrant departments, agencies, and communal administrations, a task that proved beyond the capacity of its predecessor under the 1932 law. In pursuing this goal the CPCL has developed an immense but rather indigestible body of jurisprudence applying the general principles of the linguistic legislation to the vast variety of public-sector activities.

One factor that helped to foster a better climate of opinion was a new procedural rule, imposed at the time of the reinstatement of the commission in August 1969, that decisions of the two linguistic sections in joint sessions must be based on a majority in each section. When this double majority cannot be found, the president is required to draft a brief note explaining the divergent views of his colleagues (*Emploi des langues*, undated, 132). The rule puts a premium on finding a compromise solution acceptable to both sections, and in practice the proportion of unanimous decisions has been high and increasing. For the six years from 1970 to 1975 some 80 per cent of the matters treated by the combined sections were decided unanimously, 11 per cent by majority vote, and fewer than 9 per cent remained as nondecisions. For the last two of these years 88 per cent were unanimous and only 4 per cent were nondecisions (CPCL, 1970-75).

Other prominent participants in the elaboration of language policy are the respective associations of Flemish and Francophone public servants, the Verbond van het Vlaams Overheidspersoneel (VVO) and the Association du personnel wallon et francophone des services publics (APWFSP). These organizations are quite distinct from the public service trade unions; they remain outside normal collective bargaining but as organized interest groups they defend and promote the linguistic interests of their respective memberships in the ministries, public corporations, and also in lower levels of government. The VVO also works with other Flemish associations for the general advancement of Flemish nationalist causes, while the APWFSP has campaigned unremittingly against some of the basic principles of the language laws themselves, most notably the bilingual cadre at senior levels, bilingual positions to serve the public in Brussels, and compulsory study of the second official language. In general these associations have served as an early warning system for linguistic grievances, and ministers have taken due notice of their admonitions. In the later 1970s, however, their importance seems to have declined as the main issues of public service language policy gradually became settled.

A further question of some interest is the current position of German as an administrative language. In theory, the 1963 legislation is virtually symmetrical in giving residents of the German-language region almost the same theoretical language rights as their far more numerous fellow-citizens in Flanders or Wallonie. Just as for the French and Dutch regions, the 1963 legislation makes provision for German at the level of local services, regional services, central government communication with the local or regional levels or with individuals, and in services offered outside Belgium. There is also provision for individuals to receive certified translations into German of documents in French or Dutch through the Liège provincial governor (Article 13).

In practice, services at the local level in German appear to be available without difficulty in the German-speaking region and in adjacent communes with German minority-language facilities. Complaints sent to the CPCL when residents of the German-speaking region have received documents in French rather than German seem to corroborate the general norm. The proportion of complaints to the CPCL originating in German prior to 1973 was between 1 and 2 per cent, but for 1973 to 1976 this rate rose to almost 4 per cent and for 1977 to 1980 to almost 6 per cent, no doubt reflecting increased awareness of language rights following the establishment in 1973 of the Council of the German Cultural Community. For central services, however, the situation appears less satisfactory. The prevailing impression among German-speaking informants seems to be that to correspond with central offices in German invites delays and misunderstandings due to double translation, and that the use of French or Dutch brings better and faster results. These impressions find empirical support in a recent survey of language needs in the public and private sectors, which indicated high levels of difficulty in providing services in German and also—understandably—little use of the language (CRISP, 1984, nos. 1026-27).

While limits of space preclude discussion of wider public service issues here, three general considerations may be mentioned in passing. First, the milieu of Brussels is almost as strongly Francophone as the milieu of Bern is German-speaking, and some of the social consequences of this will be explored more fully in Chapter 5. Yet in contrast with the Swiss case (see Volume 1, 139-41), this Francophone ambience has never presented a serious obstacle to the recruitment of sufficient numbers of Flemish public servants to the capital. This willingness to work in Brussels undoubtedly derives at least in part from the extensive and efficient commuting network around the capital, which provides accessible residential communes where the environment is totally Flemish.

A second point concerns the more subtle question of general bureaucratic style. While the language laws found differential acceptance among Flemings and Francophones and thus became another specific source of division between the language communities, some scholars see a common administrative style in Belgium that serves to bridge the major cleavages of language and ideology. André Molitor suggests that this style is based in turn on certain common characteristics of the Belgian civic culture, among which he identifies: a strong sense of concrete realities and a mistrust of abstract ideas; an orientation to the present; a great vitality and sense of work; a sociability manifested in small groups coupled with a mistrust of the centralized state; and a tendency to extremism in political debate that masks an underlying moderation in political action and a firm sense of the safe limits to disagreements. These traits combine to produce a role for the administration that is "reduced and secondary" when compared to that of France, but also less rigid, less formal, more oriented to practical concerns, and more closely integrated with existing political structures (Molitor, 1974, 419-28). Such a low-key bureaucracy may have its costs in terms of efficency, but on the positive side it may adjust more easily to the requirements of political and linguistic change than one that has rigid traditions of independence.

A third and final consideration is that the 1963 legislation and the discussion of the public service in this section have focused on the highly centralized structures that ruled the Belgian political system without serious challenge from 1830 to 1970. Even the regionalization law of 1980 purports to incorporate the new regional and community ministries into the existing structure of language legislation as additional *administrations centrales*, which will operate in one language only—French or Dutch— with staffs belonging to the corresponding language register, but will also be bound by the same language obligations as communal authorities in providing services to the public in special-status communes in their jurisdiction (Senelle, 1980, 226-30). Such a centralized structure has been increasingly undermined, however, by the evolution of regionalist ideas in the 1970s. To the extent that the new regional administrations take hold, build strong executives, and win some budgetary independence, success could instigate further decentralization or restructuring in central agencies. As of 1985, however, the new regional administrations are still evolving, and any discussion of their eventual impact on the rest of the administrative system can only be speculative.

F   The Judicial System

The Swiss judicial system (see Volume 1, 142-44) consists of highly diversified courts organized by the cantons capped by a few federally organized tribunals. By contrast, Belgian courts are organized on a uniform basis throughout the country. This structure, however, is quite complex, involving two levels of courts of first instance for civil and commercial matters, three for penal matters (depending on the severity of the offence), two levels of appeal courts (Cour d'appel and Cour de cassation), as well as labor courts and military courts. The law governing language usage in judicial matters is at least as complex as that for language usage in the administration, and perhaps more so on account of the special situations and legal procedures that it regulates. The central statute, the law of June 15, 1935, runs to twenty-five pages of text in each language and its various decrees of execution require forty-seven more (*Emploi des langues*, 1944). By comparison with the other language laws of the 1930s, this act proved reasonably successful in achieving its major aims, with the result that the third round of language laws in the 1960s led to only limited amendments in specific areas, the main features of the 1935 law remaining virtually unchanged. More than in the previous section, our brief sketch of this legislation will omit much of its legal detail, which has become more complex and technical through later amendments, and focus upon general principles and problems of application.

In historical perspective, traditions of bilingual judicial proceedings existed long before Belgian independence. As far back as late medieval times the rulers of Flanders, Brabant, Limburg, and Liège made various provisions for justice to be administered in the language of the parties involved, and some residues of these practices may be detected in current legislation, side by side with recent tendencies towards territorial solutions. The continuity of this tradition was broken after 1790, however, by the French occupation and by professional considerations which made the influence of the bar and the magistracy one of the strongest influences for *francisation* (Herremans, 1965, 211-12; Hayoit de Termicourt, 1936, 15-17). In 1873, following some celebrated incidents in which the right to use Flemish in the courts had been denied, Parliament provided for the optional use of Flemish as the language of procedure and of witnesses in criminal cases in Flanders, but statistics for the next decade suggest that this option was relatively little used (Clough, 1930, 140-41). Gradually, however, the use of Flemish was expanded, through further legislation, to cover its use by crown prosecutors, in appeal courts, and in the *arrondissement* of Brussels, so that in one sense the legislation of 1935 served to consolidate and extend language practices that had been developing with respect to criminal law for several decades. On the other hand, this law went much further than previous practice towards the territoriality principle, and it regulated for the first time the use of language in civil and commercial cases (Herremans, 1965, 213-15).

The 1935 law is complex, and early commentaries upon it differ rather noticeably as to its central principles (Hayoit de Termicourt, 1936, 15-24; van Hoorebeke, 1936, 9-10). Van Hoorebeke sees four basic principles, and we follow his schema here. First, in courts of first instance, whether civil or criminal, all the language of the *procédure* is governed by territoriality, Dutch in Flanders, French in Wallonie, German in the German-speaking areas, and either Dutch or French in Brussels. At the start of the proceedings, however, parties in civil cases by mutual agreement may request a change of language, and this may be given effect by transfer of the case to an equivalent court in another language region (Article 7). Similar provisions apply in criminal cases. Second, the parties in civil cases and those accused in criminal cases retain the right to testify in the language of their choice, through an interpreter if necessary, regardless of the language of proceedings. Third, the language of the pleadings by barristers follows the language of procedure, with certain closely defined exceptions (lawyers from other language regions, cases in the German areas, lawyers admitted before 1930). Finally, judgments and their execution must also follow the language of procedure. For cases introduced in the Brussels area, the language of proceedings is governed by complicated rules based on a combination of territoriality where applicable and the language of the defender, or the majority of the defenders. Further special arrangements permit the defender to request a change of language in the German areas and in communes with German-language facilities, and by amendments in 1963 similar arrangements were extended to residents of the six communes of the Brussels periphery and certain communes along the French-Dutch language frontier. These rather complicated special arrangements, however, are intended to be exceptions to the general principle of territoriality in the 1935 law.

At the level of appeal courts, the basic rule in both civil and criminal cases is to follow the language of the decision being challenged (Article 24). Similarly the highest court, the Court of Cassation, which has special responsibilities for maintaining the rule of law and the uniformity of jurisprudence by annulling defective decisions and returning them for retrial to another court of the same level (Wigny, 1952, 2: 742-45), follows the same rule except that the court may order lower court decisions in German to be handled in French or Dutch (Article 27). This relatively simple language rule does not mean that the higher courts have escaped other frictions arising from the *question communautaire*. A law of 1832 organized three courts of appeal at Gent, Liège, and Brussels for the nine Belgian provinces, placing the Flemish province of Limburg under the jurisdiction of Liège and both Antwerp and Hainaut under the jurisdiction of Brussels. In the 1960s growing demands for linguistic homogeneity made these arrangements unacceptable to the Flemish Movement, and in 1965 the Limburg Provincial Council refused to nominate candidates for the Liège court as required by law (du Roy, 1968, 72; Herremans, 1965, 238-39). Plans to enlarge the number of appeal courts were delayed by a constitutional provision which fixed the number at three (Article 104), but this barrier was removed when the constitution was amended in 1970 to establish two new courts of appeal at Antwerp and Mons. The revised Article 104, implemented by a law of June 1974, thus provides for two courts of appeal in Flanders, two in Wallonie, and one bilingual court in Brussels with jurisdiction reduced to the province of Brabant alone (Senelle, 1978, 179-80, 246-47).

A second source of Flemish concern was the composition of the Cour de Cassation. While lawyers educated in Dutch began to enter the lowest level of the magistracy in the mid-1930s, and the next two levels in the mid-1940s and 1950s respectively, this natural progression stopped abruptly at the Cour de Cassation, long a reserve of the *noblesse* and the upper bourgeoisie, where a few strong personalities firmly blocked the Flemish advance even after legislative amendments in 1967 that called for equal representation (Article 43 *quater*). As late as 1970, some forty years after the full *vernederlandsing* of the University of Gent, not one of the twenty-three judges of the court had a Dutch-language doctorate in law, though four held bilingual diplomas from Gent obtained during its brief bilingual or "Nolf" regime of the 1920s (Storme, 1970). Eventually, however, mounting pressures within the political system overcame resistance within the court, and by the early 1980s the goal of language balance in membership had been achieved. In the Brussels area the same problem of linguistic imbalance persisted into the 1960s at lower levels of the judiciary. A reply to a parliamentary question in 1964 showed that judges with Dutch-language degrees accounted for eight out of sixty-one positions in the lower courts and only two out of fifty-nine in the Brussels Court of Appeal (Herremans, 1965, 225-26).

The case load of the Cour de Cassation is organized according to specialized panels or chambers, and in designating chambers to hear cases the president takes into account the language of the dossier and the linguistic capacity of the justices concerned. Up to 1984 all cases originating in German have been handled in French or Dutch. Decisions of this court are published in both French and Dutch, but they are printed separately and unofficially—with a wide price differential in favor of the French version (*Arresten; Bulletin des arrêts*). Flemish legal circles have long stressed the importance of appointing Dutch-speaking judges and barristers to the Cour de Cassation, not only for its obvious symbolic importance but also for its essential role in the development of a Dutch-speaking legal profession and a mature Netherlandic juridical tradition, a tradition in which legal terminology would be not just a language of translation or importation from abroad but integrated with and reflective of the ongoing social development of Flemish society (Victor, 1968; Storme, 1970).

The provisions of the 1935 legislation and its decrees of execution concerning language requirements for judges, magistrates, crown prosecutors, jurymen, notaries, court clerks, and ushers occupy some thirty pages of closely printed text and have since been modified in various details. The basic principle is that magistrates and crown prosecutors must have a thorough knowledge of the language of the region concerned, as evidenced by a law diploma taken in that language or demonstrated by special examination, though some lower posts permit a simple declaration of knowledge of the language in question. At each level some posts also require a knowledge of the other "national language" (French or Dutch), and tests to establish this are organized at two levels to indicate "thorough" or "adequate" knowledge (*connaissance approfondie, connaissance suffisante*) respectively. The proportion of bilingual positions in the system as a whole is rather low, and many are specifically designated by name. Certain local magistrates in towns along the linguistic frontier must be bilingual, and a few in Liège province must show an adequate knowledge of German. For the rest, bilingualism is not a requirement, and even though some parts of a trial may take place in another official language as a matter of right, a judge may do this through an interpreter if he sees fit. Even at the highest level, most justices and counsel in the Court of Cassation are not legally required to be bilingual; by an amendment of 1967 only six judges and three counsel are obliged to demonstrate knowledge of the other official language (*Emploi des langues*, 1944; van Hoorebeke, 1936, 171-85).

The rather ambiguous position of German in the judicial system deserves notice. In spite of its limited territorial base and restricted use in the higher courts, it appears to be winning increased formal recognition as a language of justice alongside Dutch or French. Thus while one commentator in the 1930s argues that German should be considered a *langue étrangère* in every jurisdiction apart from exceptional privileged use by Belgian citizens in certain cantons of Verviers (van Hoorebeke, 1936, 23), another writing a generation later can just as firmly label German *een nationale taal van de rechtspleging* in spite of several explicit restrictions on its judicial use (Lindemans, 1973, 32). This change seems to coincide with an enhanced status for the German-language community in general since the constitutional reforms of 1970.

In spite of various shortcomings and unresolved problems, the 1935 legislation on language use in judicial matters has been widely accepted as the most effective and the most balanced of the language laws of the 1930s (Herremans, 1965, 221). Consequently the third round of language legislation in the 1960s scarcely touched the judicial realm, and the law of August 9, 1963, in particular was confined to minor territorial and organizational adjustments. Though amended several times and elaborated in many technical details (Lindemans, 1973, 5), the principles of the 1935 law have remained basically unchanged. Why, then, did this law prove more effective than its counterparts in the fields of administration and education? One of its basic features, an innovation in Belgian law, was to prescribe a penalty of nullification for acts of procedure or judgments that were linguistically irregular (Article 40). This provision has certain limits and is quite complex in its application (van Hoorebeke, 1936, 93-107), but some observers consider the nullity provision as a major reason for the successful application of the law and a more effective enforcement mechanism than a separate control agency. A slightly different perspective attributes the success of the 1935 law to the high degree of professionalism in the magistracy and to a lower level of politicization than in other sectors. In this view it is not the nullity procedure itself, but the threat it poses to professional reputation, that has led to scrupulous observance of the law in the courts.

A further question concerning language usage in the judicial system involves the availability of statutes and legal codes in Dutch. Before 1898 only the French version of any law was authentic, and unofficial translations of various statutes and codes into Dutch had no legal validity. After 1898 both versions of any new legislation had equal validity, but this still left many of the basic codes and even the constitution itself legally authoritative only in their French version. As early as 1923 a commission was created to translate the codes and the most important statutes into Dutch, but validation of the Dutch texts by Parliament proved a slow process, beset by juridical and linguistic difficulties. After 1960, under increasing political pressure, the pace quickened. The official Dutch text of the Civil Code was approved by a law passed in 1961, that of the Penal Code in 1964, and after several years of parliamentary work the authentic Dutch text of the constitution was adopted by formal constitutional amendment in 1967 (Herremans, 1965, 214-15; *Admission progressive*, 1969, 3-6). In cases of divergent legal texts, the current rule of interpretation is to seek out the intent or will (*volonté*) of the legislator (*Règlement de la Chambre*, 1975, 121), and one legal writer argues that a plurilingual legal system has advantages in allowing judges a more thorough insight into this intent (Herbots, 1973).

Another consideration is the historical tradition and the spirit of the Belgian codes themselves. In Volume 1 it was noted that Switzerland has undergone a slow legal integration over the past century that gradually displaced cantonal codes by federal ones and imposed more Germanic legal traditions on some cantonal systems that were previously inspired by French and Napoleonic influences (see Volume 1, 144). Swiss resistance to this process, as evidenced by voting patterns in referenda, appears to have been based more on religion and on defence of cantonal prerogative than on linguistic or cultural considerations, but one might expect a similar question to surface in Belgium among Flemish jurists under conditions of sharper linguistic conflict. Once again the question is complex and relevant studies appear to be lacking. In general terms one can say that the spirit of the codes themselves, in spite of strong Napoleonic influences dating from the French occupation, has not become a source of significant conflict. As a possible explanation, one may recall that the legal tradition of the Netherlands also has been strongly imprinted with French and Napoleonic influences, and further that the progressive tendencies evident in recent Netherlands penal and civil law have not proved attractive to the more traditionalist Flemish legal profession.

This section may appropriately conclude with a brief mention of a body that does not formally belong to the judicial structure at all, the Conseil d'Etat. Related vaguely to Napoleonic and pre-1830 Dutch precedents, and more directly to the tradition of the Conseil d'Etat in France, the modern Belgian version of this institution was created—after intermittent debates and an abortive earlier effort—by a law of December 1946. Its general function is surveillance over executive, legislative, and administrative acts in the interests of constitutional conformity and procedural legality. To do this, it acts partly as a juridical adviser to the executive and legislative branches, partly as an administrative tribunal. Although technically it falls under the executive branch, its independence and the difficulties of classifying its role precisely have led some scholars to regard the Conseil d'Etat as a fourth branch of government.

The legislative and administrative sections of the Conseil d'Etat are organizationally and functionally distinct. The legislative section examines and advises on the texts of draft bills, amendments, executive decrees, and their equivalents at community and regional level. Its twelve members are organized in four separate chambers or panels—two Dutch-speaking, two French-speaking—but conflicts of jurisdiction are heard by combined chambers of three Francophones and three Flemings. Decisions of this section are in the form of opinions (avis), which carry considerable political weight but are not legally binding. The administrative section is organized in five chambers—two Dutch-speaking, two French-speaking, one bilingual—and functions as an administrative court, rendering binding decisions (arrêts) on the legality of administrative actions (CRISP, 1984, no. 1055).

Although in theory the Conseil d'Etat acts as a check on the constitutionality and legality of governmental or legislative acts, and not on their political wisdom or appropriateness, the increasing complexity of the Belgian political system in recent years has made this boundary line more and more difficult to maintain. In the 1970s the Conseil became centrally involved in examining the various projects to implement the regime of communities and regions, and particularly the Egmont-Stuyvenberg accords. In the early 1980s the administrative section has had to face sensitive cases arising from gaps or grey areas in the language laws, such as whether elected communal councillors in unilingual regions must know the language of the region or must use it for council business. While some of this enhanced visibility may be traced to the delay in establishing the new Cour d'arbitrage, the removal of conflicts of legislative competence to this new body will still leave the Conseil d'Etat with a substantial conflict-regulating role in examining and assessing other linguistically sensitive measures in the context of established norms of Belgian constitutionalism.

G   The Armed Forces

In examining the language practices of the Belgian armed forces, one should note certain salient features at the start. By contrast with the longstanding Swiss concept of a citizen army, the Belgian forces evolved from a relatively small professional army in the nineteenth century to partial conscription in 1909 and to universal male military service in 1913.

Since the mid-1970s, however, the trend has been away from universal conscription in favor of a mixed force of volunteers and draftees (Young, 1982, 72-73). Second, while the Swiss army was mobilized for defensive purposes in two world wars, the Belgian forces were actively engaged and severely disorganized in both conflicts. Third, Switzerland's rigorous neutrality contrasts sharply with Belgium's post-1945 integration in NATO, which provides a linguistic environment favoring French and English over Dutch. Finally, the language practices of the Belgian armed forces have differed in certain basic respects from practices in the administrative and judicial sectors: they have not been based on the principle of territoriality; they have demanded an increasing degree of bilingualism from all commissioned officers; and the application of the principle of parity or proportionality in the linguistic distribution of officers has been more gradual than in civil administration.

The starting point for the evolution of the Belgian army was a disproportion in the forces of the United Kingdom of the Netherlands before 1830 that severely disadvantaged the southern provinces. One authority has calculated that of a total of 2,377 officers in the combined army in 1830, the future Belgian provinces, with more than half of the population, accounted for 417, or just under 18 per cent. They contributed 29 per cent of cavalry officers, but only 7 per cent of engineers, 9 per cent of artillery officers, and 13 per cent of generals (Wanty, 1957, 6-7). In the midst of the disorders that followed the Revolution, Parliament appealed in 1831 to outsiders and especially to France for help in reorganizing the armed forces and building up an officer cadre. Many Napoleonic veterans responded, and shortly afterwards the general staff was composed of twenty-four French and four Belgian officers. By 1833 there were 104 French and 44 other foreign citizens in a total officer corps of 2,407 (Lamberty, 1933, 72-73; Wanty, 1957, 39-40).

As early as October 1830, French had been declared the sole language of command and administration in the army. The linguistic orientation of the officer class was further reinforced by its position in society. Officers were paid modestly but were required to maintain a social position. An outside income was desirable. By a royal decree of 1842 marriage was authorized for only one sublieutenant in eight, one lieutenant in four, and half of the captains, and then only on condition that the wife brought to the marriage a sufficient annual income (Wanty, 1957, 227). Given the social milieu of post-1830 Belgium, such a group was bound to be overwhelmingly Francophone.

As in other domains of language usage, language rules and practices in the armed forces underwent a slow transformation under the impact of the Flemish Movement. Far in advance of its time, the Flemish Commission of 1856 called for separate Flemish and Walloon regiments, each commanded in its own language, but its recommendations were ignored. The only relevant legislation in the nineteenth century was a measure of 1888, much attenuated in Parliament, that provided for the Dutch language to be taught to officer candidates at the Ecole militaire (Clough, 1930, 169-71; Herremans, 1965, 241-42). In 1896 the Flemish leader Julius MacLeod could claim that the army, which numbered some 11,600 personnel, was 61 per cent Flemish and 39 per cent Walloon but was trained wholly in French (Lamberty, 1933, 73). Two training manuals in Dutch, produced at the initiative of Flemish officers in this period, remained without official status (Wanty, 1957, 226).

More effective legislation in 1913 imposed a knowledge of the second language (*connaissance suffisante*) on all officers and called for Flemish recruits to be instructed and addressed in their own language, though the language of commands remained French. This measure, designed to take effect in 1917, came too late to overcome the serious linguistic chasm between officers and other ranks that fuelled the Flemish Movement during the First World War. Interestingly, however, even during the last decades of the professional army a different language practice had been emerging in the militia, or *Garde civique*. Because of its territorial organization, a law of 1897 provided that militia units in Flanders would be instructed and commanded in Dutch and that its language practice in general would be subject to the law of 1878 on language usage in the administration (Herremans, 1965, 242-43; Roggen, 1965, 243).

For the regular forces, the language legislation of 1913 was followed by further laws in 1928 (Rüling, 1939, 90-96) and 1938, both of which tended to reinforce the principles of mother-tongue instruction, linguistic homogeneity of units, and bilingualism for officers and noncommissioned officers. The 1938 law, together with its executive decrees of application and several amendments, is still the basis for language usage in all the armed forces, which include the army, navy, air force, and *gendarmerie*. Like their counterparts in the administrative and judicial areas, these texts, amendments, and regulations are extremely detailed, requiring about sixty-five pages of text in each language, and only a brief summary of general principles will be attempted here (*Usage des langues à l'armée*, 1952).

The central principle of the 1938 legislation is that the recruit is trained, administered, and commanded exclusively in his mother tongue. Normally this means the language in which he has been educated, though recruits from the Brussels area may declare their mother tongue at the time of call-up (Article 19). The consequence of this is that each class of *miliciens*, normally called up at the age of nineteen, is distributed between French-speaking and Dutch-speaking units in proportions representing their percentage of the population. For recruits of German mother tongue, the army has one infantry company that is trained in German but commanded in French, as one postwar ministerial report frankly explains, because of public sensitivity to hearing military commands in German (Chambre des Représentants, 1961-62, no. 199, 7-8). In recent years this unit has attracted only about 100 recruits a year, or about 0.3 per cent of total recruits, though German-speaking units accounted for up to 0.7 per cent of recruits during the 1950s. The majority of German speakers are attracted to other units or branches of the forces, both for service reasons and for opportunities to improve their fluency in a second language (Verdoodt, 1968, 48).

The principle of linguistically homogeneous units, as a corollary of mother-tongue instruction, has been applied gradually as the operating conditions of each service have permitted. Unilingual platoons and companies were common in the 1930s, and since the Second World War army units up to battalion level or even higher have been unilingual, apart from certain support units and specialized services. In the air force, unilingual units up to wing level have existed since 1957, but in the more technical services unilingualism applies only to smaller units. In the navy, unilingual ships were established in 1954, but shore units and research ships have remained bilingual (Herremans, 1965, 253-54; Chambre des Représentants, 1979, Special Session, no. 38, 6-7). For all services, unilingual units communicate in their own language with higher military authorities and with the Defence Ministry, but in dealing with the public or with civil authorities they are expected to conform to the requirements of the laws on language usage in administrative matters (*Usage des langues à l'armée*, 1952, 14-17).

Given a structure of this kind, the burden of bilingual communication falls mainly on the officers. A good deal of the detail in the 1938 legislation and its decrees of application is concerned with defining the standards and conditions governing the various levels of language examinations that must be passed by officers and officer candidates. Basically, three levels of competence in the second official language are distinguished. First, languages account for a substantial part of the curriculum for all officer cadets in training, especially for future career officers at the Ecole militaire royale (EMR). Officer candidates must pass a test of elementary knowledge of the second language at the point of admission to EMR and a more exacting test at the completion of the course to establish *connaissance effective*, the latter concept being defined as an ability to sit as a member of a military court or to serve in a unit in an administrative and instructional capacity. Although EMR has separate French and Dutch sections for academic instruction, it has had since the 1950s a policy of alternating the two languages on a weekly basis for all service exercises (*Rapport fait*, 1953, 26). This alternating use of two official languages appears to be unique in the Belgian public sector, though it has been used extensively and effectively in the public sector in South Africa.

At the second level, every candidate for the rank of major must pass a more exacting examination (*connaissance effective développée*) to establish ability to preside over a military court and to instruct other officers in that medium. Candidates are given two chances only to pass this examination, and a second failure is a permanent barrier to any further promotion. For the decade from 1953 to 1963 Herremans reports a failure rate after two attempts of about 12 per cent among Francophone candidates, compared to 2 per cent for Flemings, a factor that aroused some antagonism in Walloon circles (1965, 251-52). This relatively demanding language requirement for *all* field-level officers further differentiates the military sector from the other major public sectors, where competence in the second language is required only selectively.

The third level of linguistic competence for officers is a full bilingualism or *connaissance approfondie*, defined as indicating a certain level of culture in the second language. It is required only for teaching staff and examiners of EMR, but those who hold it are also qualified to command unilingual units of the other language group. Studies by Jacques Brazeau in 1964 showed that 10 per cent of career officers had demonstrated this level of linguistic competence, but further analysis by linguistic groups showed 18 per cent for the Dutch register compared to 6 per cent for the French one, and some of the latter group were almost certainly older officers of Flemish mother tongue educated and trained in French in the 1930s (Herremans, 1965, 263). By 1978 these figures were 20 per cent for the Dutch register and 14 per cent for the French one, according to the minister's annual report to Parliament, but the percentages rise sharply with increases in rank, reaching 53 per cent and 30 per cent, respectively, for all officers with the rank of major or above. The same source also describes a departmental practice of allowing junior officers short-term postings to noncommand positions in units of another language in order to maintain second-language capacity (Chambre des Représentants, 1979, Special Session, no. 38, 9, 20). Finally, officers posted to German-language units must show by examination a *connaissance effective* in that language but remain listed on either the French or the Dutch register (*Usage des langues à l'armée*, 1952, 14, 36).

For noncommissioned officers, there are no general obligations to become bilingual, but candidates for promotion to the rank of sergeant must demonstrate a functional knowledge (*connaissance effective*) of the language of their prospective unit. By meeting this requirement in a second language, noncommissioned officers can qualify to serve in units of another language, including German.

The question of balanced representation of officers between the French and Dutch registers has proved more difficult. Since implementation of the 1938 act had scarcely begun before the collapse of 1940, the early postwar period saw a continuing massive imbalance between French-speaking and Dutch-speaking officers. In 1952 the Dutch register accounted for only 18 per cent of all officers, the vast majority of these being in the junior ranks. It showed only one officer above the rank of major in the air force, and only two in the *gendarmerie* (*Rapport fait*, 1953, 16, 36, 40). More complete data for the officer corps as a whole at various dates are shown in Tables 38 and 39. The first of these tables gives a profile of Dutch-speaking representation in the armed forces at intervals by branch of service and by rank; the second uses more time points to illustrate the rhythm of change by stages among junior officers, senior officers, and generals. The policy target throughout this period has been to achieve Dutch-speaking representation in each rank and branch approximately equivalent to the percentage of Dutch-speaking *miliciens* in the forces, or roughly 60 per cent. Flemish representation among noncommissioned officers has been close to this figure since the early 1960s except in the navy, where it has approached 75 per cent (Young, 1982, 68-69).

Table 38

Belgium: Armed forces officers and percentages on Dutch-language register, by branch of service and by rank, selected years, 1952-79

Category	1952		1963-64		1979	
	Total	% Dutch	Total[a]	% Dutch	Total	% Dutch
1. Total officer corps	5,111	18.5	8,175	38.9	6,608	58.0
2. By branch of service						
Army	4,085	17.1	6,230	37.1	4,120	58.2
Air Force	645	20.2	1,353	43.5	1,575	56.2
Navy	132	45.5	260	63.1	340	70.9
Gendarmerie	249	22.5	332	34.6	n.a.	n.a.
Medical Service	n.a.	n.a.	n.a.	n.a.	573	53.9
3. By rank[b]						
Lieutenant-General			8	0.0	11	45.5
Major-General			33	6.1	33	54.5
Colonel			219	11.9	241	43.2
Lieutenant-Colonel			531	13.4	525	51.8
Major			894	18.3	874	56.1
Capt.-Commandant			1,515	25.1	1,918	61.1
Captain			1,865	38.5	1,053	57.5
Lieutenant			2,089	58.1	872	57.6
Sub-Lieutenant			1,021	59.2	1,081	61.6

[a] Excludes officer-cadets and chaplains.
[b] Army and Navy data by rank unavailable for 1952.

Sources: 1952: *Rapport fait*, 1953, 16, 40; 1963-64: unpublished data and analysis prepared by Jacques Brazeau for the Canadian Royal Commission on Bilingualism and Biculturalism; Herremans, 1965, 257-62; 1979: unpublished data from the Belgian armed forces.

Table 39

Belgium: Armed forces officers on Dutch-language register, by rank categories, 1952-82 (percentages[a])

Year	Junior officers[b]	Senior officers[c]	Generals	All officers
1952	n.a.	n.a.	n.a.	18.5
1959	n.a.	n.a.	n.a.	37.3
1964	48.0	17.3	10.3	41.5
1969	55.1	26.4	23.5	48.3
1973	58.1	38.8	31.2	53.1
1976	59.2	46.5	40.0	55.9
1979	59.8	52.3	52.3	57.9
1982	60.0	56.6	50.0	59.1

[a] Percentages of total number in each category.
[b] From sub-lieutenant to captain-commandant, and equivalents in other services.
[c] From major to colonel, and equivalents.

Sources: Unpublished data supplied by Belgian armed forces; Houben, 1983, 93.

As the two tables show, the overall averages for all officers mask wide variations by rank and by branch of service. Considered by service branches, the navy, freshly re-established in 1945 after an eighty-three-year hiatus, shows the strongest Flemish representation throughout this period, which is also entirely in keeping with Belgian geography. The army, the largest and oldest of the services, has reflected most strongly the weight of Francophone tradition. A detailed analysis carried out by Jacques Brazeau in 1964 found further variations by area of specialization within each service, with Flemish representation being stronger in the technical sectors of the army and navy and among flying personnel in the air force (Herremans, 1965, 164-66). By this date the language registers had reached approximate proportionality for career army officers only at the rank of sublieutenant, for air force officers up to lieutenant, and for naval officers up to one level higher, but for no rank above these levels.

With proportionality established for junior officers, one might have expected the transition to be completed by normal progression through the ranks. As the next decade was to show, however, unforeseen difficulties arose. The favorable figures for Dutch-speaking junior officers in the registers in 1964 were based partly on noncareer officers, especially on the 1,069 *officiers de complément*, comprising 13 per cent of all officers, a category recruited temporarily after the war, mainly from the Resistance leadership, in order to rebuild the armed forces. Of these officers 66 per cent were on the Dutch register, but because they lacked formal qualifications to become career officers their chances of promotion to senior ranks were limited. Further, promotions from the rank of major upward were decided by committees of professional officers, without ministerial intervention, and here the weight of tradition appears to have delayed Flemish advancement into senior ranks. As late as 1957, one study notes, some 20 per cent of colonels in the cavalry and 25 per cent in the artillery were still drawn from the nobility (Van Gorp, 1969, 46).

The relatively slow penetration of the upper military ranks by officers on the Dutch register and the alleged hostility of the older Francophone military elite led to a certain politicization of appointments at the highest levels. Flemish nationalist circles became acutely sensitive on the issue, and nominations to top positions in the forces were closely scrutinized by the Flemish press for their linguistic implications—more closely indeed than for their possible military significance. A notable case was the *affaire Vivario* in the winter of 1967-68, when the government's nomination of an allegedly unilingual general of the land forces as chief of staff had to be withdrawn, under political pressure, in favor of the fluently bilingual head of the air force (du Roy, 1968, 72-73). A decade later, with expectations of bilingualism at upper levels more firmly entrenched, the promotion of a senior officer on the French register to command a division was sharply criticized by the Flemish press until the general held a press conference in Dutch to establish his linguistic credentials (*Soir*, 1979, June 30). Although not required by law, full-scale bilingualism has become a virtual prerequisite for all top-level appointments in the forces.

The slow rate of change in the officer corps can also be linked to certain wider factors in Belgian society. While a career in the military has been traditional for certain upper-level families, which were generally French-speaking even in Flanders, the level of esteem for the armed forces among the public at large has been rather low. In a survey already referred to that measured the degree of sympathy felt by respondents towards various groups in Belgian society (see above, 109-10), the average rating for "soldiers" (*militaires*) was the lowest of all twenty-two groups tested, and either lowest or second lowest in each linguistic region (AGLOP, 1975, variable 141). In the words of one writer, Belgium's long experience of occupations and servitudes to foreign powers has produced an attitude of "natural and instinctive antimilitarism" (Blondiau, 1967, 629). Belgian history since 1830 has also produced several distinct varieties of ideologically-linked antimilitarism, and one of these, associated with the Flemish Movement, has been founded upon the perceived inferior status of the Flemish language and the Flemish soldier in relation to the Francophone officer class (Lehouck, 1958, 226-28).

The practical effect of these traditions has been that after 1945 Dutch-speaking students were not only less qualified educationally but also less motivated towards a military career than their Francophone counterparts. Studies by Van Gorp show that from 1936 to 1939 the percentage of Dutch-speaking candidates for the Ecole militaire royale ranged from 14 to 19 per cent, and only in 1955 did the number of admissible Dutch-speaking candidates approach the proportions for the population of the same age group. A survey conducted among final-year secondary-level students in 1963-64 showed that Dutch-speaking students felt themselves to be less well informed than their Francophone counterparts about the pros and cons of a military career, less interested in such a career for themselves, and also more critical of the army, the officer corps, and the military career (Van Gorp, 1969, 126-29, 143-44, 154-56, 198-201). Similarly, among the roughly one in four *miliciens* educationally qualified to become reserve officers, a significantly higher proportion of French speakers than of Dutch speakers were interested in doing so. Similar disparities in level of interest were seen in the larger group qualified to become noncommissioned officers in the reserves (*Analyse de la population*, 1963, 27; 1965, 18-21). These intergroup discrepancies persisted in the 1970s, though smaller percentages of both groups showed interest in either officer or NCO training. While it is sometimes suggested that traditional Flemish antimilitarist sentiment has been changing (Herremans, 1965, 270), its residues still show up clearly in attitudinal data of the 1960s and 1970s.[1]

The main rules of language usage in military justice are laid down in the 1935 law on language usage in judicial matters. Unlike other jurisdictions, where territoriality is important, the choice of French or Dutch in military courts is basically left to the accused (Article 18), or to the majority of those accused (Article 21). A decree of execution of September 1935 to give effect to this principle provided that military courts would be based on two lists of officers serving in rotation, one French-speaking or bilingual, the other Dutch-speaking or bilingual (*Emploi des langues*, 1944, 136-45). In the postwar period the aim of the forces has been to achieve a generalized second-language competence sufficient to enable any career officer to sit in a military court of either official language. Thus in a matter of military justice the accused is assured of a trial in French or Dutch at his option, but—unlike the Swiss case (see Volume 1, 146)—not necessarily before members of his own language community. Since 1969 more limited arrangements have also existed for cases to be heard in German (Lindemans, 1973, 122-23, 203-204).

The original 1938 law on language usage in the army had no specific control mechanism, but an amendment of 1955 added a nine-member Commission d'inspection linguistique, composed of six parliamentarians and three senior military officers, to oversee application of the law (Article 31 *bis*). Unlike its counterpart in administrative matters, the Commission permanente de contrôle linguistique, this body has had relatively little to

---

[1] It is interesting that from 1965 to 1972, when conscientious objection was narrowly defined and somewhat exceptional, the recognized objectors were predominantly Francophones. From 1973 onward, when the concept was being debated and enlarged to include nonarmed military service, civil defence, and civil humanitarian or sociocultural service, the number of objectors grew considerably and became predominantly Flemish (CRISP, 1984, no. 1044: 28).

do. In 1977 it examined only two complaints, one of which proved un-
founded (Chambre des Représentants, 1979, Special Session, no. 38, 10-
11), and the root of this inactivity appears to be a doubt as to whether
soldiers' complaints should not more properly follow hierarchical military
channels (Lindemans et al., 1981, 69-71).

If we adopt a wider perspective and compare language policy and
practices in the armed forces with experience in other parts of the public
sector, three main points will stand out. The first is that change in the
linguistic composition of the officer corps has been relatively slow, operating mainly by intergenerational replacement. Educational standards for
career officers have remained high, and any form of *parachutage* from
other sectors, as was done for the diplomatic corps, was scarcely feasible at
the more senior levels. It was also less necessary as long as there were
enough Flemings trained in French or bilingual Francophones to command
the growing number of unilingual Dutch-language units after 1945. Second, the language policies adopted were made possible only by a strong
emphasis on bilingualism for the entire officer class, with more stringent
requirements as to both numbers and quality than for any other major
group in the public sector. This emphasis on bilingualism may be linked in
turn to the mobility factor, that is, to the essentially nonterritorial nature of
modern military service. Finally, any institution that touches virtually the
whole male population at an impressionable age, as the Belgian armed
forces have done through compulsory military service, can serve as a
powerful instrument for social integration. In 1953 a commission of inquiry
into language questions in the forces strongly recommended the banish-
ment of Flemish dialects, the exclusive use of cultivated Netherlandic (or
ABN), and the standardization of military terminology in Dutch between
the Netherlands and Belgium (*Rapport fait*, 1953, 53; Herremans, 1965,
419-20). The military authorities accepted these goals and have since made
sustained efforts to promote both oral and written use of standard Dutch in
the forces.

H   Education, Scientific Research, and Culture

The educational structure of Belgium is highly complex, not because it is
territorially decentralized as in Switzerland, but because it bears the scars
of bitterly fought battles between the forces of Catholicism and secularism.
The difficulty in tracing language policy is that it has been superimposed
upon this primary cleavage in the educational system, which remains less
unified and less standardized than other parts of the public sector. Notwithstanding the *Pacte scolaire* of 1958, it is not uncommon in Brussels to
encounter parents for whom confessionality is more important than language in the choice of a school. In addition to this basic division over
confessionality, schools in the public sector are organized by three dif-

ferent levels of government—communes, provinces, and the central administration—as well as by language regimes, and since 1980 the new community executives have also begun to examine their responsibilities and aspirations in the educational sector.

In keeping with its general principles, the constitution of 1831 contained a declaration of educational freedom, a rejection of the constraints of the United Netherlands regime. Article 17, inserted among other rights of Belgian citizens, declares:

Teaching (*enseignement*) is free. Any preventive measure is forbidden. The punishment of infractions is regulated only by law. Public education, given at state expense, is likewise regulated by law.

The very force of the reaction tended to undo some of the educational reforms of William I. Between 1826 and 1835 the total school population decreased by about 3 per cent and the proportion of pupils in state schools fell from 68 to 58 per cent (Mallinson, 1963, 33). After almost half a century of educational coexistence between Catholics and liberals, the first "School War" was precipitated in 1879 by a law of the Liberal government to modernize the school system. The Van Humbeeck law also tried to reduce clerical influence in the schools and increase control by the state, but it succeeded only in provoking a massive Catholic reaction that led to an overnight proliferation of *écoles libres*. The latter accounted for only 13 per cent of elementary enrolment in December 1878 but by December 1880 their proportion is claimed to have soared to 61 per cent, and in the four Flemish provinces to 80 per cent (Verhaegen, 1906, 132, 136).

When a Catholic government replaced the Liberals in 1884 it was the turn of the state or "neutral" system to suffer. The new Ministry of Education established in 1878 was abolished, and for three decades many educational responsibilities were relinquished to the communes. Each commune could either run a state school or "adopt" an *école libre*, but it was obliged to do both only if twenty families petitioned for a minority school. The role of the central government was reduced to a minimum; even school attendance remained voluntary down to 1914. One consequence was that by the early twentieth century Flanders was attracting international attention for one of the highest rates of illiteracy in Western Europe (Mallinson, 1963, 104-105; Rowntree, 1911, 261-72; Van de Perre, 1919, 202-204).

This context of school structures must be remembered in order to understand the evolution of language legislation in education. When the Liberal government legislated in 1883 to make Flemish the language of instruction for some subjects in secondary education, the law applied only to state schools, which by this time accounted for only a fraction of total enrolment. The *écoles libres*, constitutionally protected against state intervention, continued to teach the secondary curriculum mainly in French as a result of the *fransquillon* sympathies of the higher clergy. Only in 1910, after many unsuccessful attempts, was a partial and indirect control imposed by the introduction of a university entrance test in Dutch for students from Flanders. At the elementary level the usual language of instruction was Dutch; in 1902 only 3 per cent of the 2,364 schools in the Flemish provinces operated in French, but 90 per cent of those functioning in Dutch taught French as a second language, a practice many Flemish nationalists saw as harmful to the development of the Flemish language and culture (Clough, 1930, 149-57). The success of the secondary system in producing bilingual and even multilingual graduates, however, also won international recognition (Dawes, 1902).

The period after the First World War saw the establishment of the first Flemish sections in the *athénées*, or upper-level state secondary schools. By 1930 enrolment in the eight *athénées* in Flanders that had sections in both languages was 67 per cent in the Dutch classes and 33 per cent in French (Bauwens, 1933, 7).

A more important watershed came with the law of July 1932 on the language regime in primary and secondary education, which applied to both state-run and subsidized private schools at elementary level, and to those secondary schools governed by the secondary education act. It established the general rule that the language of instruction in Flanders, Wallonie, and the German region would be the language of the region, while in Brussels and in "bilingual communes" along the linguistic frontier it would be the child's mother tongue or usual language (*langue maternelle ou usuelle*). This example of the personality principle was not a free option, and in case of doubt the father's declaration as to mother tongue could be examined by a jury and rejected, with a further right of appeal to the minister. But the act also made certain concessions to existing practices even in the unilingual regions. Primary pupils whose language was not that of the region were given a right to instruction in their mother tongue in "transmutation classes" in the lower grades, but were to acquire the regional language well enough to transfer to it by the fourth grade. Another provision authorized the continuance at secondary level of "special linguistic sections" for certain categories of students whose previous schooling, for one reason or another, had not hitherto been in the regional language (Rüling, 1939, 112-20).

Taken in combination, these concessions made possible the perpetuation of a more or less complete Francophone school system in Flanders, contrary to the expectations of Flemish legislators. When Parliament considered the matter again in the 1960s, a parliamentary document showed a total of 7,658 pupils in various types of Francophone classes in the Flemish region (Chambre des Représentants, 1961-62, no. 398(9), 38-44). These represented only about 0.7 per cent of total regional enrolment, but at the secondary level the proportion rose to about 1.5 per cent. Concentrated in a few major towns, these classes were considered in the Flemish Movement to be an important instrument for the Francophone bourgeoisie in Flanders to maintain its privileged position (*Transmutatieklassen*, 1956). Nevertheless the importance of the 1932 legislation was that it made possible for the first time the formation of a parallel Dutch-speaking middle class on the same intellectual level as the Francophone one (Maroy, 1966, 473-74).

The chief aim of the 1963 law was to apply the central principles of the 1932 act more extensively and more rigorously. Its field of application included all education from kindergarten to the upper secondary level, all types of program, and all schools operated, subsidized, or even officially recognized by the state. The two basic principles—instruction in the regional language in Flanders, Wallonie, and the German cantons, and in the mother tongue in Brussels—were left unchanged. Minority educational facilities at the elementary level were to be available at a specified level of demand in four groups of communes: the linguistic frontier, the German region, the Malmédy communes, and the Montzen-Welkenraedt area (*Régime linguistique*, 1966a, Articles 1-6). A rather oblique reference to the 1963 law on language in administrative matters extended similar facilities to the six peripheral communes around Brussels (*Emploi des langues*, 1963, 14-17). Other exceptions related to children of military families and employees of international organizations.

Other chapters of the 1963 law and its several decrees of execution set out detailed requirements for the study of second languages and linguistic requirements for teachers and other personnel, but the more interesting sections concern its control mechanisms. In cases where the linguistic regime depended on the child's *langue maternelle ou usuelle*, enrolment in a school could only take place after a parental declaration of mother tongue on a prescribed form, which was then to be checked and verified by a special linguistic inspectorate, whose decision was in turn open to appeal to a special jury (*Régime linguistique*, 1966a, Articles 17-18; 1966b, 16-33). A second form of control was that only schools conforming to the law would have their diplomas recognized by the state (Article 19). In practice, the door was not quite closed. Private schools could still exist, without subsidies, outside the language law, and their students could have their studies recognized by passing an examination administered by a central examining board. The law could also be circumvented if students commuted to another unilingual region or boarded there. In practice these loopholes appear to have been little utilized. While there are no official school statistics on region of study by region of residence, the proportion of matriculation diplomas granted by the central examining board before and after 1963 remained constant at about 1 per cent of all diplomas.

The basic principle of territoriality in education was vigorously contested by several groups of Francophone families in Flanders, who between 1962 and 1964 initiated several complaints against the 1932 and 1963 legislation before the European Commission of Human Rights at Strasbourg as contravening the European Convention on Human Rights of 1950. After lengthy inquiry and a detailed report, the commission placed the question before the European Court of Human Rights. Despite objections from the Belgian government, the court prepared to hear the case, thereby provoking a debate in Belgium over whether the government should renew its acceptance of the court's jurisdiction (Pelloux, 1967, 216). When it did so—for two years instead of five—in November 1965, it declared that it considered the language laws to be directly linked with the structure of the Belgian state and not in conflict with the individual rights guaranteed by the convention. In a first decision in February 1967, the court rejected the government's position and declared itself competent to deal with the complex case. The second decision, on the substance of the case, was delivered in July 1968. In it the court held that the legislation, although rigorous in its provisions, was not in violation of individual human rights, primarily because it covered only public and publicly subsidized education and did not forbid private Francophone schools in the Dutch-language region. The court also accepted the principle of the unilingual region and the right of the state not to recognize linguistically nonconforming diplomas (Herremans, 1965, 198-202; Durnez, 1967, 80-83; Salmon, 1967; Levy, 1967; 1968; Maroy, 1969; Marquet, 1973; European Court, 1967-68).

On only one minor question of the six placed before it did the court find for the plaintiffs against their government. A provision that Francophone schools in a commune of the Brussels periphery should be closed to children resident outside the commune was held to be discriminatory because the same residency restriction did not apply to Dutch-language schools. One material fact in this finding was that the six communes in question—those with minority-language facilities just outside Brussels-Capital—had not been assigned to any linguistic region by the legislation of 1963 (see above, 154-55). The Belgian government did not react immediately to the court's adverse finding, but late in 1970, in the midst of more dramatic constitutional reforms, the six communes of the Brussels periphery were quietly merged into the larger *arrondissement* of Halle-Vilvoorde and thus made part of the Dutch-speaking region, where the court had found differential treatment to be admissible on public policy grounds.

The court's decision was not without comparative interest. One Swiss scholar noted that the Belgian language legislation did not go as far as a similar case in Zurich, in which the highest Swiss court upheld the right of a canton to restrict the duration of study even in a private French-language school in the interest of preserving cantonal linguistic integrity, whereas Belgian law, by contrast, left unsubsidized private schools untouched (Wildhaber, 1969-70, 36-38; and cf. Volume 1, 124).

Apart from the central question of the language of instruction, both the 1932 and the 1963 legislation contain detailed and rather similar provisions as to the place of second languages in the curriculum. At the elementary level, the 1963 law requires the teaching of a second language from the third year onwards in Brussels and in communes eligible for minority-language schools, and it also permits such teaching from the fifth year onwards in the other areas. This language must be French in Flanders and Dutch in Wallonie except in certain districts along the eastern border where it may be German. At the secondary level, the 1963 law requires only that when a second language is taught in Brussels it must be either French or Dutch (Articles 9-11). The 1932 law had done this much and more, requiring a second language—but not necessarily the other official language—in all secondary schools covered by the act (Rüling, 1939, 115).

Despite its relatively modest requirements, the second-language provisions of the 1963 law have been sharply criticized in Francophone circles from several standpoints: the too-early starting age, the number of hours devoted to a second language, the requirement to choose Dutch in Brussels, and the principle of compulsion in general. The Flemish, by contrast, have never seriously questioned the provisions for the study of French. Some evidence of these attitudinal differences shows up in educational statistics. A crude calculation for the 1966-67 school year suggests that 26 per cent of elementary pupils in French-language schools were studying Dutch and 33 per cent of those in Dutch-language schools were studying French, while in German-language schools, where the second language is taught from the first grade, 89 per cent were studying French (*Annuaire statistique de l'enseignement*, 1966-67, 16, 364-67). More detailed data are available for languages studied in secondary schools, as shown in Table 40. This table omits the technical and vocational streams and thus covers roughly half of total secondary enrolment. It also omits very small percentages of students taking Spanish or Italian as fourth languages. If we look at the cumulative totals for second, third, and fourth languages in Part B, one can conclude that in the upper years both linguistic regimes approach universality for the second official language and also for English, but then diverge in the attention given to German. One should also note that the study of Dutch as second language is more widespread in the French regime as a whole (which includes Brussels), than it is in Wallonie proper, where 68 per cent of secondary students chose Dutch and 30 per cent English as their second school language in 1972-73 (Hasquin, 1975-76, 2: 389).

A language studied in school, however, is not necessarily a language learned, and in any case Table 40 covers only one segment of the school-age population. A more representative sample of the total male population may be found in the *miliciens*. The class of 1977 were questioned on their skills in these same languages and classified as having a "fluent," "functional" or "school-level" understanding, or no understanding at all. Results for each language group as a whole and also for those from Brussels-Capital are shown in percentages in Table 41, which brings out clearly the superior second-language resources of Dutch speakers in each category and of those from the capital over the countrywide average.

Table 40

Belgium: Languages studied in secondary schools, by level and language regime, 1966-67 and 1971-72 (percentages)

Language regime and language	Lower secondary		Upper secondary	
	1966-67	1971-72	1966-67	1971-72
A Enrolment as second language				
1. French-language schools				
Dutch	82.6	69.4	86.1	83.7
English	12.7	25.9	9.8	12.7
German	4.5	4.1	3.9	3.9
2. Dutch-language schools				
French	100.0	93.8	100.0	99.9
English	—	6.0	—	0.1
German	—	—	—	—
B Enrolment as 2nd, 3rd or 4th language				
1. French-language schools				
Dutch	87.0	78.1	96.2	97.6
English	44.3	59.5	98.7	99.4
German	5.5	5.4	47.9	50.8
2. Dutch-language schools				
French	100.0	96+[a]	100.0	100.0
English	43.5	57+[a]	99.9	100.0
German	0.3	n.a.	89.2	n.a.

[a] Data on fourth language not available.

Source: Calculated from *Annuaire statistique de l'enseignement*, 1966-67, 368-71; 1971-72, 406-409.

If second-language teaching has been one source of intergroup friction in educational policy, a second is found in the teaching of history. In the post-1945 period it is the Walloons, rather than the Flemings, who have objected more strongly to the Burgundian and Belgicist school of historical interpretation, to an emphasis on the early glories of Flanders and Brabant, to an alleged neglect of regional history before 1789 and especially the history of the Prince-Bishopric of Liège (Herremans, 1951, 157; Outers,

1968, 98-107). The issue gained prominence in the years following 1945 and became the focus of several briefs and rejoinders to the Centre Harmel (Centre de recherche, 1958, Documents, nos. 154, 164, 167, 174, 175, 176, 180, 182, 183). Two decades later its longer-range effects could be seen in the publication of major cultural and intellectual histories focusing on Wallonie as a region (Genicot, 1973; Hasquin, 1975-76; Lejeune and Stiennon, 1977-81). In this cultural reorientation Walloon intellectuals were following the path chosen by their Flemish counterparts generations earlier. One result has been a closer approximation to a symmetrical model of Belgium as two intellectually self-sufficient language communities. On the Flemish side, the question of the history curriculum has widened into a more general debate on prejudice and group stereotyping in history textbooks (Maes, 1971; 1974).

Table 41

Belgium: *Miliciens* by language and level of second-language knowledge, 1977 (percentages)[a]

Group and language	Dutch speakers		French speakers	
	"fluent" or "functional"	"school-level"	"fluent" or "functional"	"school-level"
A Whole country (N = 39,272)				
Second official language	34.2	24.5	16.9	22.0
English	31.6	21.3	17.0	18.4
German	12.7	23.6	4.2	9.0
B Brussels-Capital (N = 3,292)				
Second official language	81.6	9.7	32.5	27.8
English	41.0	24.3	24.4	22.1
German	15.2	32.2	3.6	12.4

[a] Those with "no understanding" omitted.

Source: Unpublished data from the Belgian armed forces.

For four centuries prior to Belgian independence, the normal language of instruction in universities, in the Low Countries as elsewhere in Europe, was Latin. The earliest and most illustrious of these institutions was the University of Louvain, founded in Flemish Brabant in 1425. A second university, in Francophone territory, was established at Douai in 1561, but this institution was lost to the Low Countries when the town of Douai and its vicinity were annexed to France in 1667. Louvain itself was closed by the Austrian authorities in 1788, reopened after the Brabant Revolution, and closed again by the French authorities in 1797. After the fall of Napoleon, William I developed for the United Netherlands an ambitious symmetrical program of state universities, three in the north (at Leiden, Utrecht, and Groningen) and three in the south (at Gent, Liège, and Leuven). All six continued to use Latin as the language of instruction, together with Dutch in the exact sciences. Those in the south were badly disrupted by the 1830 Revolution, most faculty members abandoning their posts and returning to the north (De Smet, 1976-77, 96-98).

With the state universities in disarray, the Belgian bishops established a new Catholic university at Mechelen in 1834, and—not to be outdone—the liberals decided in the same year to establish a "free" university in Brussels. Both these new private institutions adopted French as the language of instruction, and their founding forced the authorities to review policy for the state universities. In 1835 Parliament decided to maintain two state universities at Gent and Liège—both teaching in French—and to allow the new Catholic university at Mechelen to transfer to the site of the ancient University of Louvain (Mallinson, 1963, 12-14, 38-42; De Smet, 1976-77, 99). These four institutions, two private and two state-controlled but all four teaching in French, became the core of the Belgian university system. The interval since the 1830s has seen the founding of thirteen other post-secondary institutions, including smaller Catholic colleges, specialized faculties of agriculture, engineering, or commerce, the Ecole militaire royale, and the first stages of two new state universities at Antwerp and Mons, but the four traditional universities or their successor institutions still accounted for 88 per cent of total student enrolment in 1950-51 and for 85 per cent in 1978-79 (Fondation universitaire, 1972-73, 58; Bureau de statistiques universitaires, 1979, 108). Like the elementary and secondary schools, private universities have received public financial support at virtually the same level as the state institutions since 1960.

The 1932 and 1963 language laws on education did not apply to the universities, but the latter could not remain untouched by the wider language conflict. The half-century-long struggle for the full *vernederlandsing* of the University of Gent culminated, as we have noted, in a law of April 1930 which made that university Dutch-speaking and unilingual (see above, 26-28). The force of this example led to the creation of courses in Dutch at the University of Louvain in the 1930-31 session, and in the law faculty of Brussels by 1935. At Louvain the proportion of courses offered in both languages increased to 74 per cent in 1939-40 and to 89 per cent in 1955-56 (Van Haegendoren et al., 1957, 29), by which date the university had as many Flemish students as Francophones. We have already examined how the political pressures to split this institution—by far the largest of all Belgian universities—mounted through the 1960s until they forced the downfall of the Vanden Boeynants government in 1968 (above, 114-16). The *splitsing* of Louvain/Leuven had its own demonstration effect, being followed in 1969 by a similar division of the University of Brussels into administratively autonomous Francophone and Flemish universities (CRISP, 1969, nos. 458, 463; Jonckheere and Todts, 1979, 355-69). As a result of these splits the four traditional universities became six, three French-speaking and three Dutch-speaking, with each language community having one state university, one Catholic, and one independent of church or state. The German-speaking community, which had little secondary education in German before the 1970s, has no post-secondary programs of its own. Some students at this level attend institutions in West Germany, particularly for technical courses, but the majority study in French at Belgian universities or colleges.

The problem of developing full Flemish participation in Belgian society is nowhere better illustrated than in the patterns of enrolment in higher education. For the universities the long-term trend is illustrated in Table 42, which gives university enrolment data for selected years since the 1830s. Until the 1930s, virtually all of these students studied in French. The first statistics according to language regime date from 1948-49, and from this date one can trace a steady increase in the proportion of students studying in Dutch, which in the 1980s nevertheless still falls short of the proportion of Dutch speakers in this age group.

Table 42

Belgium: Enrolment in universities, by language regime, selected years (percentages)

Year	Total students	Linguistic regime[a]	
		French	Dutch
1839-40	1,496	100	—
1879-80	4,324	100	—
1919-20	8,709	100	—
1938-39	11,566	n.a.	n.a.
1948-49	18,744	66.9	33.1
1958-59	28,275	62.0	38.0
1968-69	64,779	54.9	45.1
1978-79	89,638	50.7	49.3
1983-84	100,362	48.4	51.6

[a] A separate Dutch regime did not exist until 1930.

Sources: Bureau de statistiques universitaires, 1959, lxiv-lxvi; 1969, 17-21; 1979, 108, Table 2; and unpublished data.

Global figures, however, can be misleading, and certain refinements of these data are helpful. First of all, Table 42 includes both Belgian and foreign students, and the latter, who ranged from about 5 per cent of the total in the 1950s to 12 per cent in the 1970s, have always enrolled predominantly in French-language programs. Second, if we consider only students of Belgian nationality, the linguistic proportions differ markedly for males and females. A closer study of the figures shows that for Belgian male students the numbers in each regime were roughly equal by 1965-66, for males and females together by 1969-70, but for females separately only in 1977-78. The effect of this difference may be seen in Part A of Table 43, which shows that among university students of Belgian nationality the greatest proportionate increase since the 1950s has been in female enrolment and particularly in the Dutch regime, though this sector was still underrepresented in 1984. In absolute terms the university sector as a whole expanded rapidly during this period, but while Francophone male enrolment increased by 77 per cent in the 1960s and 1970s, female students in the Dutch regime increased more than eightfold. Part B of the same table, containing data for higher technical education, shows the same tendency for greater growth of female enrolment, especially in the Dutch sector, though in technical education Flemish representation has generally been stronger than in the universities. In spite of some short-term fluctuations, the overall proportion between language regimes on the technical side has been close to the population norms since the late 1950s.

Still another qualification to the data on university enrolments is that totals by language regimes overlook differences between provinces. One study of enrolment by provinces found that the rate of university attendance in Brabant in 1968 was more than twice that for the lowest provinces (Hainaut and Limburg), and that the four Flemish provinces actually showed a slightly higher average participation rate than did the four Walloon provinces (Amelinckx et al., 1969, Annex, 13). From this perspective the contrast is between a privileged—and mainly Francophone— centre versus a disadvantaged periphery of both language groups. In the political climate of recent years, however, attention has focused primarily on imbalances by language regime.

Emphasis on education and technological skills as keys to Flemish emancipation dates back to the influence of Lodewijk De Raet early in the twentieth century, and it remains a tenet of the Flemish Movement. The Flemish failure to penetrate the universities in proportion to their share of the population became evident in the 1950s and almost immediately became a major concern of the Flemish adult education movement and of academic research. The quest for explanations soon led back to earlier levels of education, where it was found that at the end of each of the three previous stages—elementary, lower secondary, and upper secondary—the number of Dutch speakers opting for the academic stream was below the normal proportion based on population (Coetsier, 1959; Coetsier and Bonte, 1963, vol. 1; Wieërs, 1968, 25-26). For the school year 1956-57 it can be calculated that at the lower secondary level Dutch-speaking enrolment accounted for 46 per cent of the classical section, 56 per cent of the modern languages section, 62 per cent of the technical section, and 77 per cent of the so-called "fourth-level primary," a terminal course. For the upper secondary level Dutch enrolment made up 44 per cent of the classical section, 58 per cent of the modern section, and 60 per cent of the technical section. A decade later the pattern was virtually the same, and it appears to have changed relatively little before a restructuring of the secondary system beginning in 1972-73 made further comparisons unreliable (*Annuaire statistique de l'enseignement*, 1965-66, 418, 421-22, 436-37; *Annuaire statistique*, 1976, 130-34).

Table 43

Belgium: Post-secondary students by language regime and sex, selected years (percentages)

Year	Total Students 000s	%	Male French	Male Dutch	Female French	Female Dutch	Total French	Total Dutch
A Universities[a]								
1948-49	17.8	100	84.8		15.2		65.8	34.2
1958-59	26.6	100	47.0	34.3	13.0	5.7	60.0	40.0
1963-64	33.3	100	40.3	38.2	13.6	7.9	53.9	46.1
1968-69	58.0	100	35.3	36.9	15.9	11.9	51.2	48.8
1973-74	70.4	100	31.0	36.1	17.6	15.3	48.6	51.4
1978-79	78.3	100	28.1	34.9	18.3	18.7	46.4	53.6
1983-84	88.1	100	25.5	33.5	18.9	22.1	44.4	55.6
B Post-secondary technical education[a]								
1953-54	7.0	100	74.7		25.3		52.5	47.5
1958-59	10.3	100	32.8	46.5	11.7	9.0	44.5	55.5
1963-64	17.5	100	26.8	39.7	16.4	17.0	43.2	56.7
1968-69	38.7	100	26.5	31.6	20.6	21.4	47.0	53.0
1973-74	51.4	100	23.0	33.4	18.7	24.9	41.7	58.3
1978-79	68.5	100	55.0		45.0		42.0	58.0

[a] University data are for Belgian nationality only; technical data are for total group.

Sources: A: calculated from *Rapport sur la croissance*, 1961, 28, 92; Bureau de statistiques universitaires, 1959, 163; 1969, 195; 1979, 165; Fondation universitaire, 1973-74, 68; and unpublished data; B: calculated from *Annuaire statistique*, 1968, 141; 1976, 160; 1981, 159; *Annuaire statistique de l'enseignement*, 1965-66, 429.

The possible causes of these variations are analyzed by several authors (Coetsier and Bonte, 1963, esp. vol. 2; Wieërs, 1968, 28-31; Amelinckx et al., 1969), all of whom have found both economic and sociocultural explanations. Among the former are the historic economic and social retardation of Flanders, larger families, fewer resources per child, a more limited number of university institutions and greater difficulties of access to them, and less favorable employment prospects in Flanders for university graduates. But they have also found noneconomic factors: more modest ambitions in Flemish families; the absence of an academic tradition and of a Dutch-speaking university-educated reference group; and continuing conservatism with respect to the education of women. Another analysis by Van Haegendoren suggests that confessional education in Flanders has oriented too few students towards the exact sciences (1969a, 89). In short, the differences in enrolment patterns at secondary level seem to have stemmed from complex differences in motivation and cultural environment as well as from economic considerations. One structural reform urged in Flemish educational circles was to make all secondary diplomas valid channels for university entrance, and this was done by a law of June 1964.

One final factor to be noted concerning enrolment patterns is that secondary education is subject to the language laws but university students are free to study in the language of their choice. In 1958-59 the four Flemish provinces showed 1,321 students studying in French-language programs, or 13 per cent of university students resident in these provinces. This number remained fairly steady during the 1960s but then declined to 826 by 1978-79, at which point it represented only 2.5 per cent of students from these four provinces because of massive university expansion in the interval. By contrast, students from the four Walloon provinces enrolled in Dutch-language programs represented only 0.6 per cent of the regional total in 1958-59 and 0.3 per cent in 1978-79 (Bureau de statistiques universitaires, 1959, 160-64; 1979, 151, 153).

Concern for Flemish representation in the universities has been closely matched since the 1950s by similar concern in postgraduate studies and in scientific research, which some Flemings have seen as the pinnacle of the educational system and also as the key to the further progress of their group in many different areas (Wieërs, 1968, 17). The question was brought into sharper focus in 1969 following the report of a commission of Flemish scientists appointed to study the linguistic distribution and the causes of linguistic imbalance in all types of research establishments throughout the country (Amelinckx et al., 1969). The findings of this commission, as illustrated in Table 44, indicate that in 1965 the proportion represented by the Dutch-language sector, whether estimated in terms of research units, scientific personnel, or funding, was in all cases far below the norms based on population statistics and even below the Flemish proportion of university enrolment, especially in the natural sciences. The situation was slightly more favorable in the social sciences and humanities, but these fields together accounted for only 12 per cent of total funding, leaving an aggregate French to Dutch ratio of about 70:30. Further comparison with partial data for 1967 suggested that the Dutch sector had gained a little ground in relative terms but still remained far behind the level indicated by population norms.

Table 44

Belgium: Percentage share of Dutch regime in scientific research, by sector, 1965

	Research units		Graduate personnel		Funding (millions of BFr)	
	N	% Dutch	N	% Dutch	N	% Dutch
Natural sciences	782	33	4,337	27	1,717	29
Social sciences	213	39	764	45	164	40
Humanities	141	37	426	31	74	38
Total	1,136	35	5,527	30	1,955	30

Source: Amelinckx et al., 1969, statistical section, 4, 6, and Annex I.

In seeking out causes of the imbalance the commission emphasized that it had found no evidence of discrimination against Flemish applicants for funds. Instead it emphasized once again the sociocultural aspects of the problem: in particular, the absence of an established "scientific tradition" in Flanders; more generally, the same constellation of factors that had impeded Flemish university enrolment in favor of more modest and more practical career objectives (Amelinckx et al., 1969, 5-10). In proposing remedies, the commission emphasized that no mere redistribution of existing resources would suffice because the lag of Flanders in relation to Belgium was paralleled by a further lag of Belgium in relation to Europe and of Europe in relation to the United States. It therefore proposed to "break the vicious circle of scientific underdevelopment" by a system of special supplementary grants for the disadvantaged Netherlandic sector similar to the policy of *rattrapage* or "catching-up" then being applied to Francophone institutions in Canada. The most important consideration was that university financing in general should become proportionate to the steadily increasing proportion of enrolment in the Dutch regime, but beyond this additional research funds from public sources should reflect the same proportions, and the scientific granting bodies should be organized on the basis of linguistic parity and of separate evaluation committees sensitive to the priorities of their respective cultural communities (Amelinckx et al., 1969, 14-18). This report was favorably received, and within a year the government had established a policy of special compensatory grants.

During the 1970s the question of Flemish representation merged with wider questions of science policy in general and the institutions for decision-making in this area. These institutions included a minister of science policy, a ministerial committee chaired by the prime minister for policy decisions, an interdepartmental committee of civil servants for coordination and execution, and a wider advisory council of thirty-four members drawn from the universities, scientific institutions, and the major interest groups. This last council is legally required to be balanced both linguistically and confessionally. The chief focus of decision-making is the science "budget," which is presented and debated in Parliament annually under the prime minister's estimates. This "budget" is not a departmental budget in the usual sense but a regrouping from several departments of all scientific and research-oriented activities relating to the natural and human sciences that are financed or subsidized by the public sector. In 1979 the allocations for these activities came to 43 billion Belgian francs, or about 4 per cent of the total budget of the central government.

The function of the policy process is to analyze the pattern of expenditure from three different standpoints: first, by sector or category of expenditure; second, by policy objectives; and finally, by cultural communities and regions. In terms of sectors, the proportion allocated in direct and indirect aid to universities and academic hospitals in 1979 was 64 per cent, the rest going to state-run scientific institutions, to research and development aid to industry, and to international scientific activities. In practice, close attention is paid at the planning stage to the distribution among the universities and similar institutions, because this has a direct effect on both the linguistic and the confessional balance. In the current atmosphere of linguistic and regional tension, parliamentary questioning tends to focus on the regional impact of other sectors of the science budget, and especially on the high concentration of state scientific institutions and activities in the Brussels region.

One further complication is that after the 1970 constitutional reforms some scientific activities were entrusted to the cultural councils, and after 1974 others were given to the provisional regional institutions. By 1979 this decentralization was still quite limited, only 3 per cent of the total science budget going through the cultural councils and a further 0.3 per cent through the three provisional regional administrations. For the future, however, these proportions could increase considerably, because the new regionalization legislation of 1980 gives to the new community and regional councils responsibility over "applied" scientific research relating to matters within their respective legislative powers (Senelle, 1980, 188, 194).

If scientific research was a natural corollary of Flemish concern with the university sector, another area of equal and related concern was governmental support for cultural activities. In the 1950s Flemish organizations began to collect extensive evidence from many sectors to demonstrate what they considered to be a massively unbalanced distribution of cultural resources, and to press claims for redress (Van Haegendoren et al., 1957; Van Haegendoren, 1969b). Since the 1930s the remedy usually proposed for this situation had been some form of cultural autonomy of the two communities, and in the 1950s the demands became more specific: a complete *splitsing* of the Ministry of Public Education, which was also responsible for cultural matters; a division of the entire cultural budget according to the demographic proportions of the two cultural communities; and a reorganization of national cultural institutions to split them into separate linguistic sectors, with autonomy for each sector in most activities and parity in both management and personnel (Van Haegendoren et al., 1957, 114). Even this, however, was not seen as a complete solution, since it left unresolved the question of *rattrapage*, or compensation for past imbalances in organizations and activities.

When the cultural budget was eventually split in 1969 into three categories—one French, one Dutch, and one for shared and national activities—it was decided through interparty agreement that the amounts to be allocated to each cultural community should be decided by "objective criteria" rather than by the prevailing principle of simple parity, with parity to be used only where other criteria could not be established. The experiment was an interesting one from the standpoint of resource allocation. To give effect to the new principle, the minister of Dutch education and culture commissioned two research teams from the Flemish universities (one from Leuven, the other from Brussels) to investigate the current activities and needs of the two communities in the fields of culture and sports respectively. These teams compared the language regions from the standpoint of several variables, including population, age structure, density of habitation, the numbers and size of communes, and the degree of urbanization and industrialization, and reported to the minister that approximately 60 per cent of the linguistically specific subsidies should go to the Dutch sector (Delanghe et al., 1969; Gelders et al., 1969). Predictably, neither the substance of these two reports nor the procedure was acceptable to the minister of French education and culture, who immediately commissioned two further teams from Francophone universities (Louvain and Liège respectively) to analyse the findings of the Flemish teams and prepare rejoinders (Voyé et al., 1969; Minon et al., 1969).

The Francophone critics had little difficulty in demonstrating the untenability of the original reports. In the first place, some of the data were of questionable validity. Second, and more interesting, the criteria selected as a basis for division tended to shift from one area of cultural activity to another. Thus the Flemish team tended to interpret activities showing lower expenditures in Flanders as deficiencies calling for remedial action, but those indicating lower expenditures in Wallonie as evidence of differential needs or interests between regions, selecting in each case a criterion that tended to maximize Flemish advantages. A third and more fundamental criticism was that the whole exercise of establishing external "objective criteria" as a basis for each area of expenditure is itself logically inconsistent with the principle of cultural autonomy, which presupposes that each community will establish its own priorities among areas of activity (Voyé et al., 1969, 123-26, 142-44; CRISP, 1976, nos. 727-29: 68).

The attempt to find objective guideposts led only to disagreements among academics, and the question was settled in October 1970 by a pragmatic political compromise between the two ministers of culture, which was included in a formal governmental accord in 1972. By this compromise, expenditures for education were to be divided according to various criteria of needs as indicated by existing laws and regulations, and the same criteria were to be applied to educational activities within the cultural budgets. Other more strictly cultural activities—including radio, television, arts, and letters—were to be financed as before on a parity basis. The compromise came under repeated attack from both sides, the Flemish rejecting the parity element and the Francophones rejecting the elements in the educational formula based on population, but for want of a more objective solution it served as a basis for the distribution of the cultural budget for several years. Under this formula the combination of educational items scaled more or less according to population and cultural items based on parity produced a combined grant ratio for all cultural activities of the Dutch and French Cultural Councils of approximately 54:46 for the period from 1972 to 1976 (CRISP, 1976, nos. 727-29: 34-35). The regionalization law of August 1980 specified a straightforward 55:45 ratio for the central government's grant to the new community councils for cultural and "personalizable" activities, but education grants continued to be based on "needs" as defined by statutes and regulations (Senelle, 1980, 217).

Beyond the dispute over the respective shares of the cultural communities, another area of contention has been the budget for common cultural affairs, which is presented to Parliament as part of the prime minister's estimates. As originally established at the first tripartite division in 1969, this third budget provided for national institutions in the capital, for German-language cultural activities, for international cultural relations, and for certain cultural parastatals, notably the National Orchestra, the national theatre, and the broadcasting organization. Of these the broadcasting system was by far the largest in financial terms, accounting for 53 per cent of the three cultural budgets combined in 1969. One can calculate from the budget documents for that year that the common cultural affairs budget accounted for 64 per cent of the combined total. The position of Flemish nationalist opinion has been that this common affairs budget should be reduced to a minimum or even disappear. In practice it declined significantly during the early 1970s, until in 1976 under the revised structures it represented just 23 per cent of the combined cultural budget, with the respective community budgets increasing proportionately. If we exclude broadcasting from this calculation, the common affairs proportion for all other cultural areas drops from about 23 per cent in 1969 to 10 per cent in 1976 (CRISP, 1976, nos. 727-29: 47-48), and by 1979 it was down to a mere 5 per cent of total cultural expenditures.

If the evolution of the budgetary process is a reflection of the movement towards cultural autonomy, it also has served to shape and stimulate that tendency. One example of this is the public libraries, which were placed under the cultural councils by the constitutional reforms of 1970 and the law of 1971 establishing the councils. After several years of discussion publicly supported libraries were given a new legislative and financial base in 1978 by two decrees of the respective councils. These decrees forced the bilingual communal libraries of Brussels-Capital either to become officially unilingual so as to qualify for subsidy from one of the councils or to remain financially disadvantaged under the previous legislation of 1921 (CRISP, 1979, nos. 843-44).

A similar but more highly visible case was that of amateur sport, which was also allocated to the councils in 1970 and 1971. In 1977 both the French and the Dutch councils passed *décrets* spelling out conditions for granting subsidies to amateur sports federations and associations, in both cases requiring these groups to be either unilingual bodies or organized in separate linguistic sections in order for each section to qualify for support from the corresponding council. This legislation posed a painful dilemma for organizations that had built substantial facilities in the Brussels area on the basis of linguistically mixed membership, and the dilemma was particularly acute for their Flemish members, who were usually in the minority. Some national organizations—including ping-pong players and naturists—at first opted for unity without public subsidies, but by early 1978 some forty-seven out of sixty-six national sports associations comprising an estimated 65 per cent of total membership had requested recognition as split bodies in conformity with the decrees (CRISP, 1978, nos. 791-92).

The evolution of policy with respect to education, scientific research, and culture has been accompanied by major organizational changes in the administrative agency chiefly concerned, the former Ministry of National Education and Culture. The educational sector has had a chequered administrative history. For the first century of independent Belgium there was no ministry of education except for the brief Van Humbeeck interlude from 1878 to 1884 that touched off the first Schools War. This period aside, the state's rather limited educational role was filled by the Ministry of the Interior until 1907, a Ministry of Arts and Sciences from 1907 to 1932, and after that date by a formally designated Ministry of Public Instruction, which became the Ministry of National Education and Culture after the second Schools War in 1961 (CRISP, 1974, no. 663: 2). By this date the educational sector was in the midst of a rapid expansion, which saw the departmental budget increase from 10 per cent of all central government expenditures in 1956 to 20 per cent in 1966 (Norrenberg, 1968, 374).

No sooner had the department been consolidated under its new name in 1961 than new centrifugal forces appeared. The first phase was a multiplication of ministers and secretaries of state from a single head to two in 1961 and to four in 1965, as we have already noted (see above, 186), an arrangement that persisted with minor variations in the 1970s. In 1966 the respective budgets for education and for culture were divided and presented to Parliament as two separate documents, the one for education being by far the larger. Further, a series of organizational reforms beginning in 1963 led to a gradual *dédoublement* of the major administrative divisions and a gradual increase in the authority of the directors of these divisions at the expense of the deputy minister or *secrétaire général* (Norrenberg, 1968). The process culminated in a formal splitting of the department along linguistic lines by royal decree in September 1969, with employees being assigned to one or other of the new departments according to their linguistic register and without regard to function. This made for structural distortions, hasty rearrangement of employees, new recruitment, and further financial strains. The two new unilingual departments enjoyed a virtually complete autonomy within their respective areas of jurisdiction and remained linked only tenuously for the joint administration of a few residual national institutions such as the Bibliothèque royale and certain museums. All in all, the linguistic split clearly imposed severe added strains upon a service already characterized by weak administrative traditions and strong confessional differences (CRISP, 1974, no. 663: 12-13; Molitor, 1974, 249). The establishment of new ministers with educational responsibilities in the post-1980 community executives foreshadows still further problems of divided jurisdiction whose outcome cannot yet be foreseen. More radical decentralization of control over education is understandably favored by the respective majority parties at community level (Flemish Catholics and Francophone socialists) but viewed with reserve by some other parties, most notably by Francophone Catholics. Indeed it was primarily a growing rift between the Flemish and Francophone Catholic parties over plans for the decentralization of education during the summer of 1985 that undermined the Martens V government in its final months and led to a premature dissolution of Parliament (see Appendix B below).

Yet the balance sheet is not wholly negative. One American observer has argued that cultural autonomy and administrative *dédoublement* in these sectors and others have helped to depoliticize certain issues by removing the ethnic dimension from the sectors that are twinned, thus serving to "convert politically loaded issues into technically treatable matters" (Heisler, 1974, 213). The underlying principle of cultural autonomy is that members of each group should compete only with themselves on the basis of a predetermined share of the cultural, scientific, or educational budget. In broader perspective, this can be seen as a form of affirmative action, appropriate to a situation where *laisser faire* is not trusted to produce a balanced result. In the Swiss case the public is prepared to leave intergroup allocations to the individual decisions of decentralized groups; in Belgium the question of proportionality is regulated—often after a bitter, well-publicized verbal battle—on a global or package basis at national level, where the weight of numbers can be called upon to counterbalance residual structural inequalities.

In the context of the Belgian administrative system as a whole, the educational sector has been something of a paradox. Where the general norms of the system emphasize uniformity and centralization, education has been notable for decentralization and minimal national standards. Throughout much of Belgian history since 1830 this situation has permitted variations as to both the quality of schooling and the general orientations of education, and these in turn have had differential repercussions in the language communities, reinforcing their differences. Because of the basic nature of Belgian society, the educational system has institutionalized from the beginning an enviable degree of freedom of conscience and diversity of values, but it is difficult not to see this pluralism as one of the long-term impediments to the modernization of Flemish society.

I Broadcasting

The development of broadcasting structures in Belgium has its own intrinsic interest but at the same time it provides valuable insights into the changing roles of interest groups in Belgian society over more than half a century. The first regular broadcasting services, beginning in 1923, were operated on a commercial basis by private groups, and in French only. These were followed by a private Dutch-language station in 1928. After the Prague Conference of 1929, which gave Belgium exclusive use of two medium-wave channels and joint use of a third, the government moved quickly to establish a public corporation to occupy them (Namurois, 1960, 2). A law of June 1930 created the Institut national belge de radiodiffusion (INR/NIR), which took over existing private installations and ran parallel services in French and Dutch, under a twelve-year concession, down to the German invasion of 1940.

Two features of this period, however, deserve special notice. First, while the INR retained exclusive use of the wavelengths allocated by international agreements, a number of private stations were authorized to broadcast a limited signal on other unutilized wave bands. This private regional broadcasting developed most strongly in Wallonie, and by the late 1930s Belgium had sixteen private stations, including two in Brussels, four in Flanders, and ten in Wallonie, one of which was broadcasting half its programs in Walloon dialect (Hankard, 1979, 14-15; *Radio belge*, 1973, 31-32).

Second, the ideological pluralism of Belgian society found direct expression in the programming of the state networks. Following the example of broadcasting in the Netherlands, Belgian Catholics and socialists both sought to develop their own broadcasting associations, and these were allocated blocs of programming time. By 1932 no fewer than eight of these ideologically oriented associations were sharing in the broadcasts of the two state networks, with linguistically distinct Catholic, liberal, and socialist bodies each being allocated one day a week on their respective networks, and Flemish nationalists and Walloon federalists one day a month on the Dutch and French bands respectively. The original nine-member board of directors was balanced both ideologically (three members from each of the traditional "families") and regionally (three members each from Brussels, Wallonie, and Flanders), but not linguistically. Board meetings were held exclusively in French (Hankard, 1973, 24-27; *Radio belge*, 1973, 30). Yet language did not become a major issue in the prewar period. French and Dutch spoken broadcasts had been organized separately from the start, and in 1936 an administrative restructuring created separate directorates for each network. In other respects the INR remained a unitary organization, and only occasionally were voices raised in favor of a more autonomous Flemish network (Van Dijck, 1937).

The German invasion of 1940 brought a suspension of INR activities, creation by the Belgian government-in-exile of a new broadcasting organization under government control with headquarters in London, and operation by this body of a powerful short-wave station at Léopoldville in the Belgian Congo. By September 1945 this wartime body was dissolved and the INR re-established. There were, however, two basic changes. First, the authorizations for private stations were not renewed, leaving to the INR an effective monopoly on Belgian territory. Second, and in contrast with the example of the Netherlands, the programming privileges of the ideologically based broadcasting associations were not restored, nor were they actively pursued by the associations themselves. Maurice Hankard offers a number of possible explanations for this, including the prolongation of military hostilities, major political problems including the royal question, diminishing fear of a state monopoly in broadcasting, and the integration of many former personnel from the associations into the INR itself.

From this point onwards ideological pluralism would continue to be a concern of the INR and its successor organizations, but a concern to be expressed through proportional representation of interests in their boards, staff, and programming (Hankard, 1973, 27-29). To a very limited degree the role of the prewar broadcasting associations continued after 1945 through allocation of a few programs to religious denominations, political parties, and economic interest groups on both radio and television. The immediate postwar years also saw several parliamentary initiatives, invariably unsuccessful, to restructure the INR. While most of these proposals pointed towards greater autonomy for the French and Flemish services, the strongest voices for a more radical regionalization came from critics in Wallonie, who evoked memories of prewar private stations and wartime clandestine transmitters to claim a more "authentic" *radio wallonne* (Hankard, 1979, 17-19; André-Robert, 1948; Devillers, 1952).

When structural changes finally came in 1960, the formula adopted was a tripartite one. The unitary INR was replaced by a new organization, Radio-Télévision belge (RTB/BRT), that was set up as three autonomous institutes. Two of these were independent broadcasting institutes for French and Dutch programming respectively. The third was an Institute of Common Services, jointly managed by the two broadcasting institutes, to look after services and facilities that could not easily be divided between them. Its responsibilities included technical and administrative services, broadcasts to the German-speaking region of Liège province, international services, and common cultural services such as the symphony orchestra and the central library. This institute was also responsible for buildings and equipment used by all three institutes.

The new structures gave the two broadcasting institutes ample room for innovation, and the French-language body, RTB, used this freedom to develop greater strength in regional radio programming. The 1960s also saw a tendency for the two broadcasting institutes to obtain gradual control over the personnel and functions of the Institute of Common Services. The achievement of constitutional reform and the establishment of the principle of cultural autonomy in 1970 pointed towards further reform in the structure of broadcasting, which fell almost entirely within the jurisdiction of the new cultural councils. Accordingly, a law of February 1977 dissolved the Institute of Common Services, distributing all its remaining personnel—including even the musicians of the symphony orchestra—between the two broadcasting institutes according to each individual's language register. Similarly its offices, studios, and production equipment were divided between BRT and RTB though certain "unsplittable" features, such as corridors and heating facilities, remained in co-proprietorship. A further consequence of the dissolution was that a third small institute, the Belgisches Rundfunk- und Fernsehzentrum (BRF), was created in 1977 to administer German-language radio programming to Eastern Belgium (RTB, 1976-77, 21-23).

On the Francophone side, integration of facilities and personnel from the former Institute of Common Services became an occasion for a complete structural overhaul of the French-language network. In December 1977 a decree of the Cultural Council of the Francophone Community reorganized the RTB as the RTBF, or Radio-Télévision belge de la Communauté culturelle française. A major objective of the new legislation was to reinforce the independence of broadcasting from government control and to establish stronger guarantees for ideological pluralism. Another objective was to sanction and extend the *de facto* decentralization of French-language broadcasting. The decree formally recognizes the principle of regional production centres and even provides each one with its own advisory council based on the relative strength of the political parties in the region concerned. On the basis of new and existing facilities RTBF accordingly operates three regional production centres for television (at Brussels, Charleroi, and Liège) and four for radio (at Brussels, Liège, Mons, and Namur), as well as "common production" facilities for both media in Brussels for categories of programs that remain wholly or partially centralized. For television, these include news, sports, films, some drama, and educational programs, while for radio they include musical and literary programs and international broadcasts. A major aim of decentralization has been the economic revival and cultural animation of a languishing Wallonie, but the policy has also been criticized for its dispersal of limited resources, for its debilitating effects on programming, and for administrative complexities and conflicts that one critic has labelled a "Lebanese-style pluralism" (RTBF, 1978, chaps. 1-2; Hankard, 1979; *TV 25*, 1978, 222-32; Namurois et al., 1980, 60-64; Honni, 1977).

The Dutch-language network, the BRT or Belgische Radio en Televisie, in its turn acquired a new legal framework from its own Cultural Council in December 1979 (Namurois et al., 1980, 215-25). This decree differs from the Francophone one on many organizational details, but from a more substantive standpoint it did not follow the path of decentralization chosen for the Francophone system. Although the BRT has long had regional radio programming to a limited degree on the second program (BRT 2), all of its television programming has always originated from Brussels. One explanation for this policy is Flemish determination to maintain a strong cultural presence in Brussels. Another more practical one is that centralization makes possible a better use of resources and higher-quality programming (Hankard, 1979, 26-27). One interesting innovation of the 1979 BRT decree is an added emphasis on allocating programming time on both television and radio to outside bodies in a way that is suggestive of broadcasting policy in the Netherlands and prewar Belgian practice. For this purpose up to 50 per cent of the time devoted to informational programming on television may be allocated to recognized political associations, ideological families, professional associations, and the political parties themselves, with secondment of BRT personnel and a corresponding budgetary allocation from BRT resources in proportion to the broadcasting time involved (Articles 25-32).

In long-term perspective, the development of public broadcasting in Belgium has thus followed a slow but substantial evolution from the unitary structure of the INR in 1930 to the two completely independent broadcasting systems of the RTBF and BRT of the late 1970s, each with its own legal framework, board of directors, staff, and broadcasting facilities. Further, each of these systems operates under a separate legislative authority—the community council of the cultural community concerned—except for a few residual matters still reserved to the Belgian Parliament (the ban on commercial advertising, obligations concerning governmental messages, and a right of reply for individuals or associations incorrectly or harmfully represented on a broadcast). The contrasting patterns of development within the two systems may be seen as responses to differing priorities in cultural policy: for the Francophone community, the revitalization of a languishing and increasingly disadvantaged periphery; for the Flemings, the maintenance of a viable Dutch-speaking presence in a predominantly Francophone centre.

Control by the cultural communities has also had interesting political repercussions. Although the RTBF statute calls for a balance of ideologies in staffing and programming, the balance of party forces in the French Cultural Community left the RTBF with a predominantly socialist administrative board and under a Socialist minister in the community's executive. After 1981 the control of the RTBF therefore became an issue between the Catholic-Liberal Martens V government and the Socialist opposition. To counteract socialist influence in the RTBF, the government authorized in 1983 a technical linkage between Brussels and the privately owned and commercially oriented Radiodiffusion Télévision luxembourgeoise in the Grand Duchy, an action sharply contested by the Community Council's executive. Ironically, the completion of cultural autonomy in broadcasting has more or less coincided with a substantial weakening of the public broadcasting systems, at first through the rapid spread of cable television, more recently through the founding of local and commercial radio stations in Belgium itself, a development made possible by a new broadcasting statute of 1979 (Hermans, 1983, 41-47).

From a technical standpoint, few problems arise from the nature of the Belgian terrain. A mere handful of stations is sufficient to provide medium-wave, FM, and television coverage for all of the relatively flat, compact, densely populated Belgian territory, and the main constraints arise from the limited number of frequencies and channels allocated to Belgium by international agreements. By 1966 it was possible for the RTB to report that some 99 per cent of the population was within reach of television reception and also of the three radio services intended for its own language region. Further, most of the country could also receive the radio signals broadcast in the second national language (*Monographie*, 1967, 40-41). By the later 1970s it was estimated that close to 95 per cent of households in both language regions had television sets and that even more than this level had radios (RTBF, 1978, 126; *Enkele facetten*, 1978, 13). The same openness of terrain leaves the Belgian countryside open to competition from foreign radio and television, a prospect that neighboring commercial stations have found all the more inviting in that the domestic networks have been bound by a strict ban on advertising. This competition has intensified with the spread of cable television, which increased from an estimated 10 per cent of households in 1970 to about 80 per cent in 1979, bringing in up to eleven foreign programs side by side with domestic ones (RTBF, 1978, 162-63; RTB, 1973-74, 151-67; CRISP, 1979, no. 836). As data in Table 46 indicate (below, 247), this competition from foreign stations appears to have made deeper inroads on the Francophone network than on the Flemish one.

For television, more serious technical problems stemmed from political rivalries. From 1949 to 1953 the two broadcasting communities were pitted against each other in the "battle of the lines" (lijnenslag), which set proponents of the 819-line transmission system adopted by France against those who favored the 625-line system adopted by West Germany, the Netherlands, and other European countries. Since both organizations had to depend heavily at the start on exchanged programs, the issue was an important one. The war ended with a compromise solution that some considered typically Belgian: programming in French would use 819 lines and programming in Dutch would use 625. Belgian television receiving sets would require no fewer than four picture-tube norms and would cost 25 per cent more than those of neighboring countries, but in the process a protected domestic market was created for the manufacture of these special receivers. Only in 1964 did the entire Belgian system begin to be standardized with the 625-line norm of the rest of Europe (Belgische Radio, 1979, 44; TV 25, 1978, 4; Namurois, 1960, 4). By comparison, the choice between color systems was less dramatic. In 1968 a special committee recommended choice of the PAL system for both broadcasting institutes. This meant that color receiving sets in Belgium would require a converter to pick up programs broadcast directly from France on the SECAM system; however, for those on cable the conversion could be done by the distributor (TV 25, 1978, 26; Huggett, 1969, 102-103). The wider international setting for these technical battles has been outlined by Paulu, who notes that the costs fall most heavily on those near the frontiers between technical systems (1967, 33-37).

In spite of increasing structural autonomy, the two broadcasting institutes have adopted similar frameworks of programming. In the postwar period each has offered for radio a first or "national" program, a second program largely devoted to regional broadcasts, and from 1961 onward a third program, modelled after the BBC Third Program, devoted to serious music. For television, each organization developed its own main television channel from 1953, when regular broadcasting began in both languages, until 1977, when both introduced programming on a second channel. One difference lies in the sources of this programming. The drive for decentralization of broadcasting in Wallonie has meant that the regional radio production centres in Wallonie have produced many programs for all three program services, whereas the regional radio studios in Flanders have been responsible only for the second, or regional, program. In 1975 the regional centres produced some 66 per cent of RTB radio programs, whereas the corresponding figure for BRT was about 35 per cent (RTB, 1975, 38; BRT, 1976, 197). Similarly, the second television channel is a regional service on the Francophone side but a national one in the Flemish system.

Table 45

Belgium: Domestic broadcasting time by language community, selected years (weekly averages)

	French (INR/RTB/RTBF)	Dutch (NIR/BRT)	German (BRF)
A Radio			
1952	74	77	3
1959	180	179	3
1962	237	199	14
1970	356	298	28
1978	360	363	44
1982	546	361	68
B Television			
1955	24	21	none
1959	33	32	none
1965	40	35	none
1970	48	41	none
1975	57	54	none
1978	56 + 11[a]	53 + 11[a]	none
1980	59 + 18[a]	56 + 11[a]	none
1983	71 + 35[a]	52 + 20[a]	none

[a] First and second channels.

Sources: Radio: INR, 1952, 116, 117, 124; 1959, 39; *Monographie*, 1967, 34; RTB, 1970, 22, 100; RTBF, 1978, 140; 1980, 165; 1982, 33; unpublished data from BRT.
Television: INR, 1955, 29; 1959, 47; RTB, 1965, 136; 1970, 48; 1975, 67; RTBF, 1978, 106-107; 1980, 217; BRT, 1977, 82-84; *Enkele facetten*, 1978, 41-42; 1980, 47-48; 1983, 40-41.

The evolution of domestic broadcasting time since the 1950s is illustrated in Table 45, which shows the growth of domestic programming time in each language expressed in hours per week averaged throughout the year, for certain years in which comparisons between systems are possible. These data are far from ideal because they must be assembled from a wide range of sources; some of the variations between systems and between years may arise from different methods of reckoning, especially after 1960.

Other differences arose from differences in operating conditions. In television, the 1955 data for the French channel included about eight hours a week, or 32 per cent of total programs, that were obtained from France and rebroadcast by the INR. In radio, the Dutch-language third program in the 1960s was considerably more limited than its French-language counterpart (*Monographie*, 1967, 34). Further, regional radio transmitters in Wallonie have operated separately and simultaneously (*en décrochage*) for much of this period while in Flanders regional studios were heard only consecutively on the regional network. In 1980 the periods of "disconnection" accounted for 28 per cent of total broadcasting time on the French network (RTBF, 1980, 165). In the 1980s, under community autonomy and in conditions of rapid technological change, the differences between the two systems appear to be increasing more rapidly.

Following the reorganization of broadcasting in 1960, budgetary policy was based for two decades on the principle of equal financial resources for the two programming institutes. Apart from a few minor revenues of the broadcasting institutes, broadcasting in Belgium is financed primarily from revenues from radio and television licences, which are collected by the central government and allocated in large part to the broadcasting authorities but also partly to general revenues. The principle adopted in 1960 was to provide first for the technical, administrative, and other services provided by the Institute of Common Services, and then to divide the remainder equally between the two programming institutes. In 1963 the proportion of the budget allocated to common services was 40 per cent, but as the system developed this proportion tended to increase, leaving a smaller proportion for the two programming institutes. By 1970 50 per cent of expenditures and of revenues were budgeted for common services (RTB, 1970, 120-22). After the dissolution of the Institute of Common Services, its budget and staff were integrated into those of the two programming institutes, which henceforth received the entire state grant except for a modest provision for the new German-language institute.

In spite of Flemish pressure for a distribution formula based on population figures, the principle of French-Dutch budgetary equality prevailed down to 1979. Since the constitutional reform of 1980, however, the broadcasting budgets of the RTBF and the BRT have been voted by the community councils of their respective language communities, whose main funding for cultural items including broadcasting comes from a central government grant divided in a ratio of 55 per cent for Flemings to 45 per cent for Francophones (Tournemenne, 1984, 10). Accordingly each broadcasting agency competes against other cultural claims and even health or welfare programs of its own language community,[1] and the

---

[1] For the RTBF these competing claims include those of some dozen local or community television associations, which receive modest subsidies from the executive of the French Community (CRISP, 1985, nos. 1075-76).

respective broadcasting budgets are no longer directly comparable. This change in funding is clearly an important one, but its long-run impact on broadcasting is difficult to assess.

When one turns to the question of program content, material comparing the Flemish and Francophone systems is very scarce. Since the RTB and the BRT developed separately after 1960, their audience and program research units developed independently, at different dates, and in response to divergent policy imperatives. The only study found that makes any direct comparisons of program offerings is a brief analysis of BRT evening television offerings in late 1978 prepared for the RTBF (Thoveron, 1979). This study reports that the BRT devoted more time to fiction and to entertainment, and less to information programs and sports, than the RTBF did during the study period, while cultural and documentary programs were allocated similar attention on both networks. However, the four-week period covered by this study seems a rather small sample from which to generalize. One earlier survey prepared independently probed the public's level of interest in a wide range of topics treated in the mass media, finding that respondents in Flanders showed generally lower levels of interest than in Wallonie or Brussels in most topics of domestic and international politics, and even in cultural matters. The only categories to show higher Flemish interest were sports and religious events (INBEL, 1968, 20-25). Another study, which focused on foreign and domestic news flows, found that for the periods analyzed 32 per cent of RTB news items focused on domestic events compared to 22 per cent of BRT items (Boone, 1966, 390).

In the absence of authoritative studies comparing program content, one can report on prevailing impressions and images of the two systems gathered from interviews during the 1960s and 1970s. Francophones working in the RTB saw BRT programs as more devoted to entertainment than their own, more aimed at popular tastes, less oriented to an informational function, and also more "human" than the more "serious" programming from the Netherlands. They also perceived the BRT as facing less intense competition from adjacent foreign stations and therefore catering to a less demanding public. They saw their own networks as locked in intense competition with strong foreign French-language networks, and forced to match the standards of an international Francophone clientele.

Flemish informants working in the BRT saw the RTB and the RTBF as heavily oriented towards the cultural horizons of France, as contrasted with a more "universal" orientation of the BRT that stresses primarily Netherlandic culture but also adds a healthy supplement of English, German, and French fare. They saw the BRT as more committed than the RTB to the development of domestic artists, and they also perceived it as fostering closer cultural collaboration with the Netherlands in spite of recognized differences in mentalities. These images of the networks held on either side do not match in all respects, and some of the discrepancies appear to be linked to more general group stereotypes in Belgian society.

Two areas of divergence between RTB and BRT programming relate specifically to language. First, foreign-language films shown on the BRT are generally shown in the original language with subtitles; those shown on the RTB or RTBF are usually dubbed in French. Second, and in contrast with its audience's more limited tolerance for foreign languages, the RTB and RTBF have long devoted approximately one program per week to television plays presented in various Walloon dialects, which attract significant if not spectacular audiences (Thoveron, 1971, 750-51). The BRT, reflecting more negative Flemish attitudes to the use of dialect, has a firm policy of using only standard Netherlandic or ABN for all occasions except certain popular songs, even in historical dramas where ABN is an anachronism. This is seen as an obligation to the cause of language standardization, and in a more practical vein it also facilitates coproduction of programs with the Netherlands.

One last area for comparison between Francophone and Flemish broadcasting is levels of use on each side. Here exact comparisons are difficult because available data are fragmentary. From material presented in Table 21 (see above, 86-87), it can be seen that the Flemish provinces lagged behind Wallonie and Brabant in radio licences per capita until the 1960s, but since then they have pulled slightly ahead. In television their index of sets per capita has been slightly ahead of those for other regions almost since the beginning. In color television the gap has been even wider, reflecting recent prosperity in Flanders. Estimations by the RTBF indicated that by January 1980 57 per cent of television licences in the Flemish community were for color sets, against 50 per cent in the Francophone community. The same estimates, based upon an assumed Francophone-Flemish ratio of 85:15 in Brussels-Capital, indicated that the Flemish community represented 59 per cent of all television licences and 60 per cent of residential radio licences (RTBF, 1979, 49-51).

The average duration per day of listening and viewing by the public on each system is measured and presented in so many different ways by the two organizations that meaningful comparisons seem impossible, especially over a period of time. It does appear, however, that while the volume of radio listening may be roughly similar on both sides, Francophone television viewers, with more channels in their own language to choose from, tended in the mid-1970s to watch up to half an hour more television per day than their Flemish counterparts (RTB, 1975, 2; RTBF, 1978, 77; Enkele facetten, 1978, 14). One can assemble more meaningful but still lamentably incomplete data on the division of the audience in each viewing area between domestic and competing foreign stations. These are shown for selected representative years in Table 46, but it must be remembered that this table is based on several different sources which do not always make clear the criteria on which their data are based. The figures for 1951 in this table are based on a national survey question as to radio listening the previous evening, a survey that revealed the clear predomi-

Table 46

Belgium: Audience shares of Belgian and foreign broadcasting systems, selected years (percentages)

I Francophone audience[a]	INR/RTB/ RTBF[b]	NIR/BRT[b]	France	Luxem- burg	Others
A Radio					
1951[c]	38	2	9	42	9
1962	51	2	d	36	12
1964	60	2	d	27	10
1966-67	72	1	d	11	16
1970-71	82	2	d	8	9
1973-74	71	2	d	18	9
1982	60	d	d	18	23
B Television					
1969	76	n.a.	n.a.	n.a.	n.a.
1972	69	n.a.	19	7	n.a.
1975	55	n.a.	33	9	n.a.
1978	41	n.a.	42	17	n.a.
1981	44	n.a.	35	16	n.a.
1984 (Jan.-May)	48	d	31	19	2

II Flemish audience[a]	NIR/BRT[b]	INR/RTB/ RTBF[b]	Nether- lands	France	Luxem- burg	Others
A Radio						
1951[e]	50	12	14	5	12	7
1970	77	n.a.	n.a.	n.a.	n.a.	n.a.
1975	76	n.a.	n.a.	n.a.	n.a.	n.a.
1978	80	n.a.	n.a.	n.a.	n.a.	n.a.
1981	78	1	11	d	*	9
1983	68	1	4	d	*	27
B Television						
1969	79	5	11	4	*	2
1972	69	5	21	3	*	2
1975	66	5	23	4	*	3
1978	62	3	24	4	2	5
1981	62	4	22	4	2	6
1983	59	4	25	4	3	5

* Less than 0.5 per cent.
[a] As defined by respective research organizations.
[b] Includes all radio services or television channels.
[c] Data for Wallonie only.
[d] Included in "others."
[e] Data for Flanders only.

Sources: IA: INSOC, 1951, no. 1: 9-11; Mathias and Milo, 1973, 127; *Enquête permanente*, undated, no. 63: 33; no. 72: 29; no. 80: 34; RTBF, 1982, 23; I B: RTB, 1975, 3; RTBF, 1978, 78, 163; 1979, 164; *Enquête permanente*, 1982, no. 56: 5; no. 57: 4-5; 1984, unnumbered; II A: INSOC, 1951, no. 1: 9-11; *Enkele facetten*, 1981, 83, 86; 1983, 95; II B: *Enkele facetten*, 1981, 52; 1983, 51.

nance of the privately owned Radio Luxemburg in Wallonie, in Brussels arrondissement, and in Belgium as a whole during the early postwar years (INSOC, 1951, no. 1; Thoveron, 1971, 453-55). Figures for later years come from the respective audience research units of the two organizations, each of which developed independent techniques for surveying its own clientele in its own linguistic area.

Although these figures must be used with extreme caution, the broad trends seem clear enough. In television, both organizations lost a proportion of their audience to other European networks during the 1970s, but the competition was more intense and the decline steeper on the Francophone side. At first glance this might be seen as a consequence of technical development and especially the rapid spread of cable television, but in a wider sense it may also mark the increasing integration of both Belgian communities into a common European society. In radio, the trends are less clear. While the BRT enjoyed a relatively stable domestic audience throughout the 1970s, its Francophone counterpart, which had gradually overcome the challenge of Radio Luxemburg to win a similar audience share by the late 1960s, lost ground again in the mid-1970s. Both public radio systems lost ground sharply in the early 1980s as a result of the sudden and unregulated proliferation of "free" and local private radio stations, but in the absence of any statute to regulate these competing stations it is too soon to say whether this loss of listeners will be permanent or temporary.

Apart from the two major broadcasting systems, a note should be added about radio broadcasts in German. After sporadic beginnings during the 1930s aimed at countering Nazi propaganda directed towards the German-speaking areas, these were established on a daily basis in 1945 on the return of the East Cantons to Belgium after five years of annexation to the Third Reich. Starting from a modest twenty minutes per day, programming gradually expanded in stages (see Table 45) until it averaged over eight hours per day by 1979, including morning and mid-day segments as well as evening broadcasts. Both in content and from a technical standpoint, these programs are directed towards the population of the East Cantons or "New Belgium." In recent years broadcasts have been transmitted over FM stations at Liège and Sankt Vith, and in 1975 production was transferred from Brussels to a small regional radio studio at Eupen. Under the reorganization of 1960 these German-language broadcasts were a responsibility of the Institute of Common Services, with day-to-day management alternating on a year-to-year basis between the RTB and the BRT. With the dissolution of the Institute of Common Services, a small independent broadcasting institute was created in 1977, with its own administrative council appointed by the Council of the German Cultural Community but with technical facilities for broadcasting supplied by the larger institutes. Programming in German has never extended to television, but the

East Cantons are within easy viewing range of West German programs broadcast from Köln (RTB, 1970, 100-102; 1972-73, 43-44; 1975, 51-54; Nelde, 1979a, 259-62). The new institute, the Belgisches Rundfunk- und Fernsehzentrum, has been active and expansionist, achieving continuous daytime German-language programming totalling almost 100 hours per week by April 1983 (BRF, 1983, 1, 5).

In the broad perspective of developments since the 1920s, Belgian broadcasting has given rise to minimal language conflict. Certain other issues have been far more salient, including questions of ideological balance in programming, of independence of broadcasting from government control, of monopoly powers vested in the state broadcasting system, of relaxation of the ban on commercial advertising, and of demands in Wallonie for more effective decentralization of broadcasting. One can discern in the unfolding of these issues some of the enduring divisions in Belgian society: church and state, public enterprise and *laisser faire*, centralization and local control. While each of these cleavages has had to be gradually incorporated into the broadcasting system, the language division was accommodated with minimal difficulty from 1930 onward. In this sense the evolution of broadcasting paralleled and even foreshadowed the development of cultural autonomy for the language communities in the 1970s. But this autonomy has also had its costs. The new structures provide no explicit mandate for radio or television to promote integrative values, or even mutual understanding, across linguistic boundaries. Instead they have tended to encourage linkages with the Francophone and Netherlandic language communities outside Belgium, and the current physical setting of the broadcasting system, with its divided headquarters building in Brussels, its separate studios, technical services, canteens—and even separate parking garages—tends to reduce personal contact between the professional staffs of the RTBF and the BRT to a minimum.

J The Press

Belgian daily newspapers, like their counterparts in Switzerland and the Netherlands, have historically been an opinion press, loosely compartmentalized according to the traditional ideological divisions of Belgian political life. In 1974 newspapers classed as "neutral" accounted for only 19 per cent of total circulation of dailies, the rest being identified more or less closely with the traditional ideological "families" (Luykx, 1975, 237). Though hardly giants by international standards, Belgian dailies in general have a sharply higher circulation than Swiss ones, averaging in 1970 about 47,000 copies per paper for some twenty-six Francophone papers and 80,000 per paper for fifteen Flemish ones. Fourteen papers out of forty-two, accounting for just over half of total circulation, were printed in Brussels (Gol, 1970, 37, 42-43). A further point to be noted is that the industry itself has been stagnant or declining for more than two decades. Since the late 1950s total circulation has declined gradually, apparently because of successful competition from the weekly periodical press and from broadcasting. The number of dailies rose from twenty-eight in 1852 to ninety-two in 1897, then declined to sixty-five in 1939 (Gol, 1970, 121), to thirty-nine in 1976, and to only thirty-one in 1980. More specialized areas of the subject—which will not be explored here—include the history of the censored press and the clandestine press under German occupation during the two world wars.

In historical context the long-term relationship between the Flemish and the Francophone press has been bound up with the fortunes of the respective language communities and the changing status of the two languages. One way of studying this is to analyze newspapers historically in terms of their date and place of founding and their language. Table 47, which is based on the *Tableau chronologique des journaux belges* (Bertelson, 1956), sketches this pattern over three centuries and a half, beginning in 1605, for the territory that became independent Belgium in 1830. Clearly, the method has serious limitations. It tells us nothing of the life span of each paper, its circulation, its influence, or even its frequency of publication. Further, it is only as good as the source list on which it is based, which appears to omit many of the small weeklies and regional papers founded during the past century. Nevertheless the evidence for Flanders does indicate an early predominance of Dutch papers and then a long ascendancy of French ones from the late eighteenth to the late nineteenth century. One can also note the absence of any Dutch-language paper in Wallonie. All this is consistent with other evidence of language usage presented earlier. The same source also mentions the overseas colonial press in the Congo and Ruanda-Urundi, listing thirty-two papers in French, beginning in 1898, compared with only two in Dutch, both weeklies and both founded in the 1950s.

For the modern period one can compare the relative position of the French-language and Dutch-language press in three ways. Each encounters certain problems of measurement, but by taking them together we can produce an informative profile. In the first place, by simply counting newspapers in each language one can assemble from a variety of sources the changing ratio of Francophone to Flemish papers. In 1840 there were twenty-eight dailies, all of them published in French, the first post-1830 Flemish daily being founded in 1844. By 1860 there were nine Flemish dailies in a total of fifty-five, and by 1904, twenty out of eighty-five. The number of dailies remained high until 1940 and even recovered for a time after 1945, but by 1976, after considerable rationalization in the industry, these figures had fallen to fourteen Dutch-language dailies, twenty-four published in French, and one small German-language daily in the East Cantons, the *Grenz-Echo* (Becquet, 1972-77, 1: 23; Dovifat, 1960, 23; Luykx, 1978, 530; Van Sint-Jan, 1929, 262-64). Beyond these regular dailies, a few dailies specializing in financial or sports reporting will not be considered here. Taken by themselves, these figures by title can be misleading, because the average circulation of Dutch-language papers is considerably higher than that of the others, and four of the five papers or combinations of papers with daily circulation figures above 200,000 are Flemish (CRISP, 1975, no. 682: 3).

Table 47

Belgium: Newspapers established within territory of modern Belgium, by language of paper and language region, 1605-1956

Period	Region and language of newspaper					
	Flanders		Brussels		Wallonie	
	French	Dutch	French	Dutch	French	German
1605-99[a]		5	1			
1700-79		3	4		6	
1780-89	5		1		6	
1790-99	2	3	13		6	
1800-13	3	2	5		5	
1814-29[b]	13	8	19		12	
1830-39	14	3	25	1	18	
1840-49[c]	6	4	13	1	13	
1850-59	7	6	11		8	
1860-69	5	5	7		9	
1870-79	3	5	9		6	
1880-89	1	6	13	3	3	
1890-99	5	5	18	1	15	
1900-14	6	4	8	3	8	1
1918-40	2	5	11	5	8	1
1944-56	1		9	1	2	

[a] Plus one bilingual paper (French and Dutch) in Flanders.
[b] Plus one in English in Brussels.
[c] Plus one bilingual paper (French and German) in Brussels.

Source: Compiled from Bertelson, 1956.

In the second place, one can analyze circulation data. Here the major problem is that some Belgian dailies submit their figures to an independent audit but others simply declare their circulation, especially when circulation is declining; the only penalty for overestimates is that the national news agency sets its charges according to declared circulation. While almost all of the Flemish circulation is now submitted to audit, only about 55 per cent of the Francophone circulation was audited in 1975 (CRISP, 1975, no. 682: 5). One can therefore choose between quasi-official circulation figures, based on editorial declarations or audit, and adjusted estimates made by informed students of the Belgian media.

Circulation figures before the Second World War are somewhat conjectural, but one estimate has placed total daily circulation in 1938 at about 1.7 million copies, of which 57 per cent were in French. After the Second World War total circulation soared to a reported 3.4 million in 1949, but almost all of this was unaudited. By 1958 the figure had fallen to 2.6 million after an economic recession and an increase in the practice of independent audits. The proportion of circulation in French remained at 58 per cent in 1949 and 57 per cent in 1958, but after this date it declined steadily to 53 per cent in 1965, to 51 per cent in 1969, and to 49 per cent by 1975, by which date total daily circulation—still based on a mixture of declarations and audits—had fallen to slightly over 2.3 million. The one German-language paper had a declared circulation during this period of about 13,000 to 15,000, or 0.6 per cent of total daily circulation, all the rest being Flemish (Luykx, 1978, 509, 530-31; CRISP, 1960, no. 62: 4-5; Stijns, 1957, 307). Adjusted estimates tend to be more favorable to the Flemish side. Thus one estimate for 1958 placed the Francophone share at 53 per cent, and two others in 1967 and in 1970 placed it very close to 50 per cent (CRISP, 1959, no. 1: 5; 1967, nos. 369-70: 5; Gol, 1970, 176-79). Similar corrections could be made for the 1970s. Even after this adjustment, however, it seems clear that the Francophone share of total daily circulation has remained somewhat higher than the Francophone proportion of the population.

One explanation for this discrepancy appears when we turn from circulation figures to a third criterion for comparing newspapers, readership data. These have been obtained through major consumer surveys conducted about every three years for the advertising industry, beginning in 1965 (CRISP, 1978, nos. 812-13: 3). These surveys indicate that the number of readers per copy differs considerably from one newspaper to another, and that a provincial, Catholic-oriented, Dutch-language daily may have up to twice as many readers per copy as a Francophone daily in Brussels (CRISP, 1975, no. 682: 3). The problem with these surveys is that they have been made for private clients on a confidential basis, and their full results have never been made public. Nevertheless it can be calculated from the 1969 study that 52 per cent of the copies read by respondents were in Dutch and 48 per cent in French (SOBEMAP, 1969). The spread between circulation data and readership data at this date was therefore about three percentage points.

The distribution of the daily press by language region is also interesting. If we look at circulation figures by provinces, which again are largely self-declared, they indicate that in 1966 in the four Walloon provinces only 0.2 per cent of papers sold were in Dutch and a further 0.8 per cent in German, or 1 per cent in all. In the four Flemish provinces 16 per cent of total circulation was claimed by French-language papers, and in Brabant province the ratio was 68 per cent French to 32 per cent Dutch (CRISP,

1967, nos. 369-70: 45). The readership survey of 1969 suggests a less extreme picture, however, showing that just under 2 per cent of papers read in Wallonie were in Dutch and 7 per cent of those read in Flanders were in French, the ratio for Brussels-Capital being 85 per cent French to 15 per cent Dutch (SOBEMAP, 1969). Even allowing for differing boundaries, there is a discrepancy in Flanders between declared circulation and readership reported through media surveys, which perhaps indicates a reluctance of some Francophone papers to surrender an older image of a national mission and a countrywide market for advertising. Thus the conservative Catholic daily *La libre Belgique*, founded in 1884, reported that 30 per cent of its distribution still went to Flanders (Gol, 1970, 187-88).

In terms of place of publication, the rule of linguistic territoriality is all but universal. This means that in 1975 about 51 per cent of Dutch-language circulation was published in Brussels and the rest in Flanders, while 53 per cent of French-language circulation appeared in Brussels and the rest in Wallonie. Three small French-language dailies, one in Gent and two in Antwerp, the last survivors of a long line of Francophone dailies published in Flanders, ceased publication in June 1974, leaving *Le Lloyd anversois*, a small paper specializing in financial and shipping news, as the sole exception to the territoriality principle among the dailies (CRISP, 1975, no. 680: 14; 1975, no. 682: 5; Gol, 1970, 38). French-language weeklies, however, continued to publish in Gent and Antwerp.

A few other structural characteristics of the daily press may be touched on more briefly. We have noted that the daily press is largely an opinion press, but the ideological distribution varies between the Francophone and Flemish sectors, as might be expected from interregional differences in electoral behavior discussed earlier. Table 48 gives reported circulation for both language sectors and for the total by ideological orientation, as reported by Luykx (1975). Two things stand out from this table. First, the Catholic-oriented press, already the strongest in overall terms in the 1950s, has been making further relative gains since then, while socialist and communist papers have been the chief losers. The sole Flemish communist daily became a weekly in 1959, as did its Francophone counterpart for several years from 1966 to 1974. A second point is that circulation patterns do not correspond closely with the electoral strength of the various political families. Liberal papers are considerably stronger in circulation than Liberal electoral strength would indicate, and socialist papers are far weaker than voter support for Socialist parties. Paradoxically, the relative gains of the Catholic-oriented press since the late 1950s have coincided with the waning of electoral support for the Catholic party in favor of the Volksunie and other parties.

As in the case of broadcasting, the main problems concerning the daily press lie outside the domain of language issues and intergroup relations. One major preoccupation is the declining economic viability of

Table 48

Belgium: Circulation of dailies by language and by ideological orientation, compared to voting by parties, 1958 and 1974 (percentages, with number of titles in parentheses)

Ideological "family"	Francophone papers		Flemish papers		All dailies[a]		Parliamentary vote by parties[b]	
	1958[c]	1974	1958[c]	1974	1958	1974	1958	1974
Catholic	27.1 (11)	29.0 (9)	57.5 (14)	67.0 (10)	40.0	48.4	46.5	32.3
Liberal	18.9 (6)	18.4 (5)	27.9 (2)	24.3 (2)	22.7	21.2	11.1	15.2
Socialist	17.6 (6)	13.5 (5)	13.8 (2)	8.7 (2)	16.0	11.0	35.8	26.7
Communist	1.4 (1)	1.2 (1)	0.8 (1)[c]	—	1.1	0.6	1.9	3.2
Neutral	34.9 (4)	37.9 (4)	—	—	20.1	18.8	—	—
Total	100 (28)	100 (24)	100 (18)	100 (14)	100	100	95.3	77.4

[a] Omitting one Catholic German-language daily.
[b] Omitting votes for regional and minor parties.
[c] The number of titles is for 1960, except that the Flemish communist daily became a weekly in January 1959.

Source: Calculated from Luykx, 1975, 225-26, 237-38, 242.

the newspaper industry, which has led to a series of mergers and also to attempts to diversify into cognate activities such as publication of popular magazines and free advertising flyers, printing, and even travel agencies (Gol, 1970, 115-17). In 1976 the bankruptcy of the largest Flemish chain, the *Standaard* group, had repercussions far beyond the industry itself (CRISP, 1976, no. 739). A related concern is increasing concentration of ownership in both linguistic sectors. By 1970, 69 per cent of French-language circulation was controlled by three financial groups, and another four groups controlled 86 per cent of Dutch-language circulation (Gol, 1970, 124, 176-79). In spite of these trends ownership patterns of French-language and Dutch-language dailies have remained distinct, though some groups have formed alliances to offer special rates for twinned advertising packages (CRISP, 1975, no. 682: 11). The serious problem for many observers is whether the traditional ideological pluralism of the Belgian press can be maintained in the face of these adverse economic factors.

Towards the end of the 1960s, suggestions began to be made for direct state assistance. Although the press already enjoyed indirect public assistance in the form of reduced telephone and postal rates, tax concessions, and governmental advertising, these benefits were proving insufficient. Accordingly, after prolonged discussion, Parliament passed a law in 1974 designed specifically to maintain the diversity of the daily opinion press by providing direct government subsidies to enable weaker papers to survive. This law has been much criticized both for its principle and its distribution formula—which among other features provided equal global sums for Francophone and Flemish dailies—and the search for an improved formula acceptable on all sides has been a continuing one. Nevertheless the legislation itself has been renewed from year to year and its underlying principle appears to have become a permanent feature of the Belgian political system (CRISP, 1975, no. 682: 12-24; 1978, no. 809). In 1984 these direct subsidies to the press totalled 161 million Belgian francs, which included 9 million for the German-language *Grenz-Echo*, 10 million for the national news agency, Agence Belga, and the rest divided equally between the French-language and the Dutch-language dailies.

As their primary source of domestic and international news, all Belgian dailies subscribe to the wire services of Agence Belga, while a few of the larger papers are also clients of the major international news agencies. Agence Belga also serves the Belgian broadcasting institutes, broadcasting in Luxembourg, and a large number of governmental, institutional, and private clients. One recent feature is an "à la carte" news service to private businesses, launched in 1984, which enables subscribers to receive information on a pre-selected range of topics through a system of keywords added in the header of the copy and identified and transmitted by the computer. For its own access to international news, Belga receives inputs from AFP in France (both domestic and international services), DPA in

West Germany, ANP in the Netherlands, UPI, Reuters (in English and French), TASS, and EFE in Spain. Beyond this, there are agreements with other national agencies in both East and West bloc countries and in the developing world, including a close connection with AZAP in Zaire.

In its formal structure Agence Belga is an incorporated private company, founded in 1920. Until 1940, its services were provided only in French. Originally owned by a consortium of banks and financial institutions, its shares were purchased by the country's daily newspapers after the Second World War. The board of directors, which includes representation from broadcasting as well as from the press, is carefully balanced between the Brussels and the provincial press, and also between Francophones and Flemings. The recent penury of the newspaper world has been reflected in corresponding financial stringency for Belga itself, and some critics have contended that control by the newspaper owners has inclined the board towards excessive parsimony in operations (CRISP, 1978, no. 809: 19-20). In the international field Belga has been forced to eliminate its own fulltime foreign correspondents since the 1960s and to rely increasingly on agreements with other national and international news agencies as well as a limited number of stringers abroad. For domestic news a network of five regional offices (at Antwerp, Gent, Hasselt/Genk, Liège, and Charleroi) and some 200 stringers gathers information for selection and distribution from headquarters in Brussels. In 1984 total fulltime staff in Belgium numbered 115, of whom 75 were professional journalists.

Outputs of news emanate from Brussels in Dutch and French on two separate wire networks according to the language of the client. It is policy for Belga to supply the same service on both networks and the same amount of material. In practice, it was suggested in interviews, some events may be carried in greater detail on one wire than on the other, depending on where the event originated and its relative interest for each language community. It was also suggested that the French wire probably carries relatively more news from France and the Dutch wire carries more from the Netherlands, but studies comparing news flows on each wire appear to be lacking. For the small German-language *Grenz-Echo*, Belga transmits some foreign news in German direct from DPA, while domestic Belgian news is supplied on the French wire to be selected and translated by that paper's own staff. The average output of copy on the French-language and Dutch-language services was about 30,000 words per day on each wire in 1969, but this flow had increased by 1984 to about 50,000 or more in each language, partly as a result of recent computerization of the input and output systems. These outputs were made up of foreign and domestic news in roughly equal proportions. One study of the outputs on the French wire alone in 1961 found that foreign news accounted for 57 per cent of the total for the sample period studied, but this study covered only ten days in August, the traditional holiday month in Belgium (Hoed, 1964, 274).

Since Belga's distribution of news to clients is centralized in its Brussels office, all editorial staff there must have at least a passive knowledge of the second official language, though each writes copy in his or her own language. For work on foreign news, English and German are also required. In 1969 Flemings outnumbered Francophones in the organization by about two to one, but in 1984 the two groups were in rough balance, possibly as a result of changed working conditions. As linguistic pressures mounted during the 1960s there were more requests for coverage of Flemish events by Flemish journalists and for coverage of events in Wallonie by Francophones, but there were no significant pressures for greater separation of the two services.

One significant organizational change in the handling of foreign news emerged during the early 1970s. Up to that time, news selection had been made centrally, through a single desk functioning in French, and the copy selected was then passed on for translation into Dutch. After 1970 the practice developed of having two independent desks, one for each language network, to make an independent simultaneous selection of foreign news from identical input copy. Under these arrangements it was found that the two networks tended to make different choices of sources for both stylistic and practical reasons, the French-language service selecting more material originating in French, and the Dutch-language service selecting more English copy as well as materials in Dutch from ANP. A count of Belga foreign news outputs on the French wire in August 1961 showed that 50 per cent of the material transmitted originated from AFP in France, 12 per cent from Reuters, 18 per cent from its own staff, and the rest from several other agencies and sources (Hoed, 1964, 271). For the Dutch-language service, language standardization between Belgium and the Netherlands had reached the point by the 1970s that the two national agencies could each retransmit input copy received from the other automatically, without rewriting for linguistic reasons.

On balance, Agence Belga has been successful in surmounting the sharp linguistic cleavage that has divided Belgian society since the 1960s, and also successful in bridging the continuing ideological divisions reflected in society at large and in the structure of the daily press. To the extent that governmental institutions and the electronic media have become increasingly structured according to the model of autonomous language communities, Belga has become more and more important as an agent of integration by providing an effective channel for information flows among these communities. Its most pressing problems arise more from economics than from culture. The agency's continuing financial difficulties, coupled with its dependence on the newspaper proprietors, gave rise in the later 1970s to discussion about a possible modification of its status (Van Rompaey, 1977; CRISP, 1978, no. 809: 19-23). In 1978, while this debate continued, it began to receive a share of the public subsidy to the daily press, allocated in equal amounts from the Flemish and Francophone halves of the subsidy. By 1983, however, as a combined result of cost savings from computerized operations, minor reductions in staffing, higher subscription fees from newspapers, and increased revenues from services to private clients, the agency returned to profitability after several years of substantial losses, and any immediate prospect of a change in status has faded.

The Belgian periodical press, like that of other countries, is highly diversified and not easily described in a few lines, but its development can be charted more accurately in a quantitative sense after 1966, when the deposit of copies at the national library became a requirement for all Belgian publications. Jean Gol's study of the Belgian press divides periodicals into three broad categories: first, a commercial press that includes both general-interest weeklies and reviews for a specialized readership (e.g., children) or on specialized topics; second, some 500 advertising bulletins containing minimal editorial content, which are distributed to all households in a town or region and which are often owned by daily newspapers; and third, noncommercial periodicals of opinion, which are frequently organs of political, confessional, economic, or social interest groups (1970, 152-55). In round figures, the commercial periodical press by the middle 1970s ran to about 1,000 titles, while the total number of periodicals of all kinds including yearbooks exceeded 7,000 (*Indicateur publicitaire*, 1978, 121-272; *Presse*, 1973-74, no. 80: 71).

Unlike the daily newspapers, popular general-interest and specialized weeklies gained in circulation and became quite profitable during the 1960s; one list of thirty-seven leading weeklies showed a total circulation of roughly four million copies. Some concentration of ownership has also appeared in the periodical field, and here there is a noticeable tendency for the same firm to produce either similar or identical magazines in French and Dutch, in some cases under the same title. While Belgian weeklies face strong competition from foreign imports in their domestic market, some also compete successfully in foreign markets and in a few cases sell far more copies abroad than in Belgium (Gol, 1970, 156-63). Most of this international exchange appears to be with France. Older data from the 1950s suggest that imports of weeklies and other periodicals ran well above one million copies a week, and that copies imported from France outnumbered those from the Netherlands at that time by approximately 100 to 1 (Stijns, 1957, 309). As with daily newspapers, French-language periodicals appear to have a more extensive circulation in Flanders than Dutch-language periodicals in Wallonie. Thus for *Reader's Digest*, 8 per cent of total Belgian circulation of the French version goes to the Flemish provinces, while only 0.8 per cent of circulation of the Dutch version goes to the Walloon provinces (*Indicateur publicitaire*, 1978, 142-46).

The distribution of Belgian periodicals by language for various dates is given in Table 49. For periodicals as a whole the trend indicates a dramatic increase in overall numbers and also an increase in the percentage of Dutch-language titles. A closer analysis of the 1968 and 1973 data by frequency of publication shows that the number of weeklies published in French and in Dutch was well balanced and stable in this period (46 per cent French, 47 per cent Dutch, for both years). The percentage published in Dutch tended to be lower in the categories published less frequently, in 1973 registering 38 per cent for monthlies and 36 per cent for annuals or irregular journals. These less frequently published categories, however, also showed the greatest percentage gains for Dutch-language journals over the corresponding 1968 figures (*Presse*, 1968, no. 60: 51; 1973-74, no. 80: 71).

Table 49

Belgium: Periodicals by language of publication, 1927, 1968, and 1973 (percentages)

Year	Total N	Total %	French	Dutch	German	Bilin-gual	Multi-lingual	Others
1927	2,954	100	70.2	27.2	[a]	[a]	[a]	2.6[b]
1968	4,793	100	52.2	34.0	0.8	9.9	0.4	2.6
1973	7,435	100	47.6	38.4	0.9	9.6	0.7	2.8

[a] None recorded.
[b] Including 13 or 0.4 per cent in Walloon dialect.

Sources: Bacha and Dupierreux, 1928, Preface; *Presse*, 1968, no. 60: 51; 1973-74, no. 80: 71.

The sources used for Table 49 give little information on the "bilingual" and "multilingual" categories. These can be studied in greater detail for periodicals that accept commercial advertising in the *Indicateur publicitaire*, which lists almost 1,200 journals classified by subject matter and by language of publication (1978, 121-272). Of eighty-six popular magazines listed in 1978, 48 per cent appeared in French, 36 per cent in Dutch, 15 per cent in separate French and Dutch editions, 1 per cent in German, and none in a bilingual format. For 1,079 specialized periodicals, 46 per cent were in French, 22 per cent in Dutch, 0.6 per cent in German, 11 per cent in separate French and Dutch versions (with almost a third of this group also appearing in other languages such as English or German), 15 per cent in a bilingual French/Dutch format, and 6 per cent in other bilingual or multilingual combinations or in other languages. These proportions also varied considerably from one subject sector to another.

Book publication is Belgium is highly developed, resting on strong traditions of quality printing that reach back to the early sixteenth century. Reliable statistics on book production by language, however, are difficult to establish, especially for the period before 1966, when deposit of copies in the national library was not yet a legal requirement. Even after this date the figures published in the UNESCO *Statistical Yearbook* are based on differing criteria for different years during the 1970s, making comparisons over time difficult. Table 50 shows the distribution of books published in Belgium by language for selected years over four decades, using three-year averages where data are available to reduce year-to-year variations. In general terms the table suggests that the proportion of titles published in Dutch has remained relatively stable since the 1950s.

Table 50

Belgium: Book production by language, selected years, 1938-80 (percentages)

Year	Total		French	Dutch	German	English	Other language	Two or more languages
	N	%						
1938	2,949	100	64.9	35.1	n.a.	n.a.	n.a.	n.a.
1955	2,811	100	46.5	53.5	n.a.	n.a.	n.a.	n.a.
1964-66[a]	3,543	100	40.1	55.4	0.7	1.7	0.5	1.6
1970-72[a]	4,549	100	40.2	53.3	0.7	2.4	1.0	2.4
1978-80[a]	9,354	100	36.5	56.9	0.8	2.5	0.9	2.5

[a] Three-year average.

Sources: 1938, 1955: Van Haegendoren et al., 1957, 35; 1964-80: compiled and calculated from UNESCO, 1965-67, 1971-73, 1980-82.

These data, however, must be qualified in several ways and interpreted with extreme caution. Apart from annual fluctuations and variations in criteria for what is counted as a book, many of the French and the Dutch titles are copublished with firms outside Belgium. While Belgian authors writing in Dutch are generally published (or copublished) in Belgium, many other books by non-Belgian authors published in the Netherlands are also copublished in Belgium. On the other hand, Belgian authors writing in French find it more profitable to be published by a leading Paris publisher than at home. As a result, the volume of publishing reveals little about levels of domestic authorship. From a trade standpoint, imported books account for an estimated two thirds of domestic book sales, and exports of books published in Belgium almost balance imports. In 1960 both imports and exports of books were predominantly from and towards France, but by 1979 the value of the book trade with the Netherlands was slightly ahead of that with France both for exports and imports (CRISP, 1980, no. 898: 4).

Apart from the quantitative aspects of book production, one may also note certain divergences in subject matter. One major strength of recent Flemish writing has been narrative literature, and several leading Flemish novelists have found an appreciative public in the Netherlands. On the other hand, leading Belgian authors writing in French have long tended to gravitate towards France, in many cases settling in Paris for the greater part of their careers. French-language book production in Belgium has been less oriented towards literature than towards certain specialized sectors for which Belgian publishing has gained an international reputation, notably fine arts, science and technology, religious works, and books for children. On balance, then, these differences in the structure of the publishing industry, in areas of specialization within the industry, and in the rewards of authorship combine to make book publishing a doubtful index of the cultural activity of the respective language communities.

A recurrent theme in this study of intergroup relations in Belgium has been asymmetry, and this surfaces not only in book publishing but also in reading patterns. In 1951 an INSOC survey asked the Belgian public about its reading patterns, and for those currently reading a book (about 30 per cent of total respondents), the results by region, by language of the volume, and by language or nationality of the author are shown in Table 51. This table illustrates again the more diversified linguistic and cultural influences felt in Flanders, as contrasted with a more homogeneous and France-oriented cultural milieu of Wallonie. Dating as it does from 1951, it also represents a Flanders poised on the threshold of linguistic change as a result of the educational reforms of the 1930s. The question of reading patterns was apparently never repeated, but a similar survey in the 1980s would be extremely interesting. While the language of the book being read would undoubtedly show changes, the asymmetry in cultural orientations might well persist. The published results of the 1951 survey do not allow us to analyze Flanders further, but they do show that for the whole sample the figure of 58 per cent who were reading a book in French increased to 66 per cent for women respondents, to 67 per cent for professional occupations, and to 75 per cent for respondents aged sixty-five or older (INSOC, 1951, no. 4: 23).

K   Language Issues in the Private Sector

One of the more interesting aspects of the Belgian language situation has been an increasing intervention of the legislator in the private sector. Such interventions have precedents elsewhere. In the case of Switzerland we noted the 1931 language decree of the Canton of Ticino that made Italian the priority language on the signs of all business establishments in the canton (Volume 1, 123-24). This measure was upheld by the Swiss supreme court and widely accepted thereafter as a valid and necessary exercise of cantonal sovereignty in language matters. The Belgian case is different in that the Flemish and Francophone communities are in basic disagreement over the need for intervention, over the fairness of what has been decreed, and over whether such regulation conflicts with the guarantee of linguistic liberty in Article 23 of the constitution. In these circumstances language regulation in the private sector has become one more item on the long agenda of unsettled intergroup conflicts that burden successive Belgian governments.

Table 51

Belgium: Books read by language of book and by language/nationality of author, by language regions, 1951 (percentages)

Language of book and language/nationality of author	Flan-ders	Wal-lonie	Brussels *arron-dissement*	Whole country
A Books read in French				
Author Belgian	2	8	1	4
Author French	22	53	36	34
Translated from Dutch	*	—	—	*
" " English	9	23	27	16
" " German	—	*	3	*
" " other languages	2	4	8	4
Total read in French	35	88	75	58
B Books read in Dutch				
Author Belgian	23	3	7	14
Author Dutch	8	*	*	4
Translated from French	4	*	—	2
" " English	12	3	1	8
" " German	*	—	—	*
" " other languages	6	1	2	4
Total read in Dutch	53	7	10	32
C Books read in English	5	2	4	4
D Books read in German	1	*	*	1
E Books read in other languages	6	2	11	5
Total—all languages	100	99	100	100

* Denotes 0.5 per cent or less

Source: Compiled from INSOC, 1951, no. 4: 21-27.

The notion of regulation of private language usage appeared relatively late in the evolution of the Flemish Movement, and the second wave of language legislation in the 1930s left the private sector untouched. Among possible explanations one might list the relative underdevelopment of industry in Flanders at that time, a general climate of nonintervention in the economic sphere, and the constitutional guarantees implied in Article 23 (Deleeck, 1975, 56-57). In any case the idea surfaced in the 1940s (Vandeputte, 1949) and found a first tentative legislative expression in a far-reaching law of 1948 on organization of the economy. This law called upon the new works councils to promote better labor-management relations by encouraging, among other things, use of the language of the region in a firm's internal communications and in dealing with the public authorities (Herremans, 1965, 127; Van Haegendoren, 1962, 2: 132). The new works councils were given advisory powers only, and the law had no discernible linguistic effect.

Further pamphlets on the question appeared in the 1950s, as did a rare empirical inquiry into language practice in 112 firms in four towns of East Flanders. This study found that at the plant level workers were using Nederlands almost completely, while salaried employees spoke Nederlands with workers but dealt with management in both languages and tended to see French as an avenue to promotion. Managers spoke predominantly French at higher levels and Nederlands with foremen and workers. In brief, the more closely one approached the top of the firm, the more completely was French the language of communication, and adjustment to this situation was a prerequisite for upward mobility (Deleeck, 1959, 34, 52-53; 1975, 58-59). More often the commentary was political and polemical in tone, and by the early 1960s the slogan "Taal van de arbeiders, taal van de fabriek" had acquired a certain visibility at the Flemish mass demonstrations that coincided with the third round of language laws (Rommens, 1963).

The law of August 1963 on language usage in administrative matters brought the first major change. As first tabled in Parliament, the draft bill scarcely mentioned the private sector at all but simply provided that central departments would reply to private individuals in unilingual regions in the language of the person concerned but reply to firms in the language of the region. During the committee stages two further concepts were introduced as a result of Flemish pressure. In the version finally passed, "industrial, commercial or financial" enterprises would be required to use the language of the region "for acts and documents imposed by law and by regulations," and also "for those that are directed towards their personnel." In Brussels, these documents for the firm's personnel were to be in French for Francophones and in Dutch for Flemings. A further subsection provided that firms "may add to the notices, communications, acts, certificates, and forms directed to their personnel a translation in one or more languages when the composition of the personnel justifies it." A later article on sanctions required that a firm replace documents contravening these rules, and if it failed to do so a court could order a version in the correct language to be made at the firm's expense (Emploi des langues, 1963, Articles 41, 52; 1966a, Articles 52, 59; Maroy, 1966, 489).

Almost immediately the underlying intergroup disagreements over the need for legislation were transformed into irreconcilable differences over the constitutionality and extent of application of these provisions. Did the guarantee of linguistic liberty in Article 23 apply to firms as legal persons, or did it extend only to individuals? Does a document required by law from a private firm thereby become an act of the "public authority" that may be regulated, under the same Article 23, by legislation? Since some held that the translation clause applied only to documents directed to personnel, and not to documents prescribed by law, to what extent were accompanying translations permitted or precluded? Other issues concerned the interpretation of just how many forms are "required by law" and what should be considered the operating location (*siège d'exploitation*) of a firm with plants in more than one region (De Weerdt, 1964; Henrard, 1964, 75-82; 1967; Eeckhout, 1964; Herremans, 1965, 126-29; Maroy, 1966, 490-91). Amid this welter of commentary, one can discern a tendency among Francophones to see the 1963 law as introducing certain minimal constraints upon linguistic liberty, while Flemings, with some backing from the Commission permanente de contrôle linguistique, viewed it as requiring a considerably greater degree of territorially based unilingualism for the firms to which it applied. In any event, Flemish hopes for a generalized language shift in the industrial and commercial sector were soon disappointed, and within a few years *flamingant* opinion was calling for stronger legislative measures (Van Haegendoren, 1967b, 59-63).

The opportunity for remedial action came with the constitutional reforms of 1970 and the establishment of autonomous cultural councils for the Flemish and Francophone communities. Under the new Article 59 *bis* of the constitution, the question of language regulation in the workplace in Flanders fell squarely within the competence of the new Cultural Council for the Netherlandic community, and this council, as one of its first legislative measures, enacted unanimously a comprehensive decree to regulate language relations between employers and workers in the Dutch-language region. This measure, passed in July 1973 and known as the "*Décret de septembre*" from the date of its translation and publication in the *Moniteur* seven weeks later, acquired a certain notoriety as a result of the delayed but explosive attacks mounted against it in the Francophone press during the autumn of 1973 (Cocquereaux, 1978, 91-105). The Flemish press, noting that its passage coincided with the centenary of the first legislation on language use in Flanders in 1873, saw it as a symbolic milestone marking the end of a century-old struggle.

The *Décret de septembre* continues in the same direction taken by the 1963 legislation, requiring the use of Dutch in employer-employee relations, but it differs in the increased extent and rigor of its application. Where the earlier law referred to industrial, commercial, and financial establishments only, the new decree defines worker-employer relations in the broadest possible terms. Maurice Herremans points out that by analogy with definitions in other labor legislation, these relations cover all types of enterprises, including foreign-owned multinationals in Flanders, ships operating from Flemish ports, nonprofit associations, persons working at home, domestic servants, and even family members occupied in family businesses (1978, 295-96). The decree extends not only to documents required by law and those directed to personnel but in a much wider sense to all "individual and collective contacts, oral as well as written, that relate directly or indirectly to employment" (Article 3). Personnel documents in Dutch may still be translated if the composition of the workforce justifies it, but only if this translation is requested unanimously and in writing by workers' representatives on the works council or by trade union representatives (Article 5). Enforcement is entrusted to the ministries concerned and to the Commission permanente de contrôle linguistique, whose officials are empowered to visit any firm "at any hour of the day or night without advance warning," to interrogate any manager or worker, and to see and copy any document they deem necessary to their mission (Article 7). Among the prescribed penalties are admonitions, nullification procedures for any document contravening the decree, and also penal sanctions for offenders, including fines or imprisonment up to one month, or both (*Moniteur belge*, 1973, 10091-92; Senelle, 1978, 29-34).

The thoroughness and rigor of the text of the decree were not lost upon the Francophone press, which did not hesitate to compare it to the barbarities of the wartime Nazi occupation (Todts, 1973, 887).[1] Francophone barristers attacked it vehemently as unconstitutional and ill-considered (Eeckhout, 1973a, 1973b). The Francophone public in Brussels and Wallonie quickly became aroused, and in the midst of the controversy *Le Soir* commissioned an INUSOP survey focusing on the issue. A few results from this survey are summarized in Table 52, which reveals the wide gulf on this issue between Flanders and the other two regions, with attitudes in Brussels being slightly more negative than those in Wallonie. The results also indicate that Francophones were better informed of the decree than were Flemings, as might be expected from the campaign against it in the Francophone press, though the higher level of respondents with "no opinion" in Flanders may also stem from reluctance to take a public stand. Both Wallonie and Brussels reacted sharply against the decree, in spite of a relatively high consensus among respondents in all three regions that their own workplace would be little affected. Perhaps more surprising is the strength of feeling in Brussels and Wallonie that the cultural councils ought to come to some agreement (*se concerter*) before passing a decree, a notion that appears to run against the central principle of cultural autonomy.

After the high drama surrounding its enactment, the subsequent history of the *Décret de septembre* is rather anticlimactic. Its application became part of the regular duties of the Dutch section of the Commission permanente de contrôle linguistique, which received no new staff for the

---

[1] One recent commentator has noted more calmly that the enforcement mechanisms and penalties in the decree, while more stringent than those in previous language legislation, were strictly analogous with, and even borrowed from, those in other comparable laws on worker protection (CRISP, 1984, nos. 1035-36: 13).

Table 52

**Belgium: Attitudes towards the "September Decree,"
by language region, October 1973 (percentages)**

Response category	Flanders	Wallonie	Brussels	Whole country
1. Favors decree	39	7	11	24
Opposes	7	53	62	30
Neutral, no opinion	54	40	27	46
2. Decree was necessary to correct abuses	49	11	11	31
Not necessary	21	65	73	42
No opinion	30	24	16	27
3. Cultural Councils should agree before legislating	25	53	53	38
No prior agreement needed	32	22	23	28
No opinion	43	25	23	34
4. Application will not cause problems in respondent's own firm[a]	81	66	64	74

[a] Asked only of those working in the private sector.

Source: *Soir*, 1973, November 13-17.

purpose but did complain regularly in its annual reports about the added work load. The first two years of application of the decree produced a total of thirty-seven inspections of firms in 1974 and thirty-one in 1975. Although a number of language infractions were found, the reports for these years mention only ten letters of warning and only two cases forwarded to the labor courts for prosecution, which strongly suggests that the application process has been primarily one of persuasion rather than compulsion (CPCL, 1974, 38-39; 1975, 285; Herremans, 1978, 298). While some of these cases took aim at firms still using French in employer-employee relationships, others involved firms using English. By 1978 only twelve out of ninety-six cases handled by the Dutch section concerned the 1973 decree, and even some of these decisions highlighted areas of language usage that remain outside the decree, such as communications between firm and client or between clinic and patient (CPCL, 1978, 64, 84-85). Enforcement responsibilities were also shared with the central ministries most directly concerned, the Department of Economic Affairs and the Department of Employment and Labor, which reported an even lower incidence of infractions (CRISP, 1984, nos. 1035-36: 20-22).

This contrast between seemingly draconian legislation and mild enforcement prompts a wider reflection on Belgian constitutional evolution since 1965. The development of cultural autonomy and its first institutionalization through the cultural councils created additional arenas for political decision-making that gave symbolic strength to the linguistic communities and made for more effective realization of community goals. In these early stages of the new councils, however, the decrees that emerged in these arenas seemed to carry less political legitimacy than laws passed in Parliament in spite of their equivalent legal status. Untempered by the presence of the other language community at the time of their passage, they lacked the compromises characteristic of other Belgian legislation. Their natural tendency to run to extremes of language must be considered a weakness rather than a strength, because the very rigor of the new norms would make strict enforcement counterproductive. On the other hand, the decree has not been without effect in other ways. One full-length study concludes that it has had a positive psychological impact on language use in Flanders in that workers have become more aware that their language is backed by law (Cocquereaux, 1978, 143).

The *Décret de septembre* was intended to apply only to Flanders, but its stated field of application gave rise to certain ambiguities (e.g., an employer in Wallonie or Brussels with employees working wholly or partly in Flanders), and these grey areas tended to widen as a result of judicial decisions. In the face of these uncertainties, the Council of the French Community responded in June 1982 with a decree of its own, designed to uphold the interests of Francophones in these borderline cases. Following the earlier decree, it called for the use of French by enterprises located in the Francophone region or employing personnel there. Unlike the Dutch decree, it did not impose the *exclusive* use of French, but it did claim to apply to personnel *in* the French-language region *or* to French-speaking workers, whom it further defined as those holding French-language diplomas or identity cards or even those who "habitually use French in their employment." Such a claim, if taken literally, would give the decree extraterritorial effect beyond the limits of the French-language region for which the council is competent to legislate on language matters. Further, and more seriously, it would reopen the general issue of territoriality versus personality in language policy, thereby challenging six decades of previous legislation and constitutional change. The French Community Council had moved with lightning speed to circumvent any Flemish efforts to delay or block the decree, and the executive of the Vlaamse Raad could only protest after the event. As of 1985 the obvious conflicts between the two decrees remain unresolved, awaiting the attention of the new Cour d'arbitrage (*Moniteur belge*, 1982, August 27, 9863-64; CRISP, 1984, nos. 1035-36: 23-26).[1]

---

[1] The decree of the French Community Council of 1982 was not the first on the subject of language regulation. Its predecessor, the French Cultural Council, had passed a comprehensive decree in 1978 requiring the use of French in a wide range of public-sector activities at

If we ignore the complex unresolved questions of jurisdictional overlap and conflict, the territory not covered by either decree (that is,
Brussels-Capital, the six peripheral communes, and the communes with
minority facilities along the linguistic frontier) remains under the more
limited provisions of the 1963 legislation for purposes of language regulation in the private sector. Nevertheless, there is some evidence that language behavior in the upper echelons of industry and finance has been
changing even in Brussels. Economic prosperity in Flanders and a growing
demand for Dutch-speaking personnel have brought rapid promotions to a
new generation of Flemings educated entirely in Dutch. Firms that have
been internally French-speaking have taken bilingual names and added
Flemings to their boards of directors. Some firms based primarily in Flanders and primarily Dutch-speaking in internal operations, such as the
Kredietbank, have extended their activities into other regions or across the
country. The overall result of these developments has been a growing
tendency in Brussels business circles for both languages to be used on the
basis of passive bilingualism. Just how far this change is attributable to
linguistic legislation and how far it is attributable to the increasing strength
of the economy of Flanders cannot really be determined, because the two
have gone hand in hand.

In comparative perspective, legislative intervention in the private
sector in Flanders has been distinctive for its focus on one particular sector:
the worker-employer relationship. There appear to have been no special
concerns for signs or labelling except for matters involving industrial safety,
nor for the language of professional services, nor for merchant-customer
relationships. The absence of regulation in these areas might be explained
by the guarantee of linguistic liberty in Article 23 of the constitution, but
this seems at best a partial answer because Article 23 was eroded in 1970 to
the extent that new areas for legislative intervention were created and
conferred on the cultural councils by the new Article 29 *bis* (Senelle, 1974,
53). The primary explanation for this overriding Flemish concern with
language in the workplace appears to be the widespread perception of the
language division in Flanders as a class division, in which language has
long served to reinforce class boundaries and hinder social mobility (Van
Haegendoren, 1970). The *Décret de septembre* therefore stresses the notion of *social* relations in the workplace and aims to protect the cultural
milieu of the Dutch-speaking worker, as the weaker party, against the
superior social and economic power of Francophone or allophone management. Some writers have seen the resolution of this issue as the last

all levels of government and in certain private-sector matters including employment offers
and contracts, advertising, directions for use, guarantees, and invoices. This measure,
however, was primarily directed against the growing use of English, "franglais," and foreign
borrowing, and was modelled on similar legislation in France (*Moniteur belge*, 1978,
September 9, 10133-35; Carbonneau, 1981).

major task of the Flemish Movement in Flanders itself (Deleeck, 1975, 61), but by the early 1980s the question seemed largely settled, and priorities were shifting to nonlinguistic issues. By contrast, the question of language in Brussels and its periphery remained highly salient.

One other area of importance, an area untouched by legislation, is the use of languages in the churches. Freedom of religious beliefs and of their exercise are guaranteed by Article 14 of the constitution, but certain religions are officially recognized by the state and given civil personality. A later clause, Article 117, makes the salaries and pensions of the clergy of these religions a charge upon the state, and other legislation requires communes to subsidize churches and synagogues (Wigny, 1952, 1: 340-45; Wagnon, 1964). Although this official recognition extends to four faiths—Catholic, Protestant, Anglican, Jewish—the Belgian population, as noted earlier, has been overwhelmingly of Roman Catholic background, and only Catholic services have become a focal point for linguistic controversy.

Before the increased politicization of the language issue in the early 1960s, a few sermons were delivered in French in the larger cities and towns of Flanders, and for Wallonie there is also evidence from an earlier date of services held in Flemish at Liège and Charleroi (Royer, 1973, 31). These practices were never the subject of legislation, but they were caught up in the language conflict nonetheless. In Antwerp the Vlaamse Militanten Orde (VMO) mounted public demonstrations against sermons in French for twenty-two successive weeks until the bishop intervened and ordered the sermons stopped. Similar protests were mounted in coastal towns and in the Brussels suburbs. In Leuven French-language services became a casualty of the struggle to split the university and oust the Francophone section in the later 1960s. The situation in the 1970s was one of quiet solutions. In addition to special services for allophone tourists during holiday season in both language regions, a few masses in French are still held in Flanders, but often by visiting priests rather than parish clergy, ostensibly for foreigners rather than Belgians, at unlikely hours, or in private chapels of châteaux. Not unlike the worship of the early Christian era or the Catholicism of post-Reformation England or Holland, the atmosphere of these services verges on clandestinity, and reliable information concerning them is understandably difficult to obtain.

Note on Language Usage in the Belgian Congo

After the accession of the Congo to independence in 1960, its language practices and policies prior to that date became primarily a question of historical interest. Yet the issue has some bearing on the language question in Belgium itself. It also has consequences for the new state of Zaire, which carried into independence a fainter imprint of European linguistic and cultural identity than did the former colonies of France or Britain (Erny, 1974, 52). The "language question" in the Congo before independence was in reality two distinct questions. First, there was the "internal" language question, concerning which of the multitude of local dialects, regional languages, commercial lingua francas, or international languages should be used for developmental and educational purposes in a territory characterized by extreme linguistic complexity. Second, there was the "external" question of official languages, imported from Belgium itself. Although analytically distinct, these two questions unavoidably intersected at certain points in policy terms ("Taalregeling in Kongo," 1965, 504; Van Bulck, 1948; De Boeck, 1949).

During the earliest decades of the Belgian presence in Africa, the Congo had been run as a personal fiefdom of Leopold II, and in French. When the monarch's personal rule was terminated, the Belgian Parliament established a local constitution, the Colonial Charter of 1908, which granted civil and political rights to Belgian citizens, Congolese, and foreigners domiciled there. Prominent in the chapter on rights in this charter was Article 3, which was similar to Article 23 on language rights in the Belgian constitution yet not identical with it. The colonial article repeated the principle that language usage was optional (facultatif), that it would be regulated only by formal colonial decrees, and only with respect to governmental or judicial matters. Belgian citizens in the Congo would have guarantees "similar" to those they had in Belgium, and decrees were promised within the next five years to spell out these guarantees. Finally, all decrees and regulations of a general nature were to be published in French and in "Flamand," both texts being official (Piron and Devos, 1954, 1: 10).

As matters evolved, Article 3 had little effect upon language usage in the colony. French continued to be the normal language of the administration, of private enterprises, and of social life among Europeans. The promised colonial decrees to guarantee Flemish language rights in a way similar to the language laws in Belgium failed to materialize, either in the prescribed five-year period or for decades thereafter. The sole governmental documents dealing with language usage in this period were internal administrative memoranda, none of which went beyond a reminder to officials to respect the principle of freedom of languages (Paulus, 1959, 381). In effect the freedom of languages came to mean the freedom of the civil servant and of the magistrate not to know the second official language, as it had in Flanders before the first round of language laws. In 1939 instructions from Governor-General Ryckmans sharply reminded bilingual officials of their linguistic advantage over their "less favored" colleagues and of their consequent "duty of conscience" to address unilingual superiors, colleagues, and subordinates in the language understood by the latter ("Taalregeling in Kongo," 1956, 513).

Concerning language use in the courts, the decade after 1945 saw a series of conflicting judicial decisions that created uncertainty and confusion over the right to use Dutch ("Taalregeling in Kongo," 1956, 519-50). In February 1957, almost half a century after the promise made in the Colonial Charter, these uncertainties were resolved by a colonial decree, which provided that in tribunals for Europeans either French or Dutch could be used, at the option of the accused in penal cases or of the plaintiff in civil cases. In civil cases the defendant could object to the language chosen by the plaintiff, but the judge could overrule this objection if he found that the defendant or the majority of defendants had a "sufficient knowledge" of the language in question (Piron and Devos, 1957, D12-14). Essentially, the decree was considered to have implanted in the colony a scaled-down version of the 1935 rules for courts in Brussels. It was criticized in Flemish circles because, in clarifying the rights of unilinguals, it jeopardized the rights of bilingual Flemings to a trial in their own language (*Problèmes des langues*, 1958, 23).

A crucial area for policy decisions was language use in the schools. For much of the colonial period elementary education in schools for Africans was conducted in the leading regional languages—Lingala, Kikongo, Kiswahili, and Tshiluba—even though a majority of the children had a smaller dialect or language as mother tongue (Erny, 1974, 52). This choice arose partly through the political difficulty of making an unqualified choice of French over Dutch in these schools, and partly from a perception that continuing linguistic particularism among Africans served the Belgian national interest. Even before the First World War, Count Jacques de Lichtervelde, with remarkable foresight, cautioned against the widespread use of French or even of Kiswahili in primary education: "Too exclusive diffusion of one language can be dangerous; it might become the principal factor in the creation of a real Congolese black nationality opposed to the whites" (Lichtervelde, 1913, 7). In spite of curricular changes in the 1920s and 1930s, African languages remained the vehicle for elementary education, though French made some gains as a subject of study at the primary level and as the medium of instruction at the secondary level (Polomé, 1968, 301-302).

By the 1950s, this system of vernacular education was subject to strong pressures for change in order to allow more Africans access to higher education. In October 1956 an order of the military authorities required all primary schools under army jurisdiction to switch to French as the language of instruction and to use Lingala only as a temporary bridge language for those not knowing French. By December of the same year all official primary schools were told that the language of instruction was to be French and the second language the lingua franca of the region. At the secondary level, African mission schools, staffed preponderantly by Flemish missionaries, had made a practice of using French as language of instruction but also of teaching some Dutch as a second language. After 1954 these private schools were supplemented by official interracial secondary schools that offered the basic Belgian curriculum leading to university entrance. Francophones attending these schools objected to the compulsory study of Dutch, and the issue became whether these schools should follow the model of Brussels, with its compulsory second national language, or that of Wallonie, with freedom of choice. In Flemish circles the reaction to these changes was to view the Congo as a sort of contractual condominium of the two Belgian language communities that had been terminated unilaterally by the imposition of French upon the Africans. In the end most Flemish opinion accepted French-medium elementary schools for African children, but continued to press for instruction in Dutch as a second language in all these schools as a matter of national interest (*Talenprobleem*, 1957, 18-26; *Problèmes des langues*, 1958, 24-25). Walloon partisans, by contrast, argued just as strongly that African interests were best served by a generalized official unilingualism in the educational and administrative fields (Burton et al., 1958).

In spite of vast distances and limited numbers, education for Europeans managed to duplicate most of the divisions of schools in Belgium. There was a private Catholic sector, the *écoles libres*, and an official sector. Both sectors offered classes in French and in Dutch at the primary and secondary levels, but the Flemish system was less complete and for many regions it involved costlier boarding schools at a distance. In higher education there was a private Catholic university at Léopoldville, founded in 1954, and a state university in Elisabethville, founded in 1956. The latter made provision for some courses in Dutch as well as in French. For various social and practical reasons, however, enrolment in the Dutch educational sector in the mid-1950s reached only about 10 per cent of total European enrolment, a level far below the proportion indicated by Flemish activity in the Congo (*Problèmes des langues*, 1958, 20-22; *Talenprobleem*, 1957, 29-32; Verthé, 1959, 105-109).

Although Flemish opinion at home was still less outward-looking than that of Brussels or Wallonie, Flemings participated extensively as individuals in what was then viewed as the burden of colonialism. In the field of Catholic missions it was estimated that roughly 80 per cent of Belgian personnel were Flemish. A Dutch-speaking section of the training program for colonial administrators was begun in 1936, and by 1939 it accounted for 45 per cent of the candidates. Many Flemings found employment in commercial or industrial enterprises operating in the colony, and still others came as independent settlers. There are no firm language statistics for these sectors, but in the 1950s overall Flemish participation was estimated at about 60 per cent of the European population; it was further estimated that 14 per cent of this white population was in colonial administration, 15 per cent in Catholic missions, 5 per cent in Protestant missions,

45 per cent in private enterprises, and a further 18 per cent were independent colonists ("Taalregeling in Kongo," 1956, 466, 477, 480).

Beginning from the 1940s, one can trace a certain Flemish cultural awakening in the Congo, as a result perhaps of the successes of the Flemish Movement at home and the wartime prominence of the Congo as the only unoccupied territory of Free Belgium. From 1943 broadcasts in French and in Dutch from Léopoldville became the major voice of the Belgian government in London. In 1947 schooling in Dutch became available for children of Flemish families ("Taalregeling in Kongo," 1956, 484). Dutch-language periodicals were founded, notably a monthly review in 1942, a weekly in 1951, and a literary quarterly in 1955. Dutch-language books in public libraries, almost nonexistent in 1942, increased to 6 per cent of holdings by 1950 and to 19 per cent by 1958. The major Flemish cultural foundations and other organizations in Flanders began to take an increased interest in the colony. In several towns a series of Flemish social circles or *vriendenkringen* began to offer an alternative to French as the normal language of social contact. Some Flemish opinion was prepared to accept the predominance of French in official and commercial life and even as the language of instruction in the schools, while concentrating instead on intensified Dutch-language cultural activity as the main mission for Netherlandic civilization in the Congo (*Problèmes des langues*, 1958, 6-13; Verthé, 1959, chap. 3).

The last decade of Belgian rule in the Congo saw Flemish thought in the colony take on a certain visionary quality that illustrates in yet another context the frequently cited Flemish penchant for romanticism. The new literary reviews began to bring forth the first fruits of a Flemish-African literature, marked by new perspectives and different world images, and acknowledging a distant kinship with the successful—but Calvinist— example of Afrikaans literature far to the south. As a rich and sparsely populated land 80 times the size of Belgium, or—as some preferred to say—128 times the size of Flanders (*Problèmes des langues*, 1958, 13), the Congo offered a vista of almost limitless space for future European expansion and settlement. Flemish intellectuals in the colony left behind the traditional and the familiar to observe and celebrate a new world of experience under African skies (Verthé and Henry, 1961). Some saw an emergent Léopoldville-Cape Town axis, a vast belt of Netherlandic cultural influence extending from the equator to the Cape of Good Hope, a Flemish equivalent of the vision of Cecil Rhodes. As events were soon to demonstrate, however, these visions were mere apparitions, and they vanished like morning mist in the harsh dawn of the Léopoldville riots of January 1959 that heralded Congolese independence.

The failure of the Flemish dream in Africa was unrelated to language policy, but from a more limited linguistic perspective we may note that in the last years of Belgian rule the Congo could offer its Dutch-speaking population bilingual official gazettes and legal codes, Dutch-language schools and radio broadcasting, and a significant Flemish cultural presence. The net result, however, was admittedly a *bilinguisme mitigé*, and it did not alter the fact that European life in the colony was overwhelmingly French-speaking at the level of business, industry, and public life. The example of the Congo could only serve to strengthen Flemish convictions of the ultimate wisdom of unwavering territorial unilingualism in Belgium itself.

Chapter 5

Contemporary Problems

Where ethnic or linguistic conflict has become general and pervasive throughout a political system, as it has been in Belgium for much of the twentieth century, it may appear somewhat arbitrary to select certain special areas for more detailed analysis. In Switzerland, as Volume 1 demonstrated, some of the more salient conflicts in recent decades have been primarily regional or local in their manifestations, and one can trace their evolution as more or less independent issues in the appropriate regional arenas. In Belgium many aspects of the linguistic and cultural struggle can be similarly localized in one language region or even in a smaller geographical area, but the rules of the political system—at least as it functioned up to the constitutional reforms of 1970 and 1980—have dictated that the solutions must be pursued primarily in the national political arena, through channels already strained by an accumulation of other questions. Even strictly localized Belgian issues are therefore less easy to isolate and analyze independently of the functioning of the system as a whole.

Notwithstanding this basic difference from the Swiss political system, there are good reasons for looking more closely at certain specific engagements in the wider Belgian language struggle. Among observers and partisans alike there is virtually unanimous agreement that the highly complex "Brussels question" has become the largest and most difficult of the community issues still outstanding in the 1980s. After Brussels, the choices become less obvious. Among various possibilities, there are two other issues that illustrate somewhat contradictory tendencies. The conflict over the Voer (or Fouron) district shows how a question of apparently minor significance can persist as a conflict within the political system over a long period, escalating and reinforcing other intergroup differences along the way. On the other hand, the issue of the Francophone minority in Flanders, once highly salient, has become virtually silent and neglected. Consequently, by a curious reverse logic it may be instructive to examine how a system in which intergroup conflict is generalized can also occasionally turn a major issue into a nonissue. These three issues also have a certain sociological rationale in that they illustrate at least four distinct relationships and processes, namely (1) the class relationship in Flanders between Francophone elites and Flemish masses, (2) the frictions between Walloons and Flemings along the language frontier in the Voer and other border communes; and the double tendency of the Brussels agglomeration (3) to assimilate non-Francophone immigrants and (4) to exert outward urbanizing pressures on the surrounding Flemish countryside. Since much of the background for these issues has been developed in earlier chapters, the first two at least can be treated rather briefly.

A   The Francophone Minority in Flanders

In the polemics of the language struggle, the Francophone population of Flanders has been frequently and severely criticized but seldom seriously analyzed. One of the rare full-length profiles of this group, clinical and perceptive though hardly sympathetic—a study that ranges widely over the historical, psychological, sociological, and cultural aspects of the question—has been written by an Antwerp magistrate under the pseudonym of Dirk Wilmars (1968). Among other perceptions, Wilmars sees the Francophones as composed of several distinct groups, which he assesses separately in terms of their openness to Netherlandization. There are the relatively few titled nobility, whose traditions and patterns of life are inseparably linked with an upbringing in French. There is a small, wealthy upper bourgeoisie, whose international lifestyle isolates it from close contact with the local population and from Netherlandic influences. There are those in liberal professions, which have been increasingly influenced by educational reform and language legislation. Finally, he sees a category of snobs and parvenus, possessing little culture or education and often having successful commercial backgrounds, who see in *francisation* an easy route to higher social status (1968, 184-96).

Wilmars also explains just why he considers this heterogeneous Francophone minority to be undeserving of recognition of its language rights. Basically, it is not an ethnic group but a social class, and a privileged one in terms of incomes and occupational structures. It is also an elite that voluntarily severed its connections with the Flemish masses, leaving them uneducated and culturally deprived. To grant recognition to these Francophones as a distinct minority group, he argues, would be undemocratic and unfair to the Flemish masses. Moreover, in practical terms the Francophone group is small and scattered widely throughout the Flemish region. Although Wilmars's essay is analytical and has more nuances than the polemical literature of the Flemish Movement, it tends in the same general direction. He estimates that much *francisation* has been of relatively recent origin, finding that in a small sample of thirty families in the Antwerp region only eight had genuinely Francophone grandparents. What emerges clearly if somewhat indirectly in this analysis and others is that the Francophone element in Flanders is not the consequence of *in*migration but of the long historical coexistence of the two languages in Flanders. In this sense it is authentically Flemish and also largely accessible to Netherlandization, except for "the nobility, certain circles of the upper bourgeoisie, and the incurable snobs" (Wilmars, 1968, 175-78, 199).

The Francophone population of Flanders, long a prime target of the Flemish Movement, is now seldom mentioned. Such a dramatic reduction in conflict deserves careful analysis, but there is a notable absence of serious studies of the transformation. From an historical standpoint, it is clear that Francophone elites resisted the program of the early Flemish Movement strongly and for a time successfully. Their political power, which was almost total in the nineteenth century, was much reduced by the coming of manhood suffrage in 1893 and effectively broken by the abolition of plural voting in 1919. Their near monopoly of the liberal professions was doomed by Netherlandization in the universities and by the language laws, which meant that the legal profession in particular, but also medicine, engineering, and certain other disciplines important in the public sector, were opened on equal or even preferential terms to Dutch speakers. At the social level, the situation is far less clear. Wilmars predicts a transitional period of one or two generations before a cultivated, Dutch-speaking intellectual elite, with a mastery of correct Netherlandic idiom, can reach the level of cultural attainment achieved by the Francophone elites, and in the interval the Netherlandization of Francophones will remain closely tied to the replacement of Flemish dialects by standard Netherlandic or ABN (1968, 180-81, 196-97).

From an official or legislative standpoint, the Francophones of Flanders no longer exist. In a sociological sense, however, a minority of this size, historical importance, and economic resources does not vanish overnight. Yet it is also worth noting that the language laws of 1962-63 did not produce the dramatic consequences that might have been imagined beforehand. There was no discernible wave of *out*migration of French speakers from Flanders, though many Francophones may be hidden without trace in the vast wave of daily commuters from Flanders to Brussels. Nor was there any exodus of industries, any diversion of new investment, attributable to the language laws. The extent of Francophone migration to Brussels may be gauged from a 1974 survey of migrants from Flanders resident in the capital, which found that 9 per cent of the sample studied were of French mother tongue. Further, Francophones constituted 7 per cent of immigrants before 1963 and 12 per cent in the period from 1963 to 1970 (*Wetenschappelijk onderzoek*, 1974-75, 3: 4-8). These figures suggest some Francophone overrepresentation among migrants before 1963 and some further increase after that date, but these numbers are still moderate in relation to the total Francophone population in Flanders. In the absence of evidence to the contrary, one may assume that many

Table 53

Flanders: Francophones as a percentage of total population, by provinces, selected *arrondissements*, and cities, 1846-1947

Territory	Total population in 1947 000s	Speaking French only						Speaking French only or most frequently				
		1866	1890	1910	1920	1930	1947	1846	1910	1920	1930	1947
Antwerp province	1,281	0.8	1.7	1.3	1.2	1.5	0.8	1.7	3.4	3.6	4.1	3.0
Antwerp (*arrondissement*)	784	1.1	2.4	1.7	1.7	2.1	1.0	2.6	4.7	5.0	5.6	4.2
Antwerp (commune)	263	1.9	2.9	2.7	2.5	3.3	1.8	4.4	7.5	7.9	8.8	7.4
East Flanders	1,217	1.0	1.0	0.8	1.0	1.2	1.0	1.7	2.3	3.5	3.4	3.1
Gent (*arrondissement*)	441	1.0	1.1	1.1	1.5	1.8	1.1	2.1	3.8	6.8	6.0	4.9
Gent (commune)	166	2.2	2.1	2.0	2.9	3.5	2.0	5.1	7.7	13.9	11.8	9.6
West Flanders	996	4.1	3.7	3.6	3.8	4.7	4.3	5.3	6.2	6.7	8.3	8.3
Brugge (*arrondissement*)	199	1.0	1.1	1.1	1.1	1.7	1.3	1.4	2.7	3.5	4.5	3.9
Brugge (commune)	53	2.4	2.6	1.9	2.1	2.3	1.4	3.2	5.5	7.3	7.7	5.9
Limburg	460	4.5	3.9	3.3	3.1	3.2	2.0	5.0	4.5	4.4	4.6	3.4
Arrondissement of Leuven	317	3.2	3.2	3.0	2.8	3.4	2.6	4.4	5.6	5.8	6.5	5.7

Source: Compiled from census reports of years concerned.

families adjusted incrementally to the changing linguistic situation of Flanders without physical displacement.

Although we cannot fully compensate for the absence of systematic studies of these adjustment patterns, we can review and summarize evidence from several sources that enables us to trace in outline the evolution of Francophones in Flanders under the impact of the language laws. This profile can be constructed from three main sources of information. First, official census figures give the numbers of unilingual Francophones from 1866 to 1947 and the number speaking French "most frequently" from 1910 to 1947. Second, the evolution of linguistic preferences since 1947 can be measured less directly by means of other data from the public and private sectors, including the language choices of *miliciens* and of university students, school statistics, and the consumption patterns of the various mass media. A third resource is secondary analysis of data collected through surveys. Some of these data have already been introduced in earlier chapters; the question now is to reassemble them and assess their collective significance.

The comparative size of the linguistic minorities in Flanders and Wallonie was first outlined in Table 4 (above, 40). For Flanders the census data are elaborated and extended to selected *arrondissements* and communes in Table 53, which shows more fully the chronological and spatial distribution of Francophones in Flanders up to 1947. With few exceptions the percentages of unilingual Francophones and of Francophone predominance rose gradually to a peak in 1930 and then fell even more uniformly by 1947, undoubtedly reflecting the language laws of the 1930s. Although the province of West Flanders as a whole stands considerably ahead of the others in this table, roughly three quarters of its Francophones on each side of the table can be traced to border communes in the Mouscron-Comines area that were transferred to Wallonie by the language law of 1962. If these are removed, West Flanders looks quite similar to the other provinces. The effect of comparing provinces with major cities and their immediate *arrondissements* is to suggest that while critical masses of Francophones were to be found in large cities and towns, the linguistic minority was in fact widely dispersed geographically throughout the whole of Flanders.

For the post-1947 period we can assemble several kinds of less direct evidence:

1. *Military service.* As noted earlier (above, 43-44), *miliciens* have a choice of language for their compulsory military service, and this information can be analyzed by provinces and *arrondissements*. For the four Flemish provinces the proportion choosing French-language units was 3.6 per cent in 1953 and 4.0 per cent in 1963, the last class to be recruited before provincial boundaries were adjusted to the linguistic frontier. As a result of these territorial adjustments the proportion of Francophones in

1964 fell sharply to 2.6 per cent, but it then continued to fall, receding to 1.4 per cent in 1970 and to a mere 1.1 per cent in 1977.

2. *University students.* Enrolment in Francophone programs from the four Flemish provinces fell from 13 per cent of total university enrolment from those provinces in 1958-59 to 2.5 per cent in 1978-79. However, much of this percentage change is accounted for by rapid expansion of the Dutch sector. Francophone enrolment in absolute numbers held steady during the 1960s but then declined by 38 per cent between 1968-69 and 1978-79 (Bureau de statistiques universitaires, 1969, 193, 195; 1979, 151, 153; cf. above, 227-30).

3. *School enrolments.* While military service and university education offer a linguistic choice, the lower levels of education are more restricted. The total number of children recorded as attending French-language classes in Flanders was only 2,435 in 1976. They made up an infinitesimal group when compared against total Dutch-language enrolment, about 0.2 per cent at elementary level and 0.02 per cent at secondary level (*Annuaire de statistiques régionales*, 1978, 62, 206). Presumably these classes exist only in communes with minority-language facilities. By contrast, a parliamentary document listed 7,658 such pupils for the school year 1961-62, which was still only about 0.7 per cent of enrolment in the Dutch regime at the time, whereas in 1902 2.6 per cent of *schools* in Flanders were conducted in French (Chambre des Représentants, 1961-62, no. 398(9),38-44; Clough, 1930, 155). There are no official statistics on students who commute from one language region to another, nor any separate statistics on boarding schools, and at least one private, nonrecognized, nonsubsidized French-language school exists in Antwerp. Nevertheless the number of exceptions to the rule of Dutch-language education at primary and secondary level in Flanders appears to be totally insignificant.

4. *Newspaper readership.* Approximately 7 per cent of all newspapers read in Flanders in 1969 were published in French, but only 2.4 per cent of survey respondents reported reading *only* French papers. Since roughly one person in three read no newspaper at all, this latter figure represents 3.5 per cent of those who did read newspapers (SOBEMAP, 1969).

5. *Broadcasting.* In 1969 some 7 per cent of survey respondents in Flanders listened to French-language RTB radio and 5 per cent watched RTB television, but only 3 per cent of those who utilized Belgian broadcasting were tuned *only* to French-language programs. If we include data for foreign broadcasting and newspapers, the percentage using media of both languages goes up and the percentage of non-users decreases, but those using *only* French-language media remain around 2 to 3 per cent of the regional population (SOBEMAP, 1969).

Considered together, these post-1947 data suggest the continuing existence of a French-speaking—but not necessarily unilingual—minority of about 2 to 3 per cent of the population of Flanders. The data on *miliciens* and universities also suggest that this group still includes some young people. But these conclusions fall short of certainty. Although the "French-only" component appears to be of similar proportions across several sectors, there is no proof that it refers to the same nucleus of Francophone families in each sector. In the case of media data from the 1969 SOBEMAP survey, however, we can select for further analysis those who show linguistically consistent behavior across several media sectors, including daily newspapers, Belgian radio, Belgian television, foreign radio, and foreign television. This is done in Table 54, which compares those who used French-language media *exclusively* and those who used them *predominantly* against the total number of respondents in the Dutch-language region. These two groups together made up 3.9 per cent of the sample population. One might argue for inclusion of the next adjacent group in terms of media usage, the 4.9 per cent of the sample who used French and Dutch media equally, but only 18 per cent of this group read a French-language newspaper and their socioeconomic profile is distinctly closer to the average for the whole sample than to that of the other users of French media in almost every category analyzed here.

The findings of this analysis are interesting in several respects. The distribution by age is at first rather puzzling, but it becomes clearer if we reflect that bilingual skills often increase with age and with experience in the workforce. If we group the two categories of French media users together they give a combined result of 35 per cent under thirty-five years old, 36 per cent aged between thirty-five and fifty-four, and 29 per cent aged fifty-five or more, which is almost identical with the sample as a whole. This similarity of age profiles is significant, because it argues that the use of French-language media was stable from one age cohort to another at this date.

In other respects the profile that emerges in this survey tends to confirm the popular image of Francophones in Flanders as a privileged group. The users of French-language media tended to be better educated, of higher social class, better placed occupationally, and better off financially than the sample as a whole. They were more amply supplied with automobiles, telephones, bathtubs, and a whole host of appurtenances and comforts that are often seen as evidence of success in contemporary societies. In spatial terms, further analysis showed a slight tendency for these groups to be overrepresented in the Antwerp area, the Brussels periphery, and urban areas generally, with slight underrepresentation in rural communes. By provinces, they were overrepresented in Brabant and underrepresented in the peripheral provinces of Limburg and West Flanders. But there is another side to this profile. The Francophone minority in Flanders—at least when measured by these criteria of media usage—is also represented in noticeable numbers among those with modest education,

Table 54

Flanders: Selected socioeconomic characteristics of users of French-language media,[a] 1969 (percentages)[b]

Characteristic	French media exclusively (N = 141)	French media predominantly (N = 89)	Total respondents for Flanders (N = 5,938)
Age			
15-34	38	29	33
35-54	36	36	35
55 or over	26	35	32
Total	100	100	100
Education			
primary only	38	17	53
upper secondary or post-secondary	41	51	19
Social class			
upper or middle (A, B)	43	55	22
skilled or unskilled worker (C1, C2)	57	45	77
Selected occupational categories			
professional and managerial	18	18	4
middle management	10	13	7
employees	9	25	13
skilled workers	13	13	19
unskilled workers	14	4	22
inactive or retired	19	13	17
Family income (monthly)			
under 20,000 BFr	70	56	81
30,000 BFr or over	9	16	4
Percentages of households having			
automobile	63	73	57
telephone	50	64	32
bathroom with bath	54	75	42
Percentage taking vacation in 1968			
in Belgium	33	27	21
abroad	31	46	20

[a] For the construction of the media index, see above, 44-45.
[b] Percentages for age, education, class, occupation, and income run vertically, with some categories omitted.

Source: Computer runs based on SOBEMAP, 1969.

lower social status, unskilled jobs and average incomes, in rural areas, and in every province of the Dutch language region.

Taken by themselves, these structural and behavioral data are hardly sufficient. To complete the picture one must resort to interviews and to the few memoirs and essays that touch on the question. One such document is by Hubert d'Ydewalle, a member of a landed family in West Flanders, who served as burgomaster of the village of Beernem until his arrest in 1944 by the German occupation forces and subsequent death in captivity. His posthumously published essay *Noblesse en Flandre* recognizes the past isolation and even ostracism of the nobility from the Flemish Movement and calls for measures of redress. The Flemish milieu, he asserts, "is our milieu," and the elites of Flanders must become bilingual in order to continue their traditional mission of moral and cultural leadership of the Flemish masses. The political weakness of the Flemish Movement was that the nobility had remained aloof from it, leaving the leadership to demagogues and extremists, who were self-made men, *novi homines* drawn from minor bourgeoisie. Against these tendencies, the nobility in Flanders have a political role to play, an educational and cultural mission to fulfil, and a religious example to set, particularly as a landed gentry in the rural milieu (Ydewalle, 1946).

The journalist Charles d'Ydewalle—a cousin of Hubert d'Ydewalle—has left a personal memoir that is less directly focused on the social issue but more evocative of the traditional aristocratic milieu, particularly as it existed in the distant era before the First World War. In his *Confession d'un Flamand*, Charles d'Ydewalle sketches in vivid detail the milieu of his childhood in a family that had been French-speaking for generations. Domains of language were clearly marked, but by status rather than by wealth: "We spoke Flemish to rich farmers and French to poor bourgeois" (1967, 30-31). Political values were "Belgian" without qualification, but the cultural and literary model was fashioned on France and its illustrious civilization. At school, he recalls, "I found the battle of 11 July 1302 [Golden Spurs] . . . *parfaitement regrettable*" (1967, 53-54). The political culture was traditional, conservative, aristocratic, and "the Flemings, all dialect speakers, were a little like the people of the Third World," having nothing in common with the gallicized aristocracy (1967, 39).

As a consequence of the Flemish Movement and the language laws, this Francophone aristocracy was thrust aside. Ydewalle depicts the social revolution in Flanders with the stark clarity of the losing side: "For us, 1913 was the twilight. . . . Innocently, we were aliens, although of the same complexion and the same blood group" as the rest of Flemish society, an object of resentment to the Flamingants, whereas on the other side "the sons of cowherds and gardeners are now ministers" (1967, 25). There is a touch of pathos to Ydewalle's picture, but it evokes no sympathy on the Flamingant side. In a preface to Wilmars's book, Théo Lefèvre, a former prime minister and himself a Fleming of French mother tongue and middle-class origins from Gent, refers pointedly to "this treason of one part of the elite" and calls for them to reintegrate themselves with the rest of the population (Wilmars, 1968, 14). If public concern for the well-to-do and the powerful is seldom in abundant supply, this rule is confirmed empirically for Flanders in a national survey of 1975, in which "the rich" received the fourth lowest ranking on sympathy scales (after "Brusselers," "soldiers," and "political dissidents") of some twenty-two social groups in Belgian society (AGLOP, 1975, variables 122-43; and cf. above, 109-10).

For other evidence, especially as to recent linguistic behavior, one must rely on interviews. In the composite picture that emerges from oral sources one can discern two broad tendencies. First, there is a generation of Francophones whose careers in the army, in diplomacy, and in the public sector generally were blighted by blocked promotions and early retirements during the 1960s as a result of more rigorous linguistic policies. For those from Flanders in this group, there is a double undercurrent of bitterness at having been politically ostracized by Dutch-speaking Flemings and sacrificed at the altar of territorial unilingualism by Francophones from Wallonie. They find a further cruel irony in the contrast between Walloon indifference to their fate and the frenzy that arose over the relative handful of Francophones surrendered to Flanders by the transfer of the Voer communes.

On the other side, there is another more flourishing Francophone group in Flanders, generally of a younger generation and in some cases children of the first group, for whom adaptation to Dutch as a working language has not proved a serious barrier. In the public sector these Francophones appear on the Dutch-language registers, having arrived there either by transfer or by Dutch-language educational diplomas, and many have risen rapidly. For public functions their language is the same ABN variety of Dutch that is increasingly expected of all educated persons in Flanders. Their children go almost invariably to Dutch-medium schools. The difference is that many of these Francophones do not master a local Flemish dialect but retain French as their home language and usual language of social life. However, the rise of a new Dutch-speaking elite has meant that cultivated Nederlands is also heard increasingly at even the most exclusive social events, where only French would have been spoken in the 1950s, and this second group is at home in both languages.

In the absence of systematic studies of the Francophone group in Flanders, our conclusions should be taken less as firm findings than as hypotheses to be explored further. Essentially, the Flemish Movement in Flanders accomplished a social revolution, which opened up a wide range of positions in the public sector to *novi homines* and encouraged the formation of new elites. But if social revolutions produce winners, they also produce losers, and in this case those who paid the price were the dispossessed Francophones, many of whom were ill equipped to live by the new language rules. Their losses in Flanders, however, were in many cases limited to one generation, by which time linguistic adaptation enabled many of their children to assume positions equivalent to those of their grandparents. For many of these families this linguistic adjustment has not so far demanded a surrender of cultural identity, which to all appearances remains predominantly French-oriented as before. The tentative conclusion for Flanders is that many Francophone elite families have been able, after a transitional period, to adjust to the change of language patterns and to retain a significant share of their traditional position in Flemish society. Paris, as Henri IV decided in 1593, was worth a Mass, and Antwerp or Gent, as these families have discovered more recently, may well be worth a second language.

B   The Voer Question

As noted in Chapter 4 (above, 152-53), the six small communes (as they then were) of the Voer district were transferred from Liège province to Limburg and from Wallonie to Flanders as a result of the legislation of November 1962 to fix the linguistic frontier and create language regions that were as homogeneous as possible. At the other end of the language frontier the same law transferred the much more populous Mouscron-Comines district from Flanders to Wallonie, and in all some forty-nine communes and twenty-two parts of communes were transferred from one region to the other by this legislation. Only in the case of the Voer communes did serious political complications arise.

At first glance the Voer district appears a most unlikely place for any kind of social conflict. Its six small villages, heavily agricultural in economic activity and strongly Catholic both in daily life and in political allegiance, had a combined population at the 1961 census of only 4,299 persons in a territory of about twenty-five square miles. Long a feudal dependency of the Netherlands, the area was annexed to Liège during the French occupation and remained with Liège after 1815. Cut off from Dutch Limburg after the boundary adjustments of 1839, it came increasingly within the economic orbit of the nearby industrial cities of Liège and Verviers, both solidly Francophone. In this respect it differs significantly from the other linguistic enclave, the Comines area, which is economically oriented less towards its former province of West Flanders than towards the major industrial metropolis of Lille, just across the border in France.

From a linguistic standpoint, the Voer lies in the transitional zone between Dutch and German dialects described in Chapter 2 (above, 60-61). Some Francophone sources contend that the dialect spoken there is in fact a form of Low German rather than Dutch, but this argument does not appear to have been advanced seriously before the proposed transfer to

Limburg in 1962. The Walloon linguist Elisée Legros, who traced the dialectal frontier with painstaking care, did not hesitate to describe these communes as *"dialectalement flamandes"* though also *"assez fortement francisées"* and even familiar with Walloon dialect "because of their position and the desire of the inhabitants" (1948, 64). The census of 1846 showed the area to be about 90 per cent Flemish-speaking, and in 1930 some 76 per cent of the total population recorded Dutch as their only or most frequently spoken language (CRISP, 1979, no. 859: 7). Since some Francophones contest these results as having been unduly influenced by the Abbé Veltmans, a local curé and militant of the Flemish Movement, one may note that all six communes showed overwhelming majorities speaking Dutch only or predominantly in 1910 and four of them did so again in 1920, but the other two showed a temporary decline in 1920, to 62 per cent in St. Martens-Voeren and to 36 per cent in Remersdaal, followed by a recovery in 1930 (Meeus, 1975, 60-61). In 1947, however, five of the six communes showed narrow pluralities or majorities for French over Dutch as the most frequently used language—in one case by 164 to 163, plus one German speaker—and these results were in turn contested by the Flemish Movement as having been too much influenced by the contemporary hue and cry against wartime activists.

Under the 1932 language laws the Voer was considered part of the Dutch-language region for administrative and educational purposes, even though it remained part of a Walloon province. The 1947 census results—publication of which was delayed for the contested areas until 1954—put this status in doubt. The six communes were then given a special bilingual administrative regime with French preponderant. The language of instruction in communal schools remained Dutch (or in fact local patois) but with reinforced teaching of French as a second language. The Liège provincial government maintained a Dutch-speaking section to deal with the Voer and with other Dutch-speaking communes in the Landen area. In the central administration, some services to the Voer were provided through regional offices in Liège while others, including school inspection, taxation, employment services, agriculture, and customs administration, were handled from regional offices in Limburg. This hybrid regime, developed in consultation with local interests, gave rise to no visible friction before 1962. The Centre Harmel, which studied the entire length of the linguistic frontier in great detail, found its Francophone and Flemish members divided over a formula for the Voer communes. In the end, as a compromise, its final report recommended a special bilingual regime for the area, to be developed in consultation with local interests and promulgated by special royal decree (CRISP, 1979, no. 859: 10-12; Schreurs, 1961).

When the Lefèvre-Spaak Christian Social-Socialist coalition government assumed office in May 1961, it was formally committed to regulate the linguistic issue as a high priority. In November the new minister of the interior, Arthur Gilson, a Christian Social Francophone from Brussels, introduced the government's bill to fix the linguistic frontier permanently and to modify certain administrative boundaries to reflect the frontier. Following the recommendations of the Centre Harmel, this bill left the Comines and the Voer areas in their respective provinces of West Flanders and Liège but with special linguistic status, as an alternative to establishing administrative enclaves beyond the ends of the existing linguistic frontier. When the bill was examined in a committee of the lower house, some members took exception to these departures from the general principle of linguistic homogeneity. A Walloon Socialist from West Flanders called for the transfer of Mouscron-Comines to Hainaut, and his plea was supported by a Socialist colleague from Liège, who conceded the transfer of the Voer communes to Limburg in the name of the same principle, but also—allegedly—because the transfer of these solidly Catholic communes would leave the Socialists within reach of an absolute majority in the Provincial Council of Liège. Although Flemish members hesitated and the minister himself opposed the changes, the committee eventually approved them overwhelmingly. Against further opposition from Walloon Christian Social members, they were accepted by the lower house as a whole in February 1962. Passage through the Senate later in the year proved even more difficult, because by summer local opposition to the transfer in the Voer had spread more widely throughout Liège province and even to Wallonie as a whole. However, by this time Flemish opinion had reluctantly accepted the double transfer, and it had become politically and psychologically impossible to call into question one side of the transfer without also reopening the issue of Mouscron-Comines and other communes lost by Flanders. In the end the only way out of a dangerous impasse was to press forward. The government put pressure on its Francophone senators and the legislation was passed in final form, with certain additional minority guarantees for the transferred areas, on October 31 (CRISP, 1979, no. 859: 12-17; Hasquin, 1975-76, 2: 341-42; Herremans, 1965, 33-34; *Soir*, 1979, June 22, July 10).

Although accounts differ as to who should bear the blame, there seems little doubt that the committee of the lower house that first considered the Gilson bill made a serious error in ignoring local opinion in the Voer during its deliberations. While early warning signals were visible, and not least from Minister Gilson himself, local interests were clearly overridden and sacrificed to the symmetry of a general principle. By summer and autumn the warning signs were unmistakable, but by this time there was no other way out. The Voer transfer had become part of a package that could no longer be dismantled without serious or even fatal consequences for the government itself. Unlike the Swiss system, where issues can be isolated, decentralized, and resolved in a limited context, the centralization of the

Belgian political system and its tendency to work through interconnected package deals make it cumbersome and unforgiving of errors. Once the government's course had been set, the consequences followed with the inevitability of a Greek tragedy. Ironically, one of the first victims was Gilson himself, who soon found himself pilloried and hanged in effigy as a traitor to the Francophone cause, his political career in ruins.

Time heals many political wounds, but the issue of the transfer has dominated politics in the Voer region at every subsequent election. Immediately before the final vote on the Gilson bill, in October 1962, the Provincial Council of Liège authorized a commission of inquiry and a vote in the six communes to ascertain popular feelings on the transfer. At this vote 93 per cent of those voting, or 63 per cent of all eligible voters, opted to remain in Liège. One third of the electorate did not participate, and it is generally accepted that most of those in favor of the transfer boycotted this vote. At all subsequent elections the pro-Liège irredentists organized either special lists under the label "Retour à Liège" or campaigns of abstention by casting blank or spoiled ballots. Thus at regular communal elections in 1964, 1970, 1976 and 1982 the "Retour à Liège" lists obtained 59 to 63 per cent of the vote and about two thirds of local council seats. In four national elections similar lists won 57 per cent of the vote in 1965, 62 per cent in 1968, 57 per cent in 1974, and 53 per cent in 1977. At the 1971 national election 60 per cent of the voters cast blank or spoiled ballots, as did 59 per cent in 1978, and 54 per cent in 1981. At the first election for the European Parliament in June 1979, where Voer voters had a choice only among Flemish lists, 51 per cent cast spoiled or blank ballots. The voting data therefore show that while the pro-Liège group has been a permanent majority since the transfer, there is a far-from-negligible pro-Limburg Flemish minority, comprising approximately 40 per cent of the electorate, which votes predominantly for the Flemish Social Christian party (CVP) or for the Volksunie. The vote for socialist and liberal parties has been negligible during this period (CRISP, 1979, no. 859: 18-22; 1981, no. 943: 11).

Similar and even stronger tendencies emerged in education. Before 1962 the six communes had only Dutch-language communal schools, but French-language classes were available in adjacent communes. In 1961-62 some 64 per cent of the 639 school-age children in the area attended the communal schools while 36 per cent attended classes in Walloon communes. The 1963 law on languages in education gave the Voer a right to request minority-language educational facilities in French, but efforts to obtain such classes were met with insensitivity and procrastination on the part of the Limburg and central government authorities. This administrative heavy-handedness only increased the determination of the pro-Liège faction and led Walloon organizations to conduct a ten-year successful campaign for the financial support of privately run classes and transport arrangements, an appeal that served to sensitize the whole of Francophone Belgium to allegations of Flemish oppression in the Voer. By 1969-70 some 65 per cent of the school population attended these private classes or schools in adjacent Walloon communes, and by 1978-79, when French-language communal schools had been established alongside the Dutch-language classes, 62 per cent of area pupils were in the French schools (CRISP, 1979, no. 859: 23-25; *Soir*, 1979, June 23).

Since 1963 several successive Belgian governments have attempted to resolve the Voer issue without success. During the post-election negotiations in 1968 two proposals to retransfer the area to Liège were promptly rebuffed, but then an interparty agreement undertaken by the new Eyskens government undertook to place the area in an "autonomous canton" outside any province and directly under the central government. To do this required an amendment of the constitution, and this was added to the ongoing agenda of constitutional reform negotiations then in progress. In December 1970 Article 1 was accordingly amended to allow Parliament to create such direct dependencies through legislation passed by special majorities, including majorities from both linguistic groups in each house and a two-thirds majority of all votes cast. This rigorous procedure was designed to protect the Brussels area from a similar fate, but in fact it more or less blocked legislation on the Voer as well. A 1971 bill to create a separate Voer canton, though signed by all ministers of the government, encountered backbench CVP opposition. The next Eyskens government attempted to mollify Flemish opposition by leaving the extraprovincial Voer canton *within* the Netherlandic linguistic region, but this was promptly declared unconstitutional by the Conseil d'Etat in September 1972. Two months later the Eyskens government fell (CRISP, 1979, no. 859: 28-30).

The next coalition, headed by the Walloon Socialist Edmond Leburton, adopted a more pragmatic policy. In May 1973 it eased certain administrative barriers and preconditions by executive decree, allowing minority-language classes to be established without further delay in each of the six small communes. This action eased the tension somewhat until August 1976, when the Conseil d'Etat, in response to a complaint from local Flemish groups, annulled the decree on grounds of incompatibility with the specifications of the language legislation. This new barrier to French-language classes was removed a few months later by the fusion of the six Voer communes into one under the general reorganization of municipal government, which took effect from January 1977, but not before an infuriated Francophone population had regrouped its forces to capture ten out of fifteen seats on the new council of the consolidated commune of Voeren or Fourons. The new commune now fulfilled all legal requirements for minority-language schools, but the minister of Dutch education still delayed recognition, adding to the growing frustration on the Francophone side (*Soir*, 1979, June 23; CRISP, 1979, no. 859: 23-25).

From 1976 onward one can trace a gradual resurgence of the Voer issue both locally and in the national arena. The pro-Liège faction had been mobilized afresh by the events of that year, and the communal council of the integrated Voeren commune saw its inaugural sitting annulled because some councillors insisted on taking the oath in French. In September 1977 some Fouronnais attended the thirtieth Fête du peuple jurassien in faraway Delémont in the newly emerging Swiss canton of Jura (see Volume 1, 193-94), and they returned with a new vision of a *peuple fouronnais*. They remodelled their own autumn fête to imitate the Jura example and formed an activist political association, Action fouronnaise, as well as a militant youth group.

The local Flemish minority, looking with some anxiety at these developments in an area that had been officially part of Flanders for some fourteen years, appealed to various national Flemish associations for support and assistance. In contrast with the Swiss case—in which citizens of other cantons generally refrained from taking sides in the long struggle between the Jurassiens and the Bernese cantonal authorities—their appeal was immediately answered, and each new step on the Francophone side was matched by a response in kind. The most visible of these reactions were sympathy marches and demonstrations by militant organizations, most notably by the Taal Aktie Komitie and the resuscitated paramilitary Vlaamse Militanten Orde, or VMO, which had the negative effect of persuading even more Francophones to join Action fouronnaise (*Soir*, 1979, June 23-25). From early 1978 the scale of violence gradually escalated from tire slashings and property defacement to Molotov cocktails, gunfire, and physical injuries, until by late 1979 some Belgian students of the problem were seriously worried about the possibilities of a major explosion of violence.

Instead of growing or diminishing, however, the level of violence continued at roughly the same level and was characterized by sporadic mass demonstrations, burnings of automobiles—including a few with Netherlands plates as a reprisal for alleged laxity of the Dutch authorities in allowing Flemish militants to organize across the border—and the burning of a Flemish school. The authorities took an increasingly firm line against mass demonstrations, bussing in small armies of gendarmes to bar entry to outsiders. They successfully prosecuted the uniformed VMO and imprisoned their leader under an antifascist law of 1934 that banned private militias. Meanwhile other Flemish organizations found a way to counterattack and to open a second front at the other end of the language frontier by demonstrating in support of a Dutch-language school for the small Flemish minority in Comines. There the Francophone communal council, playing into their hands, successfully evaded and refused a request from Flemish parents until the central government was forced to intervene and establish the minority-language school to which the language laws entitled them.

In 1982 matters in Voeren took a new turn when the leader of the Francophone Action fouronnaise, José Happart, fresh from an acquittal in a Liège court for his part in the 1979 violence, contested the communal election on the "Retour à Liège" list, topped the poll, and at once announced his intention to be named burgomaster of the commune for the period 1983-89 and his refusal to yield to a more moderate candidate. His sole platform was return of the commune to the province of Liège. The normal Belgian procedure is that burgomasters are nominated by the communal council, proposed by the minister of the interior, and appointed by the King—acting, presumably, on ministerial advice. When Happart's name was proposed, the Vlaamse Raad addressed a unanimous request to the King not to accept it, while the Council of the French Community—also unanimously—requested its acceptance (Soir, 1982, November 18-19). Even in such a totally unpromising situation, which in January 1983 briefly threatened the survival of the Martens V government, interparty negotiation eventually produced a way to split the difference: Happart would be named burgomaster, but only after a year's delay to December 31, 1983—which could be rationalized as allowing him time to learn Dutch—and he would serve under the supervision of a new adjunct-commissioner of the *arrondissement* appointed to oversee Flemish interests (Deweerdt, 1984, 414-19; Smits, 1984, 476-82; CRISP, 1983, no. 1019: 21-22). The example of Voeren then became similar to and linked with a few other Flemish communes with linguistic facilities in which the rights of elected Francophone officials to exercise their mandate in French were being increasingly challenged by the Flemish parties and defended by the French ones.

But the Happart case soon spread beyond Voeren. The disputed burgomastership had given the young activist national prominence, and the Francophone Parti socialiste offered him a place—although he was not a socialist—on its list for the 1984 election for the European Parliament. Standing as an independent, Happart won 235,000 personal votes, the only Francophone candidate to exceed 100,000, and thereby contributed significantly to the party's advance from four seats in 1979 to five in 1984. Although this electoral strategy enabled the Parti socialiste to capture votes from the declining Rassemblement wallon and the FDF, there was a price to be paid. Happart's candidacy widened and embittered the split between the Parti socialiste and the Flemish Socialistische Partij, and his initial refusal to join the Parti socialiste led the socialists in the European Parliament to exclude him from membership in their group. When the veteran socialist Ernest Glinne was ostracized by the Parti socialiste for refusing to back Happart at Strasbourg, he could remind the 1984 party congress, with some irony, that he had been similarly disciplined in 1963—as the sole socialist to vote against the original transfer of the Fourons to Limburg (Lettre de Belgique, 1984, no. 38: 14-16).

Why has the Voer conflict persisted and intensified for more than two decades? This conflict is a classic example of how disagreement over an apparently minor issue can return to haunt its perpetrators. In part, one may trace the persistence of the question to the immobilism of the Belgian political system and its incapacity to find a solution or even a remedial measure. The sense of alienation among local Francophones appears to have a twofold origin: their double frustration at being overlooked during the passage of the 1962 legislation and at being denied redress for more than a decade afterwards. The situation is worsened by the existence once again of a minority complex on both sides: the pro-Flemish group because they are a local minority in the Voer, and the pro-Liégeois because they are an insignificant minority in the province of Limburg. The combination of political immobilism, alienation, and minority consciousness has created almost an ideal climate for appeals to extraparliamentary methods, and both sides, as if in unconscious justification of such appeals, have not hesitated to accuse the other of Nazi-style tactics.

Among other complicating factors, there has been a conspicuous absence of room to manoeuvre in the search for a solution. The constitutional and legal framework has left the traditional Belgian method of conflict resolution by compromise or "splitting the difference" substantially unavailable in this case—except in conjunction with other issues. Unlike the Brussels area, some sort of either/or solution, a subordinate-superordinate linguistic relationship, is specified by the language laws in the clearest possible terms. To make matters worse, the issue cuts close to the most sensitive interests and core values of both sides: for the Francophones, the basic human freedom to choose one's own language; for the Flemings, the inviolability of historically indisputable Netherlandic territory. For the latter, the Voer is simply Flemish irrespective of recent language behavior; for the former, the Limburg administration has been an odious and repressive tyranny.

The very incongruity of the Voer issue, its infinitesimal size combined with irreconcilable antagonisms, has helped to make it a continuing media event in Belgium and even abroad. As such, it has proved useful to organizations that owe their existence or their continuing strength to the *question communautaire*. These include, as noted earlier, the regional political parties, the major cultural foundations, and other associations that promote cultural activism. We have already described in Chapter 3 how pressures from regional parties and cultural associations have widened linguistic cleavages in the traditional parties, preventing the adoption of moderate policies out of a fear of further electoral losses to the regional parties (above, 142-46). This has meant that few political leaders have an overriding interest in "solving" the Voer issue or others like it, while many significant interest groups in the national political system derive tangible benefits from continuance of the conflict—as long as it remains at a moderate level—in the form of membership maintenance and heightened group loyalty. Since the pro-Liège Francophones in the Voer were clearly the aggrieved party after the legislation of 1962, activist Walloon organizations in particular can win added advantage by keeping the issue alive and using it as a bargaining counter in other contexts.

These conclusions may seem to imply criticism of the Belgian political system, but one must end with a note of caution. The obvious alternative to the Belgian system of intergroup bargaining in one central arena would be a Swiss-style decentralization of linguistic and cultural disagreements to regions, provinces, or communes, where they would be examined in that context and settled according to local criteria. But such an alternative may not be readily available in Belgium, because the structural and sociological conditions of language predominance in the Belgian setting might well intensify the cumulative pressures of French upon Dutch under a decentralized political system. As long as these pressures continue, one crucial barrier against them will be the Flemish majority in a central parliament. These underlying structural factors appear to be a major reason why important provisions of the language laws, and especially those concerning communes with minority-language facilities, have been excluded from the competence of the new community councils.

C The Problem of Brussels

It is somewhat misleading to speak of a "Brussels problem"; closer examination reveals no less than five major issues that divide the language communities either directly or indirectly. In the first place, there is the process of *francisation* of the Brussels area population, which in a century and a half has changed a predominantly Flemish city into a predominantly Francophone one. Second, there is the territorial expansion of the metropolis, which in the same period has added twenty-one more communes to the urban core and threatened many adjacent ones in Flemish Brabant. Third, there is a need for a coordinated system of metropolitan government for the urbanized area. Fourth, in a Belgium that is increasingly regionalized around language boundaries there is a growing need for effective regional planning and economic development for the Brussels area, since Flanders and Wallonie have both been developing their own regional frameworks for economic development. Finally, Brussels must serve as an appropriate national capital for all of Belgium, and this question in turn has both practical and symbolic aspects. Analytically, these questions can be identified and examined separately. From a political perspective, they are inevitably interrelated, but they are differently perceived and assigned different priorities by the different groups in question. What seems to be generally agreed is that Brussels—in one aspect or another— has become the largest outstanding issue dividing the language communities.

In historical perspective, the experience of Brussels as a capital can be traced back to Burgundian times and beyond, but its pre-eminence dates from the reign of the Emperor Charles V. Although situated in solidly Flemish countryside, Brussels was exposed early to French influences through the royal courts of Brabant and Burgundy, and again in the seventeenth and eighteenth centuries when French had become the universal language of intellectual and cultivated discourse throughout Europe. Austrian domination in the eighteenth century led to the predominance of French in governmental circles. Yet French was spoken natively by a relatively small circle. Verlooy, who deplored the neglect of Nederlands in a celebrated essay of 1788, estimated the French-speaking population of Brussels at about 5 per cent of the total, but this minority included the nobility and the upper bourgeoisie (Lindemans, 1963, 9). The French Revolution brought several thousand French-speaking exiles to Brussels after 1789, and this influx was followed by French military invasion in 1794 and two decades of coercive *francisation*. Down to the end of the *ancien régime* municipal administrative documents were in Latin or Flemish, with notarial acts in Flemish or French according to the parties involved, but after 1794 all these documents were written exclusively in French (Stengers, 1979, 89, 135-44).

Before 1800, the urban population still lived within the historic pentagon defined by the second wall of the city, constructed in the fourteenth century. Even in 1830, when Brussels became the capital of independent Belgium, old maps in the City Hall museum show only very minor ribbon development extending towards the immediately adjacent villages. A special language census in the commune of Brussels in 1842 revealed that 61 per cent of the population spoke Dutch or Flemish and 38 per cent spoke French or Walloon. Two districts out of eight, comprising the east and southeast sections of the upper town, had a majority of French speakers, and even the two western districts across the River Senne had Francophone minorities of 12 and 20 per cent (Mols, 1960, 157; 1961, 137-38; Kruithof, 1956, 212, 220). Further change was under way. Charles Baudelaire, who spent two desperately poverty-stricken years in Brussels from 1864 to 1866 and who left copious notes for a savagely critical portrait of Belgian society, included a vivid testimony on the language situation: "People do not know French; *nobody* knows it, but everyone *pretends* not to know Flemish. This is the fashion, but the proof that they know it very well is that they tell off their servants in Flemish" (1941, 42; 1953, 76). Although a biased witness in other respects, he seems credible here for the bourgeoisie that he knew.

By 1846, the date of the first national census, the spread of population into adjacent communes was becoming more marked, and for the next century we can trace the growth of the capital area and its changing linguistic composition with reasonable precision. This can be done in two ways. One can trace the growth and linguistic composition of the urbanized area as it expanded from census to census as in Part B of Table 8 (above, 48), or one can take the post-1963 boundaries of Brussels-Capital and trace the linguistic composition of this territory from 1846. Table 55 follows the second of these alternatives, tracing the linguistic evolution of the nineteen communes of Brussels-Capital, which were reduced from twenty-two by annexations in 1921. In 1846 it can be estimated that only about half of these communes were urbanized significantly, but these accounted for close to 90 per cent of the total population, the rest being solidly Dutch-speaking smaller communes of the outer ring. No matter which method of reckoning is used, the general trend in these data is unmistakable, though it stands out a little more sharply by this "territorial" method. Closer study of the figures by individual communes shows that the commune of Brussels, with its expanding boundaries, is quite close to the language proportions for the metropolitan area as a whole for most of this period, while the suburbs vary quite widely above and below the regional averages. In 1846 only one commune, Saint-Josse-ten-Noode, showed a razor-thin plurality of French over Dutch. By 1890 this plurality—ignoring bilinguals—was found in three communes, and by 1900 in six, including Brussels itself. By 1930 French was predominant in twelve out of nineteen communes, and by 1947 in all nineteen, by margins ranging from less than 1 per cent in Evere to an overwhelming 78 percentage points in Ixelles.

Table 55

Brussels: Population and language distribution in Brussels metropolitan area communes, 1846-1947 (percentages)[a]

Year	Total population		French only	Dutch only	French and Dutch	French only or mainly	Dutch only or mainly
	000s	%					
1846	212	100	—	—	—	32.0	66.7
1866	309	100	19.3	46.2	31.7	—	—
1880	437	100	23.2	42.0	26.2	—	—
1890	520	100	20.7	29.6	44.7	—	—
1900	626	100	22.3	25.5	42.8	—	—
1910	762	100	27.1	23.2	40.8	48.7	45.5
1920	806	100	31.6	16.4	46.7	58.7	37.8
1930	892	100	37.1	14.3	42.7	62.7	33.7
1947	956	100	37.0	9.5	43.9	70.6	24.2

[a] The table omits minor categories (German speakers, those without an official language, other combinations, etc.).

Source: *Wetenschappelijk onderzoek*, 1974-75, 1: 11-20.

As a result of the suppression of the language questions in the census there have been no further census data since 1947, but the linguistic evolution of the Brussels area has continued and can be traced through a number of studies, estimates, and other indicators of linguistic behavior. One of the first studies of this kind was undertaken by Leo Lindemans, who, distrusting the "subjective" elements of the 1947 census, attempted what he termed an "objective language census" through a sampling of communal electoral registers. By this means he found that 27 per cent of the electorate were immigrants from Dutch-speaking communes, and for those born in the Brussels area he then estimated the percentage born to Dutch families by estimations based on the date and commune of birth and other data in the registers. Overall he estimated that some 53 per cent of the 1948 electorate were of Flemish or Netherlandic origin, and a repetition of the experiment on the 1966 electoral lists revealed that this proportion had fallen to 47 per cent. While Lindemans's method has been justly criticized as having little bearing on current language *behavior*, it is instructive as an approximate indicator of the point from which language transfer began. The first Lindemans study also served to highlight the extent of Flemish immigration into the Brussels area and its subsequent *verfransing*, which was particularly high in communes of high Francophone concentration (Lindemans, 1951, 3-8, 77-84; 1968, 3-9, 33-35; *Wetenschappelijk onderzoek*, 1974-75, 1: 26-33).

In 1969 a survey of the Brussels area conducted by Kluft and Van der Vorst, two Flemish researchers of the Institute of Sociology of the University of Brussels, asked four separate questions concerning language and cultural identity. Some 27 per cent of respondents declared themselves of Dutch mother tongue, but only 13 per cent used Dutch "most frequently"; 17 per cent used Dutch for mental calculations, and 18 per cent felt they belonged to the Dutch-speaking community. A small middle group that varied from 3 to 6 per cent could not be attributed to either language, and the rest were Francophones. Using a weighted index, the authors suggested that the Dutch community made up only 18 per cent of the sample, but this sample, based on electoral registers of citizens, excluded foreign workers resident in Brussels (*Wetenschappelijk onderzoek*, 1974-75, 1: 39; Monteyne, 1972, 21-24; CRISP, 1970, nos. 466-67: 11). Even so, the figure was lower than that suggested by any previous study or census, and the leakage of preliminary results to the press in late 1969, when delicate constitutional negotiations were in progress, caused a sharply negative reaction in Flemish nationalist circles. The rector of the Flemish section of the university promptly dissociated his institution from the results, and as a result of external pressures and alleged errors in interpreting data from the sample no final version of this study was ever published. The fragments available through the press, however, suggest that this study was based on honest and useful research, capable of yielding significant structural, attitudinal, and cognitive information on the Brussels language communities at a critical point in the political evolution of Belgium and some two decades after the last language census.[1]

Several other indicators tend to come close to the result arrived at by Kluft and Van der Vorst. A second survey of the Brussels population, sponsored externally by the Institute for Peace and Conflict Research in Copenhagen but carried out by the same research team, issued a preliminary report in which the Flemish represented 18 per cent of a first subsample of 500 (Boserup, 1969, 14), but the analysis of the full sample and publication of full results of this study also appear not to have been carried out. The proportion of *miliciens* from Brussels-Capital doing compulsory military service in Dutch-language units averaged 15 per cent from 1964 to 1966, and remained reasonably stable at 16 per cent in 1970 and 17 per cent in 1977 (*Analyse de la population*, 1964, 9; 1965, 9; and unpublished data from the armed forces). In 1968 the proportion of identity cards issued to Belgian citizens in Dutch in Brussels was 13.6 per cent, and 12.3 per cent of drivers' licences were in Dutch (CRISP, 1970, nos. 466-67: 13; Monteyne, 1972, 22). In 1969 10.4 per cent of university students in Brussels-Capital were in the Dutch-language sector, but with improved Dutch-language education this figure rose to 11.9 per cent by 1978. Other possible indicators are school enrolments (see below, Table 58, 315) and voting for Flemish lists at national or communal elections.

On the other hand, some Flemish authorities see these figures as unrepresentative of the underlying cultural situation, and argue that official documents such as identity cards or drivers' licences tend to reflect the predominant language of the milieu rather than the first language of a bilingual applicant. Monteyne, after reviewing various other estimates, suggests a figure for the Flemish community in Brussels of around 24 per cent (1972, 23), and a survey made in 1967 for the Francophone Rassemblement pour le Droit et la Liberté (RDL), which classified bilingual respondents carefully according to the language used at home among family members, concluded that 27 per cent of the population of the nineteen communes were Dutch speakers by this criterion (*Que veulent les Bruxellois*, 1968, 10, 36). One partial explanation for these differing estimates appears to be variations in what is being measured. In the Brussels context it seems very likely that results will differ significantly according to whether one is measuring mother tongue (by whatever definition), language used at home, or language most frequently used outside the home.

The fact of *verfransing* of the Brussels population is admitted by all. If there is disagreement between the language communities as to its extent,

---

[1] The study also found a marked tendency for respondents of *both* language groups to overestimate the percentage of Dutch speakers in Brussels-Capital, a tendency that could be partly explained by the fact that the 1947 census and all subsequent estimates had indicated figures well above the survey findings (*Soir*, 1969, September 18).

these differences become enormously wide and irreconcilable concerning its causes. Among Francophones this language shift has almost invariably been seen as a voluntary exchange undertaken by the Brussels population as a step towards modernization and realization of the superior benefits of a cosmopolitan culture. The Brabant patois of Brussels, in this view, has receded exactly as did the various patois of Wallonie, in favor of French as the only possible language of culture and of the schools (Perin, 1962, 81-82). An earlier Francophone author typically suggested that the linguistic contest in Brussels was not between two languages but between a language and a dialect, since the only true *language* in the Brussels agglomeration was French (Remouchamps, 1936, 62). Flemish circles have viewed the process quite differently. For them *verfransing* has been involuntary, the result of strong social pressures from more wealthy and powerful elements in Brussels society, pressures that the economically and culturally weaker lower classes have little capacity to resist. In a situation where the two language communities have had manifestly unequal access to resources, the debate over the voluntary or forced nature of *verfransing* is reminiscent of Thomas Hobbes's argument in Chapter 21 of *Leviathan* that an action undertaken for fear of death may still be considered the act of a free agent.

Although the positions on either side remain far apart, the structural factors underlying the process of *verfransing* can be documented quite fully as a result of several surveys. From the two studies by Kluft and Van der Vorst and by Boserup one can draw a reasonably complete socioeconomic profile of the two language communities in the later 1960s, and this is done in outline in Table 56. The Dutch-speaking community was found to be about 18 per cent of the sample in both surveys, and not surprisingly the two surveys produced quite similar profiles for some variables, though only one result for each is presented here. The general result from both surveys indicates a clear but not overwhelming social and economic advantage for the Francophone group on every variable available for examination, though it may be noted as a refinement that the Dutch speakers were rather better off in terms of higher-level occupations than in terms of self-rated social class. Boserup emphasizes the importance of Flemish underrepresentation in middle-level occupations, and a consequent tendency for the upper-level and lower-level Flemish groups to be isolated from one another by an intermediate terrain of white-collar employment where the vast bulk of the workforce has been Francophone: "the Flemish are not prevented from entering middle-class occupations, but simply disappear as Flemings once they have entered them" (1969, 11-12).

One can look at these socioeconomic indicators from another perspective by drawing upon the SOBEMAP survey of the same year, which enables us to analyze the Brussels population according to its patterns of use of the mass media. In terms of daily newspapers, radio, and television,

Table 56

Brussels-Capital: Selected socioeconomic characteristics by language communities, 1969 (percentages)

Characteristic	French-speaking respondents	Dutch-speaking respondents
1. Education		
post-secondary	21	6
higher secondary	21	14
lower secondary	27	33
elementary only	31	47
Total	100	100
2. Occupation		
professional, managerial	17	14
independent	23	23
employees	38	20
workers	21	43
Total	99	100
3. Income (BFr per month)		
over 22,000	22	11
13,000-22,000	30	24
7,000-13,000	28	31
under 7,000	20	34
Total	100	100
4. Social class (self-rated)		
upper, upper middle	30	6
middle	42	43
lower middle	9	16
working class	17	33
no information	2	3
Total	100	101
5. Percentage of households having		
automobile	55	46
telephone	65	44
bathroom	65	43

Sources: 1, 2, 3: Kluft and Van der Vorst survey, as reported in *Laatste Nieuws*, September 18, 1969; 4, 5: Boserup, 1969, Tables 4 and 5.

this survey showed that 53 per cent of Brussels respondents used only French-language media, 7 per cent used only Dutch-language sources, 6 per cent used none of these categories of media, and the remaining 34 per cent used media of both languages. This last group can be further subdivided: 21 per cent used mainly French media, 5 per cent used mainly Dutch media, and 9 per cent used both more or less equally, but the socioeconomic profiles of these three subgroups are so similar that we have grouped them together in Table 57. From this table it can be seen that users of media of both languages, the majority of whom may be presumed to be from Flemish or mixed-language families, are more closely compara- ble in socioeconomic status with users of French media than with those who used only Dutch media. In other words, these data tend to confirm the general impression that upward social mobility for the Flemish population in Brussels is related to capacity to function in French.

A more recent study under the auspices of the Netherlandic Cultural Commission for the Brussels Agglomeration has examined in some detail the concomitants of *verfransing* among immigrants to the capital area from Flanders, focusing upon four main spheres: cultural life, social contacts, economic activities, and administrative practices (Louckx, 1975b). Even though many questions in this survey were thrown in doubt by the inability or unwillingness of respondents to give meaningful answers, the number of usable variables remains quite large. Perhaps the most striking result that emerges is the enormous effect of linguistically mixed marriages upon intergenerational language transfers. In homogeneous Dutch-language marriages 81 per cent of the children attended Dutch-language schools and 14 per cent were educated entirely in French, whereas in mixed Dutch-French marriages 19 per cent of the children were educated wholly in Dutch and 74 per cent wholly in French. The language of the spouse had similar effects on the language used at work, with friends, by the children with their friends, and with administrative authorities. In other findings, Louckx's data indicate that the *verfransing* of children is higher for respon- dents resident in communes that are predominantly Francophone, for those either in unskilled or in high-level occupations as distinct from intermediate ones, and for families where the parents have been educated in French or where the child has first learned French. *Verfransing* of respondents themselves at the workplace is higher in predominantly Fran- cophone communes, for those working in the private sector, for working women rather than for men, and for the more highly educated.

Another structural factor that appears significant is the situation of the languages themselves. Baetens Beardsmore, who has done the most exten- sive study to date of the regional French spoken in Brussels (1971), has elsewhere called attention to the close symbiotic relationship between French and the local Brabant dialect of Flemish. His research revealed a readiness among many dialect speakers in situations of deference to switch to French rather than to the less familiar standard Dutch or ABN, and he even found linguistic evidence of "systematic convergence" between regional French and Brussels Flemish despite the vast distance between the standard languages (De Coster et al., 1971, 78-82). The survey by Boserup had noted that high-status Dutch speakers in Brussels were separated from low-status Dutch speakers by Flemish underrepresentation at the middle levels, which were mainly Francophone (1969, 11-12). Sociolinguistic research further suggests that many of these upper-level speakers, usually well educated, intellectually inclined, and often immigrants from Flanders, literally speak a different language from that spoken at lower social levels.

This point emerges with great clarity in an earlier study by Louckx based on in-depth interviews with some ninety-five native-born Flemish Brusselers from the largely working-class, historically Flemish communes of Anderlecht and Molenbeek-Saint-Jean. Though quantitative results were not attempted, these interviews showed a marked tendency, especially among some older respondents, to see ABN as a "foreign" language in Brussels, a form of snobbism, pretentious, artificial, associated with Antwerp and with Flemish extremism. In general the older, fluently bilingual Brusselers in this sample revealed a highly instrumental attitude to language: as one typical respondent remarked, "*Een Brusselaar spreekt alle talen.*" Some younger respondents were less willing to be accommodating. These interviews also make it clear that some had asked for and received their identity cards in French because it was the presumed language of the municipal employee at the counter, while others accepted French-language documents without complaint even though their applications had been filled out in Dutch. Still others were unaware of the language of their identity card until they checked it (Louckx, 1975a, 40, 57, 61-65, 98-103). This indifference to the language of official documents tends to cast grave doubts upon all estimates of the relative size of the linguistic communities based on this criterion.

Beyond the structural concomitants of *verfransing* lie more subtle questions of identity and aspirations. One observer, the late Leo Cappuyns, first vice-governor of Brabant, suggested that three widely divergent estimates of the Netherlandic element in Brussels were each correct in a certain sense. About 50 per cent, as first suggested by Lindemans, were of Flemish stock. Of this number, he suggested, about a third actively desired integration as Francophones. Another third preferred to retain a Flemish cultural orientation but were disinclined to resist environmental pressures, while the remaining third were prepared to resist these pressures resolutely (1967, 20).

Thanks to the surveys, one can supplement this estimate with empirical findings. In the Kluft-Van der Vorst survey of Brussels-Capital, 47 per cent of the Dutch-speaking respondents identified themselves simply as Flemings, 37 per cent as Dutch-speaking Brusselers, 11 percent as French-

Table 57

Brussels: Selected socioeconomic characteristics by patterns of media usage, 1969 (percentages)[a]

Characteristic	French media exclusively (N = 710)	Both French and Dutch media (N = 462)	Dutch media exclusively (N = 92)	Neither French nor Dutch media (N = 87)
1. Age				
15-34	32	43	32	32
35-54	33	33	26	21
55 or over	35	24	42	46
Total	100	100	100	99
2. Education				
primary only	20	16	33	29
upper secondary or post-secondary	51	51	32	47
3. Social class				
upper or middle (A, B)	53	54	35	43
skilled or unskilled worker (C1, C2)	47	46	65	57
4. Occupational categories				
professional and managerial	16	13	4	18
middle management	18	15	8	11
employees	17	23	28	21

Table 57—Continued

Characteristic	French media exclusively (N = 710)	Both French and Dutch media (N = 462)	Dutch media exclusively (N = 92)	Neither French nor Dutch media (N = 87)
skilled workers	9	11	7	3
unskilled workers	5	5	8	1
inactive or retired	22	16	29	32
5. Family income (BFr per month)				
under 10,000	19	15	29	33
30,000 or over	10	10	5	9
6. Percentage of households having				
automobile	64	66	57	57
telephone	67	65	53	56
bathroom with bath	69	69	50	63
7. Percentage taking vacation in 1968				
in Belgium	51	55	42	36
abroad	44	45	36	36

[a] For items 1 to 5 percentages run vertically, with some categories omitted. For the construction of the index, see above, 44-45. This survey treats Brussels as twenty-five communes, adding the six peripheral communes to Brussels-Capital.

Source: Computer runs based on SOBEMAP, 1969.

speaking Brusselers, and the rest with other groups. Of the French-speaking respondents, 65 per cent identified themselves as French-speaking Brusselers, 20 per cent as Walloons, 9 per cent with the French of France, and the rest with other groups. In the Louckx survey of Flemish immigrants, respondents from linguistically homogeneous marriages identified overwhelmingly as Flemings (76 per cent) or as "Brussels Flemings" (16 per cent), but those from linguistically mixed marriages showed more varied responses, including 47 per cent identifying as Flemings and 14 per cent as "Brussels Flemings" (*Soir*, 1969, September 18; Louckx, 1975b, 68, 131).

In more general terms, these surveys point towards a certain complexity and absence of symmetry. The sense of an independent identity as "Brusselers" seems to be more widely and more strongly felt on the Francophone side. Among Dutch-speaking respondents the sense of Flemishness is clearly stronger among those who are immigrants from the Flanders region. Among native-born Brusselers of Flemish origin, Louckx found strong pro-Belgian, antifederalist views, with marked antipathies to Flemish nationalism and to the regional political parties of both sides (1975a, 124-51), a finding also noted by other observers (Aubry, 1971, 22-23). Beyond those findings, however, one can discern faint outlines of subtle cross-pressures and multiple loyalties that are not fully explored in the empirical studies available so far. At the risk of oversimplification, one might hypothesize that in the 1970s on the Dutch-speaking side there were many "Brussels Flemings" but few "Flemish Brusselers" (though some were *Brusselaars* without qualification), while among the French-speaking population "Francophone Brusselers" probably outnumbered "Brussels Francophones" (Herremans, 1980, 339). Our nomenclature here assumes the existence of multiple or compound loyalties of unequal intensity, with the primary one being represented by the noun and the secondary one by the qualifying adjective.

The Kluft-Van der Vorst study also explored the readiness of bilingual respondents to reply in the second language when addressed in it in a shop. Some 50 per cent of French speakers and 84 per cent of Dutch speakers reported an adequate understanding of the second language, and of these bilinguals 71 per cent of Dutch speakers said they "always" replied in French and 12 per cent "never" did so, while 57 per cent of French speakers said they "always" replied in Dutch while 25 per cent "never" did so (*Soir*, 1969, September 18). In part this difference may be linked to differences in fluency in the second language, but it may also be partly attitudinal, and here it would be useful to see further analysis of those not willing to use their second language. For many native-born Brusselers, however, individual bilingualism appears as both a positive personal value and a part of the mission of Brussels as a capital. As one of Louckx's Brussels-born subjects rather picturesquely expressed it, "*Een Brusselaar is bilingue en Belge avant tout*" (1975a, 137). In this milieu the language conflict in the capital tends to be seen as something imported by Flemish and Walloon immigrants, and "real" or autochthonous Brusselers perceive intuitively—and no doubt correctly—that the capital area stands to lose from any reduction in its role as a bridge and mediator between the other regions.

In the expansion of the Brussels metropolis, *verfransing* has been especially characteristic of the urbanizing communes at the edge of the metropolis. Thus at the census of 1846 Saint-Josse-ten-Noode and not Brussels itself was the first commune to show a slight French-speaking plurality. A decree of 1891, applying the law of 1889 on language use in judicial matters in Flanders, excluded Brussels and five surrounding communes from the operation of the law. The area designated bilingual for purposes of the 1921 language law on administrative matters was extended to seventeen communes, but this was reduced to sixteen by the language law on administrative matters of 1932. The language law on judicial matters of 1935 extended the bilingual regime to three more suburban communes, and the same three communes were also added to the law on languages in administrative matters by an amendment of 1954 (Lindemans, 1963, 20-21). The perimeter around these nineteen communes was then fixed by law as the limit of Brussels-Capital as a result of the suppression of the language census and the passing of the linguistic legislation of 1963.

But while legislation imposed a formal limit to the Brussels agglomeration, there is much evidence that the drift to the suburbs and its accompanying language shift have continued. One can see this in the changes between the 1930 and 1947 censuses, and it appears again—though not from official sources—if one compares the 1947 census figures with the results of a study of the Brussels suburbs carried out by Kluft and Jaspers for the Institut de Sociologie in 1969 and reported by the Brussels daily press and by CRISP (1970, nos. 466-67: 18-34). Map 2 indicates, by three successive figures, the percentages of those speaking only or mainly French in these communes at the 1930 census, at the 1947 census, and as indicated by the 1969 study. For the nineteen communes of the agglomeration and for some others not included in the 1969 survey, only the first two of these figures are available, while beyond the outer periphery the percentage of Francophones living north of the linguistic frontier was minimal in 1947 and apparently remained low into the 1970s. The general trends uncovered by the Kluft-Jaspers study indicated larger increases of Francophones at the southern and eastern edges of the agglomeration, while further out, and especially at the northern edge, the language proportions appeared more stable and in a few instances even became more favorable to Dutch speakers. One must, of course, treat these figures with caution. The 1947 census is suspect in Flemish eyes, and the 1969 figures are based on survey research. In the absence of any official census, some Francophone estimates of the *francisation* of the Brussels periphery have run to unjustifiable extremes (Martens et al., 1976, 464; CRISP, 1963, no. 224: 14-15, 20).

Map 2

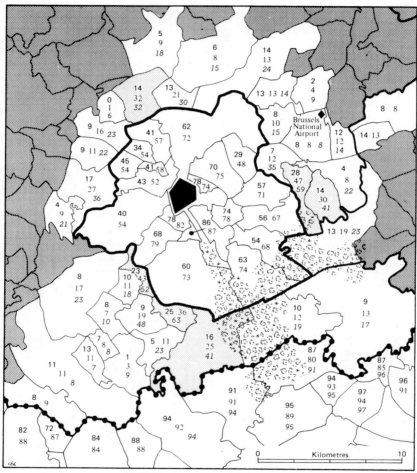

BRUSSELS AND SURROUNDINGS
Increasing Francophone Concentration 1930-1969

5 Percentage French-speaking, 1930 census	▬▬▬ Brussels Agglomeration
5 Percentage French-speaking, 1947 census	●—●—● Language Frontier
5 Percentage French-speaking, 1969 survey	▬▬ Limit of Arrondissement
▨ Less than 5 per cent French-speaking in 1947 and not included in 1969 survey	▫ Communes with minority-language facilities
⬟ The "Pentagon"—historic walled centre of Brussels	░ Soignes Forest

Source: Carte Administrative de Belgique, Edition Provisoire (1977).

The effect of linguistic legislation and especially of the more rigorous legislation of 1963 on the urban expansion of Brussels is difficult to assess. The legislation of the 1930s was not taken seriously by many communal administrations, and even after 1963 most Francophone opinion appears to have assumed that the six peripheral communes with minority-language facilities would sooner or later be incorporated into Brussels-Capital. By the early 1970s, however, there was evidence from studies by geographers that urbanization was spreading out rather unevenly around the capital area. A study by Jouret (1972) sought to delineate the urban area in terms of some fourteen criteria of urbanization and concluded that by these criteria some sixty-one communes should be included within the urbanized zone. The interesting feature of this zone is that it stretches southward across the language boundary into Wallonie. The same study shows that in the 1960s the periphery as a whole was growing faster than Brussels-Capital, the communes with facilities faster than the other communes of Flemish Brabant, and the adjacent communes of Walloon Brabant just south of the language frontier most rapidly of all (Jouret, 1972, 108).

A second study of urbanization reinforces these findings by tracing the level of activity in the real estate market for selected years from 1912 to 1978 through a study of newspaper advertisements. It finds that by 1968 the active zone extended even more deeply into Wallonie, that for the entire period studied the most active axes of growth had been those to the southeast and south of the central pentagon, and that language considerations have apparently been one of the factors in this evolution (Vandermotten, 1971). What stands out from these and other geographical studies is the elliptical shape of the expanding urbanized area, with the faster growing end extending southeast into Wallonie. In the communes along the northern, western, and northeastern edges of Brussels-Capital, the urbanized zone has rather sharply defined limits, while to the south and southeast urbanization extends further into the countryside, but so far less intensively. It seems likely that language is one factor underlying this asymmetrical pattern of development.

At the attitudinal level, the Flemish position on this double process of expansion and *verfransing* is vividly epitomized by the image of the Brussels *olievlek* or "oil stain," a double form of pollution destroying the physical and human environment of the Flemish countryside. Francophones have responded for decades by an appeal to one of their dearest core values, the principle of linguistic liberty. Conspicuously lacking in their value system is any recognition of the principle widely accepted in Switzerland that an immigrant from one language region to another should adjust to the language of the region. In the Brussels suburbs, because of differences in social status between language groups, the evidence strongly suggests a reverse adjustment by the indigenous Flemish population to Francophone norms. Louckx found evidence that native-born Dutch-speaking Brusselers, for whom language loyalty was not a basic value, were sympathetic to the extension of full bilingual status to the communes of the periphery (1975a, 129-30). The indigenous Flemish population of the periphery, however, is not Brussels-born and appears to be more open to political mobilization against *verfransing* through Flemish nationalist parties.

A second image that has long haunted many Flemings is the spectre that the linguistic "island" of Brussels will expand until it links up with Wallonie as a peninsula or salient in the language frontier. Academic studies of urbanization in the Brussels area suggest that this linkage is already well on the way to realization. A 1959 mail survey conducted by the Fondation Charles Plisnier showed that two thirds of Brusselers and half the Walloon respondents favored precisely what the Flemings feared (CRISP, 1960, no. 56: 19). The Flemish Movement, on the other hand, has for decades been firmly determined that this linkage must not happen in any legal sense, and hence the terminology of the debate over the language boundary, as Paul Levy has noted, has closely resembled that of a military campaign (1954b, 390-93). Municipal politics has been especially polarized in Sint-Genesius-Rode (Rhode-Saint-Genèse), the commune that forms the bridge or neck of the potential peninsula, where the two sides were almost equal at the 1976 and 1982 communal elections.

What the Flemings see as necessary defence is interpreted as anti-French imperialism on the Francophone side. This group in turn remains insensitive to the sociological imperialism inherent in its own slogans of linguistic liberty. The Brussels conflict is important because nowhere else in Belgium has there been so much contact across language lines under such unequal conditions. Ever since the regulation of the language question in Flanders itself, the Flemish Movement has given top priority to finding institutional remedies to counterbalance this inequality of social condition between the language communities in and around Brussels.

The quest for an improved institutional framework for the language communities in the Brussels area has been a crucial component of the general quest for language legislation and constitutional reform. The general features of this quest have been dealt with in earlier sections and need not be recapitulated here. Other aspects have focused on the special problems of the Brussels area. Among the control agencies, for example, the Commission permanente de contrôle linguistique has a jurisdiction over the entire country, while the vice-governor of Brabant has a special mandate to watch over the application of the language laws in Brussels-Capital and the six peripheral communes, as well as to coordinate the agglomeration's regional planning. The struggle for institutional reforms, which has been contested on virtually every detail, has been aimed both at strengthening the cultural position of the Dutch-speaking population in the agglomeration and also at curbing the urban area's tendencies towards physical expansion into the countryside.

The complicated question of extending the boundaries of the agglomeration gave rise to a major governmental crisis that threatened the Lefèvre-Spaak government during parliamentary consideration of the language laws in 1963. An early ministerial proposal to establish minority-language facilities both in the Flemish periphery and in three adjacent Walloon communes south of the linguistic frontier broke down over implacable opposition from the latter. In the end a delicate compromise was reached that left six peripheral communes as a special administrative *arrondissement* with limited French-language minority facilities and a Dutch-language administration, but not *formally* attached to either Flanders or Brussels-Capital. Each side viewed the result rather differently. What the Flemish saw as sensible containment of the "oil stain" became for the Francophone press a *carcan*, an "iron collar" to strangle the capital. While Flemings continued to look on the special *arrondissement* as if it were part of Flanders, Francophones in these communes and in Brussels continued to press for full bilingual status and incorporation into Brussels-Capital. These pressures proved unsuccessful, and after seven years the six peripheral communes were formally incorporated into the Dutch-language region by a law of December 23, 1970, just one day before the vote on the new constitutional Article 3 *bis* to recognize and entrench the four language regions in the constitution (Maroy, 1972, 175; CRISP, 1963, nos. 213-14; 1970, nos. 466-67: 6; 1971, no. 535: 22-24). For Flemish parliamentarians this settlement of the boundaries of Brussels has been accepted as definitive and irreversible; for their Francophone colleagues it is still being contested in the 1980s.

The problem within the Brussels agglomeration was to strengthen the institutional framework for the Dutch-speaking minority, and here the first attempts were made through the language laws on administrative matters of 1932 and 1963. The 1932 act imposed on the sixteen communes then composing the capital area an obligation to serve the general public in both French and Dutch, but it left the choice of an internal language of administration to the municipal councils, most of which chose to operate exclusively in French. The 1963 act was much more specific concerning the enlarged Brussels-Capital of nineteen communes. In addition to a reinforcement of external bilingualism in dealing with the public, communes were required in their internal administration to handle each file in French or Dutch according to the language in which it originated, whether from a member of the public, an employee, or a unilingual region. Internal as well as external documents were to be bilingual, and all employees except trades personnel and workers were to have an elementary knowledge of the second language. Further, the principle of language registers for personnel adopted in the central administration was also to apply in the nineteen communes, and "at least 50 per cent" of positions in communal administrations and their subordinate public bodies were to be filled on the basis of parity between French-speaking and Dutch-speaking applicants, the rest being left to municipal option. After ten years, that is, by 1973, all posts of director-level and above in municipal administration were to be staffed on a parity basis (*Emploi des langues*, 1959, 4-5; 1963, 24-29).

During the discussions of constitutional reform in the later 1960s it became obvious that the implementation of these language norms was making little progress. In a ministerial document prepared for the discussions it was reported that by 1969 eight communal administrations out of nineteen had no Dutch-speaking director and eighteen had no Dutch-speaking director-general. All mayors or *bourgmestres* were Francophones[1] and some were unilingual. Findings were similar for municipal councils, committees of public assistance, and health services. Three communes had deliberately reserved all appointments for Francophones since 1964 (*Soir*, 1969, December 4; "Brussel," 1970, 122-23). In the face of such noncompliance, attention shifted to alternative forms of institutionalization that might help to circumvent resistance at the level of individual communes.

Machinery to achieve this was embodied in two new constitutional provisions, Articles 108 *bis* and 108 *ter*, which had the more general purpose of providing a basis for metropolitan or regional government above the level of communes. Article 108 *bis* provided a framework of institutions and powers for *agglomérations* of urban communes and for *fédérations* of nonurban communes, to be created as Parliament saw fit. Article 108 *ter* provided additional special linguistic and cultural safeguards for the Brussels agglomeration within the new general framework. In the case of the Brussels area, with its nineteen separate municipal administrations, nineteen police departments, and nineteen independent mayors and communal councils, and cooperating only on a voluntary basis, the need for some form of closer coordination and planning was particularly acute. Metropolitan government had long been blocked for two reasons. First, it had been imposed briefly under the German occupation during the Second World War and promptly suppressed in 1944, which gave the idea strongly negative associations. Second, the nineteen communal councils were important as political bases for many members of Parliament and even ministers, and as such were jealously guarded from encroachments. In the 1960s ten of the nineteen Brussels area mayors were also members or ex-members of Parliament and a total of twenty-three parliamentarians including several ministers and ex-ministers were members of the nineteen communal councils (Cappuyns, 1967, 5; "Brussel," 1970, 109).

The central feature of the additional cultural safeguards provided for the Brussels agglomeration by the revised constitution and its implement-

---

[1] This document appears to have overlooked one Flemish burgomaster (in Berchem-Sainte-Agathe).

ing legislation of July 1971 was a form of compulsory cultural separation for electoral purposes. Candidates for the new Agglomeration Council were to be identified as to their linguistic community and nominated only by members of that community. The executive or *collège* of the Agglomeration Council was to be elected by the council on a quasi-parity basis of six members from each community plus a president elected at large. Two further provisions gave the representatives of each community an "alarm-bell" procedure similar to Article 38 *bis* at the level of the central Parliament whereby a measure threatening that community could be sent back to the executive for reconsideration, and also established separate Dutch and French cultural commissions for the agglomeration with competence to regulate cultural and educational matters for their respective communities in the capital area (Senelle, 1978, 277-81; Maroy, 1972, 170-73).

As matters turned out, the first results ran counter to expectations. At the first election for the new Agglomeration Council in November 1971, the FDF and some parts of the PLP formed a last-minute common front that presented a joint list of French-speaking and Dutch-speaking candidates, each duly nominated by the requisite number of French-speaking or Dutch-speaking voters respectively as required by law. This list, under the name Rassemblement bruxellois, managed to capture an absolute majority of seats on the Agglomeration Council, including thirty-one out of fifty-three Francophone seats and even eleven out of thirty Netherlandic ones. On this basis they then secured nine out of thirteen seats on the executive of the agglomeration, including the presidency and three of the six Flemish seats. The Flemish press reacted strongly, interpreting the result as yet another manifestation of Brussels's antipathy to the Flemish cause. From an institutional standpoint, such a result precluded any resort to the "alarm-bell" procedure to protect the Flemish minority in the council, since the Flemish members representing the Rassemblement bruxellois were largely under the sway of the latter's Francophone leadership (CRISP, 1972, nos. 553-54; De Witte, 1976, 19). All in all, the Brussels Agglomeration Council proved an acute disappointment to segments of Flemish opinion that had looked to it for a more effective Flemish presence in Brussels politics, and the tendency in Flemish nationalist circles during the 1970s was to scale down its political importance, leaving it mainly as an intercommunal coordinating body for technical matters. When the regular communal elections were held in 1976 and again in 1982 the membership of the Agglomeration Council was not renewed, even though some parties had exhausted their original list of substitute members.

More significant and more successful than the Agglomeration Council itself have been its two offshoots established by the same legislation of July 1971, the Dutch and French Cultural Commissions of the Brussels Agglomeration. Elected by the respective linguistic groups of the Agglomeration Council, and working under the respective national ministries of education and of culture, these two commissions were given a broad mandate to promote the educational and cultural objectives of their respective communities in the Brussels area through policy development, subsidies to cultural organizations, advice to other authorities, and the passing of regulations and decrees within their areas of jurisdiction. On the Flemish side in particular the Nederlandse Commissie voor de Cultuur, or NCC, which has represented four political parties with a slight nationalist majority, has been important as the first representative political body for the Flemish community in Brussels. As such it has served as a catalyst in promoting and coordinating the activities of a wide variety of Flemish voluntary associations previously present in the capital, thereby giving a certain legitimacy and visibility to the Flemish community that had been lacking in the political process at the communal level (CRISP, 1977, nos. 776-77; De Witte, 1976, 51-56).

Because the experiment in power-sharing on the Agglomeration Council ended in disillusion and disappointment, the predominant Flemish reaction during the 1970s was to consolidate and expand the sphere of community autonomy. The 1971 legislation provided for cultural autonomy in the capital with primary reference to education and culture, including sports and leisure activities. In subsequent negotiations, particularly in the Egmont-Stuyvenberg agreements, the tendency was to widen the principle to include health care and welfare programs among the matters "personalized" according to language. These agreements, however, could not be implemented, and the later negotiations leading to the regionalization legislation of 1980 set aside the question of Brussels in order to reach agreement on other aspects of regionalization. Further progress on Brussels issues was then delayed by the severity of the economic crisis, and the basic choice between more effectively bilingual institutions and more radical community autonomy in Brussels has remained under discussion during the early 1980s. The issue poses difficult questions for both sides, especially since some Flemish opinion in the capital considers a radical splitting of cultural or leisure activities such as sports associations or publicly supported libraries to be counterproductive in cases where there already exists an effective Flemish presence in mixed-language organizations or institutions (CRISP, 1978, nos. 791-92; 1979, nos. 843-44).

The same law of July 1971 that established the Brussels Agglomeration Council also created four other agglomerations (for Antwerp, Gent, Charleroi, and Liège) and five federations of nonurban communes around Brussels. The professed aim of these federations was to establish municipal bodies in the wider periphery of Brussels strong enough to deal effectively through coordinating committees with the powerful Brussels agglomeration in matters of joint concern. A further aim was clearly to submerge communes with significant Francophone minorities in the wider, more rural Flemish periphery and especially to hinder the growing efforts of the six communes with facilities to build a coalition with Walloon and Brussels Francophone groups to achieve full bilingual status. In spite of local protests, the six communes were included in the federations as part of a larger parliamentary package deal that resembled in certain respects the bargaining over the linguistic frontier in 1962 (CRISP, 1971, no. 535: 24-30).

These federations, however, were short-lived, becoming superfluous with the countrywide reform of communal boundaries that took effect in 1976. The fusions of communes, completed under a Francophone minister of the interior, in effect rescued the six peripheral communes with minority-language facilities because as early as 1971 legislation had forbidden any fusions between communes having different linguistic regimes. On the other hand, several other communes of the periphery having significant Francophone minorities without legally recognized minority-language facilities were fused with more homogeneous Flemish communes to create larger units radiating outward from Brussels in a pattern designed to resist further Francophone encroachment (CRISP, 1976, no. 735; Michel, 1976). These institutional barriers to Francophone territorial expansion seem likely in the long run to reinforce the tendency for the Brussels area to develop more rapidly towards the south into Walloon communes adjacent to the language frontier.

One crucial institutional factor from a linguistic standpoint is the educational structure in the capital area. Historically, the evolution of language practices in Brussels area schools is quite diversified and difficult to document in detail, but enough evidence exists to suggest that for half a century after the Revolution of 1830 most official teaching in Brussels itself was offered in French to generations of Flemish-speaking students, many of whom understood little or nothing of what was said in the classroom. Some Flemish was taught as a subject in these schools, but it was given little weight in the curriculum and was in some cases taught by instructors whose own mastery of the language was limited. Not until 1878 was Dutch introduced systematically into a few primary classes as language of instruction, largely as a result of efforts by a sympathetic communal councillor, Charles (or Karel) Buls, who had been struck by the poor pedagogical results of an all-French system. Practices in the écoles libres in this period are less well documented, but some classes in the Catholic system appear to have been conducted in Flemish. Still further linguistic variations appear in some of the suburbs: while Ixelles and St. Josse prescribed only French in the classroom, Molenbeek and St. Gilles began the lower grades in Flemish (Boon, 1969).

The establishment of Dutch-language classes in several communes in the 1870s did not lead to a comprehensive Flemish system. Even Buls himself, who went on to serve for almost two decades as the last Flemish burgomaster of Brussels, recognized the greater utility of French for Flemish pupils. What emerged under a variety of forms was a parallel network of bilingual or dual-medium schools that used Dutch as a transitional language in the early grades and prepared Flemish children either for secondary education in French or for employment in a predominantly Francophone milieu with greater success than the single-medium French system. Although this system attracted international attention in educational circles, its precise extent is not well documented. The unilingual French system continued and even predominated, attracting many children from Flemish households. According to official reports, eight communes of the capital area in 1900 had only unilingual French-medium communal schools at elementary level, and as late as 1960 this was still the case for five communes in the enlarged agglomeration. Schools that were not unilingual French were in many cases bilingual. One source for 1929 reports that 64 per cent of elementary schools offered unilingual French classes, 32 per cent were bilingual, and only 4 per cent had unilingual Dutch classes. Only in 1932 did the new language legislation call for a complete Dutch-medium education system, and in practice the records show that some bilingual classes persisted—in spite of the language laws—well into the post-1945 period (Swing, 1980a, 39-45, 79-80; Lindemans, 1963, 90-91, 95-96).

There can be little doubt that the asymmetry of the school system and its strong leaning towards French reflected faithfully the wishes of many Flemish parents, who saw in French-language or bilingual education the only avenue of upward mobility for their children. For several decades the principle of mother-tongue education was contested in the name of freedom of parental choice, of the frequently cited *liberté du père de famille* to select for his children the appropriate educational options, both religious and linguistic. For more than a century after 1830, however, parents in several Brussels-area communes, especially if they were secular-minded and wanted official schools, faced a simple Hobson's choice of French-language schooling or none at all. A complete Dutch-language system of equivalent quality scarcely existed until the 1960s, and its absence long constituted one of the major Flemish grievances with respect to the capital.

The evolution of enrolment in Dutch-language classes becomes easier to trace after 1932 and is shown in Table 58. What stands out first from this table is the peaking of enrolment during the Second World War and apparently also during the First World War, though here the relevant peacetime data seem to be unavailable. One may also note the drop in Dutch-language elementary enrolment following passage of the 1932 law on language use in the schools. In both wars attempts were made by Flemish activists, with some backing from the German occupation authorities, to enforce the principle of mother-tongue education. The percentage of elementary students in Dutch classes more than doubled after a leading Flemish militant, Flor Grammens, was appointed president of the Commission permanente de contrôle linguistique in 1940 and began inquiries which led to the transfer of several thousand children of Flemish origin to Dutch-language classes. After 1945, during the general pursuit of Flemish activism, the enrolment pattern quickly reverted to approximately the prewar level, and Grammens, whose defence was that he had only applied existing prewar Belgian legislation, was sentenced to six years in prison (Aelvoet, 1957, 39; Deleu et al., 1973-75, 1: 610-12; Scheuermann, 1942, 57-59). The experience of both world wars left the principle of mother-tongue education indelibly associated with constraint and foreign occupation. As Wilmars comments, Flemish Brusselers can sense very quickly which way the wind blows and in 1940 they adjusted quickly and pragmatically to the stronger side (1971, 72). It would be a mistake, however, to assume that constraint and pragmatism were nonexistent before 1939 or after 1945.

Table 58

Brussels agglomeration: Numbers and percentages of students in Dutch-language classes, selected years[a]

Year	Nursery schools		Elementary schools	
	N (000s)	%	N (000s)	%
1916-17	5.5	35.6	19.8	28.0
1931-32	n.a.	n.a.	14.3	22.6
1933-34	n.a.	n.a.	13.3	19.2
1938-39	3.3	23.2	13.2	19.3
1942-43	6.8	42.1	22.6	39.7
1946-47	4.0	24.1	14.4	25.9
1951-52	3.7	20.4	11.5	20.2
1957-58	4.7	18.8	14.1	18.0
1960-61	5.7	18.1	13.8	17.1
1965-66	6.1	15.9	15.2	16.3
1970-71	6.1	13.6	15.0	14.4
1975-76	5.4	12.6	11.8	12.3
1977-78	4.9	12.3	10.6	11.4
1979-80	4.4	12.1	9.5	10.7
1981-82	4.7	12.6	8.6	10.1
1983-84	5.6	14.8	8.3	10.2

[a] The number of communes included varies according to changes in agglomeration boundaries.

Sources: 1916-17: De Cneudt, 1918, 128-29; 1931-34: Van Wezemael, 1937, 7; 1938-58: Lindemans, 1963, 87, 93; 1960-78: Swing, 1980a, 138-39; *Feiten en meningen*, 1967, nos. 3-4: 201; 1979-84: data from French and Dutch ministries of national education.

Another period of administrative constraint occurred from 1967, when the executive decrees implementing the 1963 education law were first applied, until 1971, when the principle of language choice was restored. In this period more than 47,000 declarations of home language were examined by ministry inspectors of both language groups, but only a minute percentage of cases were contested by the parents or between the inspectors themselves and carried to appeal tribunals. Even fewer children—in all just fifty-three over a four-year period—were placed in Dutch-language rather than French-language schools as a consequence of the policy. A close study of enrolment patterns for this period on a year-by-year basis suggests that the application and later relaxation of linguistic controls made little if any discernible difference in the general trend of enrolment in Dutch-language classes. In 1971 the principle of *liberté du père de famille* was restored for Brussels residents as a concession to Francophones. This step was part of a package deal that in return conceded to Flemings a systematic construction program of new schools and several major noneducational benefits, including the Brussels Agglomeration Council, the federations of communes around Brussels, and the incorporation of the six communes with facilities into Flanders (Swing, 1980a, 111-15; Ruys, 1973, 192-93; Hasquin, 1975-76, 2: 414-15).

Since 1971 the restoration of freedom of choice has led to intensive advertising campaigns each year as the two educational systems compete for declining numbers of students. The Flemish authorities, the first to advertise widely, have tended to stress the career advantages of bilingualism in the Brussels milieu. In the later 1970s their French counterparts responded vigorously, emphasizing that French is the child's passport to the outside world. For those resident outside Brussels-Capital, even in communes with facilities, mother-tongue education and linguistic inspection of parental declarations have remained obligatory.

The enrolment pattern in Dutch-language classes suggested by Table 58—wartime years excepted—is one of steady decline, but the situation is not quite as dark as bare statistics might at first suggest. Approximately one child out of four in Brussels is non-Belgian, and these children, mainly offspring of foreign workers from Mediterranean countries, go almost exclusively to French-language schools. Further, both school systems currently attract a substantial fraction of their enrolment from families resident in the suburbs just outside Brussels-Capital, which makes these data somewhat imprecise as an indicator of language trends in the nineteen communes. By adjusting for these factors one Flemish source estimated that for Belgian children resident in Brussels the proportion attending Dutch classes was around 21 per cent in 1970, while another suggested a figure of 18 per cent for 1974, or just slightly above the percentage of voters who supported Flemish electoral lists (Garré, 1970, 131; De Witte, 1976, 50). From this perspective the Flemish presence in Brussels is far from the point of disappearance, and the implementation of cultural autonomy since 1970 has brought significant qualitative improvements in Dutch-language education in the capital. Indeed while significant numbers of

Flemish families in Brussels continued to send their children to Francophone schools, the late 1970s brought the first modest enrolments of Francophone children in the agglomeration's Dutch-language schools, which were beginning to attract attention for the high quality of their teaching of both official languages. By 1984 one source estimated the number of *vrais francophones* in these schools at almost 1,000 out of a total enrolment of about 13,000 (Herremans, 1980, 347-48; *Soir*, 1984, April 25). The enrolment data from 1980 to 1984 suggest a relative stabilization in Dutch-language enrolment at the elementary level and a modest recovery in kindergarten classes to the levels of the later 1960s. However, a more detailed study by Deprez and colleagues (1982b) reveals a significant degree of cross-linguistic enrolment in both directions, a tendency that clearly runs against the original intent of the language laws.

Two further problems of institutional reform for the capital area concern electoral boundaries and regional economic planning. The electoral *arrondissement* of Brussels still coincides with the pre-1963 administrative *arrondissement*, which is now divided into the two administrative *arrondissements* of Brussels-Capital and Halle-Vilvoorde. Flemish nationalist opinion has long sought separate electoral *arrondissements* as well in order to limit the political influence of Brussels and discourage Francophone expansion beyond the agglomeration boundaries. Local Francophone opinion has just as firmly opposed any such split. In 1978 the Egmont-Stuyvenberg agreement proposed a compromise solution: the electoral split would be effected, but Francophones in the six communes with facilities and in specified districts of certain other peripheral communes would have the right to opt for a fictitious domicile in one of the Brussels-Capital communes and would then enjoy voting rights as well as administrative and judicial services in the commune of their choice (*Pacte communautaire*, 1978, 55-59). The Egmont package as a whole, however, proved unacceptable to the Flemish electorate, which made its displeasure amply clear at the 1978 general election. Since agreement on the re-gionalization of 1980 was achieved only by postponing all discussion of the Brussels question at that stage, the question of electoral boundaries for Brussels remains on the agenda of unsolved problems.

The move to regionalization has also left its mark on economic institutions, which have been restructured to reflect increased interest in economic decentralization and regional development. By legislation of 1970, regional economic planning functions for Wallonie and Flanders were officially vested in two regional economic councils, which superseded advisory councils organized earlier by the private sector. The same law created several regional development societies—including five for the four provinces of Flanders and Flemish Brabant and one for Wallonie as a whole—to handle the more technical aspects of regional development. The new act treated the Brussels area inconsistently. A seventh regional development society was established for Brussels-Capital, but the corresponding policy body, the regional economic council, was created for the whole province of Brabant, with consequent overlaps in jurisdiction with the other two regional economic councils.

The effect was to leave the capital area endowed with somewhat ill-matching institutions for planning and coordinating economic development. The mandate of the new regional economic council extended to the whole of Brabant, but only concurrently with the councils for Wallonie and Flanders, and that of the regional development council covered only the nineteen communes of Brussels-Capital, whereas the private-sector predecessor of these two bodies, the Conseil économique de la région bruxelloise, had been concerned with the whole of the pre-1963 Brussels *arrondissement*. Those concerned with the economic development of the Brussels urban area tried to win recognition for it as a regional economic and geographic entity comprising both Brussels-Capital and its immediate Flemish hinterland, in spite of the difference in language regimes. Their efforts to this end, however, were unsuccessful (CRISP, 1972, no. 584; 1973, no. 587; nos. 616-17: 31-36), and the economic vulnerability of the capital area has been heightened by its further failure to obtain institutions as a political region matching those granted to Flanders and Wallonie in the regionalization legislation of 1980.

This institutional weakness has gone hand in hand with regional development priorities that have given very little to the economically advantaged Brussels area. In matters of economic planning and development, Flanders and Wallonie have found much common ground as parts of a disadvantaged periphery seeking to reduce the relative advantages of a privileged centre. Some voices, particularly in Flanders, have called for more radical measures, including decentralization of the tertiary sector and the parceling out of some central government services to other cities on the model of the Netherlands. The arithmetic of the Belgian party system makes it easy for Flemish Christian Social members and Walloon Socialists to combine against a strongly bourgeois, mainly Francophone Brussels. The consequence of this concerted move against the centre has been slower economic growth for both Brussels-Capital and the Brussels periphery. The problem is most acute for some communes of the inner urban core, where the additional social costs of a large immigrant population and the loss of well-to-do residents to the suburbs during the 1970s have brought chronic fiscal crisis, a problem that Flemish parliamentarians at the national level have been little disposed to alleviate as long as the councils of these same communes maintain their opposition to Flemish aspirations for cultural parity in the capital (Heisler, 1977, 44).

A final aspect of the "Brussels question" stems from the special role of Brussels as the capital of a plurilingual country. The problem is by no means unique to Belgium. We have noted earlier the difficulties that

Switzerland has faced in attracting sufficient Francophone public servants to Bern (see Volume 1, 139-42), and the same question surfaces again in Ottawa, where Francophone Canadians encountered a virtual absence of French-language administrative services and an inadequate educational system until the 1970s (McRae, 1969). In any plural society there are potential problems in reconciling the outlook of the local population of the capital with the linguistic and cultural imperatives of the country as a whole. In the case of Belgium, however, the difficulties are compounded by special structural and attitudinal factors, by the importance of the capital to both sides, and by the need since 1970 to develop new institutions for the capital within an emerging framework of regionalization.[1]

The issue of linguistic and cultural parity for Flemings and Francophones in Brussels is therefore a concern not only for the Dutch-speaking minority in the capital itself but for the entire Flemish population of Belgium (Gerlo, 1968a). In a special sense it symbolizes the final phase of the Flemish Movement and the emancipation of the Flemish people from a tutelage that dates back to 1830 and even earlier. Further, Flemish political circles see parity in Brussels as one side of a carefully balanced package deal, which they claim in exchange for the parity conceded to the Francophone community at the national level in spite of its numerical inferiority. Francophones, who obtained guarantees of parity at national level in the Cabinet and in other respects through the 1970 constitutional revisions, argue that the two cases are dissimilar and that any form of political parity in Brussels would be "undemocratic" given the large disproportion between linguistic groups in the capital.

Understandably, the two sides have long been far apart on the issue of an acceptable institutional status for Brussels within the reformed Belgian state structure. The early stages of the debate on decentralization and federalism were bedeviled by rivalries between proponents of two regions and those who advocated three, with the Brussels area as an autonomous third region. Flemish opinion, keenly sensitive to anti-Flemish attitudes in Brussels, has always opposed placing Brussels on an equal footing with Flanders and Wallonie, leaning instead towards some form of condominium or *rijksgebied* that would make the capital area a joint dependency of the two language communities. Most Francophone spokesmen have favored a three-region model with substantial autonomy for Brussels, if only because they oppose Flemish parity in Brussels and feel threatened by it.

There are, however, visible nuances and divisions in Francophone opinion. Francophone Christian Social politicians, speaking from a minor-

---

[1] After the 1980 reforms the question of a capital also arose for the new regional and community councils. While the Walloon Regional Council promptly designated Namur as capital of Wallonie, both the French Community Council and the Vlaamse Raad opted for Brussels.

ity position, tend to stress the common interests of the Francophone community as a whole, while Walloon Socialists and the FDF in Brussels have a sharper sense of loyalty to their respective regions. Many Walloons are just as wary as Flemish federalists about the dangers of centralization, while many Brusselers would prefer to see Brussels's historical role as a centre continue undisturbed. Thus one Francophone defender of Brussels could write, with perhaps unconscious irony, that "Brussels has no imperialist desire . . . [it] wishes simply to live in an integrated and normally outstretched metropolitan area" (Desmarets, 1967, 18). A typical Flemish view is that Brussels must be structured "not as an arrogant third region, but as an open city, where both ethnic communities can live freely and meet each other as equals" (De Witte, 1976, 72).

As in other contentious areas of Belgian politics, the preliminary resolution of the problem took the form of a compromise. The 1970 constitutional revisions formally recognized *both* the bipartite *and* the tripartite models, that is, the two main cultural communities (Articles 3 *ter*, 59 *bis*) and the three regions (Article 107 *quater*). But these articles enunciated broad principles only and merely established a framework for a more intensive debate, extending over most of the next decade, on how to implement them. In this process the bipartite model enjoyed certain strategic advantages in that the cultural councils were established almost at once by a law of July 1971 and have functioned continuously since that date, being reorganized as community councils in 1980. By contrast, regionalization on a tripartite basis has come slowly, hesitantly, and with a number of false starts and setbacks extending over almost a decade, a delay that might be attributed both to divisions of opinion within the Francophone community and to its overall numerical inferiority. The 1980 legislation establishing political and administrative structures for Flanders and Wallonie was made possible only by an agreement early in the negotiations to postpone consideration of the Brussels region, on which positions appeared irreconcilable.

One factor that has made resolution of the Brussels question unusually difficult is that under a regime of cultural autonomy the Belgian language communities live increasingly in separate worlds served by separate communication networks. In such a setting it becomes easier for each side to build up sharply opposing perceptions of the linguistic situation. Among Francophones the myth of the inevitable and irreversible *francisation* of Brussels remained strong even in the 1970s and delayed recognition by Francophones of the emerging Dutch-language cultural networks built by a dedicated Flemish elite. On the Flemish side, some nationalist opinion went beyond claims of cultural parity to dream unrealistically about a Flemish "reconquest" of Brussels. Extremism on both sides contributed to hardened attitudes, to political stalemate, and to the exclusion of Brussels from the regionalization legislation of 1980. But even a failure to act or a postponement may appear in retrospect as a form of decision. The force of this observation will be increasingly apparent to the extent that regional institutions take hold in Flanders and Wallonie, for Brussels entered the 1980s without a corresponding framework and therefore remains dependent on the central government in matters within regional jurisdiction. As long as this regional framework is lacking, its absence emphasizes the political obstacles to realization of the tripartite model.

Chapter 6

The Ambiguity of the Belgian Case

The theoretical problem posed by the Swiss case in Volume 1 was relatively straightforward. The central issue was to explain the signal success of Switzerland in combining linguistic and cultural pluralism with political stability and low levels of social conflict. The one major anomaly in this picture was the departure from prevailing Swiss norms represented by the Jura conflict. In spite of the relative simplicity of this question, the answers offered in recent social science literature and the factors described in Volume 1 suggest a wide range of possible explanations based on Swiss historical traditions, on social structures, on attitudinal patterns, and on political institutions.

In the Belgian case, the theoretical issue is more complex, because the problem is in fact a double one. First, there is the question of why linguistic conflict has been so intense, so persistent, so fundamentally intractable over more than a century. A second question then arises of why this prolonged and severe conflict has not propelled the Belgian political system into mass violence, civil war, or political separation. When set off against the Swiss case, Belgian interethnic relations appear highly troubled. If, however, we shift the frame of reference to Cyprus, Lebanon, or Northern Ireland, the Belgian political system reveals unexpected capacities for the containment of conflict within well-defined and manageable limits. Any adequate theoretical summary of the Belgian case must account satisfactorily for both of these dimensions, for the presence of conflict as well as for its limits.

Not surprisingly, many of the existing studies of Belgium, especially those undertaken by foreign observers, have focused on the conflictual aspects. Thus Dunn's comparative study of Switzerland and Belgium is framed around a polar contrast between Swiss "linguistic harmony" and Belgian "linguistic and cultural differences," though he does note the historical paradox that in the mid-nineteenth century Switzerland had been "split by strife" while Belgium was "calm and prosperous" (1970, 7-9). On the other side, some Belgian authors and informants tend to dismiss or minimize the language issue as an artificial issue, created—or at least perpetuated—by political elites for political ends. Relatively few studies have emphasized both the conflictual elements and the conflict moderating influences operating simultaneously. Among those that do, Val Lorwin's work is noteworthy for balancing a set of reasons for the "intractable" nature of the linguistic-regional conflict against a corresponding list of "factors for unity" (1966, 174-78; 1974, 197-201). The combination of acute linguistic conflict and avoidance of overt violence has also been noted by Aristide Zolberg, who observes that "there is, beneath the acrimonious tone of Belgian crisis politics, a degree of collusion among the antagonists that serves to keep them in check" (1977, 106).

The existing studies of Belgium, however, do not focus neatly on the themes of conflict and conflict regulation. The phenomena or processes being investigated vary considerably from one study to another. Thus Francophone authors have tended to produce pessimistic, conflict-oriented studies with such titles as *Le divorce belge* (Outers, 1968), *La guerre des belges* (du Roy, 1968), or even the more extreme *La Belgique est-elle morte?* (Dayez, 1969). Partisans of the Flemish cause, on the other hand, have tended to place the conflict in more positive contexts of social change, political development, mass mobilization, increasing democratic participation, and group emancipation (De Raet, 1939; Van Haegendoren, 1962; Gerlo, 1966; Elias, 1969; Lamberty, 1971-73; Ruys, 1973). Other authors show similar variations. A number of English-speaking scholars, as Luc Huyse has noted in a review article (1975b), have been attracted to themes of social segmentation and political accommodation. James Dunn (1970) focuses his comparative study of language conflict in Belgium and Switzerland around party systems. Aristide Zolberg sees the linguistic conflict arising from cultural reactions to broad developmental changes and increased social mobility in Flanders in the nineteenth century (1974; 1976).

In spite of the variety of objectives in these studies of Belgium, explanations offered for linguistic conflict or alternatively for its regulation or moderation can be found under each of the four main categories that we have examined in earlier chapters, as in the Swiss case previously examined. That is, conflict levels have been linked by different scholars (1) to Belgian historical traditions, (2) to the social structures, (3) to attitudinal factors, and (4) to formal political institutions. A few examples will illustrate this range of explanations.

For historians of the Pirenne school, Belgium is a natural political unit founded on a much older political culture combining French and Germanic influences, a culture in which linguistic pluralism is incidental and secondary. For Pieter Geyl, on the other hand, the separation of the common Netherlandic stock between the northern and southern provinces was an historical accident arising from the fortunes of war. For Shepard

Clough, trained in Carleton Hayes's seminar on nationalism in the 1920s, the Flemish Movement was a typical nationalist movement having "much in common" with others of its kind and time (1930, v, 1-2).

Explanations in terms of social structure are abundant, but different observers, as Dunn notes, have reached "radically different conclusions as to whether or not the cleavages are cross-cutting" (1970, 14). Lipset and Rokkan see a "gradual deepening of cleavages" leading towards "a polarization between French-speaking, secular and industrial Wallonia and Nederlands-speaking, Catholic and agricultural Flanders" (quoted in Dunn, 1970, 14). Val Lorwin, on the other hand, lists this cleavage structure among the "factors of unity." "Each great factor of division—religion, class, party—is also a factor of national cohesion across regional and language boundaries" (1966, 178). "This discrepancy," as Dunn rightly observes, "calls for a much closer investigation of the Belgian cleavage structure" (1970, 15). But if disinterested foreign scholars can reach such divergent views of cleavage factors, it is scarcely surprising that Flemish and Francophone Belgians differ even more radically in their perceptions of other structural factors, including most obviously the distribution of economic resources (Quévit, 1978; Van Haegendoren, 1978).

Explanations of conflict in terms of attitudinal and value differences between language groups are similarly plentiful. Some writers have suggested that divergence in core values is comprehensive and even total. On the Flemish side, Lode Claes has emphasized the "different reactions of the two parts of Belgium to all the great political issues and crises" of the postwar period (1963-64, 43). On the Walloon side, Jean Beaufays sees the difficulty in resolving Flemish-Francophone conflict as stemming from a "totally divergent conception of law" (1977, 22). Even more damaging to intergroup relations is the persistence of attitudes of superiority among Francophones. Val Lorwin, in a telling phrase, lists the survival of "reflexes of underdogs" among Flemings and of "overdogs" among Walloons— attitudes that have outlasted the conditions that created them—as one of the reasons for intractability of the conflict (1966, 175). On the other hand, some attitudes help to moderate conflict. One of the key components of the Belgian political culture, Zolberg contends, is the habit of not pushing matters to extremes, of "splitting the difference" (1977, 103-106).

One recent and more nuanced explanation of conflict levels in terms of attitudes argues that Belgium's "mixed record" in managing political conflicts is a function of a distinctive pattern of ideological space among the political elite. A three-country empirical study showed that the ideological space of parliamentarians in Italy was strongly unidimensional, but in Switzerland and Belgium it was pluridimensional. In Belgium, however, the linguistic-regional cleavage clearly surpassed the others in salience, whereas in Switzerland the three most salient cleavages were closely comparable with one another (Dierickx and Frognier, 1980).

Finally, many sources have attributed the level of conflict to the pattern of formal political institutions. Lorwin, writing before the constitutional reforms of 1970, lists the absence of effective organization of the linguistic communities and regions as one of the factors of "intractability" (1966, 174). Similarly, Derek Urwin refers to "communalism" in Belgian politics in the 1960s as a "non-institutionalized cleavage" and attributes the system's continuing inability to accommodate the language issue in part to the latter's "non-institutionalization in the party system" (1970, 330, 340). Earlier, Lode Claes pointed to the paradox of abandonment of "the internal logic of the unitary structure" through various devices to maintain intergroup equilibrium without a corresponding acceptance of "the logic of federalism" to replace it (1963-64, 47). Concerning institutional causes, however, there is no need to multiply specific authorities, because the entire public debate on institutional reform since the mid-1960s has been premised on the assumption that the language conflict could be resolved or reduced through institutional changes. The major disagreements in that debate have centred not on whether change is needed but on different institutional options to accommodate conflicting group objectives.

The examples given above are illustrative rather than exhaustive, but it appears unproductive to attempt a full survey. The existing literature on the Belgian language question is quite diversified in focus and its contribution to conflict analysis is often incidental or superficial. As an alternative, it seems more useful to review and assess the more important sources of conflict and of conflict moderation or regulation encountered in previous chapters. Once again, as in the Swiss study, the factors relevant to the Belgian case can be grouped loosely around the themes of the first four chapters, that is, around historical traditions, socioeconomic structures, attitudinal questions, and formal political institutions respectively. These four categories, however, are not closed compartments, and it is important to be sensitive to interrelationships and interactions between factors in different categories.

As was the case in Volume 1, the primary objective of this preliminary assessment of the Belgian case is a faithful description and comprehensive understanding of linguistic conflict in one particular setting, not an analysis of its wider comparative or theoretical implications. Later on, when the four case studies are complete, many of these factors will be taken up again in a comparative context, together with others that may be relatively insignificant or neutral in a strictly Belgian context, for both theoretical and policy purposes. These wider questions, however, belong to the final phase of the inquiry. Our method in this first phase is frankly intuitive, founded upon a feel for the total Belgian situation together with some awareness of language conflicts elsewhere and of the general literature. The problem is to identify what has been important in the Belgian context, and to understand why it has been important in that setting.

On the historical side, the pattern of Belgian and pre-Belgian history points to a number of factors that served to generate or intensify conflict. The long heritage of cultural isolation and stagnation under foreign rule seems crucial as a source of Flemish underdevelopment. Its importance is heightened by the double demonstration effect of prosperity in the Dutch Republic during the same period and also in the Flemish provinces themselves in earlier periods. Policies of forced *francisation*, whether by administrative decision or by social pressure from elites, led to resentment and ultimately to reactions from the target groups. The French revolutionary heritage in Belgium also reinforced linguistic conflict by driving the language communities further apart, whereas in Switzerland it assisted the linguistic minorities but also found both sympathizers and opponents in each language group.

More insidious sources of conflict seem to lie in the reactive impact of successive changes in language policy, which produced an escalating dialectic of linguistic hostility. Thus policies of *francisation* under French occupation after 1794 led to countervailing efforts after 1815 to promote Dutch. This in turn led to policies favoring French again after 1830, which in turn engendered the Flemish Movement. Its successes before and after 1900 in turn aroused Wallonie. Flemish collaboration with the German occupation in both world wars was in each case a response to previous repression and frustration, but it evoked even more severe repression in 1919 and 1945. Finally, perhaps because of the openness of Belgium to external influences, there appears to be some international linkage between domestic language conflict and wider Franco-German tensions, at least in certain periods.

On the other side, certain elements in this historical tradition have served to moderate either linguistic conflict specifically or domestic conflict in general. Prolonged foreign domination fostered a cautious political culture that favored negotiation and acquiescence over intransigence or force. Religious unity in the face of the Protestant northern provinces bridged the linguistic cleavage and aided nation-building efforts after 1830. The long-term stability of the linguistic frontier made it a source of relatively little friction, even after linguistic conflict became significant in other ways. The cross-cutting of the language frontier and various early political boundaries created strong traditions of cultural coexistence in Brabant, Flanders, and Limburg. Finally, early traditions of communal autonomy and pluralism left a heritage of vigorous local government that mitigated the impact of excessive centralization and *francisation* after 1830.

A second category of factors comprises those relating to socioeconomic structures. Here we encounter some difficulty, in that some structural elements that would appear at first glance to favor stability and moderation have in fact worked in the opposite direction in the Belgian setting. A prime example is the near equality in numbers of the two main language communities, which comes even closer to a balance of power if economic resources and social status are also considered. Yet at the attitudinal level this near equality translates into a double minority complex fed by reciprocal fears and resentments. The two communities have also had relatively the same proportions over time, but this stability has been overshadowed by its asymmetrical components, so that Francophones fear higher Flemish birth rates and growing regional imbalance while Flemings in turn resent language transfers to French. In short, these structural features are viewed through an attitudinal prism clouded by pre-existing hostility.

Our earlier analysis showed that the intersection of the two cleavages of language and religious observance was neither completely overlapping nor completely cross-cutting, but rather somewhere in between. In Belgian experience this angle of intersection has proved highly conflictual, perhaps because political rhetoric and popular stereotypes are prone to exaggerate the degree of overlapping. Further, while per capita income and per capita production in Flanders and Wallonie were roughly equal in the early 1970s, they were converging from opposite directions. Once again attitudes ignored this relative equality to focus on relative disadvantage, the Flemings stressing past economic deprivation and the need for compensation, the Walloons demanding special measures to rejuvenate aging economic structures and halt the relative decline.

Finally, the very presence of Brussels as a large, predominantly Francophone capital in Flemish territory and its relentless urban expansion into the countryside have been major sources of intergroup tension and linguistic conflict. One can imagine a vastly different evolution of the entire *question communautaire* if the capital had been either located south of the linguistic frontier or developed in less centralized fashion. This means that much of the attitudinal intensity of the Flanders-Brussels confrontation can be attributed to an accident of geography and to policy decisions that preceded the earliest manifestations of the language question.

On the whole, then, structural factors give rise to several major sources of conflict, not so much from their overall effects—which in many respects point towards rough balance and stability—as from selective or biased perceptions of their asymmetrical components. The general problem seems to lie less in the structural elements themselves than in the way that they are presented to and perceived by language groups already imbued with hostile attitudes and mobilized along community lines.

On the other side, one can observe other structural factors that operate to moderate the level of conflict. Flemish-Walloon antipathies are to some extent softened by their common interest in resisting the predominance of Brussels. Increasing socioeconomic development in Flanders has diminished economic and occupational inequality between language communities, and political inequality was reduced to insignificant dimensions by earlier reforms of the electoral system and of parliamentary representation. Social inequality between the language groups, more difficult to confront by direct policy measures, is gradually shrinking as a result of the spread of cultivated standard Dutch. Strictly speaking, we should not assume that the reduction of these inequalities directly reduces present levels of conflict; more accurately, it removes conditions that earlier helped to generate and maintain conflict. Finally, the lower profile of the Francophone minority in Flanders since the 1960s may be considered a rather rare but reasonably successful example of conflict regulation.

The third category of factors relates to perceptions and attitudes, and also to how these are organized at the level of associations and political parties. As already noted, hostile attitudes between language groups were generated in the course of Belgian history, and they have been reinforced by interaction with certain structural factors. Further sources of conflict may be found in the images of the groups themselves, which not only diverge considerably but reveal other-group stereotypes considerably more negative than autostereotypes. Further, perceptions of Francophone superiority feelings show up prominently in these stereotypes. Intergroup sympathy ratings appear to be substantially lower in Belgium than in Switzerland, which argues for lower levels of affective integration in Belgian society. There is also evidence of differences between Francophones and Flemings in orientations to other nations and to external reference groups, which are not necessarily conflictual in themselves but afford a foundation for intergroup disagreements on policy questions.

Since 1945, Flemings and Walloons have been sharply polarized over a series of major political issues. They stand further apart on a left-right scale than do the Swiss language groups, and in major confrontations there is some tendency for the linguistic division to be reinforced with class or religious arguments. The Flemish Movement attacked the French-speaking minority in Flanders more as an unduly privileged social class than as a language group, and the attack was largely successful in its language objectives.

Despite all the evidence of hostile attitudes, however, the picture must be qualified by several factors favoring conflict moderation. There are on both sides perceptions of pragmatism and willingness to compromise. There is substantial consensus on the basic rules of the political game and on general goals and priorities of Belgian society. More important, the linguistic crisis has been displaced since 1980 by economic concerns, just as it in turn had followed episodes of intense religious conflict (the "Schools War") and class conflict (the General Strike of 1960-61).[1] The

---

[1] One may add certain nuances to this pattern. As the events of 1985 have shown, certain residues of earlier conflicts tend to persist or resurface, providing subtle linkages between issues dominant currently and those dominant in the recent past (see Appendix B below).

Belgian pattern of conflict adjustment is therefore sequential rather than balanced, and many observers see the high salience of linguistic conflict as temporary, cyclical, and likely to subside as other issues become more active.

Linguistic conflict is also moderated by the patterns of mobilization of attitudes and beliefs into organizations and political parties. This mobilization is extensive, but in general the lines of segmentation both for parties and for other organizations have been largely religious and ideological rather than linguistic. Since no one political party can expect to win a parliamentary majority, the rule is that coalition governments are shaped through negotiation and compromise. Until the late 1960s, the three traditional political parties dominated the political scene, but this supremacy was undermined by the rise of three regional parties and subsequently by heightened linguistic strains and splits within the traditional parties. The resulting multiparty system has clearly increased the difficulties of working the parliamentary system, but the level of conflict is not perceptibly higher than before. Indeed the acceptance of regional parties as possible coalition partners after 1974 tended to legitimize these parties as full partners in the system and thus to regularize and regulate the linguistic conflict rather than to increase it.

A more ambiguous factor in attitude mobilization is the Belgian practice of deciding all major issues in one central parliamentary arena. This has decided disadvantages in that it increases the complexity of the political game, and also keeps minor issues alive and even favors their escalation, if only to preserve them as useful bargaining counters and devices for maintaining group solidarity. On the other hand, the continuing presence of all participants in this single arena tends to moderate the extremes of linguistic conflict through political socialization and parliamentary decorum. Since 1970 constitutional reform and regionalization have modified this system, surrendering part of this centralization in return for greater autonomy for language communities and regions. It is too early to assess whether this tradeoff will raise or lower the general level of conflict, but one can still argue that the 1980 reforms left all the really important or sensitive issues *between* language communities to be settled in the central parliamentary arena as before.

The fourth category concerns the role of formal institutions. Since their general purpose is to reduce or regulate conflict, it is logical to consider institutional factors conducive to conflict moderation before those tending to heighten conflict. Whether intergroup hostility can be more effectively reduced by one form of institutionalization or another is often a difficult matter of political judgment, but the *general* effects of institutionalization as contrasted with noninstitutionalization are more clear. In the Belgian setting the case can be made repeatedly that the regulation of linguistic relationships by law or by other formal institutional arrangements tends to regularize, control, channel, and even moderate the intensity of intergroup conflict. This means that while hostility or resentment may continue at a high level, its *expression* takes more regular, more stylized, and ultimately less violent forms. In such a setting even nonparliamentary and extra-legal forms of protest are regularized and exercised according to well understood and widely accepted norms of the political culture. Using a distinction developed in the General Introduction between conflict and violence (see Volume 1, 23-25), one can say that levels of hostility in Belgium are quite high but levels of overt violence remain within generally acceptable limits.

The institutional devices that work towards moderation are many, but virtually all of those encountered in the preceding pages may be classified under four headings: (1) those promoting *fair representation* of the language communities; (2) those promoting *cultural autonomy* for these communities; (3) those designed to secure *compliance* from unwilling individuals or groups; and (4) those designed to maintain or improve *intergroup linkages* across language lines.

The first of these categories is the one most frequently encountered in earlier chapters. The long and often bitter struggle for equal or proportional Flemish participation in Belgian political life extends to virtually every component of the political system. Among the more prominent examples of this quest for fair representation one can list the successive extensions of the franchise; proportionate parliamentary representation for Flanders and Wallonie; linguistic parity on parliamentary committees; linguistic parity in the Cabinet; fair representation in the public service and in public corporations; proportionate funding in higher education and in scientific research; equality in educational resources, especially in Brussels; and equal funding for broadcasting systems. In a few areas the representational question required special remedial measures, as in the Ministry of External Affairs, or it met unexpected delays, as in the senior ranks of the armed forces and in the supreme court, but by the end of the 1970s this aspect of institutionalization was more or less complete and important sources of Flemish discontent had been removed. While most of these developments have been designed to satisfy Flemish claims, one might also include in this category devices to protect Francophones from Flemish numerical predominance, such as the "alarm-bell" procedure in Parliament.

The second category, devices to promote *cultural autonomy*, is rather later in its origins and is still incomplete in the early 1980s. Prominent among these developments have been the tracing of an exact linguistic frontier and the principle of unilingual regions; the formation of homogeneous army units after 1938; the gradual splitting of culturally sensitive departments and portfolios in the 1960s; the separation of the broadcasting systems; and the division of the two major bilingual universities. The principle was greatly expanded by the constitutional changes of 1970, being extended to cultural organizations, leisure and sports associations, and eventually to health care and welfare functions. One can view the regionalization legislation of 1980 as a further extension of the autonomy principle, the full significance of which remains to be seen. The tendency for these measures to reduce levels of conflict appears to be both in their reduction of cross-linguistic contacts and in their enlargement of each group's control of its own environment.

The third category of devices, those aiming at *compliance*, consists in various control agencies and mechanisms established specifically to oversee institutional arrangements that have evoked substantial, intense, and organized opposition within the system. In one sense the foremost of these mechanisms is the corpus of the linguistic laws themselves, with all its meticulous detail. Beyond this legislative base, however, there are special and differing avenues of enforcement for each of the four main areas covered by the linguistic legislation. The administrative sector is governed by the Commission permanente de contrôle linguistique, as well as by specific agencies for the Brussels, Voer, and Comines-Mouscron areas. For the judiciary there are nullity procedures for linguistically defective acts. For the armed forces there are annual ministerial reports to Parliament and a separate control commission. In education the two separate departments have monopoly control in their respective unilingual regions, which creates problems and vexations for legally protected minorities but also facilitates compliance with regional norms. For Parliament itself, and for the new community and regional councils, there is the Conseil d'Etat and the new Cour d'arbitrage, established under the 1980 legislation on regionalization to handle jurisdictional conflicts. In general the control function is not an agreeable one, and it would be difficult to show that conflicts are resolved or even reduced by these devices. They are, however, regularized and channelled in legally specified ways, with opportunities for exchange of views, mediation, and compromise, with the result that the potential for extreme frustration and violence is thereby lessened.

Finally, there are institutional devices to maintain *intergroup linkages* between the language communities. These linkages have become fewer and more tenuous in contemporary Belgium, because emphasis during the 1960s and 1970s was very much on building community autonomy. The only significant innovation in this area is provision in the regionalization legislation of 1980 for an intergovernmental coordination committee to prevent or regulate conflicts among the new councils or between any of them and the national government. There are, however, some older linkages, and these may well take on new significance as community autonomy increases. The foremost of these is undoubtedly the Cabinet itself, backed by other agencies of the central government. Parliament is another body of this kind, and its linkage role was vastly improved in the 1930s through technological innovation in the form of simultaneous translation facilities. In the informational field, the bridging role played by the national press agency, Agence Belga, should not be forgotten. Some Belgian observers worry that these remaining linkages may prove too weak or insufficient, particularly from the standpoint of communication and value formation. There is the further point that the eventual role of Brussels, historically a strong factor for linkage as well as a source of linguistic contention, was left unsettled in 1980. The capital seems likely to become less important as a linkage factor in future to the extent that community segmentation in the urban area increases.

Up to this point we have considered formal institutions as devices for moderating conflict, but one may also ask whether institutionalization can sharpen conflict or even generate it. The answer for Belgium appears to be that conflict is most closely associated with an absence of appropriate institutions or alternatively with their breakdown or failure. In broad perspective, the primary elements of the Belgian language conflict were generated prior to the establishment of institutions offering appropriate channels for language-group aspirations. Beyond this, however, we have also noted certain areas of institutional failure, and we may then ask whether this failure is due to faulty institutionalization or to the basic intractability of the conflict. In the Voer issue (see above, 285-93), the primary cause appears to be faulty political judgment on the part of the political elite, and better alternatives might have been found. In the establishment of the Brussels Agglomeration Council, pre-existing levels of attitudinal intolerance might well have precluded any other power-sharing alternatives at the time. These are, of course, value judgments, and in other cases the answer may be less clear. Nevertheless the broad lesson from Belgian experience appears to be that formal institutionalization of relations between language groups does not by itself heighten language conflict and does in fact tend to moderate it, though it may fail to produce significant improvements in mass attitudes at points where conflict is especially acute.

With the completion of this survey of the language situation in Belgium, the inquiry as a whole has reached the halfway point. The cases of Switzerland and Belgium have been examined; those of Finland and Canada still lie ahead. It seems appropriate to conclude this phase with a few comparative observations that emerge from the first two studies, with a glance forward towards the two to follow; for if Switzerland and Belgium appear at first sight to be noteworthy primarily for their differences from one another, they also show some basic similarities that should not go unnoticed. Further, some of these similarities serve to differentiate these two cases significantly from the language situations of Finland, or Canada, or both these countries. Only a few central features of these four systems will be mentioned at this stage; more systematic comparisons must wait until the four case studies have been completed.

To begin with factors that have shaped the historical environment, the terrain comprising modern Belgium has been open to outside influences, not easily defensible, an area of contact and of easy communication, whereas Switzerland has been a mountain fortress, easily defended, though also positioned astride major trading routes and a point of frequent cultural contact. Both countries have dense populations in limited space, in contrast with the abundant terrain and relatively sparse populations of Finland and Canada. Both Belgium and Switzerland have strong early antecedents for cultural pluralism in what Hans Daalder has labeled the "ancient pluralism" of vigorous mercantile cities and local loyalties (McRae, 1974, 113-14), but Belgium diverged sharply from this path after 1830. The attempt in Belgium to build a centralized state on the model of France has run into fundamental challenges in the twentieth century. Both Belgium and Switzerland have early traditions of linguistic coexistence but rather late achievement of linguistic equality. However, this equality was realized under vastly different circumstances, and Switzerland was the only country of the four that never developed any significant mass movement of subcultural ethnic nationalism.

A comparison of structural factors shows both similarities and differences. Both Belgium and Switzerland show relative stability over more than a century in the proportions of their larger language groups, a stability that contrasts visibly with changing linguistic ratios in Finland. In both countries the components of language stability are asymmetrical, balancing demographic advantage on one side against net internal migration gains and language transfers on the other. Both countries had relatively high linguistic homogeneity over much of their territory before language became a salient political issue. The relative numbers of the two largest language groups, however, are far closer to equality or balance in Belgium than they are in Switzerland or Finland or Canada. On the other hand, the major languages in Switzerland are closer to equality of international status than are those of Belgium, so that equality of *languages* and of language communities at the international level at least partially compensates for more extreme numerical disparity of language groups at the domestic level.

Other significant but subtle differences concern the structure of social cleavages. In Switzerland the Protestant-Catholic religious cleavage cross-cuts the language cleavage almost exactly. In Belgium this particular cleavage is missing, but that between practising and nonpractising Catholics partially reinforces the language division. In Switzerland the language cleavage is never linked to a cleavage of social class. In Belgium this linkage is made frequently, though the objective evidence is complex enough to give rise to varying interpretations.

The most dramatic differences between Belgium and Switzerland surface in the area of attitudes. The very high salience in Belgium of the language question itself contrasts starkly with the unobtrusive and secondary role of language in Switzerland. While the Belgian language communities have been sharply divided over a whole series of political crises since 1945, language seldom colors political issue alignments in Switzerland, and then only moderately, across a limited range of issues. If Belgium is famous for its simultaneous minority complexes among all three language groups, Swiss political culture emphasizes generosity to minorities and avoidance even of the concept of minority status. Where Belgium is still burdened by public attitudes of sociocultural superiority and inferiority in intergroup relations, Switzerland has a well established and widely accepted ethos of linguistic equality. If the multilingual society is reluctantly accepted in Belgium as an unpleasant necessity, it is welcomed in Switzerland as a cultural bonus and an economic asset. It is hardly surprising that these strong attitudinal differences should translate into differing patterns of political action. Where Belgium has experienced language as a mainspring for important political movements, cultural associations, and regionally based political parties, such organizations have been insignificant as a factor in Swiss federal politics.

Notwithstanding these wide attitudinal differences over language, there are some similarities in general value systems and their political organization that can be all too easily overlooked. Both Belgium and Switzerland are societies characterized by deeply ingrained religious and ideological pluralism, which led in both cases to considerable associational segmentation around the traditional political alignments of liberalism, socialism, and political Catholicism. Both countries have highly developed systems of democratic politics, based on electoral systems that closely reflect voter preferences and political decision-making founded on a broad consensus of the participant political groups. There are some differences here between the Swiss principle of grand coalitions embracing all major parties and the Belgian general rule of reliance on lesser coalitions, but the major contrast is between these two systems and the more primitive Canadian system of majoritarian government abetted by a weighted electoral system.

At the institutional level, the Belgian and Swiss political systems differ fundamentally concerning the locus of decision-making, with the former channelling all major decisions into one central parliamentary arena and the latter distributing responsibilities between the cantons and the Confederation in a relatively decentralized federal system. Even though the Belgian system has undergone innovative decentralization since 1970 and the Swiss system—conversely—has experienced a slow trend towards stronger federal authority, the two systems remain far apart in this respect. In the specific area of language policy, perhaps the most striking difference lies in the Belgian attempt to regulate language usage in all public sectors in the most meticulous detail, in contrast with Switzerland's reliance on a few slender constitutional norms buttressed by custom, judicial decision, and wide public consensus. On this point, Switzerland is once again unique among the four cases studied, though neither Finnish nor Canadian language legislation quite matches the Belgian system in attention to detail.

In spite of these fundamental differences in political systems and in implementation of language policy, Belgium and Switzerland are quite similar in one crucial way. Both countries base their language policies primarily on the principle of linguistic territoriality, with stable, publicly maintained language boundaries. There are specific exceptions to this rule in both countries, but in Switzerland the rule extends even to the language practices of the four officially plurilingual cantons. The primacy of the principle of fixed territoriality may appear unremarkable at this stage of the inquiry, but it will take on greater significance as the focus shifts to Finland, where the territoriality and personality principles have been mixed and variable, and to Canada, where the appropriate principle is disputed and the long-run outcome remains uncertain. The two case studies to follow will examine more thoroughly the alternatives to territoriality as a basis for language accommodation.

Appendices

Appendix A
Abbreviations

It may be helpful to add a list of political parties, interest groups, and institutions that are referred to by abbreviation or acronym in the text, with short forms in both French and Dutch where appropriate. Certain survey organizations and research institutes cited mainly as sources (AGLOP, CACEF, CEPESS, CERE, CRISP, INBEL, INSOC, NIPO, SOBEMAP) are omitted here but identified further in the Bibliography.

ABN	Algemeen beschaafd Nederlands (i.e., standard cultivated Dutch)
Agalev	Anders gaan leven (Flemish ecology party)
APWFSP	Association du personnel wallon et francophone des services publics
BASS	Belgian Archives for the Social Sciences
BRF	Belgisches Rundfunk- und Fernsehzentrum
BRT	Belgische Radio en Televisie
CGER/ASLK	Caisse générale d'épargne et de retraite
CPARCLB	Commission permanente pour l'amélioration des relations entre les communautés linguistiques belges
CPCL/VCT	Commission permanente de contrôle linguistique
CSC/ACV	Confédération des syndicats chrétiens
CVP	Christelijke Volkspartij (Flemish Catholic party)
Ecolo	Parti écologique (Francophone ecology party)
EMR/KMS	Ecole militaire royale
FDF	Front démocratique des francophones (Brussels regional party)
FGTB/ABVV	Fédération générale du travail de Belgique
INAMI/RIZIV	Institut national d'assurance maladie-invalidité
INR/NIR	Institut national belge de radiodiffusion/Belgisch Nationaal Instituut voor Radio-omroep
MPW	Mouvement populaire wallon
NATO/OTAN/NAVO	North Atlantic Treaty Organization
NCC	Nederlandse Commissie voor de Cultuur
NIR	See INR
ONEM/RVA	Office national de l'emploi
ONSS/RVSZ	Office national de sécurité sociale
PDB	Partei der Deutschsprächigen Belgiër (German-speaking regional party)
PLP	Parti de la liberté et du progrès (Francophone Liberal party to 1976)
PRL	Parti réformateur libéral (Francophone Liberal party from 1979)
PS	Parti socialiste (Francophone Socialist party)

PSC	Parti social chrétien (Francophone Catholic party)
PVV	Partij voor Vrijheid en Vooruitgang (Flemish Liberal party)
RDL	Rassemblement pour le Droit et la Liberté
RTB	Radiodiffusion-Télévision belge
RTBF	Radio-Télévision belge de la Communauté culturelle française
Sabena	Société anonyme belge pour l'exploitation de la navigation aérienne
SDR/GOM	Société de développement régional
SP	Socialistische Partij (Flemish Socialist party)
ULB	Université libre de Bruxelles
Verdinaso	Verbond van Dietsche Nationaal-solidaristen
VEV	Vlaams Economisch Verbond
VMO	Vlaamse Militanten Orde
VNV	Vlaams Nationaal Verbond
VVB	Vlaamse Volksbeweging
VVO	Verbond van het Vlaams Overheidspersoneel

Appendix B
A Postscript on the Events of 1985

The Social-Christian/Liberal coalition ministry formed by Prime Minister Wilfried Martens after the November 1981 election (usually designated Martens V) was the first Belgian government in two decades to last for an entire electoral period. Its final months in office, however, were marked by a series of issues that demonstrated the continuing presence of communal and linguistic tensions in spite of governmental efforts to focus attention upon problems of the Belgian economy. On July 4, 1985, on a relatively minor educational matter, the Francophone parties in Parliament invoked for the first time the "alarm-bell" procedures for protection of a linguistic community (see above, 183). Before this issue could be resolved in Cabinet, a more serious ministerial split developed between its Francophone Catholic (PSC) and Francophone Liberal (PRL) members over the responsibilities of a PSC minister of the interior for the Heysel stadium soccer riots. The crisis culminated in the resignation of the six PRL ministers on July 15, followed the next day by resignation of the government, which the King held in suspense. After delicate negotiations, all ministers returned to their previous portfolios, but the price of the settlement was a severely amputated legislative agenda for the coalition, an advancement of the scheduled 1985 general election from December to October, and a loss of prestige and credibility for the government.

The July crisis can be seen as a somewhat clumsy pre-election manoeuvre of a type that has precedents in Belgian coalition politics. Though not a communal issue in itself, its effect was to reduce the time available to resolve another more serious issue, the question of decentralizing jurisdiction over education from the central Parliament to the community councils. While all other major parties were willing to designate the appropriate constitutional articles for amendment by the post-election parliament, the Francophone Catholics (PSC) insisted adamantly that agreement on suitable guarantees for the *écoles libres* had to come first. The result was a major impasse among the coalition partners, most notably between the PSC and the Flemish Catholics (CVP), who strongly favored decentralization.

When this impasse persisted through August and proved unbridgeable, the government dissolved Parliament prematurely, in advance of the autumn session, on September 2, remaining in office itself in a caretaking role. As a consequence of this early dissolution, no parliamentary declaration of constitutional revision could be passed, and the 1985 Parliament is therefore not empowered to amend the constitution. Additionally, a parliamentary committee that had been studying the Brussels question did not deliver a report; the transitional system of representation for communities and regions remained unchanged; and the outgoing government presented no budget for 1986.

Notwithstanding these setbacks, and contrary to the expectations of many observers, the four government parties collectively held their own at the general election on October 13 and even managed a marginal gain of two seats in the Chamber of Representatives. The main regional parties continued to decline, the Volksunie dropping from twenty seats to sixteen, the FDF from six seats to three. The Rassemblement Wallon lost its last two seats to disappear from the lower house altogether, but perhaps mainly because its program of Walloon regionalism has been largely adopted by the other Francophone parties. While the Socialist opposition parties also gained slightly in this election, the way was clear for a renewed centre-right coalition.

Although the four coalition partners and the choice of prime minister were never in doubt, the formation of a ministry proceeded slowly. A negotiating committee consisting of Martens as *formateur* and three delegates from each of the four parties met intensively for more than a month to work out a detailed, wide-ranging interparty agreement for a new national coalition. Simultaneously, Francophone and Flemish delegates worked separately on priorities for their respective regional and community executives. When these negotiations culminated in a sixty-page governmental accord, a new, carefully balanced Martens cabinet, comprising the prime minister, four other Flemish Catholics (CVP), three Flemish Liberals (PVV), four Francophone Liberals (PRL), and three Francophone Catholics (PSC)—the same formula as Martens V—was announced and sworn in on November 28.

Bibliography

The Flemish Movement has occupied the attention of hundreds and even thousands of intellectuals in Belgium for more than a century. The resulting bibliography is several times too vast for any outside scholar to cover thoroughly. Unlike the bibliography for Switzerland in Volume 1, where virtually every reference that seemed of interest could be followed up, the bibliography of this volume can only claim to be an intelligent sampling of available material and a record of works examined and found useful in preparing this study. For ease of reference, all the categories of material used—books, articles, documents, periodicals, newspapers, and data sets—are arranged in a single alphabetical order. More extensive bibliographies may be found in Herremans (1965, vol. 2), Verdoodt (1973; 1983), and Alen and Van Speybroeck (1977).

L'Admission progressive de la langue néerlandaise dans les textes officiels de la Belgique, 1969. Heule, Brussels, and Namur: UGA.

Aelvoet, H., 1957. *Honderd vijfentwintig jaar verfransing in de agglomeratie en het arrondissement Brussel, 1830-1955*. Brussels: Simon Stevin.

AGLOP, 1975. *Le citoyen belge dans le système politique*. A machine-readable data set held in the Belgian Archives for the Social Sciences (BASS) at Louvain-la-Neuve.

Alen, A., 1980. "La réforme de l'Etat: la nouvelle constitution et ses lois d'exécution," *Documents-CEPESS* 19, nos. 2-3.

_____ , and P. Van Speybroeck, 1977. "La réforme de l'Etat belge de 1974 jusqu'au Pacte communautaire," *Documents-CEPESS* 16, nos. 5-6. Includes a comprehensive bibliography for the period 1970-77, 329-84.

Amelinckx, S., et al., 1969. *Participation des francophones et néerlandophones à la recherche scientifique en Belgique*. Brussels: Ministre de la politique et de la programmation scientifiques. Mimeographed.

Amelunxen, C., 1971. "The History of the German-speaking Minority-group in Belgium," *Plural Societies* 2, no. 4: 39-45.

Analyse de la population de la classe de milice, various years. Brussels: Forces armées belges, Centre de recherches des facteurs humains. The 1965 edition appears under the name of U. Bouvier.

André, R., 1983. *La population de la Wallonie dans la dualité démographique de la Belgique*. Brussels: Fondation Charles Plisnier and Charleroi: Institut Jules Destrée.

_____ , et al., 1969. *Aspects de la démographie de Belgique: population et logement en Wallonie*. Brussels: Fondation Charles Plisnier.

_____ , et al., 1984. *Analyse statistique de la population de la Wallonie et perspectives à l'horizon 2031*. Brussels: Centre de Démographie de l'Institut de Sociologie, Université libre de Bruxelles.

André-Robert, E., 1948. "A propos de la radio wallonne," *Nouvelle revue wallonne* 1: 37-43.

Annales parlementaires/Parlementaire handelingen. Brussels.

Annuaire de statistiques régionales, various years. Brussels: Institut national de statistique. Series begins in 1976.

Annuaire statistique de la Belgique, various years. Brussels: Institut national de statistique. Title varies slightly.

Annuaire statistique de l'enseignement, various years. Brussels: Ministère des affaires économiques and Ministère de l'éducation nationale.

Arango, E. R., 1961. *Leopold III and the Belgian Royal Question*. Baltimore: Johns Hopkins Press.

Les archives du Conseil de Flandre (Raad van Vlaanderen), 1928. Brussels: Dewarichet.

Armstrong, C. A. J., 1965. "The Language Question in the Low Countries: The Use of French and Dutch by the Dukes of Burgundy and their Administration." In J. R. Hale, et al., eds., *Europe in the Late Middle Ages*. Evanston: Northwestern University Press, 386-409.

Arresten van het Hof van Cassatie, various years. Brussels: Bruylant. Series begins in 1937.

Aubry, L., 1971. "Qu'est-ce qu'un Bruxellois?" *Nouvelle revue wallonne* 17:21-23.

"L'Autonomie culturelle... sa réalisation constitutionnelle et légale," 1971. *Cahiers-CEPESS*, no. 3.

Bacha, E., and R. Dupierreux, 1928. *Périodiques belges: répertoire par titres et par sujets*. Brussels: Dewit.

Baetens Beardsmore, H., 1971. *Le français régional de Bruxelles*. Brussels: Presses Universitaires.

Baeyens, H., 1963-64. "The Development of the Brussels Agglomeration," *Delta* 6, no. 4: 79-89.

Bährens, K., 1935. *Die flämische Bewegung: Europäisches Problem oder innerbelgische Frage*. Berlin: Volk und Reich Verlag.

Ballegeer, J. H., 1984. "Diplomacy in Plural Societies: The Cases of Canada and Belgium." Unpublished M.A. research essay, Carleton University.

Banks, A. S., and R. B. Textor, 1963. *A Cross-polity Survey*. Cambridge: M.I.T. Press.

Barnes, S., 1964. "Political Culture and Christian Trade Unionism: The Case of Belgium," *Relations industrielles* 19: 354-78.

Bartier, J., 1968. "Partis politiques et classes sociales en Belgique," *Res Publica* 10, special issue no. 2: 33-106.

Basse, M., 1930-33. *De Vlaamsche beweging van 1905 tot 1930*. 2 vols. Gent: Van Rysselberghe and Rombaut.

Baudart, E., 1945. *L'Avenir de la Wallonie*. Brussels: Editions universitaires.

Baudelaire, C., 1941. *La Belgique toute nue*. Edited by L. Gerin. Brussels: Editions de la Nouvelle revue Belgique.

_____, 1953. *Pauvre Belgique*. Edited by J. Crépet and C. Pichois. Paris: Louis Conard.

Bauwens, L., 1933. *Régime linguistique de l'enseignement primaire et de l'enseignement moyen*. Brussels: Edition universelle.

Beaufays, J., 1973. "La politique économique régionale de la Belgique." In A. Fischer, et al., *Etudes sur le régionalisme en Belgique et à l'étranger*. Brussels: Bruylant, 229-351.

_____, 1977. "La Belgique: la fin de l'état unitaire." Paper presented to the C.I.R.S.H. Colloque pluridisciplinaire international, May 9-10, 1977.

_____, et al., 1985. *La problématique fouronnaise*. Liège: Service de politologie régionale, Université de Liège. Etudes et recherches, no. 33.

Becquet, C. F., 1972-77. *Le différend wallo-flamand*. 2 vols. Couillet: Editions Institut Jules Destrée.

"The Belgian Periodical Press," 1968. In *Belgian News*, October 1968. Brussels: Ministry of Foreign Affairs and External Trade.

Belgische Radio & Televisie handboek, [1979]. Brussels: BRT-Persdienst.

Bertelson, L., ed., 1956. *Tableau chronologique des journaux belges*. Brussels: Section bruxelloise de l'Association générale de la presse belge.

"Le bilinguisme passif et son utilisation en Belgique," 1967. *Bulletin mensuel de l'Union des anciens étudiants de l'U.L.B.* 40, no. 340: 31-36.

Bindoff, S. T., 1945. *The Scheldt Question*. London: Allen and Unwin.
Bischoff, H., 1930. *Notre troisième langue nationale*. Bruxelles: Imprimerie coopérative Lucifer.
———, 1931. *Die deutsche Sprache in Belgien: ihre Geschichte und ihre Rechte*. Eupen: Esch.
Blondiau, A., 1967. "Opinion publique et défense nationale en Belgique," *Res Publica* 9: 621-34.
"Het Boek in België," 1976. *La presse/De pers*, no. 91: 15-22. Reprinted from the Kredietbank *Weekberichten*, October 8, 1976.
Boeynaems, M., 1967. "Cabinet-formation," *Res Publica* 9: 471-506.
———, 1973. "Les années 1970 et 1971 sur le plan communautaire et linguistique," *Res Publica* 15: 881-914.
Bogaert-Damin, A. M., and L. Maréchal, 1978. *Bruxelles: développement de l'ensemble urbain, 1846-1961*. Namur: Presses universitaires de Namur.
Bonis, J., 1969. "L'affaire Merckx et la sociologie," *Revue nouvelle* 50: 179-86.
Boon, H., 1969. *Enseignement primaire et alphabétisation dans l'agglomération bruxelloise de 1830 à 1879*. Leuven: Publications universitaires.
Boone, L., 1966. *De sociaal-politieke betekenis van de radioberichtgeving: een vergelijkende studie over herkomst, inhoud en vorm van de informatie in de B.R.T., R.T.B., en buitenlandse omroepen*. Leuven: Warny.
Boserup, A., 1969. "Brussels Study: Differences in Socio-economic Status." Unpublished working paper. Copenhagen: Institute for Peace and Conflict Research.
Bossier, H., 1950. "De zaak Coucke en Goethals: geschiedenis van een mythe," *Nieuw Vlaams Tijdschrift* 4: 1078-1112.
Bourassa, H., [1919]. *La langue, gardienne de la foi*. [Montréal]: Bibliothèque de l'Action française.
Bouvier, U. See *Analyse de la population de la classe de milice*.
Bouwen, R., 1965. "Groepscohesie in etnisch-homogene en etnisch-heterogene groepen met verschillende gezindheid: onderzoek naar de samenhang van groepsdiscussies door inhoudsanalyse." Unpublished thesis for the *licence*, University of Leuven.
Brackelaire, M., 1958. "De gezindheid van Vlaamse meisjesstudenten tegenover de Walen: Sociaal-psychologisch onderzoek naar het verband tussen de gezindheid en het contact." Unpublished thesis for the *licence*, University of Leuven.
Bracops, J., 1960. "Réplique [à Ludovic Moyersoen]," *Res Publica* 2: 27-32.
Brassinne, J., 1977. "Bilan des conseils culturels et des conseils régionaux," *Res Publica* 19: 179-219.
[Brazeau, J.,] 1965. "L'emploi des langues en matière militaire." Unpublished working paper prepared for the Canadian Royal Commission on Bilingualism and Biculturalism.
———, 1966. "Essai sur la question linguistique en Belgique." 4 vols. Ottawa: Royal Commission on Bilingualism and Biculturalism. Contains three volumes of appendices of documentary material. Mimeographed.
BRF (Belgisches Rundfunk- und Fernsehzentrum), various years. *Tätigkeitsbericht*. Eupen: BRF.
BRT (Belgische Radio en Televisie), various years. *Jaarverslag*. Brussels: BRT.
Brugmans, H., 1972. "'Flamands' et 'Hollandais': les complexes reciproques," *Septentrion* 1: 59-74.
"Brussel: bindteken of splijtzwam?" 1970. *Neerlandia* 74: 97-148. Special issue devoted to the Brussels question.
De Brusselse Post, various dates.

De Brusselse randgemeenten: een onderzoek naar de residentiële en taalkundige ontwikkeling, 1964. Antwerp: Kultuurraad voor Vlaanderen.

Bulletin de statistique, various years. Brussels: Institut national de statistique.

Bulletin des arrêts de la Cour de cassation, various years. Brussels: Bruylant.

Bureau de statistiques universitaires, various years. *Rapport annuel.* Brussels: Fondation universitaire.

Burton, J., et al., 1958. "Les langues au Congo," *Nouvelle revue wallonne* 10: 8-18.

Bustamante, H., et al., 1978. "Bilingual Education in Belgium." In B. Spolsky and R. L. Cooper, eds., *Case Studies in Bilingual Education.* Rowley, Mass.: Newbury House, 3-21, 501-504.

CACEF (Centre d'action culturelle de la communauté d'expression française), various years. *Revue de presse.* Namur.

Caeymaex, C., 1912. *De talen op onzen kansel.* Leuven: Drukkerij "Nova et vetera." Reprinted from *La vie diocésaine,* May 1912.

Cappuyns, L. L., 1967. Untitled brief to the Meyers Commission. Mimeographed.

Carbonneau, T. E., 1981. "Linguistic Legislation and Transnational Commercial Activity: France and Belgium," *American Journal of Comparative Law* 29: 393-412.

Carlier, A., 1950. "Le fédéralisme en Belgique et l'exemple suisse," *Nouvelle revue wallonne* 3: 21-40.

Carson, P., 1969. *The Fair Face of Flanders.* Gent: Story-Scientia.

Carton de Wiart, H., 1933. "Psychologie du peuple belge," *Revue des deux mondes* (103rd year) 15: 527-37.

Census. See *Recensement.*

Centre de recherche pour la solution nationale des problèmes sociaux, politiques et juridiques en régions wallonnes et flamandes (Centre Harmel), 1958. *Documents* and *Rapport final.* 11 vols. Brussels: Ministère de l'Intérieur. Multilithed. The *Rapport final* was also printed as a parliamentary document dated April 24, 1958, Session 1957-58, no. 940.

CEPESS (Centre d'études politiques, économiques et sociales), various years. *La vie politique en Belgique.* Brussels. Monthly, mimeographed.

CERE (Centre d'études pour la réforme de l'Etat), 1937-38. *La réforme de l'Etat.* 2 vols. Brussels: CERE.

Ceuleers, J., 1978. "Dagboek van een kabinetsformatie," *Res Publica* 20: 229-71.

_____ , 1980. "De splitsing van de Belgische Socialistische Partij," *Res Publica* 22: 373-82.

Chambre des Représentants, various years. Working documents of Parliament (identified by session and number).

Chaput, G., and R. de Falleur, 1961. "La production et l'investissement des régions flamande, wallonne et bruxelloise," *Cahiers économiques de Bruxelles,* nos. 10-11: 177-208, 373-91.

Chaput-Auquier, G., 1962. "Les produits intérieurs provinciaux, 1948-1953-1959," *Cahiers économiques de Bruxelles,* no. 13: 5-35.

Chavanne, J., 1961. "Que veulent les Wallons?" *Revue nouvelle* 34: 132-42.

Claes, L., 1961. "Flamands et francophones," *Revue nouvelle* 17: 166-77.

_____ , 1962. *Het Vlaams complex.* Reprinted from *Streven* 16, no. 1.

_____ , 1963-64. "The Process of Federalization in Belgium," *Delta* 6, no. 4: 43-52.

_____ , 1973. "Le mouvement flamand entre le politique, l'économique et le culturel," *Res Publica* 15: 219-36.

_____ , 1985. *De afwezige meerderheid.* Leuven: Davidsfonds.

Claeys, P. H., 1973. *Groupes de pression en Belgique.* Brussels: Editions de l'Université de Bruxelles and Editions du CRISP.

Claeys-Van Haegendoren, M., 1967. "Party and Opposition Formation in Belgium," *Res Publica* 9: 413-35.

Clark, G. N., 1926. "The 'Great Netherlands' Idea," *Edinburgh Review* 243: 240-52.

Clark, S., 1984. "Nobility, Bourgeoisie and the Industrial Revolution in Belgium," *Past and Present*, no. 105: 140-75.

Cliquet, R. L., 1960. "On the Differential Population Development of the Flemings and the Walloons and its Influence on Flemish-Walloon Relations," *Homo* 11: 67-88.

_____ , 1968. "De studie van de biologische fertiliteit en de anticonceptie in het raam van de nationale enquête over de huwelijksvruchtbaarheid," *Population et famille* 15: 1-37.

Clough, S. B., 1930. *A History of the Flemish Movement in Belgium.* New York: Smith. Reprinted 1968, New York: Octagon.

_____ , 1945. "The Flemish Movement." In J. A. Goris, ed., *Belgium.* Berkeley and Los Angeles: University of California Press, 108-26.

Cocquereaux, J., 1978. *De vernederlandsing van het bedrijfsleven: het september decreet van de Nederlandse Cultuurraad.* Berchem/Antwerp and Amsterdam: Maarten Kluwer.

Coetsier, L., 1959. *De actuele deelname van beide taalgroepen aan het Belgisch opleidingswezen en de maatschappelijke gevolgen ervan.* Gent: Laboratorium voor teogepaste psychologie.

_____ , and A. Bonte, 1963. *Doorstroming naar de universiteit.* 2 vols. Antwerp: Kultuurraad voor Vlaanderen. Vol. 3, by J. L. Wieërs, appeared in 1964.

Collard, E., 1952. "Commentaire de la carte de la pratique dominicale en Belgique," *Lumen vitae* 7: 644-52.

Commission flamande 1859: Installation, délibérations, rapport, documents officiels, 1859. Brussels: Verbruggen.

Coppieters, F., 1974. *The Community Problem in Belgium.* 2nd rev. ed. Brussels: Institut belge d'information et de documentation.

_____ , 1984. *Les structures politiques des communautés et des régions en Belgique.* Brussels: Institut belge d'information et de documentation.

Coulon, M., 1962. *L'autonomie culturelle en Belgique.* 2nd ed. Brussels: Fondation Charles Plisnier.

Covell, M., 1981. "Ethnic Conflict and Elite Bargaining: The Case of Belgium," *West European Politics* 4: 197-218.

_____ , 1982. "Agreeing to Disagree: Elite Bargaining and the Revision of the Belgian Constitution," *Canadian Journal of Political Science* 15: 451-69.

_____ , 1983. "Belgium's New Regional Institutions," *Canadian Journal of Netherlandic Studies* 4, no. 2/5, no. 1: 82-88.

CPCL (Commission permanente de contrôle linguistique), various years. *Rapport annuel/Jaarverslag* (Brussels). Printed in alternate years as a Senate or a Chamber of Representatives document since 1965.

Craeybeckx, J., 1970. "The Brabant Revolution: A Conservative Revolt in a Backward Country?" *Acta historiae Neerlandica* 4: 49-83.

CRISP (Centre de recherche et d'information socio-politiques), various years. *Courrier hebdomadaire.* Brussels.

Curtis, A. E., 1971. *New Perspectives on the History of the Language Problem in Belgium.* Ann Arbor: University Microfilms. Ph.D. dissertation, University of Oregon.

Cuypers, G., 1965. "Stereotypie en projectie: stereotype beeld van de Walen bij Vlaamse studenten." Unpublished thesis for the *licence*, University of Leuven.

Daelemans, J., 1963. "De federalistische opvattingen in de belgische pers: een inhoudsanalyse 1919 tot 1963." Unpublished thesis for the *licence*, University of Leuven.

_____ , 1966. "Systematisch overzicht van het federalizatieproces," *Politica* 16: 249-64.

Daenen, I., 1960. "Methodes van observatie van kleine groepen: toepassing van de methode van R. F. Bales." Unpublished thesis for the *licence*, University of Leuven.

Daenen, J., 1978-79. "Les vacances de la population belge en 1976," *Bulletin de statistique* 64: 823-33; 65: 471-88.

Damas, H., 1971. "Les migrations pendulaires en Belgique: situation au 31 décembre 1961," *Population et famille*, no. 25: 1-58.

Daubie, C., 1972. "Les techniques de protection des minorités," *Annales de droit* 32: 207-44.

_____ , 1975. "Le Pacte culturel: de sa genèse à son application," *Res Publica* 17: 171-99.

_____ , 1981. "Le Sénat de Belgique: perspectives et esquisse d'une réforme," *Administration publique* 5: 101-18.

Dawes, T. R., 1902. *Bilingual Teaching in Belgian Schools*. Cambridge: Cambridge University Press.

Dayez, E. C., 1969. *La Belgique est-elle morte?: Dossier sur la crise belge*. Paris: Fayard.

De Bakker, B., and M. Claeys-Van Haegendoren, 1973. "The Socialist Party in the Socialist System and in Organised Socialism in Belgium," *Res Publica* 15: 237-47.

de Bie, P., 1951. *Représentations de Benelux*. Reprinted from *Bulletin de l'Institut de recherches économiques et sociales de l'Université de Louvain* 17: 637-710.

_____ , 1965. "Aspects socio-culturels des classes ascendantes en Belgique," *Cahiers internationaux de sociologie* 39: 91-111.

Deblaere, G., et al., 1967. *Regionale welvaartsverschillen in België*. Antwerp: Standaard.

_____ , et al., 1974. "La navette de la population active vers Bruxelles," *Eco-Brabant*, nos. 4-5: 21-42.

De Bo, L. L., 1873. *Westvlaamsch idioticon*. Brugge: Gaillard.

De Boeck, L. B., 1949. "Taalkunde en de talenkwestie in Belgisch-Kongo." In Institut royal colonial belge, Section des sciences morales et politiques, *Mémoires* 17, no. 1.

Debuyst, F., 1967. *La fonction parlementaire en Belgique: mécanismes d'accès et images*. Brussels: CRISP.

Declerck, R., 1961. "La province," *Res Publica* 3: 205-16.

De Clercq, B. J., 1968. *Kritiek van de verzuiling*. Lier: Van In.

De Cneudt, R., 1918. *De vervlaamsing van het lager onderwijs in Groot-Brussel*. Brussels: Hessens.

De Coster, S., et al., 1971. *Aspects sociologiques du plurilinguisme*. Brussels: AIMAV and Paris: Didier.

De Croo, H. F., 1965. *Parlement et gouvernement: problèmes institutionnels à travers une session parlementaire*. Brussels: Bruylant.

De Groeve, H. E. A., et al., 1968ff. *Code linguistique*. Heule, Brussels, and Namur: UGA. Several volumes, with loose-leaf bindings. Vol. 1 includes basic language laws in administrative matters and their decrees of application.

De Hoog, B., 1983. "L'union linguistique entre la Belgique et les Pays-Bas," *Septentrion* 12, no. 1: 48-57.

Dehousse, F., 1961. "Le problème des structures politiques de la Belgique," *Res Publica* 3: 297-305.

De Jonghe, A., 1967. *De taalpolitiek van Koning Willem I in de Zuidelijke Nederlanden (1814-1830)*. Sint-Andries-bij-Brugge: Darthet.

Delanghe, L., et al., 1969. "Objektieve kriteria: Wetenschappelijke benadering van de objektieve behoeften in beide kultuurgemeenschappen." Part I: Kultuur. Leuven: Katholieke universiteit te Leuven. Mimeographed.

Deleeck, H., 1959. *De taaltoestanden in het Vlaams bedrijfsleven*. Brussels: Arbeiderspers.

_____ , 1963. "De vervlaamsing van het bedrijfsleven en de jongste taalwetgeving," *Gids op maatschappelijk gebied* 54: 845-56.

_____ , 1975. "L'emploi des langues dans les entreprises flamandes," *Septentrion* 4, no. 1: 55-62.

Deleu, J., et al., 1973-75. *Encyclopedie van de Vlaamse Beweging*. 2 vols. Tielt and Utrecht: Lannoo.

Delfosse, J., 1964. "La législation linguistique et le malaise wallon," *Revue nouvelle* 40: 510-15.

Delfosse, P., 1979. "La formation des familles politiques en Belgique," *Res Publica* 21: 465-93.

Delmartino, F., 1982. "La régionalisation de la Belgique: réforme fédéraliste ou opération de décentralisation." Paper presented at the Twelfth Congress of the International Political Science Association, Rio de Janeiro, August 1982.

Delpérée, F., 1973. "La Belgique: état fédéral?" *Revue du droit public et de la science politique en France et à l'étranger* 88: 607-60.

Delplace, L., 1899. *La Belgique sous Guillaume I, roi des Pays-Bas*. Leuven: Istas.

Delruelle, N., 1970. *La mobilité sociale en Belgique*. Brussels: Editions de l'Institut de sociologie.

Delruelle-Vosswinkel, N., 1972. *Les notables en Belgique*. Bruxelles: Editions de l'Université.

Delruelle, N., et al., 1966. "Les problèmes qui préoccupent les Belges," *Revue de l'Institut de sociologie* 39: 291-341.

_____ , et al., 1970. *Le comportement politique des électeurs belges*. Brussels: Editions de l'Institut de sociologie.

Deneckere, M., 1954. *Histoire de la langue française dans les Flandres, 1770-1823*. Gent: "Romanica Gandensia."

De Nolf, R., 1968a. *Federalisme in België als grondwettelijk vraagstuk*. Antwerp: Nederlandsche Boekhandel.

_____ , 1968b. "The Federalism in Belgium as a Constitutional Problem," *Res Publica* 10: 383-406.

_____ , 1968c. "Pragmatische federalisering in België," *Streven* 21: 858-67.

Deprez, K., et al., 1982a. "Anderstaligen in het nederlandstalig onderwijs te Brussel," *Ons erfdeel* 25: 92-99.

_____ , 1982b. "Anderstaligen in het nederlandstalig basisonderwijs in Brussel: wie en waarom?" *Taal en sociale integratie* 6: 231-63 (with abstract in English).

De Raet, L., 1939. *Over Vlaamse volkskracht*. Antwerp: Standaard. Selected writings edited by Max Lamberty.

De Raeymaeker, O., 1965. "De diplomatieke loopbaan," *Politica* 15: 209-22.

Dereymaeker, R., 1966. "Situation actuelle de la statistique régionale," *Etudes statistiques et économétriques*, no. 14.

Dersin, A., 1981. "Souveraineté régionale et finances publiques: approche par les recettes et les masses budgétaires," *Res Publica* 23: 213-38.

Deschouwer, K., 1982. "Het profiel van de Brusselse FDF-kiezer (1968-1978)," *Taal en sociale integratie* 6: 141-65.

Des Cressonnières, J., 1919. *Essai sur la question des langues dans l'histoire de Belgique*. Brussels: Lamberty.

Desmarets, J., 1967. "Bruxelles: terre de discorde ou d'union," *Revue générale belge* 103, no. 10: 1-18.

De Smet, R. E., et al., 1958. *Atlas des élections belges, 1919-1954*. Brussels: Institut de sociologie.

De Smet, W. M. A., 1976-77. "L'emploi des langues dans l'enseignement universitaire en Belgique," *La monda lingvo-problemo* 6: 95-106.

Des Ombiaux, M., 1921. *Psychologie d'une capitale: Bruxelles*. Paris and Brussels: Librairie Moderne.

De Somer, P., 1966. "Taalproblemen en hoger onderwijs," *Onze alma mater* 20: 151-63.

Desonay, F., and A. van Duinkerken, 1963-64. "Two Ways of Looking at Flanders," *Delta* 6, no. 4: 33-42.

de Stexhe, P., 1972. *La révision de la Constitution belge, 1968-1971*. Brussels: Larcier and Namur: Société d'études morales, sociales et juridiques.

Destrée, J., 1912. *Lettre au Roi sur la séparation de la Wallonie et de la Flandre*. Brussels: Weissenbruch.

_____ , 1923. *Wallons et Flamands: la querelle linguistique en Belgique*. Paris: Plon.

Devillers, A., 1952. "Pour une radio wallonne authentique," *Nouvelle revue wallonne* 4: 218-28.

De Vreese, W., 1899. *Gallicismen in het Zuidnederlandsch: proeve van taalzuivering*. Gent: Siffer.

de Vries Reilingh, H. D., 1954. *België: lotgenoot in de Lage Landen*. Meppel: Boom.

De Vroede, M., 1975. *The Flemish Movement in Belgium*. Antwerp: Kultuurraad voor Vlaanderen.

Dewachter, W., 1967. "The General Elections as a Process of Powerachievement in the Belgian Political System," *Res Publica* 9: 369-411.

_____ , 1975a. "Problemen en oplossingen voor het aktuele beleid," *Res Publica* 17: 501-15.

_____ , 1975b. "Beeld van de machtstruktuur in België," *Res Publica* 17: 545-62.

De Weerdt, I., 1964. *Het taalgebruik in het bedrijfsleven*. Antwerp: Vlaams Economisch Verbond.

Deweerdt, M., 1984. "Overzicht van het Belgische politiek gebeuren in 1983," *Res Publica* 26: 413-72.

De Wilde, L. O. J., 1958. *Kultuur- en levenskansen van Vlaanderen in Kongo*. Brussels: Lodewijk De Raetfonds.

De Witte, K., 1976. *Brussel 2000*. Leuven: Davidsfonds.

Dhondt, J., 1947. "Essai sur l'origine de la frontière linguistique," *L'antiquité classique* 16: 261-86.

D'Hoogh, C., and J. Mayer, 1964. *Jeunesse belge: opinions et aspirations*. Brussels: Institut de sociologie.

Dierickx, G., 1978. "Ideological Oppositions and Consociational Attitudes in the Belgian Parliament," *Legislative Studies Quarterly* 3: 133-60.

_____ , and A. P. Frognier, 1980. "L'espace idéologique au Parlement belge: une approche comparative," *Res Publica* 22: 151-76.

Doms, P., 1965. "L'emploi des langues dans les Chambres législatives en Belgique," *Res Publica* 7: 126-40.

Dosfel, L., 1910. *De Belgische wetten op het gebruik der nederlandsche taal*. Brugge: Houdmont-Carbonez.

Doucy, A., et al., 1971. *L'opinion publique belge: le parlement; l'Europe; les finances publiques; la politique culturelle.* Brussels: Editions de l'Institut de sociologie.

Dovifat, E., ed., 1960. *Handbuch der Auslandspresse.* Bonn: Athenäum and Köln-Opladen: Westdeutscher Verlag.

Dumont, F., 1965. *L'irrédentisme français en Wallonie de 1814 à 1831.* 2nd ed. Charleroi: Institut Jules Destrée. First edition, 1938

Dunn, J. A., 1970. *Social Cleavage, Party Systems and Political Integration: A Comparison of the Belgian and Swiss Experiences.* Ann Arbor: University Microfilms. Ph.D. dissertation, University of Pennsylvania.

————, 1974. "The Revision of the Constitution in Belgium: A Study in the Institutionalization of Ethnic Conflict," *Western Political Quarterly* 27: 143-63.

Dupont, J. A., 1947. "Le génie wallon," *Revue de psychologie des peuples* 2: 353-70.

Durnez, G., 1967. "Straatsburg/Strasbourg," *Ons erfdeel* 10, no. 4: 80-83.

du Roy, A., 1968. *La guerre des belges.* Paris: Editions du Seuil.

Duvieusart, J., 1975. *La question royale: crise et dénouement, juin, juillet, août 1950.* Brussels: CRISP.

L'économie flamande: ombres et lumières, 1967. Brussels: Economische Raad voor Vlaanderen.

Eeckhout, J., 1964. "La langue de l'entreprise," *Journal des tribunaux* 79: 4-5.

————, 1973a. "Les langues des entreprises," *Journal des tribunaux* 88: 483-84.

————, 1973b. "Le décret de septembre et le barreau," *Journal des tribunaux* 88: 697.

Elias, H. J., 1963-65. *Geschiedenis van de vlaamse gedachte.* 4 vols. Antwerp: Nederlandsche Boekhandel.

————, 1969. *Vijfentwintig jaar Vlaamse Beweging, 1914-1939.* 4 vols. Antwerp: Nederlandsche Boekhandel.

Emery, W. B., 1969. *National and International Systems of Broadcasting.* East Lansing: Michigan State University Press. Includes Belgium (ch. 7) and Switzerland (ch. 19).

Emery-Hauzeur, C., and E. A. Sand, 1974. "Naissances désirées et non désirées: étude descriptive," *Population et famille,* no. 31: 1-26.

Emploi des langues en matière administrative, 1959. Brussels: Moniteur belge. Consolidation of the law of June 28, 1932, and its decrees of execution.

Emploi des langues en matière administrative, 1963. Brussels: Moniteur belge.

Emploi des langues en matière administrative: coordination des lois, 1966a. Brussels: Moniteur belge. Coordinated text of the law of August 2, 1963, and earlier legislation.

Emploi des langues en matière administrative: arrêtés royaux d'exécution du 30 novembre 1966, 1966b. Brussels: Moniteur belge.

Emploi des langues en matière administrative, undated. Brussels: Ministère de l'Intérieur. Office consolidation of the legislation, decrees of execution, and relevant parliamentary documents up to 1973.

Emploi des langues en matière judiciaire: loi du 15 juin 1935; arrêtés royaux d'exécution, 1944. Brussels: Moniteur belge.

Encyclopedie van de Vlaamse Beweging. See Deleu et al.

Enkele facetten van het kijk- en luisteronderzoek, various years. Brussels: BRT Studiedienst. Published annually by the BRT Research Service.

Enquête permanente sur les programmes, various issues. Brussels: RTB. A series of RTB research studies on radio audiences in Wallonie and Brussels.

Enquête socio-économique, avril 1977, 1978. 3 vols. Brussels: Institut national de statistique.

Erny, P., 1974. "Vie universitaire au Zaire," *Education et développement*, no. 97: 48-56.

Etienne, J. M., 1968. *Le mouvement rexiste jusqu'en 1940*. Paris: Colin.

Etudes statistiques, various years. Brussels: Institut national de statistique. Early numbers appear under the title *Etudes statistiques et économétriques*.

European Court of Human Rights, 1967-68. *Case "Relating to Certain Aspects of the Laws on the Use of Languages in Education in Belgium."* 4 vols. Strasbourg: Council of Europe. The two judgments are in Series A, the pleadings and documents in Series B, with parallel texts in French and English.

Fayat, H., 1966. *Het Brusselse vraagstuk*. Gent: Julius Vuylsteke-Fonds.

Féaux, V., 1963. *Cinq semaines de lutte sociale: la grève de l'hiver 1960-1961*. Brussels: Institut de sociologie.

Feiten en meningen, various years. Antwerp: Kultuurraad voor Vlaanderen.

Filley, W. O., 1950. "Foreign Policy in Multinational Democratic States, 1914-1945: The Influence of Secondary Nationalities." 2 vols. Unpublished Ph.D. dissertation, Yale University.

Fischer, A., et al., 1973. *Etudes sur le régionalisme en Belgique et à l'étranger*. Brussels: Bruylant.

Fischer, H., and U. P. Trier, 1962. *Das Verhältnis zwischen Deutschschweizer und Westschweizer: Eine sozialpsychologische Untersuchung*. Bern and Stuttgart: Huber.

Fitzmaurice, J., 1983. *The Politics of Belgium: Crisis and Compromise in a Plural Society*. London: Hurst.

"Les Flamands parlent aux Européens," 1968. *Synthèses*, no. 269. Special number with articles by several authors.

"La Flandre et les Flamands," 1980. Special issue of *Socialisme* 27: 329-95.

Flandricismes, wallonismes et expressions impropres dans la langue française, 1830. 4th ed. Brussels: Rampelbergh. Published anonymously but attributed to the Abbé Poyart, later revised and updated by L. Quiévreux. Antwerp and Brussels: Moorthamers, 1928. The first edition is listed as Brussels, 1806.

Fondation universitaire, various years. *Rapport annuel*. Brussels: Fondation universitaire.

Fondation universitaire. Bureau de statistiques universitaires. See Bureau.

Fonson, F., and F. Wicheler, 1910. *Le mariage de Mlle. Beulemans*. 3rd ed. Paris: Librairie Théatrale du "Nouveau siècle."

Fonteyn, G., 1979. *Les Wallons: faire surface*. Brussels and Leuven: Oyez.

_____ , 1983. *Fourons: une histoire Happart*. Antwerp: Soethoudt.

Fouillée, A., 1903. *Esquisse psychologique des peuples européens*. 2nd ed. Paris: Alcan.

Fox, R. C., 1965. "Medical Scientists in a Château." In N. Kaplan, ed., *Science and Society*. Chicago: Rand McNally, 334-51.

Fraeys, W., 1977. "Les élections législatives du 17 avril 1977," *Res Publica* 19: 495-513.

_____ , 1979. "Les élections européennes de 1979," *Res Publica* 21: 411-26.

_____ , 1982. "Les élections législatives du 8 novembre 1981: analyse des résultats," *Res Publica* 24: 129-49.

Fredericq, P., 1906-1909. *Schets eener geschiedenis der Vlaamsche Beweging*. 3 vols. Gent: Vuylsteke.

Frese, A., 1918. *Deutsches Land in Belgien*. Berlin: Stilke.

Friedrich, C. J., 1975. "The Politics of Language and Corporate Federalism." In J. G. Savard and R. Vigneault, eds., *Les états multilingues: problèmes et solutions*. Québec: Les presses de l'Université Laval, 227-42.

Frognier, A. P., 1975. "L'axe gauche/droite," *Res Publica* 17: 471-78.

F. T., 1963. "Un gouvernement impopulaire?" *Les dossiers de l'Action sociale catholique* 40: 619-26.

Galderoux, M., 1959. "Le recensement des langues nationales parlées," *Dossiers de l'Action sociale catholique* 36: 583-609.

Gallus (pseud.), 1969. *Benelux: 20 millions de Néerlandais?* [Brugge]: Desclée De Brouwer. Preface by L. Outers.

Garré, G., 1970. "Frontlijn: Nederlandstalig onderwijs," *Neerlandia* 74: 129-32.

Geen talentelling, 1959. Brussels: Vlaams Aktiekomitee Brussel en Taalgrens.

Geerts, G., et al., 1977. "Successes and Failures in Dutch Spelling Reform." In J. A. Fishman, ed., *Advances in the Creation and Revision of Writing Systems*. The Hague and Paris: Mouton, 179-245.

Gelders, H., et al., 1969. "Objektieve kriteria: Wetenschappelijke benadering van de objektieve behoeften in beide kultuurgemeenschappen." Part II: Sport. Brussels: Vrije Universiteit te Brussel. Mimeographed.

Genicot, L., 1973. *Histoire de la Wallonie*. Toulouse: Privat.

Géoris-Reitshof, M., 1962. *L'extrême-droite et le néo-fascisme en Belgique*. Brussels and Paris: Pierre de Méyère.

Gérain, R., 1975. "La responsabilité politique des ministres devant les conseils culturels," *Res Publica* 17: 31-52.

Gérard-Libois, J., and J. Gotovitch, 1972. "L'an 40: la Belgique occupée," *Res Publica* 14: 137-46.

Gerlo, A., 1966. *De Vlaamse Beweging op nieuwe banen*. Antwerp: Ontwikkeling.

————, 1968a. "Un statut national pour Bruxelles," *Synthèses*, no. 269: 42-47.

————, 1968b. "Une structure double pour l'Université libre de Bruxelles," *Synthèses*, no. 269: 68-71.

Geschiere, L., 1950. *Eléments néerlandais du wallon liégeois*. Amsterdam: Noord-Hollandsche Uitgevers.

Geyl, P., ca. 1920. *Holland and Belgium: Their Common History and Their Relations*. Leiden: Sijthoff.

————, 1925-30. *De Groot-Nederlandsche gedachte*. Vol. 1, Haarlem: Tjeenk Willink. Vol. 2, Antwerp: "De Sikkel."

————, 1955. *Debates with Historians*. Groningen and Djakarta: Wolters. Esp. ch. 9, "The National State and the Writers of Netherlands History."

————, 1960. *Noord en Zuid: eenheid en tweeheid in de Lage Landen*. Utrecht and Antwerp: Spectrum.

————, 1964. *History of the Low Countries: Episodes and Problems*. London: Macmillan; New York: St. Martin's Press.

Gilissen, J., 1951. "Etude statistique de la répression de l'incivisme," *Revue de droit pénal et de criminologie* 31: 513-628.

————, 1958. *Le régime représentatif en Belgique depuis 1790*. Brussels: Renaissance du livre.

————, 1963. "Military Justice in Belgium," *Military Law Review*, no. 20: 83-105.

————, 1968. "La Constitution belge de 1831: ses sources, son influence," *Res Publica* 10, special issue no. 2: 107-41.

Gillouin, R., 1930. *De l'Alsace à la Flandre: le mysticisme linguistique*. Paris: Editions Prométhée.

Gilson, A., et al., 1983. *La répartition des compétences entre l'Etat, les Communautés et les Régions*. Brussels: Centre d'étude des institutions politiques.

Glejser, H., 1967. "Le revenu des régions belges," *Cahiers économiques de Bruxelles*, no. 33: 263-72.

Goffart, V., 1969. "La crise de Louvain, du 1er janvier au 31 mars 1968," *Res Publica* 11:31-76.

Gol, J., 1970. *Le monde de la presse en Belgique.* Brussels: CRISP.

Goosse, A., 1979. "Le français de Wallonie." In R. Lejeune and J. Stiennon, eds., *La Wallonie, le pays et les hommes.* N.p.: Renaissance du livre, 3: 173-81.

Goris, J. A., 1943. *Du génie flamand.* New York: Roseau pensant.

Gotovitch, J., 1967. "La légation d'Allemagne et le Mouvement flamand entre 1867 et 1914," *Revue belge de philologie et d'histoire* 45: 438-78.

Goudsblom, J., 1964. "Het algemeen beschaafd Nederlands," *Sociologische gids* 11: 106-24.

Grammens, M., 1961. "Vlamingen in Belgische diplomatie," *Streven* 14: 1079-85.

Grégoire, M., et al., 1958. *Aspects de la société belge: recueil de conférences.* Brussels: Librairie encyclopédique.

Grootaers, L., 1924. "Quelques emprunts entre patois flamands et wallons," *Leuvensche Bijdragen* 16: 43-64.

Haesaert, J., 1947. "Psychologie de l'ethnie flamande en Belgique," *Revue de psychologie des peuples* 2: 371-402.

Hamelius, P., 1894. *Histoire politique et littéraire du mouvement flamand.* Brussels: Rozez.

————, 1921. *Introduction à la littérature française et flamande de Belgique.* Brussels: Office de publicité.

Hankard, M., 1973. "La Radio en Belgique à travers 50 ans d'existence." In G. Thoveron, ed., *La radio hier et aujourd'hui.* Brussels: RTB.

————, 1979. "Histoire cursive, en six épisodes, de la communautarisation et régionalisation de la Radio-télévision belge," *Dossiers du CACEF*, no. 64: 13-27.

Hanse, J., et al., 1971. *Chasse aux belgicismes.* Brussels: Fondation Charles Plisnier.

Hasquin, H., ed., 1975-76. *La Wallonie, le pays et les hommes; histoire, économies, sociétés.* 2 vols. [Brussels]: Renaissance du livre.

Haust, J., 1933a. *Dictionnaire liégeois.* Liège: Vaillant-Carmanne.

————, [1933b]. *Le dictionnaire liégeois et les germanistes.* Groningen, The Hague, and Batavia: Wolters. Reprinted from *Mélanges de philologie offerts à Jean-Jacques Salverda de Grave.*

Hayoit de Termicourt, R., 1936. *L'emploi des langues en justice.* Brussels: Larcier.

Heisler, M. O., 1974. "Institutionalizing Societal Cleavages in a Cooptive Polity: The Growing Importance of the Output Side in Belgium." In M. O. Heisler, ed., *Politics in Europe.* New York: McKay, 178-220.

————, 1977. "Managing Ethnic Conflict in Belgium," *Annals of the American Academy of Political and Social Science* 433: 32-46.

Hemmerechts, K., 1964. *Het Triëst van het Noorden.* Leuven: Davidsfonds.

Henrard, M., [1964]. *L'emploi des langues dans l'administration et dans les entreprises privées: Loi du 2 août 1963.* Heule: UGA.

————, 1967. "Législation linguistique et entreprise privée," *Annales de droit et de sciences politiques* 27: 245-65.

Herbots, J., 1973. *Meertalig rechtswoord: rijkere rechtvinding.* Gent: Story-Scientia.

Hermans, M., 1983. *La RTBF et les partis politiques.* Liège: Département de science politique, Université de Liège. Etudes et recherches, no. 30.

Herremans, M. P., 1948. *La question flamande.* Brussels: Meurice.

————, 1951. *La Wallonie: ses griefs, ses aspirations.* Brussels: Editions Marie-Julienne.

————, 1963. *Le contentieux Flamands-Wallons.* Reprinted from *Socialisme* 10, no. 56: 185-205.

————, 1965. "Le bilinguisme et le biculturalisme en Belgique." 2 vols. Ottawa: Royal Commission on Bilingualism and Biculturalism. Vol. 2 has an extensive bibliography, 426-514. Mimeographed.

————, 1978. Comment on "Typologie sur l'emploi des langues dans l'entreprise privée." In J. G. Savard et al., *Minorités linguistiques et interventions: essai de typologie.* Québec: Centre international de recherche sur le bilinguisme, 292-98.

————, 1980. "Les Flamands bruxellois," *Socialisme,* nos. 160-61: 339-49.

Hill, K., 1974. "Belgium: Political Change in a Segmented Society." In R. Rose, ed., *Electoral Behavior: A Comparative Handbook* (New York: Free Press; London: Collier Macmillan, 29-108.

Hocepied, C., 1984. "De activiteitsgraad van de Belgische senatoren tijdens de zitting 1982-1983," *Res Publica* 26: 645-61.

Hodges, M. H., 1972. *The Belgian Political Elite: A Study of the Composition and Transformations of the Political Elite in Belgium Since the End of World War Two.* Ann Arbor: University Microfilms. Ph.D. dissertation, Georgetown University.

Hoed, J., 1964. "De l'information des quotidiens belges de langue française en matière de politique étrangère," *Res Publica* 6: 269-79.

Höjer, C. H., 1946. *Le régime parlementaire belge de 1918 à 1940.* Uppsala and Stockholm: Almqvist and Wiksell.

Holvoet, L., and M. Platel, 1980. "De regeringsvorming Martens I," *Res Publica* 22: 333-70.

Honni, M., 1977. "La RTB comme si vous y étiez," *Revue nouvelle* 66: 211-21.

Hotterbeex, M., ed., 1981. *Quelle autonomie pour la communauté germanophone belge?* Liège: Département de science politique, Université de Liège. Etudes et recherches, no. 20.

————, 1983. *Brève histoire politique de la réforme communautaire de l'Etat belge.* Liège: Département de science politique, Université de Liège. Etudes et recherches, no. 38.

Houben, K.,1983. "Wet en werkelijkheid inzake het taalevenwicht in het Belgisch officierencorps," *Res Publica* 25: 83-93.

Houben, R., et al., 1984. *Waarheen met België?/Que pourrait devenir la Belgique?* Brussels: Centre d'étude des institutions politiques.

Houtman, W., 1963. *Vlaamse en Waalse documenten over federalisme.* Schepdaal: "Het Pennoen."

Hoyaux, J., 1972. "Situation actuelle à Bruxelles et en Wallonie." In *Première conférence des minorités ethniques de langue française.* Delémont: Comité permanent des minorités ethniques de langue française, 47-60.

Huggett, F. E., 1969. *Modern Belgium.* London: Pall Mall Press.

Humblet, J. E., 1963. "Les Wallons et l'étude des langues vivantes," *Revue nouvelle* 37: 59-67.

————, 1980. "Emergence des communautés et des régions en Belgique." In J. Dofny and A. Akiwowo, eds., *National and Ethnic Movements.* Beverly Hills and London: Sage, 77-89.

Huyse, L., 1969. *L'apathie politique: étude sociologique.* Antwerp and Brussels: Erasme.

————, 1970. *Passiviteit, pacificatie en verzuiling in de belgische politiek.* Antwerp and Utrecht: Standaard.

————, 1974. "Un regard sociologique sur la question linguistique en Belgique," *Septentrion* 3, no. 3: 23-25.

————, 1975a. "The Language Conflict in Belgium," *Sociological Contributions from Flanders* 4: 83-89.

————, 1975b. "Vijftien Angelsaksische auteurs over politiek, verzuiling en compromisvorming in België," *Res Publica* 17: 413-31.

INBEL (Institut belge d'information et de documentation), 1968. *Etude de l'opinion en Flandre, en Wallonie, et à Bruxelles sur certains problèmes politiques, économiques et sociaux en Belgique.* Brussels: SOBEMAP.

"L'incivisme devant nous," 1948. *Revue nouvelle* 8: 34-63.

L'indicateur publicitaire pour la Belgique et le Grand-Duché de Luxembourg, 1978. Brussels: Chambre d'Agences-Conseils en Publicité.

Inglehart, R., 1971. "The Silent Revolution in Europe," *American Political Science Review* 65: 991-1017.

INR (Institut national belge de radiodiffusion), various years. *Rapport annuel.* Brussels: INR.

INSOC, various years. Brussels: Institut universitaire d'information sociale et économique. A regular series of opinion surveys, under various titles, published in periodical form from 1946 to 1964.

Les institutions politiques de la Belgique régionalisée, 1973. Brussels: CRISP. Dossiers du CRISP, no. 6.

"In welke taal publiceren?" 1966. *Onze alma mater* 20: 164-72.

Irving, R. E. M., 1980. *The Flemings and Walloons of Belgium.* London: Minority Rights Group.

Janne, H., 1962. "Les données économiques et sociales devant les positions fédéralistes," *Socialisme* 9: 671-97.

————, ca. 1964. An untitled collection of data on economic comparisons of regions. Cf. Janne and De Greef, 1962, and Janne, 1967. Mimeographed.

————, 1967. *Les données économiques et sociales des trois grandes régions belges.* Brussels: Fédération bruxelloise du Parti Socialiste Belge.

————, and G. De Greef, 1962. *Les données économiques et sociales devant les positions fédéralistes.* Brussels: Imbruco.

Jaspar, E. J. E. M. H., 1952. "Het Belgische volkskarakter gezien door een Nederlander," *De Vlaamse gids* 36: 8-11.

Jennissen, E., and P. de Mont, ca. 1911. *Séparation administrative.* Gent: Plantyn.

Jonckheere, J., 1970. "Les recensements linguistiques en Belgique et au Canada." Unpublished M.A. thesis, Université de Montréal.

Jonckheere, W., and H. Todts, 1979. *Leuven Vlaams: splitsingsgeschiedenis van de Katholieke Universiteit Leuven.* Leuven: Davidsfonds.

Jouret, B., 1972. *Définition spatiale du phénomène urbain bruxellois.* Brussels: Editions de l'Université de Bruxelles.

Kabugubugu, A., 1970. "Changement et constance des attitudes d'étudiants flamands envers les Wallons, la Flandre, la Belgique et Bruxelles." Unpublished Ph.D. dissertation, University of Leuven.

————, and J. R. Nuttin, 1971. "Changement d'attitude envers la Belgique chez les étudiants flamands," *Psychologica Belgica* 11: 23-44.

Karush, G. E., 1977. "Industrialisation et changements de la population active en Belgique de 1846 à 1910," *Population et famille,* no. 40: 37-76.

Katz, D., and K. W. Braly, 1933. "Racial Stereotypes of One Hundred College Students," *Journal of Abnormal and Social Psychology* 28: 280-90.

————, and K. W. Braly, 1935. "Racial Prejudice and Social Stereotypes," *Journal of Abnormal and Social Psychology* 30: 175-93.

————, and K. W. Braly, 1967. "Verbal Stereotypes and Racial Prejudice." In M. Fishbein, ed., *Readings in Attitude Theory and Measurement.* New York: Wiley, 32-38.

Kelly, G. A., 1967. "Biculturalism and Party Systems in Belgium and Canada," *Public Policy* 16: 316-57.

————, "Belgium: New Nationalism in an Old World," *Comparative Politics* 1: 343-65.

Kendall, W., 1975. *The Labour Movement in Europe*. London: Allen Lane.

Kern, R., 1983. "Zur Sprachsituation im Arelerland." In R. Jongen et al., eds., *Mehrsprachigkeit und Gesellschaft*. 2 vols. Tübingen: Niemeyer, 2: 70-87. Linguistische Arbeiten, no. 134.

Kerr, H., D. Sidjanski, and G. Schmidtchen, 1972. *1972 Swiss Voting Study* (ICPSR 7342). A machine-readable data file from the Inter-University Consortium for Political and Social Research, University of Michigan.

Khol, A., 1970. "Zur Diskriminierung im Erziehungswesen: Das Sachurteil des Europäischen Gerichtshofes für Menschenrechte vom 23. Juli 1968 in den belgischen Sprachenfällen," *Zeitschrift für ausländisches öffentliches Recht und Völkerrecht* 30: 263-320.

Kint, G., ca. 1966. *L'enseignement en langue néerlandaise dans l'agglomération bruxelloise*. Translated by A. Borquet. 2 vols. Brussels: no publisher listed. Foreword by the Minister of National Education, Frans Grootjans.

Kirschen, E. S., 1962. "L'économie bruxelloise face au fédéralisme," *Cahiers économiques de Bruxelles*, no. 14: 159-66.

Kittell, A. E., 1967. "The Revolutionary Period of the Industrial Revolution: Industrial Innovation and Population Displacement in Belgium, 1830-1880," *Journal of Social History* 1: 119-48.

Kohn, H., 1957. "Nationalism in the Low Countries," *Review of Politics* 19: 155-85.

Kossmann, E. H., 1978. *The Low Countries, 1780-1940*. Oxford: Clarendon Press.

Kruijt, J. P., 1959. *Verzuiling*. 2nd ed. Zaandijk: Heijnis.

_____, and W. Goddijn, 1968. "Verzuiling en ontzuiling als sociologisch proces." In A. N. J. Den Hollander et al., eds., *Drift en koers: een halve eeuw sociale verandering in Nederland*. 3rd ed. Assen: Van Gorcum, 227-63.

Kruithof, J., 1956. "De samenstelling der Brusselse bevolking in 1842," *Tijdschrift voor sociale wetenschappen* 1: 159-221.

Kurth, G., 1896-98. *La frontière linguistique en Belgique et dans le nord de la France*. 2 vols. Brussels: Société belge de librairie.

Het Laatste Nieuws, various dates. Brussels.

Lagrou, L., 1960. "Gezindheid en interactiestructuur." Unpublished thesis for the *licence*, University of Leuven.

Lamberty, M., 1933. *Philosophie der Vlaamsche Beweging en der overige sociale stroomingen in België*. Brugge: Cayman-Seynave.

_____, 1948. *De Vlaamse Beweging nu*. Antwerp: Nederlandsche Boekhandel.

_____, 1951. *Lodewijk de Raet, grondlegger van een vlaamse volkspolitiek*. Antwerp: Die Poorte.

_____, 1968. "La question flamande," *Res Publica* 10, special issue no. 2: 143-55.

Larochette, J., 1947. "Les rapports entre Wallons et Flamands," *Revue de psychologie des peuples* 2: 447-62.

Laurent, E., [1971]. *La Bande noire de l'Entre-Sambre-et-Meuse: Coecke et Goethals étaient-ils innocents?* Brussels: Print Express.

Laurent, P. H., 1969a. "*Bilinguisme passif*: A Belgian Bureaucratic Experiment." Paper presented at the Annual Meeting of the American Political Science Association, New York, September 1969.

_____, 1969b. "The Reversal of Belgian Foreign Policy," *Review of Politics* 31: 370-84.

Leclercq, J., 1930. *Une vue d'ensemble de la question flamande*. Brussels: Editions de l'A.J.C.B.F.

Ledent, M., 1964. "Le stéréotype du flamand chez les francophones, avec recherche du rôle éventuel de la projection." Unpublished thesis for the *licence*, University of Louvain.

Lefèvre, P., 1977. "Le Rassemblement Wallon au gouvernement: défi au gouvernement ou défi au parti?" *Res Publica* 19: 391-406.

—————, 1980. "Le FDF: seize ans d'expérience pluraliste," *Res Publica* 22: 385-99.

Legris, M., 1965. "Le contrôle linguistique ou le dialogue difficile," *Dossiers de l'Action sociale catholique* 42: 809-22.

Legros, E., 1948. *La frontière des dialectes romans en Belgique.* Liège: Vaillant-Carmanne.

Lehouck, F., 1958. *Het antimilitarisme in België, 1830-1914.* Antwerp: Standaard.

Leirman, W., et al., eds., 1968. *Dossier Leuven: feiten, cijfers en beschouwingen.* Leuven: Boekengilde De Clauwaert.

Lejeune, R., and J. Stiennon, eds., 1977-81. *La Wallonie, le pays et les hommes: lettres, arts, culture.* 4 vols. [Brussels]: Renaissance du livre.

Leniere, J., 1966. "Sociaal-psychologisch onderzoek naar auto- en heterostereotypen bij Vlamingen en Walen," *Tijdschrift voor sociale wetenschappen* 11: 159-68.

Leplae, C., 1955. "Différences culturelles entre instituteurs d'expression française et flamande," *Bulletin de l'Institut de recherches économiques et sociales* 21: 709-54.

—————, 1956. "Différénces culturelles entre instituteurs flamands, francophones et hollandais," *Bulletin de l'Institut de recherches économiques et sociales* 22: 731-41.

Leroy, R., 1976. *Le dynamique du chômage et de l'emploi: Belgique, 1947-1973.* Brussels: Commission des communautés européennes.

Lettre de Belgique/Brief uit België, various years. Brussels: Ministère des affaires étrangères. A weekly press review.

Levy, P. M. G., 1938. "La statistique des langues en Belgique," *Revue de l'Institut de sociologie* 18: 507-70.

—————, 1950. "Un conflit de la politique et de la technique: les recensements des langues en Belgique," *Revue nouvelle* 11: 517-22.

—————, 1954a. "Un recensement sort de la clandestinité," *Revue nouvelle* 20: 85-92.

—————, 1954b. "La frontière linguistique existe-t-elle?" *Revue nouvelle* 20: 384-94.

—————, 1959. "Le recensement linguistique du 1er janvier 1960 ou naissance, vie et mort d'un recensement," *Res Publica* 1: 58-69.

—————, 1960a. *La querelle du recensement.* Brussels: Institut belge de science politique.

—————, 1960b. "Pas de recensement linguistique?" *Revue nouvelle* 31: 261-74.

—————, 1962. "La mort du recensement linguistique," *Revue nouvelle* 36: 145-54.

—————, 1964. "Quelques problèmes de statistique linguistique à la lumière de l'expérience belge," *Revue de l'Institut de sociologie* 37: 251-73.

—————, 1967. "Y a-t-il des juges à Strasbourg?" *Revue nouvelle* 45: 258-76.

—————, 1968. "Le couperet de Strasbourg," *Revue nouvelle* 48: 205-15.

—————, 1974. "The Feed-back of the Legal Use of Statistical Data, or, the End of a Languages Census." Paper presented at the Eighth World Congress of Sociology, Toronto, August 1974.

Lichtervelde, J. de, 1913. *La question des langues au Congo belge.* Brussels: Institut de sociologie Solvay.

Lijphart, A., 1968. *The Politics of Accommodation: Pluralism and Democracy in the Netherlands.* Berkeley and Los Angeles: University of California Press.

_____ , 1981. *Conflict and Coexistence in Belgium: The Dynamics of a Cultur-ally Divided Society*. Berkeley: Institute of International Studies, University of California.

Lindemans, L., 1951. *Proeve van een objectieve talentelling in het Brusselse*. Antwerp: Standaard.

_____ , [1963]. *Het vraagstuk Brussel uit Vlaams oogpunt*. Brussels: Simon Stevin.

_____ , 1968. *Huidige taalverhoudingen in de Brusselse agglomeratie*. Brussels: Simon Stevin.

_____ , 1973. *Taalgebruik in gerechtszaken*. 2nd rev. ed. Gent and Leuven: Story-Scientia.

_____ , et al., 1981. *De taalwetgeving in België*. Leuven: Davidsfonds.

"Liquider la répression," 1959. *Revue nouvelle* 29: 25-49.

Lobelle, J., 1982. "Le Québec et la Flandre: étude comparative de situations sociolinguistiques," *Anthropologie et sociétés* 6: 131-39.

Lorwin, V. R., 1962. "The Politicization of the Bureaucracy in Belgium." Unpublished paper.

_____ , 1965. "Constitutionalism and Controlled Violence in the Modern State: The Case of Belgium." Paper presented at the Annual Meeting of the American Historical Association, San Francisco, December 1965.

_____ , 1966. "Belgium: Religion, Class, and Language in National Politics." In R. A. Dahl, ed., *Political Oppositions in Western Democracies*. New Haven and London: Yale University Press, 147-87.

_____ , 1972. "Linguistic Pluralism and Political Tension in Modern Belgium." In J. A. Fishman, ed., *Advances in the Sociology of Language*. The Hague and Paris: Mouton, 2: 386-412.

_____ , 1974. "Belgium: Conflict and Compromise." In K. D. McRae, ed., *Consociational Democracy*. Toronto: McClelland and Stewart, 179-206.

_____ , 1975. "Labor Unions and Political Parties in Belgium," *Industrial and Labor Relations Review* 28: 243-63.

Louckx, F., 1975a. *Wetenschappelijk onderzoek van de taaltoestanden in de Brusselse agglomeratie: autochtone Brusselaars op de tweesprong*. Brussels: Nederlandse Commissie voor de Cultuur van de Brusselse agglomeratie.

_____ , 1975b. *Nederlandstalige inwijkelingen in de Brusselse agglomeratie*. Brussels: Nederlandse Commissie voor de Cultuur van de Brusselse agglomeratie.

_____ , 1981. "De Brusselse Vlamingen tussen assimilatie en integratie," *Kultuurleven* 48: 537-46.

_____ , 1982. *Vlamingen tussen Vlaanderen en Wallonie*. Brussels: V. U. B. Uitgaven. Published as vol. 5 of *Taal en sociale integratie*.

Luykx, T., 1969. *Politieke geschiedenis van België van 1789 tot heden*. 2nd rev. ed. Amsterdam and Brussels: Elsevier.

_____ , 1975. "De opinierichtingen in de Belgische dagbladpers," *Res Publica* 17: 223-44.

_____ , 1978. *Evolutie van de communicatie media*. Brussels: Elsevier Sequoia.

Lyon, M., 1971. *Belgium*. London: Thames and Hudson.

Mabille, X., 1978. "L'évolution des partis politiques en 1977," *Res Publica* 20: 273-77.

Mackey, W. F., 1981. "Urban Language Contact: Common Issues in Brussels and Abroad," *Taal en sociale integratie* 3: 19-37.

Mackie, T. T., and R. Rose, 1974. *The International Almanac of Electoral History*. London and Basingstoke: Macmillan.

Maes, F., 1953. "La langue, la loi, la liberté (le point de vue flamand)," *Revue nouvelle* 17: 635-39.

Maes, L. T., ed., 1971. *Onderzoek naar de voorordelen in de Nederlandstalige geschiedenishandboeken bestemd voor het secundair onderwijs in België.* Gent: Pedagogisch Centrum, Rijksnormaalschool, and Vilvoorde: Informatie- en documentatiecentrum Anne Frank.

———, 1974. "Prejudice and its Impact on the Teaching of History," *Memo from Belgium,* no. 165.

Magenau, D., 1964. *Die Besonderheiten der deutschen Schriftsprache in Luxemburg und in den deutschsprachigen Teilen Belgiens.* Mannheim: Bibliographisches Institut.

Malengreau, G., 1953. "De l'emploi des langues en justice au Congo," *Journal des tribunaux d'outre-mer* 4: 3-6.

Mallinson, V., 1963. *Power and Politics in Belgian Education.* London: Heinemann.

Marneffe, A. de, 1934-36. *Comment la Belgique fut beulemanisée.* 2 vols. Charleroi: Table Ronde.

Maroy, P., 1966. "L'évolution de la législation linguistique belge," *Revue du droit public et de la science politique en France et à l'étranger* 82: 449-501.

———, 1969. "L'arrêt de Strasbourg du 23 juillet 1968," *Annales de droit* 29: 169-201.

———, 1972. "Le statut spécial de Bruxelles et de son agglomération," *Annales de droit* 32: 165-86.

Marquet, F., 1973. *Commentaire critique de la Convention européenne des droits de l'homme, de son organisation judiciaire, et de l'arrêt du 23 juillet 1968.* Antwerp: privately published by the author.

Martens, M., et al., 1976. *Histoire de Bruxelles.* Toulouse: Privat.

Martens, P., 1962. *De Zuidnederlandse taalgrens voor het Belgisch Parlement.* Heusden: privately published by the author.

———, 1970. "De Voerstreek sinds de taalwetten van 1962-63," *Ons erfdeel* 13: 159-62.

Mast, A., 1972. Review of "La Constitution belge revisée," special issue of *Annales de droit* 32, nos. 2-3. In *Res Publica* 14: 875-79.

Mathias, T., and T. Milo, 1973. "Evolution du public de la radio de novembre 1969 à septembre 1972." In G. Thoveron, ed., *La radio hier et aujourd'hui.* Brussels: RTB.

Maystadt, P., 1972. "Les communautés culturelles et les régions," *Annales de droit* 32: 119-40.

McRae, K. D., ed., 1969. *The Federal Capital: Government Institutions.* Ottawa: Queen's Printer. Studies of the Royal Commission on Bilingualism and Biculturalism, no. 1.

———, ed., 1974. *Consociational Democracy: Political Accommodation in Segmented Societies.* Toronto: McClelland and Stewart.

———, and H. L. Black, 1977. "National News Agencies with Special Reference to Plurilingual Countries," *Communication et information* 2: 228-57.

Meertens, P. J., 1950a. "Ce qu'on a dit des Pays-Bas," *Revue de psychologie des peuples* 5: 11-32.

———, 1950b. "Le caractère néerlandais et ses variétés régionales," *Revue de psychologie des peuples* 5: 33-49.

Meeus, B., 1971. "Sociologische analyse van het taalgebruik: het gebruik van het ABN en het dialect in België," *Politica,* new series, 21: 228-45.

———, 1974a. "A Sociolinguistic Profile: Urban-Rural Differences in the Use of Dutch in Belgium." Paper presented at the Eighth World Congress of Sociology, Toronto, August 1974.

———, 1974b. "Onderzoek naar de toestand van het ABN en het dialect in België," *De gids op maatschappelijk gebied* 65: 391-413.

———, [1975]. *De taaltoestanden in België.* Brussels: Mens en Ruimte.

Memnon (pseudonym for D. Ryelandt), 1967. "Le malaise bruxellois," *Revue générale belge* 103, no. 4: 87-93.

Merkblatt über die Grundsätze für die Anwendung der drei Landessprachen in Belgien, [1916]. Brussels: Druckerei des General-Gouvernements. Preface by General von Bissing.

Meyers, P., ca. 1968. "Rapport d'activités, 20.10.1966-16.2.1968." [Brussels]: Commission permanente pour l'amélioration des relations entre les communautés linguistiques belges. Mimeographed.

Meynaud, J., et al., 1965. *La décision politique en Belgique*. Paris: Colin.

Micha, R., and A. De Waelhens, 1949. "Du caractère des Belges," *Les temps modernes* 4: 413-42.

Michel, J., 1976. *La fusion des communes*. Brussels: Cabinet du Ministre de l'Intérieur.

Minon, P., et al., 1969. "Observations sur les rapports 'Objektieve kriteria.' " Liège: no publisher indicated. Mimeographed.

Molitor, A., 1974. *L'administration de la Belgique: essai*. Brussels: Institut belge de science politique and CRISP.

————, 1979. *La fonction royale en Belgique*. Brussels: CRISP.

————, 1981. "La régionalisation dans les états d'Europe occidentale," *Administration publique* 5: 205-27.

Mols, R., 1960. "Bruxelles et les Bruxellois," *Revue de psychologie des peuples* 15: 6-44, 131-75.

————, 1961. *Bruxelles et les Bruxellois*. Brussels: Librairie de l'édition universelle.

————, 1964a. "Le problème bruxellois: son aspect démographique," *Revue nouvelle* 39: 140-58.

————, 1964b. "Le problème bruxellois: le 'plus grand Bruxelles,' " *Revue nouvelle* 39: 249-69.

————, 1971. "La pratique dominicale en Belgique," *Nouvelle revue théologique* 93: 387-425.

Moniteur belge/Belgisch staatsblad, various years. Brussels.

Monographie 1966/1967: réponse au questionnaire de la RAI, [1967]. Brussels: RTB.

Monteyne, A., ca. 1972. *Brussel: cijfers, prognoses*. Brussels: Dosfelinstituut.

Moortgat, A., 1925. *Germanismen in het Nederlandsch*. Gent: Vanderpoorten.

Morsa, J., 1963. "Tendances récentes de la fécondité belge," *Population et famille*, no. 1: 18-50.

————, 1964. "Tendances récentes de la mortalité en Belgique," *Population et famille*, no. 2: 16-40.

————, 1965. "Fécondité, nuptialité et composition par âge," *Population et famille*, no. 5: 83-112.

————, 1966. "L'immigration en Belgique (1890-1954)," *Population et famille*, nos. 9-10: 41-72.

————, 1970. "Une enquête nationale sur la fécondité: II. Sterilité—pratiques contraceptives," *Population et famille*, no. 20: 37-91.

————, and G. Julémont, 1971. "Une enquête nationale sur la fécondité: III. Pratiques contraceptives 1966-1971," *Population et famille*, no. 25: 141-49.

Moureau, L., and C. Goossens, 1958. "L'évolution des idées concernant la représentation proportionnelle en Belgique," *Revue de droit international et de droit comparé* 35: 378-93.

Moureaux, S., et al., ca. 1970. *Bruxelles sacrifiée: la verité sur le plan Eyskens*. Brussels: Fédération PLP de l'arrondissement de Bruxelles.

_____ , and J. P. Lagasse, 1984. *La Cour d'arbitrage: juridiction constitution-nelle*. Brussels: Larcier.

Moyersoen, L., 1960. "Le problème des frontières linguistiques," *Res Publica* 2: 20-27.

Mughan, A., 1979. "Modernization and Ethnic Conflict in Belgium," *Political Studies* 27: 21-37.

Namurois, A., 1960. "Le nouveau statut de la radiodiffusion en Belgique," *Revue de l'U.E.R.*, no. 63: 2-10.

_____ , et al., 1980. *Statuts*. Brussels: RTBF. Etudes de radio-télévision, no. 27.

Nelde, P. H., 1978. "Sprachkonflikt und Sprachwechsel in Brüssel." In P. S. Ure-land, ed., *Sprachkontakte im Nordseegebiet*. Tübingen: Niemeyer, 19-41. Linguistische Arbeiten, no. 66.

_____ , 1979a. *Deutsch als Muttersprache in Belgien: Forschungsberichte zur Gegenwartslage*. Wiesbaden: Steiner.

_____ , 1979b. *Volkssprache und Kultursprache: Die gegenwärtige Lage des sprachlichen Übergangsgebietes im Deutsch-Belgisch-Luxemburgischen Grenzraum*. Wiesbaden: Steiner.

_____ , 1979c. "French Interferences among a German-speaking Minority." In P. S. Ureland, ed., *Standardsprache und Dialekte in mehrsprachigen Gebieten Europas*. Tübingen: Niemeyer, 105-24. Linguistische Arbeiten, no. 82.

_____ , et al., 1981. "Minderheitenproblematik an der romanisch-germanisch Sprachgrenze." In P. S. Ureland, ed., *Kulturelle und sprachliche Minder-heiten in Europa*. Tübingen: Niemeyer, 219-64. Linguistische Arbeiten, no. 109.

Nielsen, F., 1980. "The Flemish Movement in Belgium after World War II," *American Sociological Review* 45: 76-94.

NIPO (Nederlands Instituut voor de Publieke Opinie en het Marktonderzoek), various dates. "Berichten." Amsterdam. Mimeographed.

Norrenberg, D., 1968. "La gestion du Ministère de l'éducation nationale et de la culture," *Res Publica* 10: 373-81.

Les nouvelles institutions de la Belgique: le régime définitif prévu par le pacte d'Egmont et l'accord du Stuyvenberg, 1978. Brussels: CRISP.

Nuttin, J., 1970. "Sub-group Formation, Dominance, Task-orientedness, and Contact in Heterogeneous Cultural Groups." In *NATO Conference: Special Training for Multilateral Forces, July 22-26, 1969*. Brussels: NATO, 188-208.

_____ , 1976. "Het stereotiep beeld van Walen, Vlamingen en Brusselaars: hun kijk op zichzelf en op elkaar," *Mededelingen van de Koninklijke Academie voor Wetenschappen, Letteren en Schone Kunsten* (Literature Section) 38, no. 2.

Nuttin, J. M., Jr., 1958. "Gezindheid van Vlaamse studenten tegenover de Walen: Sociaal-psychologisch onderzoek naar het verband tussen de gezindheid en het contact." Unpublished thesis for the *licence*, University of Leuven.

_____ , 1959. "De ontwikkeling van de gezindheid tegenover de Walen en het persoonlijk contact." Unpublished doctoral dissertation, University of Leuven.

_____ , 1959-60. "Die ontwikkeling van de gezindheid tegenover de Walen en het persoonlijk contact," *Tijdschrift voor opvoedkunde* 5: 315-33.

Obler, J., et al., 1977. *Decision-making in Smaller Democracies: The Consociational Burden*. Beverly Hills and London: Sage.

Olyff, F., 1940-47. *La question des langues en Belgique*. 2 vols. Hasselt: Editions du Moulin.

L'opinion publique belge et l'université de Louvain, 1967. Leuven: "Non Ever-tetur."

Orianne, P., 1967. "La politique provinciale et communale," *Res Publica* 9: 553-82.

Orlemans, J., 1961. "Invloed van etnisch-heterogene groepssamenstelling op de verwachting der groepsleden ten aanzien van de groepsprestatie." Unpublished thesis for the *licence*, University of Leuven.

Outers, L., 1968. *Le divorce belge*. Paris: Editions de Minuit.

Paardekooper, P. C., 1962. "*Er zijn geen Belgen!*": *Zes kauserieën*. Amsterdam and Antwerp: Standaard.

Pacte communautaire: réforme des institutions, 1978. Brussels: Secrétariat d'Etat à la réforme des institutions. Text of the Egmont-Stuyvenberg Pact.

"Le Pacte culturel," 1971. *Cahiers-CEPESS*, no. 4.

Paulu, B., 1967. *Radio and Television Broadcasting on the European Continent*. Minneapolis: University of Minnesota Press.

Paulus, J. P., 1959. *Droit publique du Congo belge*. Brussels: Institut de sociologie.

Pauwels, J. L., 1956. "La situation linguistique dans le Nord de la Belgique," *Orbis* (Leuven) 5: 116-22.

Pecheux, J., 1950. *Evolution de la presse en Belgique*. Brussels: Institut géographique militaire.

Peeters, C. H., 1930. *Nederlandsche taalgids: woordenboek van Belgicismen*. Antwerp: "De Sikkel."

Pelloux, R., 1967-68. "L'arrêt de la Cour européenne des droits de l'homme dans l'affaire linguistique belge," *Annuaire français de droit international* 13: 205-16; 14: 201-16.

Perin, F., 1960. *La démocratie enrayée: Essai sur le régime parlementaire belge de 1919 à 1958*. Brussels: Institut belge de science politique.

————, 1962. *La Belgique au défi: Flamands et Wallons à la recherche d'un état*. Huy: Imprimerie coopérative.

————, 1968. "Mythes et réalités dans les idéologies du pouvoir," *Res Publica* 10, special issue no. 1: 77-91.

Petri, F., 1937. *Germanisches Volkserbe in Wallonien und Nordfrankreich*. 2 vols. Bonn: Röhrscheid.

————, 1977. *Die fränkische Landnahme und die Entstehung der germanisch-romanischen Sprachgrenze in der interdisziplinären Diskussion*. Darmstadt: Wissenschaftliche Buchgesellschaft.

Picard, E., 1906a. "Essai d'une psychologie de la nation belge," *Revue économique internationale*, 3rd year, vol. 4: 251-97.

————, 1906b. *Essai d'une psychologie de la nation belge*. Brussels: Larcier.

Picard, H., 1955. "De talentelling in en rond Brussel," *De Vlaamse Gids* 39: 5-22.

Picard, L., 1963. *Evolutie van de Vlaamse Beweging van 1795 tot 1950*. 3 vols. Antwerp and Amsterdam: Standaard.

Pinon, R., 1957. "De la 'Commission des griefs flamands' à l'autonomie culturelle," *Nouvelle revue wallonne* 9: 21-31.

Piot, F., 1975. "La régionalisation dans le système politique belge," *Documents-CEPESS* 14, nos. 4-5.

Pirenne, H., 1900. *La nation belge*. 3rd ed. Brussels: Lamertin.

————, 1948-52. *Histoire de Belgique des origines à nos jours*. 5th ed. 5 vols. Brussels: Renaissance du livre.

Piron, M., 1970. "Le dictionnaire des populations de l'Europe: l'article Wallons," *Revue de psychologie des peuples* 25: 84-89.

————, ca. 1975. "Français et dialecte en Wallonie." In *Taaltoestanden in België, mede in Europees Verband*. Brussels: Mens en Ruimte, 26-42.

————, 1979. *Anthologie de la littérature dialectale de Wallonie: poètes et prosateurs*. Liège: Mardaga.

Piron, P., and J. Devos, 1954-58. *Codes et lois du Congo belge*. 2 vols. and four supplements. Brussels: Larcier and Léopoldville: Edition des Codes et lois du Congo belge.

Platel, M., 1980. "De Volksunie, 1977-1979," *Res Publica* 22: 401-29.

Pohl, J., 1979. *Les variétés régionales du français: études belges, 1945-1977*. Brussels: Editions de l'Université de Bruxelles.

Polomé, E., 1968. "The Choice of Official Languages in the Democratic Republic of the Congo." In J. A. Fishman et al., *Language Problems of Developing Nations*. New York: Wiley, 295-311.

Population: relevé décennal, 1831 à 1840, 1842. Brussels: Ministre de l'Intérieur.

Pourquoi Pas? Brussels. Published weekly.

Prayon-van Zuylen, A., 1892. *De Belgische taalwetten*. Gent: Siffer.

La presse/De pers, various years. Brussels: Association belge des éditeurs de journaux.

Les problèmes des langues au Congo-belge et au Ruanda-Urundi/De taalproblemen in Belgisch-Kongo en Ruanda-Urundi, 1958. Brussels: Stichting-Lodewijk De Raet.

Pro Flandria Servanda, 1920. The Hague: Nijhoff.

Le public de la radio en 1967-68, ca. 1968. Brussels: RTB. Audience research report, no. 63.

Putanier, H., 1955. *L'agglomération bruxelloise et le problème linguistique*. Brussels: Editions Librairia.

Quairiaux, Y., and J. Pirotte, 1978. "L'image du Flamand dans la tradition populaire wallonne depuis un siècle," *Res Publica* 20: 391-406.

Quertainmont, P., 1977. "La controverse de la 'culturalisation' ou de la 'régionalisation' des crédits budgétaires," *Res Publica* 19: 623-43.

Que veulent les Bruxellois?, ca. 1968. Brussels: Rassemblement pour le droit et la liberté.

Quévit, M., 1978. *Les causes du déclin wallon*. Brussels: Editions vie ouvrière.

La radio belge a 50 ans, 1973. Brussels: RTB.

Rapport fait à Monsieur le Ministre de la Défense nationale par la Commission mixte chargée de l'étude du problème linguistique qui se pose au sein des forces armées, 1953. Brussels: Institut géographique militaire.

Rapport sur la croissance des populations estudiantines, 1961. Brussels: Conseil national de la politique scientifique.

Rapport sur la situation économique de l'arrondissement de Bruxelles (121 communes), 1968. Brussels: Conseil économique de la région bruxelloise.

Rayside, D. M., 1976. *Linguistic Divisions in the Social Christian Party of Belgium and in the Liberal Parties of Canada and Quebec*. Ann Arbor: University Microfilms International. Ph.D. dissertation, University of Michigan.

_____ , 1978. "The Impact of the Linguistic Cleavage on the 'Governing' Parties of Belgium and Canada," *Canadian Journal of Political Science* 11: 61-97.

Recensement de la population, various years. Brussels. Title varies before 1961, and dates refer to census years rather than year of publication.

Recueil des lois et arrêtés royaux de la Belgique, 1831-36. Brussels. Bilingual edition, 13 vols. Title varies.

Reed, T. H., 1924. *Government and Politics of Belgium*. Yonkers-on-Hudson: World Book Company.

"La réforme de l'Etat belge," 1980. Special issue of *L'Europe en formation*, no. 240: 9-112. Articles by eighteen authors.

"La réforme de l'Etat de 1980 et de '1990,'" 1984. Special issue of *Res Publica* 26: 289-402.

Régime linguistique dans l'enseignement: loi du 30 juillet 1963, 1966a. Brussels: Ministère de l'éducation nationale et de la culture.

Régime linguistique dans l'enseignement: arrêtés royaux d'exécution du 30 novembre 1966, 1966b. Brussels: Ministère de l'éducation nationale et de la culture.

Règlement de la Chambre des Représentants de Belgique, 1975, [Brussels].

Remiche, J., 1947. "Regards sur Liège," *Revue de psychologie des peuples* 2: 418-29.

Remouchamps, J. M., 1936. *La francisation des arrondissements de Bruxelles, Arlon et Verviers au cours d'un demi-siècle (1880-1930)*. Brussels and Liège: Editions de la Défense wallonne.

Renard, A., 1961. "A propos d'une synthèse applicable à deux peuples et à trois communautés," *Synthèses*, no. 186, 204-36.

Renard, C., 1966. *La conquête du suffrage universel en Belgique*. Brussels: Fondation J. Jacquemotte.

Rens, I., 1965. "Les garanties parlementaires contre la minorisation et la révision constitutionnelle en Belgique," *Res Publica* 7: 189-221.

Rezsohazy, R., and J. Kerkhofs, 1984. *L'univers des Belges: valeurs anciennes et valeurs nouvelles dans les années 80*. Louvain-la-Neuve: CIACO.

Rock, P., and L. Schevenhels, eds., 1968. *Adult Education and Leisure in Flanders*. Brussels: Ministerie van Nederlandse Cultuur.

Roggen, I., 1965. "Soldats-citoyens et citoyens-miliciens," *Res Publica* 7: 231-53.

Rombauts, J., 1962. "Gedrag en groepsbeleving in etnisch-homogene en etnisch-heterogene groepen." Unpublished doctoral dissertation, University of Leuven.

—————— , 1962-63. "Gedrag en groepsbeleving in etnisch-homogene en etnisch-heterogene groepen," *Tijdschrift voor opvoedkunde* 8: 25-55.

Rommens, L., 1963. *Het nederlands in ons bedrijfsleven*. Brussels: BRT.

Romus, P., 1968. "L'évolution économique régionale en Belgique depuis la création du Marché commun (1958-1968)," *Revue des sciences économiques* 43: 131-74.

Roosens, C., 1983. "Les agents des services extérieurs du Ministère belge des affaires étrangères: aspects linguistiques de leur statut (1831-1982)," *Administration publique* 7: 271-82.

Rowat, D. C., ed., 1973. *The Government of Federal Capitals*. Toronto: University of Toronto Press.

Rowen, H. H., 1965. "The Historical Work of Pieter Geyl," *Journal of Modern History* 37: 35-49.

Rowntree, B. S., 1911. *Land and Labour: Lessons from Belgium*. London: Macmillan.

Royer, R., 1973. *Histoire de Rénovation wallonne*. Brussels: Bonivert-Liedts.

RTB (Radiodiffusion Télévision belge), various years. *Rapport d'activités*. Brussels: RTB.

RTBF (Radio-Télévision belge de la Communauté culturelle française), various years (1977ff.). *Rapport d'activités*. Brussels: RTBF.

Rudolph, J. R., 1977. "Ethnonational Parties and Political Change: The Belgian and British Experience," *Polity* 9: 401-26.

Rüling, H., 1939. *Das Sprachenrecht Belgiens*. Halle: Niemeyer. Contains extensive texts of 1930s language legislation in French and German.

Ruys, M., 1973. *The Flemings: A People on the Move, A Nation in Being*. Translated by H. Schoup. Tielt and Utrecht: Lannoo.

—————— , 1975. "Le gouvernement Tindemans face au problème communautaire belge," *Septentrion* 4, no. 1: 63-66.

Ryelandt, D., 1951. "Agences de presse," *Revue générale belge*, no. 67: 80-95.

Salmon, J. A., 1967. "Le quatrième arrêt de la Cour européenne des droits de l'homme," *Journal des tribunaux* 82: 341-48.

Salverda de Grave, J. J., 1906. *De Franse woorden in het Nederlands*. Amsterdam: Müller.

_____ , 1913. *L'influence de la langue française en Hollande d'après les mots empruntés*. Paris: Champion.

Sauvy, A., 1962. *Le rapport Sauvy sur le problème de l'économie et de la population en Wallonie*. Liège: Conseil économique wallon.

Schama, S., 1972. "The Rights of Ignorance: Dutch Educational Policy in Belgium, 1815-1830," *History of Education* 1: 81-89.

Scheuermann, F., 1942. *Sprachenfreiheit und Sprachenzwang in Belgien*. Köslin: Hendess.

Schillings, H., 1965. "Die deutsche Volksgruppe in Belgien," *Europa ethnica* 22: 9-18.

Schreurs, A. H., 1948. *Liège, terre de France*. Liège: "Jeune France."

_____ , 1953. *La route de Wallonie*. Liège: Faculté de droit de Liège.

_____ , 1956. "L'aspect sociologique du régionalisme et la réalité wallonne sur le plan économique et social," *Nouvelle revue wallonne* 8: 25-31.

Schreurs, F., 1960. *Les congrès de rassemblement wallon de 1890 à 1959*. Charleroi: Institut Jules Destrée.

_____ , 1961. "La fixation de la frontière linguistique," *Nouvelle revue wallonne* 13: 85-92.

Seiler, D. L., 1975. *Le déclin du "cléricalisme": structure du comportement politique du monde catholique wallon*. Brussels: Institut belge de science politique.

Sénat (Belgium), various years. Working documents of Parliament (identified by session and number).

Senelle, R., 1970. "The Political, Economic and Social Structures of Belgium," *Memo from Belgium*, nos. 122-24.

_____ , 1972. "La révision de la Constitution, 1967-1971," *Textes et documents*, nos. 279-81.

_____ , 1974. "La Constitution belge commentée," *Textes et documents*, no. 301.

_____ , 1978. "La réforme de l'état belge," *Textes et documents*, no. 315.

_____ , 1979. "La réforme de l'état belge: II," *Textes et documents*, no. 319.

_____ , 1980. "La réforme de l'état belge: III. Les structures régionales prévues par les lois des 8 et 9 août 1980," *Textes et documents*, no. 326.

Servais, P., 1970. "Le sentiment national en Flandres et en Wallonie: approche psycholinguistique," *Recherches sociologiques*, no. 2: 123-44.

"La situation économique des régions linguistiques," 1963. *Les dossiers de l'Action sociale catholique* 40: 1-14.

Smeyers, J., 1959. *Vlaams taal- en volksbewustzijn in het Zuidnederlands geestesleven van de 18de eeuw*. Gent: Koninklijke Vlaamse Academie voor Taal- en Letterkunde, sixth series, no. 83.

Smits, J., 1984. "Belgian Politics in 1983: Communitarian Struggles Despite the Economic Crisis," *Res Publica* 26: 473-502.

SOBEMAP, 1969. *Etude sur les lecteurs de la presse belge et luxembourgeoise*. A machine-readable data file prepared by the Société belge d'économie et de mathématique appliquées (SOBEMAP) for the Centre d'étude belge des supports de publicité (CEBSP).

Le Soir, various dates. Brussels.

S[oudain] de N[iederwerth], C., 1857. *Du flamand, du wallon et du français en Belgique*. Liège: Redouté.

Soumeryn, G., 1973. "L'article 107 *quater* ou le régionalisme en Belgique." In A. Fischer et al., *Etudes sur le régionalisme en Belgique et à l'étranger*. Brussels: Bruylant, 353-89.

Spitaels, G., 1967. *Le mouvement syndical en Belgique*. Brussels: Editions de l'Institut de sociologie.
Spoo, M., 1955. "Gezindheid en contacten: Een sociaal-psychologisch onderzoek van de houding van de Vlaamse student tegenover de Waalse student." Unpublished thesis for the *licence*, University of Leuven.
De Standaard, various dates. Brussels.
Statistique générale de la Belgique: exposé de la situation du Royaume, 1851-1860, 1865. Brussels: Lesigne.
Statistiques démographiques, various years. Brussels: Institut national de statistique.
Statistiques financières, various years. Brussels: Institut national de statistique.
Stengers, J., 1950-51. "Sentiment national, sentiment orangiste, et sentiment français à l'aube de notre indépendance," *Revue belge de philologie et d'histoire* 28: 993-1029 and 29: 61-92.
_____, 1959. *La formation de la frontière linguistique en Belgique ou de la légitimité de l'hypothèse historique*. Brussels: Latomus.
_____, 1965. "Belgium." In H. Rogger and E. Weber, eds., *The European Right*. Berkeley and Los Angeles: University of California Press, 128-67.
_____, ed., 1979. *Bruxelles: croissance d'une capitale*. Antwerp: Fonds Mercator.
Stijns, M., 1957. "The Flemish Press and Other Press Problems in Belgium," *Gazette* 3: 301-19.
Stoetzel, J., 1983. *Les valeurs du temps présent: une enquête*. Paris: Presses universitaires de France.
Storme, M., 1970. "De taaltoestanden in het Hof van Cassatie," *Rechtskundig Weekblad* 33: 1129-1134.
Stracke, D. A., [1913]. *Was Vlaanderen altijd tweetalig als nu?* Antwerp: "Veritas."
Suenaert, L., 1983. "Les besoins en langues modernes/étrangères: une enquête dans les services publics en Flandre et en Wallonie." Unpublished thesis for the *licence*, Université catholique de Louvain.
Swing, E. S., 1973. "Separate but Equal: An Inquiry into the Impact of the Language Controversy on Education in Belgium," *Western European Education* 5, no. 4: 6-33.
_____, 1980a. *Bilingualism and Linguistic Segregation in the Schools of Brussels*. Québec: Centre international de recherche sur le bilinguisme.
_____, 1980b. "Schools, Bilingualism and Community Tensions: The Brussels Experience After 1971." Paper presented to the Annual Meeting of the Comparative and International Education Society, Vancouver.
_____, 1981. "The Politicolinguistics of Education in Belgium," *Word* 32: 213-24.
_____, 1982. "Education for Separatism: The Belgian Experience." In B. Hartford et al., eds., *Issues in International Bilingual Education: The Role of the Vernacular*. New York and London: Plenum Press, 265-90.
Le système de la décision politique en Belgique, 1977. Brussels: CRISP. Dossiers du CRISP, no. 11.
"De taalregeling in Kongo: documenten," 1956. *Band* 15: 417-571. Special double issue dealing with many aspects of official language usage.
Taaltoestanden in België, mede in Europees Verband, ca. 1975. Brussels: Mens en Ruimte.
Taeldeman, J., 1978. "Französisch-Flämische Sprachinterferenz in Flandern." In P. S. Ureland, ed., *Sprachkontakte im Nordseegebiet*. Tübingen: Niemeyer, 43-66. Linguistische Arbeiten, no. 66.
Het talenprobleem in het onderwijs van Belgisch-Kongo, 1957. Gent: Julius Vuylsteke-fonds.

Les taux de chômage en Belgique, 1976. Brussels: Office national de l'emploi.

Telemachus (pseudonym for Jan Grootaers), 1963. "Approche sociologique de la question linguistique," *Revue nouvelle* 38: 303-14.

ter Spill, J. H. W. Q., 1924. "Belgique et Hollande," *Le flambeau*, 7th year, vol. 2: 151-72.

Thoveron, G., 1971. *Radio et télévision dans la vie quotidienne*. Brussels: Editions de l'Institut de sociologie.

Thoveron, J., 1979. *Les programmes de télévision diffusés par la BRT*. Brussels: RTBF.

Tindemans, L., 1969. *Autonomie culturelle 69*. Brussels: Van Ruys.

_____ , 1971. *L'autonomie culturelle*. Brussels: Van Ruys.

Todts, H., 1961-71. *Hoop en wanhoop der Vlaamsgezinden*. 3 vols. Leuven: Davidsfonds.

_____ , 1973. "Het 'Décret de septembre,'" *Kultuurleven* 40: 881-88.

Tournemenne, M., 1984. *Les budgets de l'Etat, des Régions et des Communautés en Belgique*. Brussels: CRISP. Dossiers series, no. 20.

Toussaint, N., 1935. *Bilinguisme et éducation*. Brussels: Lamertin.

De transmutatieklassen, 1956. Brussels: Vermeylen-fonds.

Trim, R., 1983. "Sprachtod in Altbelgien-mitte?" In R. Jongen et al., eds., *Mehrsprachigkeit und Gesellschaft*. 2 vols. Tübingen: Niemeyer, 2: 157-68.

Trollope, F. M., 1834. *Belgium and Western Germany in 1833*. 2 vols. Brussels: Wahlen.

Tulippe, O., et al., 1965. *Démographie wallonne*. Brussels: Fondation Charles Plisnier.

Turney-High, H. H., 1953. *Chateau-Gérard: The Life and Times of a Walloon Village*. Columbia, South Carolina: University of South Carolina Press.

TV 25, 1978. Brussels: RTBF.

Uitterhaegen, R., 1963. "De stereotiepen van de Waal bij Vlaamse en Waalse studenten." Unpublished thesis for the *licence*, University of Leuven.

UNESCO, various years. *Statistical Yearbook*. Paris: UNESCO.

Urbain, R., 1958. *La fonction et les services du premier ministre en Belgique*. Brussels: Librairie Encyclopédique.

Urwin, D., 1970. "Social Cleavages and Political Parties in Belgium: Problems of Institutionalization," *Political Studies* 18: 320-40.

Usage des langues à l'armée, 1952. Brussels: Ministère de la Défense nationale.

Valkhoff, M., 1931. *Les mots français d'origine néerlandaise*. Amersfoort: Valkhoff.

_____ , 1944. *L'expansion du néerlandais*. Translated by J. Sépulchre. Brussels: Editions lumière.

Van Assche, W., 1972. "De taalgroepen in het parlement," *Tijdschrift voor bestuurswetenschappen en publiekrecht* 27: 242-54.

Van Bellinghen, J. P., 1978. "De organisatie van de Belgische diplomatie." In P. Van de Meerssche, ed., *Belgisch buitenlands beleid en internationale betrekkingen: Liber amicorum Professor Omer De Raeymaeker*. Leuven: Leuven University Press, 689-701.

Van Bogaert, E., 1968. "Het taalevenwicht in de Belgische diplomatie." In T. Luykx, ed., *Liber amicorum August De Schryver, Minister van Staat*. Gent: T. Luykx, 681-90.

Van Bol, J. M. R., 1983. "Les ressources des communautés et des régions en 1982," *Administration publique* 7: 32-58.

Van Bulck, G., 1948. "Les recherches linguistiques au Congo belge." In Institut royal colonial belge, Section des sciences morales et politiques, *Mémoires*, no. 16.

Van Campenhout, M., et al., 1967. "Emploi et remunération du travail par branche d'activité industrielle, dans les provinces et régions linguistiques, de 1955 à 1964," *Etudes statistiques*, no. 15.

Van Cauwelaert, E., 1971. *Taalvrijheid: een kritische motivering van de taalwetgeving.* Antwerp: Nederlandsche Boekhandel.

Van Cauwelaert, F., 1946. "Foreign Policy, 1918 to 1940." In J. A. Goris, ed., *Belgium.* Berkeley and Los Angeles: University of California Press, 129-47.

Van den Bosch, A., and E. Gouverneur, [1970]. *Population et pratiquants dans les doyennés et diocèses de la Province écclesiastique belge.* Brussels: Centre interdiocésain.

_____ , and E. Gouverneur, 1974. *Statistiques de base des doyennés et diocèses de la Province ecclésiastique belge.* Brussels: Centre interdiocésain.

Van den Brande, A., 1967. "Elements for a Sociological Analysis of the Impact of the Main Conflicts on Belgian Political Life," *Res Publica* 9: 437-70.

Van den Daele, G., 1950. *De achterstand en de minderwaardige behandeling der Vlamingen in de Belgische administraties.* Gent: "De Week."

Van den Hoof, A., 1965. "Attitude van Franstalige en Nederlandstalige militairen tegenover de andere taalgroep: Sociaal-psychologisch onderzoek naar het verband tussen attitude en contact, voor en na samenwerking." Unpublished thesis for the *licence*, University of Leuven.

Van de Perre, A., 1919. *The Language Question in Belgium.* London: Grant Richards.

Vandeputte, R., 1949. *De vervlaamsing van het bedrijfsleven: de volgende phase van de Vlaamse strijd.* Antwerp: Standaard.

Van der Elst, F., 1968. "L'avenir de la Volksunie," *Res Publica* 10, special issue no. 1: 101-109.

Van der Haegen, H., 1981. "Neuf cent mille étrangers en Belgique," *Bulletin de statistique* 67: 3-10.

Van der Molen, U., 1951. "Le problème des langues dans l'administration belge." Brussels: Ministère de l'instruction publique. Mimeographed.

_____ , [1959]. *Het gebruik der talen in bestuurszaken.* Reprinted from A. Vranckx et al., eds., *Administratief lexicon.* Brugge: De Keure.

Vandermotten, C., 1971. *Le marché des terrains à bâtir dans la région bruxelloise, 1912-1968.* Brussels: Editions de l'Institut de sociologie.

van der Straten-Waillet, F. X., 1963-64. "Between the Fatherlands and Europe: A Belgian Looks at the Low Countries," *Delta* 6, no. 4: 13-23.

_____ , 1968. "Indrukken over de vergeliking van het belgische en nederlandse maatschappelijke en politieke leven." In T. Luykx, ed., *Liber amicorum August De Schryver, Minister van Staat.* Gent: T. Luykx, 739-45.

Van Dijck, J. G. R., 1937. *Vlaanderen wenscht een zelfstandige omroep.* Turnhout: Van Mierlo-Proost.

Van Elst, J., 1961. "Gezindheid en discussiegehalte: een inhoudsanalyse van discussies in kleine groepen." Unpublished thesis for the *licence*, University of Leuven.

Van Gorp, G., 1969. *Le candidat officier: aspects sociologiques du futur Corps des officiers belges.* Leuven: Wouters.

Van Haegendoren, M., 1962. *De Vlaamse Beweging nu en morgen.* 2 vols. Hasselt: Heideland.

_____ , 1965. *The Flemish Movement in Belgium.* Antwerp: Flemish Cultural Council.

_____ , 1967a. "Taalhomogeniteit," *Ons erfdeel* 11, no. 1: 78-87.

_____ , 1967b. "Un seul secteur négligé? La flamandisation des entreprises," *Ons erfdeel* 11, no. 2: 52-63.

_____, 1968. "Morphologie du Mouvement flamand," *Synthèses*, no. 269: 92-96.

_____, 1969a. *Zwartboek van de Vlaamse achterstand in het wetenschappelijk onderzoek*. Heverlee: privately published.

_____, 1969b. *Zwartboek van de culturelle achterstand van Vlaanderen*. Heverlee: privately published.

_____, 1969c. "Nederlandstaligen en Franstaligen in het wetenschappelijk onderzoek in België," *Ons erfdeel* 13, no. 1: 158-61.

_____, 1970. "Belgium and Its Double Language Boundary," *La monda lingvo-problemo* 2: 17-20.

_____, 1978. *Het geld van de Vlamingen*. Leuven: Davidsfonds.

_____, and H. D. de Vries Reilingh, 1959. *Noord-Zuid verbinding: samenhorigheid en samenwerking van de Lage Landen*. Tielt and The Hague: Lannoo.

_____, et al., 1957. *De Nederlandse cultuur in België*. Brussels: Stichting-Lodewijk De Raet.

van Haeringen, C. B., 1960. *Netherlandic Language Research*. 2nd ed. Leiden: Brill.

Vanhamme, M., 1968. *Bruxelles: de bourg rural à cité mondiale*. Antwerp and Brussels: Mercurius.

van Hoorebeke, A., 1936. *L'emploi des langues en justice: commentaire critique de la loi du 15 juin 1935*. Brussels: Bruylant.

Van Horenbeeck, H., 1961. "Groepssamenstelling en interactiestructuur: Een onderzoek van etnisch homogene en heterogene groepen bij middel van de observatiemethode van R. F. Bales." Unpublished thesis for the *licence*, University of Leuven.

Van Houtte, J. A., 1961. "Le sentiment national belge au XIXe siècle," *Revue générale belge* 97, no. 2: 1-24.

Van Impe, H., 1968. *Le régime parlementaire en Belgique*. Brussels: Bruylant.

Van Loey, A., 1945. *La langue néerlandaise en pays flamand*. Brussels: Office de Publicité.

_____, 1954. "Les mots français en néerlandais." In Académie royale de Belgique, *Bulletin de la classe des lettres et des sciences morales et politiques*, fifth series, 40: 277-90.

_____, 1958. "Les problèmes du bilinguisme en Belgique," *Etudes germaniques* 13: 289-302.

Van Lommel, R., 1965. "Groepscohesie in etnisch homogene groepen en etnisch heterogene groepen met verschillende gezindheid." Unpublished thesis for the *licence*, University of Leuven.

Van Malderghem, R., 1981. "Enkele elementen van het kiesgedrag in Brussel: een analyse van het F.D.F.-elektoraat," *Taal en sociale integratie* 3: 155-72.

Van Molle, P., 1972. *Het Belgisch Parlement/Le Parlement belge, 1894-1972*. Antwerp: Standaard Wetenschappelijke Uitgeverij.

Vanneste, A. M. S., 1974. "Aspects sociolinguistiques de la Flandre française: étude diachronique et synchronique." Paper presented to the Eighth World Congress of Sociology, Toronto, August 1974.

Van Passel, F., and A. Verdoodt, 1975. "Bilinguismes en Belgique," *Quaderni per la promozione del bilinguismo*, nos. 9-10.

Van Pelt, H., 1974. *De omroep in revisie: ontwikkeling van het radio- en televisiebestel in Nederland en België*. Leuven: Acco.

van Raalte, E., 1948. "Van Nederlands-Belgische toenadering tot samenwerking, 1848-1948," *Etudes internationales* 1: 203-19.

Van Rompaey, C., 1977. "L'amont et l'aval: Belga et l'AMP," *Revue nouvelle* 66: 170-71.

Van Sint-Jan, R., 1929. "Die politische Presse Belgiens," *Zeitungswissenschaft* 4: 1-24, 65-87, 129-55, 193-212, 257-77, 321-42.

Van Slambrouck, H., 1967. "Het stereotype van de Waal en van de Vlaming bij Vlaamse studenten." Unpublished thesis for the *licence*, University of Leuven.

Van Springel, J., 1969. "Trends in Belgian Newspaper Ownership Concentration," *Gazette* 15: 201-206.

Van Waelvelde, W., and H. Van der Haegen, 1967. *Typologie des communes belges d'après le degré d'urbanisation au 31 décembre 1961*. Brussels: Ministère des affaires économiques. Reprinted from *Bulletin de statistique* 53: 722-75.

Van Wauwe, L., 1971. *Fédéralisme: utopie ou possibilité?* Paris: Pichon and Durand-Auzias.

Van Wezemael, J., 1937. *Bruxelles: trait d'union ou pomme de discorde?* Brussels: Editions le Rouge et le Noir.

Vehicules à moteur neufs mis en circulation, various years. Brussels: Institut national de statistique. Title varies slightly.

Verdoodt, A., 1968. *Zweisprachige Nachbarn: Die deutschen Hochsprach- und Mundartgruppen in Ost-Belgien, dem Elsass, Ost-Lothringen und Luxemburg*. Vienna and Stuttgart: Braumüller.

————, 1973. *Les problèmes des groupes linguistiques en Belgique*. Leuven: Institut de linguistique de Louvain. A bibliography with commentary, indispensable for serious study of language questions in Belgium.

————, 1976. "The German and German Dialect Speakers in Belgium." In H. and A. L. V. Haarmann, eds., *Sprachen und Staaten: Festschrift Heinz Kloss*. Hamburg: Stiftung Europa-Kolleg, 1: 211-28.

————, 1977. *Linguistic Tensions in Canadian and Belgian Labor Unions*. Québec: Centre international de recherche sur le bilinguisme.

————, ed., 1978. "Belgium." Special issue of the *International Journal of the Sociology of Language*, no. 15.

————, 1980. "De toekomst van België in de publieke opinie," *Kultuurleven* 47: 654-63.

————, 1983. *Bibliographie sur le problème linguistique belge*. Québec: Centre international de recherche sur le bilinguisme.

Verhaegen, P., 1906. *La lutte scolaire en Belgique*. Gent: Siffer and Brussels: Dewit.

Verhulst, A., 1968. *Belgium's Historical Position in Europe*. Antwerp: Kultuurraad voor Vlaanderen.

Verlinden, C., 1955. *Les origines de la frontière linguistique en Belgique et la colonisation franque*. Brussels: Renaissance du livre.

Vermeylen, A., 1918. *Quelques aspects de la question des langues en Belgique*. Brussels: "Le Peuple."

Vermylen, H., 1966. "Enkele co-varianten van de gezindheid van Vlamingen tegenover Walen." Unpublished thesis for the *licence*, University of Leuven.

De vernederlandsing van het bedrijfsleven, 1973. Brussels: Cultuurraad voor de Nederlandse Cultuurgemeenschap.

Verthé, A., 1959. *Vlamingen in Kongo: hun werkende aanwezigheid en hun innerlijke kultuurstrijd*. Leuven: Davidsfonds.

————, 1965. *België buiten zijn grenzen*. Brussels: België in de Wereld.

————, and B. Henry, 1961. *Geschiedenis van de Vlaams-Afrikaanse letterkunde*. Leuven: Davidsfonds.

Victor, R., 1961. "Taaltoestanden in het militair gerecht," *Rechtskundig weekblad* 24: 1879-88.

————, 1968. "De vernederlandsing van het rechtswezen in België." In T. Luykx, ed., *Liber amicorum August De Schryver, Minister van Staat*. Gent: T. Luykx, 772-83.

Vidick, G., 1967. "Les partis politiques belges: démocratie ou oligarchie," *Res Publica* 9: 353-68.

Vindex, 1951. *Le fédéralisme*. Brussels: Hottelet.

Vlaemynck, F., and G. Fauconnier, 1974. *Het vraagstuk "Leuven" (1968) in de spiegel van de Belgische pers*. Leuven: Centrum voor communicatiewetenschappen, Katholieke Universiteit Leuven.

Voyé, L., 1973. *Sociologie du geste religieux: de l'analyse de la pratique dominicale en Belgique à une interprétation théorique*. Brussels: Editions Vie ouvrière.

————, et al., 1969. "Analyse sociologique du rapport 'Objektieve kriteria.'" Leuven: Université catholique de Louvain. Mimeographed.

VVO (Verbond van het Vlaams Overheidspersoneel), various years. *Activiteitsverslag*. Brussels.

Wagnon, H., 1964. "La condition juridique de l'Eglise catholique en Belgique," *Annales de droit et de sciences politiques* 24: 59-86.

Waleffe, B., 1968. *Some Constitutional Aspects of Recent Cabinet Development in Great Britain and Belgium*. Brussels: Bruylant.

————, 1971. "Le Roi nomme et révoque ses ministres": la formation et la démission des gouvernements en Belgique depuis 1944. Brussels: Bruylant.

La Wallonie en alerte: pétition adressée à Messieurs les Présidents des deux Chambres par cinquante-trois académiciens contra "la minorité perpetuelle" de la Wallonie, 1949. Liège: Thone.

Wanty, E., 1957. "Le milieu militaire belge de 1831 à 1914." In Académie Royale de Belgique, Classe des lettres et des sciences morales et politiques, *Mémoires* 52, no. 3.

Warland, J., 1940. *Glossar und Grammatik der germanischen Lehnwörter in der wallonischen Mundart Malmedys*. Liège: Faculté de Philosophie et Lettres and Paris: Droz.

Wetenschappelijk onderzoek van de Brusselse taaltoestanden, 1974-75. Brussels: Nederlandse Commissie voor de Cultuur van de Brusselse Agglomeratie. A multivolume report with working papers produced by Mens en Ruimte and the Centrum voor Sociologie, VUB. Title varies slightly.

Wieërs, J. L., 1968. "L'enseignement et la recherche scientifique en Belgique," *Synthèses* 23, no. 269: 24-32.

Wigny, P., 1952. *Droit constitutionnel: principes et droit positif*. 2 vols. Brussels: Bruylant.

————, 1969. *Comprendre la Belgique*. Verviers: Marabout.

————, 1972. *La troisième révision de la Constitution*. Brussels: Bruylant.

Wildhaber, L., 1969-70. "Der belgische Sprachenstreit vor dem Europäischen Gerichtshof für Menschenrechte," *Schweizerisches Jahrbuch für internationales Recht* 26: 9-38.

Wilkens-Weyland, H. R., 1972. "Die Brüsseler Region als Nationalitätenproblem," *Europa ethnica* 29: 50-55.

Willems, L., 1913. *De Middeleeuwsche taaltoestanden in Vlaamsch-België*. Sint-Amandsberg: Verhaeghe.

Willems, M., 1980. "Bibliografie van de studie van het Belgisch Parlement," *Res Publica* 22: 289-301.

Willemsen, A. W., [1954a]. *De Vlaamse Beweging voor 1914*. Schiedam: Roelants.

————, [1954b]. *De Vlaamse Beweging na 1914*. Schiedam: Roelants.

_____, 1969. *Het Vlaams-nationalisme: de geschiedenis van de jaren 1914-1940*. 2nd ed. Utrecht: Ambo. First edition, 1958.

_____, 1974-75. *De Vlaamse Beweging*. 2 vols. Hasselt: Heideland-Orbis. Parts 4 and 5 of the collective work *Twintig eeuwen Vlaanderen*. 15 vols.

Wilmars, D. (pseudonym for Jozef van Alsenoy), 1968. *Le problème belge: la minorité francophone en Flandre*. Translated by E. Knaeps. Antwerp: Editions Erasme.

_____, 1971. *Diagnose Brussel*. Antwerp and Utrecht: Standaard.

Wilmots, J., 1983. "Nederlands/Hollands/Vlaams—An Untranslatable Title," *Canadian Journal of Netherlandic Studies* 4, no. 2/5, no. 1: 28-32.

Wils, L., 1955. *De ontwikkeling van de gedachtinhoud der Vlaamse Beweging tot 1914*. Antwerp: Standaard.

_____, 1972. *De houding van de politieke partijen tegenover de Vlaamse Beweging in de 19e eeuw*. Heule: UGA.

_____, 1974. *Flamenpolitik en aktivisme: Vlaanderen tegenover België in de eerste wereldoorlog*. Leuven: Davidsfonds.

Wilwerth, C., 1980. *Le statut linguistique de la fonction publique belge*. Brussels: Editions de l'Université de Bruxelles.

Wind, B. H., 1937. "Les contributions néerlandaises au vocabulaire du français belge," *Neophilologus* 22: 81-98, 161-67.

_____, 1947. "De quelques curiosités syntaxiques propres au français belge," *Neophilologus* 31: 161-65.

_____, 1960. "Nederlands-Franse taalcontacten," *Neophilologus* 44: 1-11.

Witte, E., et al., eds., 1978ff. *Taal en sociale integratie*. Brussels: Centrum voor interdisciplinair onderzoek naar de Brusselse taaltoestanden. An irregular series containing six volumes to 1982.

_____, et al., 1984. *Le bilinguisme en Belgique: le cas de Bruxelles*. Brussels: Editions de l'Université de Bruxelles.

Wood, R. E., 1980. "Language Maintenance and External Support: The Case of the French Flemings," *International Journal of the Sociology of Language*, no. 25: 107-19.

Ydewalle, C. d', 1949. *A Belgian Manor in Two World Wars*. Translated by E. Sutton. London: Macmillan.

_____, 1967. *Confession d'un Flamand*. Paris and Brussels: De Meyere.

Ydewalle, H. d', [1946]. *Noblesse en Flandre*. Brussels: Editions Lesigne.

Young, C., 1965. *Politics in the Congo: Decolonization and Independence*. Princeton: Princeton University Press.

Young, W. L., 1982. *Minorities and the Military*. Westport and London: Greenwood Press.

Zakalnyckyj, W., 1978. "Les structures de l'Etat belge prévues par le pacte communautaire," *Bulletin de documentation* (Ministère des finances), no. 3 (March), 139-85.

Zolberg, A. R., 1974. "The Making of Flemings and Walloons: Belgium, 1830-1914," *Journal of Interdisciplinary History* 5: 179-235.

_____, 1976. "Les origines du clivage communautaire en Belgique," *Recherches sociologiques* 7: 150-70.

_____, 1977. "Splitting the Difference: Federalization without Federalism in Belgium." In M. J. Esman, ed., *Ethnic Conflict in the Western World*. Ithaca: Cornell University Press, 103-42.

_____, 1978. "Belgium." In R. Grew, ed., *Crises of Political Development in Europe and the United States*. Princeton: Princeton University Press, 99-138.

Zoller, H., 1963. "Les différences objectives entre Flamands et Wallons." Unpublished thesis for the *licence*, University of Louvain.

Index